ACKNOWLEDGEMENTS

I would like to thank:

my editor, Michael "shadow" Goodwin, my copyeditor, Peggy Nauts, our production coordinator, Lisa Brazieal, and the whole staff at Peachpit—especially executive editor Marjorie Baer, whose enthusiasm and patience contributed immeasurably to this book.

all of the film editors who agreed to be interviewed. I only wish I could include everyone's ideas—I learned so much from all of you.

Mark at A.C.E., the countless agents and agents' assistants who helped to set up the interviews, and Dawn Walters, who transcribed them.

the cast and crew of *Want* and the entire Bare Witness Productions group, Eric Peltier, and of course, Daniel Gamburg, who has always been willing to do whatever I ask, no matter how strange or difficult (even if I'm taking pictures).

Brian, Randy, Will, and the rest of the Yak Herders, past and present. We done changed the world; please keep on making it better.

Lisa Brenneis, for giving me the crazy idea to take this thing on in the first place and for supporting me throughout, even if it was just to see someone share her pain.

my loving family, PSW, KAW, AJW, HDR, and KFM.

And most of all, I would like to thank Divi Crockett for so very much help, support, trust, dedication, inspiration, and love.

— Michael Wohl

CONTENTS

CHAPTER 3: EDITING PATTERNS 89

CHAPTER 6: ADVANCED EDITING 233

CHAPTER 8: SPECIAL EFFECTS   343

The Invisible Art

Unless you're a film professional or a serious fan, you may have never heard names like Walter Murch or Thelma Schoonmaker—even though they are editing geniuses without whose work films like *The English Patient* and *Raging Bull* would never have been possible. In the filmmaking industry, they are more than merely famous; they are superstars.

So why don't you know their names?

Perhaps it's because at its best, film editing is an invisible art. While the cinematographer shoots pretty pictures that catch your eye and movie stars' faces grab your attention (they'd better, considering how much they cost), the editor's job is to make her work completely invisible. Although some filmmakers, such as Oliver Stone and Jean-Luc Godard, have chosen a cinematic style that draws attention to the filmmaking process, if you work professionally as a film editor (or aspire to), you're usually trying as hard as you can to keep anyone from noticing your editing work. In fact, the better the editing, the harder it is to observe and explain.

It's All Film

I use the terms "film," "video," "program," "show," and "movie" more or less interchangeably. Even though most of the content you'll be working with probably originates on video and may end up being distributed on video, "film" is still widely accepted as the best way to refer to the media that combine moving images with sound. Thus, the term "filmmaking" refers to the art of creating projects in all those different media.

Thousands of film and video editors are at work every day, cutting TV programs, news reports, video games, corporate training videos, movies, commercials, and many other projects. And whether you know it or not, in many cases when you say to yourself, "Wow, that film was great!" it's the work of the editor that you're applauding.

> **CUTTING** Another word for film editing. For many years, editing involved physically cutting pieces of film, scraping off some of the emulsion, applying special cement, and reassembling the pieces using a handy gadget called a splicing block. In this book, I will use the term generally to refer to any aspect of the editing process.

THE MAN BEHIND THE EDITING MACHINE

When I first became interested in filmmaking, I went to my local theater and watched Francis Ford Coppola's *Apocalypse Now* more than 20 times in a row. I went back every day, until the ticket taker started letting me in for free. I'm not sure if it was out of admiration or pity.

The reason I kept going back was that I was trying to deconstruct the film and figure out why it was so powerful—a difficult process, since films are designed precisely to defeat that kind of analysis. Every day I would sit there watching the screen, trying to catalogue the visual, aural, and story elements. And every day I got caught up in the film's seductive dramatic content and technique, and I would lose track of my analysis. Still, each day I got a little further into the film before I lost focus, until finally I could pretty much describe how the film was constructed, shot by shot.

Most people don't want to know how film works; they don't want anything to spoil the magic. Because deep down film *is* magic—which is part of what attracts some of us to learning how it works. Personally, I've always been drawn to things that seem impossible: I seek to understand the things that baffle me. So ever since my experience with *Apocalypse Now,* whenever a particular film really appeals to me, I go to see it again and again, until I can deconstruct it.

Becoming a Filmmaker

It wasn't long before I decided to try my hand at making movies myself, so in 1988 I enrolled in San Francisco State University. SFSU boasts a small, intensive film-production program that's highly respected in the filmmaking community. The focus is on film as a medium for artistic expression, rather than as a tool for entertainment or (God forbid) commerce.

Of course, if you're looking for a career in the real world of filmmaking, it's useful to know a particular skill set and excel at it. So I supplemented my artistic education at SFSU with an internship at a corporate video production house, where I honed my editing skills. I had also been writing screenplays for many years, and as I became more interested in directing, I looked for opportunities to work with actors as well.

Shortly after I graduated from film school, I produced, directed, and edited my first fiction film, *Theatereality,* but I kept working at the production house as an editor, assistant director, and video technician. Because I had taught myself basic computer skills, I became the company's computer expert as well.

Building Final Cut Pro

One thing led to another, and one day I woke up to find myself working at Adobe Systems, testing an early version of Adobe Premiere—one of the first digital desktop editing systems. Almost no one on the design team had any experience actually editing video; that was where I came in. Working closely with Randy Ubillos, the architect and lead engineer of Premiere, I reported bugs and helped design features for the forthcoming release.

When Randy resigned from Adobe to create a new division at Macromedia—one that would be responsible for building the ultimate next-generation tool for desktop video production—he invited me to join the team designing what would eventually become Final Cut Pro. Part of my job was heading a mini production studio within Macromedia where we could test the software on real-world projects.

The development of Final Cut Pro took nearly four years—far longer than had been expected—and in the meantime, Macromedia decided that a professional video-editing tool no longer fit the company's product strategy. In the summer of 1998, Apple took over the project and guided our focus squarely towards *DV.* Nine months later, Final Cut Pro version 1.0 was born.

> ***DV*** *The term "digital video" (in lowercase) refers to any video information that is stored digitally, but the acronym DV (in uppercase) refers to the latest digital technology for recording video images and the specific format it uses. That format may be further specified as MiniDV, DVCAM, or DVCPRO. Some variants include DV50 and DV100.*

During its entire development, I was using the software at whatever prototype stage it was at to cut my shows. This allowed me to make recommendations about improving the workflow and how the features would hold up in the real world. The engineers could look over my shoulder and observe how the program worked on an actual project. Everyone agreed that this process was one reason Final Cut Pro became such a useful—and successful—application. Indeed, many other software projects of all types (including Adobe Premiere) have adopted this technique as part of their development cycle. Perhaps it's this, more than the specific features of Final Cut Pro, that constitutes my real legacy to the world of software development.

Once Final Cut Pro was out in the world, my job was to teach people how to use it. In addition to building the tutorial that shipped with the software and constructing the demos Apple used at trade shows and sales meetings, I taught Final Cut Pro to Apple sales teams, product reps, and demo artists.

Back to the World of Filmmaking

All this was fun, but it was taking me further and further away from filmmaking. Finally, in September 1999, I left Apple to get back to *using* the tools rather than building them. I didn't totally give up on teaching, though. In the last few years I've led classes on Final Cut Pro, digital video production, cinema as an online medium, and related topics for places like the American Film Institute, DV Creators, and San Francisco State University.

These days I'm able to devote more time and energy to creating digital video projects of my own. Before leaving Apple I cofounded a theater company called Bare Witness Productions (www.barewitness.com) that produces short films using improvisational techniques both in front of and behind the camera. We go to real locations and use wireless mics and tiny DV cameras to perform and record improvised dramatic scenes. Then we edit the pieces and post the results on our Web site.

My current project (in addition to this book) is *Want,* a feature film about the culture of consumption. We shot for 34 days over a three-month period using PAL DVCAM, and I am currently editing the film with Final Cut Pro 2.0. *Want* should be finished just about the same time this book is published, so if the film festival circuit likes us, you may be hearing more about this film.

I will be using examples and anecdotes from my recent real-life projects throughout this book to illustrate and elaborate on various editing techniques and concepts. I hope this real-world anchor will give these lessons an element of truth that will help turn dry concepts into practices and techniques that are alive and easy to remember.

FINAL CUT PRO AND THE DIGITAL REVOLUTION

The last few years have seen nothing less than a bona fide revolution in the world of filmmaking. This is due in large part to new technologies, particularly DV; digital editing systems like Final Cut Pro; *FireWire;* the Internet; and computers powerful enough to process the huge data files produced by multimedia applications without taking all day to do it.

> **FIREWIRE** *FireWire (or IEEE 1394) allows high-speed data transfer over inexpensive cables. FireWire is the technology that connects your DV tape deck to your computer and transmits video, audio, and timecode information all at once, and very quickly. Before FireWire, connecting a deck to a computer meant hooking up as many as six different cables and having a special interface on the computer to plug all those cables into.*

What makes these technologies revolutionary is not so much their capability as their affordable price. Less than ten years ago, it would have cost at least $250,000 to set up a modest digital film production facility. Today, you can buy equipment and software that let you achieve the same professional production level for $25,000 or less.

All this is having a profound impact on our society—and it's far broader than simply making it possible to produce professional video on the cheap. Revolutionary technology is opening up the powerful medium of film to millions of people who had no previous access. This means we'll be hearing more voices—and that means new ways of shooting, editing, and thinking that will inevitably transform film in ways that are unimaginable today.

But the technology just gets you started. To become a successful film editor, you need to learn how to see the invisible art, how to understand and speak the secret visual language that editors use to build effective film sequences.

LANGUAGE CLASS, LESSON ONE

Whether you call it film or video, the moving image is a universal language, one that the whole world understands but only a limited few have taken the time to learn to speak.

As an editor, the biggest part of your job is to learn to deconstruct and understand the components of film language. You need to be able to do it in your sleep. I must warn you here and now that this may have a significant and detrimental impact on your ability to actually enjoy popular culture. Rather than relaxing and letting the filmmakers take you for a pleasant ride, you'll find yourself obsessively analyzing the media you see. This can have a dire effect on your personal relationships as well. Nothing spoils a first date like a detailed dissertation on the continuity errors in the romantic comedy you're watching.

Learning the Language

You'll also need to understand the common terms and specialized vocabulary used in the world of film and video production, as well as some terms that are specific to computer use and software operation. As we go along, I'll provide boxed definitions of terms that are potentially confusing or obscure. Also, you'll find a glossary in the back of the book summarizing these terms.

Turn Off the Sound

Want to see how it works? Turn off the sound.

Get a copy of your favorite movie or television show, and watch it *with the sound turned off.* Without the distraction of dialogue, sound effects, or musical score, it's easier to pay close attention to the visual elements that make up a sequence. For instance, duration: How long are the *shots?* Are they consistent or inconsistent in length (long and short shots intermixed)?

> **SHOT** *Every time the camera frames a different angle or image of the events being filmed, the resulting video or film is a shot. The word also refers to different ways of framing the action, as in "close shot" and "long shot."*
>
> **CUT** *A transition between shots in which the second image replaces the first image instantaneously.*

Are the shots connected by *cuts? Dissolves? Wipes?* Other special visual effects?

DISSOLVE *A transition between shots in which the first shot starts to fade out while the second image is fading in. In the middle of the dissolve, both shots are briefly superimposed.*

WIPE *A transition between shots in which the second image replaces the first image by taking some recognizable shape such as, for instance, an expanding circle or a moving diagonal line.*

Watch the sequence again, still without sound. This time pay attention to the *edit points* in each shot—the precise moment when one shot ends and the following shot begins. What's happening before and after each edit point? How are the pictures on either side of the edit point connected? Is the connection visual? Spatial? Emotional?

Now go back and watch the show a third time—this time with the sound on. What are the elements that make up the soundtrack? Music? On-camera dialogue? Off-camera speech? Sound effects? Background noise or *room tone?*

ROOM TONE *Unless you're in outer space, the environment around you has a characteristic sound. In a house it might be the soft hum of the refrigerator and the ticking of a clock. In a park it could be wind in the trees and a chattering squirrel. These sounds make up what filmmakers call room tone, an important consideration when recording and editing the soundtrack.*

Listen to how the sound interacts with the visual elements, how it bridges transitions and complements or contrasts with the visual content. Pay attention to the edit points for the sound: Where does each sound element start and end? Compare the audio edit points to the visual edit points. Notice how much, or how little, the sound affects the visual content.

The more you learn how to deconstruct the media you watch, the better you'll get at creating media of your own. After trying this exercise a few times, you'll start to do this sort of deconstruction automatically as you watch, without having to roll the show back. And you'll discover that your visual vocabulary is growing fast, making you a more effective editor and filmmaker.

THE GAME PLAN

Even if you don't plan to become a full-time video editor, or if producing video content is only a hobby or a small part of your current job, knowing the tools of this trade will benefit you in ways you may not realize. Consider that 15 years ago basic computer skills were widely seen as geeky esoterica; today they are a prerequisite for nearly any job. In just the same way, as technology continues to advance, video will become more and more commonplace in all types of communication. This book will teach you the basic editing concepts you'll need to prepare for that day.

We'll start by going over the basic elements of what film editing is all about. Then I'll move on to show you how to use Final Cut Pro like a pro. You'll learn to edit with skill and finesse and make the most of the program. Some of the techniques we'll explore are fairly basic, and some are quite advanced.

Final Cut Pro Not Required

Final Cut Pro is a powerful, versatile tool for sound editing, video editing, performing some kinds of special effects, and managing the *post-production* of film and video projects. And because it is my tool of choice, I will generally refer to it when I describe how to perform various editing operations.

> **POST-PRODUCTION** *Everything that happens after the film is shot, including editing, sound design, special effects, and so on. Also known as post.*

However, this book is aimed at teaching you how to become a competent, professional editor, not just a technician who knows the ins and outs of Final Cut Pro. The editing strategies I'll describe don't depend on using Final Cut Pro. They should be equally useful no matter what editing system you're using, whether it's an Avid, an old-fashioned splicing block, or some hot new program neither you nor I have heard of yet. Sometimes, finding the best solution to a particular problem may require a tool other than Final Cut Pro. In such cases I'll show you how to integrate that tool with the rest of your workspace.

Now that you have some idea what this book is, let me tell you what it is *not:*

This book is not a comprehensive manual. Final Cut Pro 2.0 comes with a 1,400-page tome detailing every option of every feature. Lisa Brenneis's *Final Cut Pro 2 for Macintosh: Visual QuickPro Guide,* also published by Peachpit Press, is another great resource to help you learn how each tool and feature works.

Nor is this book intended for absolute beginners at digital video. I won't tell you how to install your software, nor what hardware you should buy, nor how to hook it up. You'll need a basic familiarity with Macintosh operating procedures, and it will be extremely helpful if you have access to a Final Cut Pro workstation in order to try out the techniques described herein.

MORE THAN MAKING MARKS ON PAPER

We are all media consumers. Virtually anyone living in today's technological culture sees thousands of hours of professionally produced video and film every year. Images are used to communicate information, entertain, educate, and persuade—sometimes all at the same time. But even with the latest technology at your fingertips, filmmaking is not a simple medium to master. Sure, the tools are getting cheaper and simpler to use, but it is still easy to tell the work of a professional from that of an amateur.

Merely having paper and pencil does not make someone a writer. Writing is more than making marks on paper. It's a craft that requires a deep understanding of language, principles, and techniques—all of which will vary widely depending on the intended result. Film editing is just the same. Sure, anyone with a couple of thousand dollars can buy a computer and a video-editing application like Final Cut Pro—but that doesn't mean he knows how to edit.

By the time you complete this book, you will have learned to recognize a wide variety of editing situations and know exactly how the pros handle them. (You don't have to follow the "rules," of course, but at least you'll know which ones you're breaking.) And no matter what type of shows you'll be editing, the quality of your work will improve.

Not only will this book change the way you use your editing software, it will change the way you think about film.

> ### Keystroke Names
>
> *Whenever I specify a single-letter keystroke (as in, "To bring up the dialog box, press ⓣ") that letter will be printed in uppercase for readability. However, that doesn't mean you should type it in uppercase. In fact, I want you to hit that key without pressing ⓈⱧⒾⒻⓉ. On the rare occasions that I'll ask you to type something in uppercase, I'll include ⓈⱧⒾⒻⓉ followed by a hyphen, as in, "Press ⓈⱧⒾⒻⓉ-Ⓣⱽ." (The hyphen means press both keys simultaneously.) Bottom line: Unless you see a ⓈⱧⒾⒻⓉ, all letter keys should be typed lowercase.*

CHAPTER ONE

The Editor's Job

A movie is shaped three times. It is written; then it is produced; and finally, it is edited.

It all begins when a screenwriter lays out a vision for the film. He conceives characters and their dialogue or narration. He structures the dramatic events that constitute the plot and interweaves the themes that ultimately give meaning to the work.

Next, a producer acquires the rights to the script, and assembles a cast and crew to transform the written words into moving images and sounds that will be recorded on film or tape.

The most important person the producer will hire is the director, who instills the script with her own interpretation, emphasizing certain elements and downplaying others, adding tiny touches and deeper insights. Together, these collaborators revise the script to work within the financial restrictions and limitations of production logistics. Then they pick locations, hire actors, specify shots and *camera angles,* and start filming the scenes. With every individual decision they make, they shape the raw material of the film in their own unique way.

CAMERA ANGLE *Refers to camera position: high angle (camera shooting down from above the set), low angle (camera shooting up at the set from the ground), and so on.*

WHERE THE EDITOR FITS IN

Once a film is shot, the raw footage is handed over to an editing team, which continues to revise and adapt the material, shaping it into its final form. The editor will make her own changes to the vision—sometimes out of necessity (for instance, compensating for shots that are missing or have technical problems), sometimes through her own creative artistry. The editor may change the order of the scenes or the shots within a scene. She may decide to omit a shot that tells the audience what to think, or she may add one that foreshadows a dramatic event.

Sometimes a story may even be rewritten in the editing room—which means everything from its basic structure to the emotional tone, the underlying theme, and the way the audience feels about the characters gets revamped. Although a well-directed film usually won't require such drastic restructuring, there may be ideas present in the material, latent in the script, or concealed in the director's unconscious choices that are invisible to either writer or director. Often decisions made in the editing room reveal elements previously undiscovered in the original story or shooting script. A great editor can sense these hidden themes and bring them to light.

For instance, several years ago I cut a show about Ron, a mentally retarded man who was trying to find love. The director had an annoying habit of composing his shots with some foreground object obscuring part of the frame. When I asked him why, he just said he liked the way it looked—but as I assembled the scenes, I began to realize that in a certain way the images reflected Ron's difficulty seeing and understanding the world clearly and his inability to interact with it effectively.

Although the "obscured" shots cropped up throughout the film, I decided to use them most often in the early scenes. Then, after the climax, when Ron makes a real emotional connection with the woman he loves, I stopped using them entirely. The result was a subtle but effective way to help the audience understand the character's unique view of the world. The director reaped critical accolades praising him for this visual touch. At first I was irritated that he got all the credit, especially since he had hardly noticed how my editing was helping to get an important story point across. But I later realized the technique had really come from his insight, albeit an unconscious one—although it wasn't until I sensed it in the editing room that I was able to make it work.

The writer creates a story, and the director gives it vision—but it's the editor who tells it.

FOOTAGE *All the video and audio shot during production.*

THE EDITING PROCESS

Editing involves a lot more than simply cutting film. An experienced editor knows how to work in creative collaboration with the director, the producer, and even the writer. And he understands that most editing decisions are based on the special nature and design of every film or video project. Part of the craft of editing is treating each project uniquely, shaping it to find how the material can best be communicated.

What Kind of Film Are You Making?

Often it's the big questions that never get asked, and the biggest question of all is: What the heck are you trying to do, anyway? People make films for all sorts of reasons, but for the most part they can be sorted into four main categories: films that inform, educate, persuade, and entertain.

Once you know which category (or categories) your film falls into, you'll be able to determine the answers to many of the smaller questions that will occur during the editing process.

These four ideas will lead you in four different editing directions. Confusing them, or trying to follow too many of them at once, may destroy the integrity of the project and undermine its potential. Don't kid yourself. If you're making an instructional video about building materials, don't get caught up trying to entertain when you should be educating. Likewise, if you're creating an ad to sell designer perfume, don't try to teach the viewer how to make her own.

Of course, there's always overlap. Some projects may inform at one point, educate at another, and entertain at a third. And some films fall outside of this simplified structure altogether. Still, knowing where you stand in terms of your intent will help you make a better show.

Films That Inform

What I mean by "inform" is simply providing facts about a given subject. For instance, an informative film about eggs would not attempt to convince the audience that eggs are good or bad for people's health but might show, among other things, how they are brought to market in rural China. This type of film would generally be classified as a documentary, or perhaps as a corporate communications piece. If your goal is to inform, some editing strategies might be:

- Clearly identify the content as information. This can be done with graphics or special effects, sound cues, or subtler editing techniques such as pacing. For instance, you would tell your story in chronological order, making sure to stop at important points and discuss why they matter.

- Summarize important content. At the end of each section, or at the end of the film, reiterate the essential information that you want the audience to take home with them. You can do this with a graphic chart or a list, or sometimes by replaying selected scenes with a narrator reminding the viewer what their significance is.

Films That Educate

While "informing" and "educating" do overlap a bit, the goal of an educational film is generally not just to supply viewers with information but to show them how to use that information. For instance, if the egg film were re-edited to be educational, it might explain how to select eggs at a market; how to identify their origin, age, and cholesterol content; and how to ensure against taking home a package with a cracked egg in it. If your goal is to educate, some editing strategies might be:

- Break down the subject or task into small, clearly identifiable parts. For example, tell your viewers that choosing eggs includes noting their expiration date, checking the level of refrigeration they're stored at, inspecting each egg for cracks, and checking the carton for signs of contamination. You would probably use specific shots or sequences to illustrate each of these points.

- Provide assignments or tasks to help the viewer apply what she's learned. For example, send the viewer out to buy some eggs, and include a sequence where she can look at the eggs while you show a sample package on-screen.

- Repeat important steps more than once. Learning is based on repetition. The more you repeat critical information, the more likely the viewer is to retain it.

Films That Persuade

Persuading is a cross between informing and entertaining. A good persuasive film doesn't feel preachy or didactic. At their best, such films are entertainment that leaves you with a particular message: For instance, if you want to persuade your audience that eggs are the best food for breakfast, lunch, and dinner, you might base your show around a happy family that eats lots of eggs. If your goal is to persuade, some editing strategies might be:

- Show both sides of an issue. Neglecting to acknowledge the opposing view leaves an audience suspicious. For instance, you could acknowledge that because eggs don't have much fiber, the happy family might want to eat some salad on the side now and then with their omelette.

- Focus on the micro view first, and then extrapolate to the macro. For example, start by telling the story of one family and its egg consumption habits, and then expand to show how the whole community benefits.

- Pay extra attention to your soundtrack. Music will affect the emotions of your viewers far more powerfully than purely visual information.

Films That Entertain

Entertainment refers to shows that deliver levity, distraction, or amusement. Entertainment can also provide emotional release such as empathy. An entertaining egg movie could tell the story of a chicken desperate to keep her eggs from being eaten. She follows a customer home and devises elaborate obstacles to prevent his family from cooking her eggs. If you are trying to entertain your audience, some editing strategies might be:

- Hide the evidence of filmmaking artifice. You want to disguise the fact that a crew of 52 people worked for three days in order to make a scene that runs for only ten minutes on-screen. A great deal of editing technique is about concealing this artifice.

- Use editing techniques that emphasize suspense, humor, and action (see Chapter 3, "Editing Patterns").

- Create an emotionally engaging story.

Know Your Tools

Whether you're editing on an Avid, Final Cut Pro, or a Steenbeck flatbed, the better you know your production tools, the better you'll do. Of course, just knowing which toolbar holds which bells and whistles won't tell you when to use them, but familiarizing yourself with time-saving shortcuts and compound features available in your editing tool will free up more of your brain power for making those creative decisions.

It's equally important to know what your tool *can't* do. Don't try to drive nails with a screwdriver. Sure, it sort of works…but wouldn't you be happier using a hammer? For example, Final Cut Pro has some robust *compositing* (see Chapter 8, "Special Effects") and audio capabilities, but other tools like Discreet Combustion or Avid ProTools are better suited for accomplishing complex tasks in those areas. Likewise, you could probably edit a feature film in Adobe After Effects, since it's geared toward creating special effects, but why would you want to?

> **COMPOSITING** *The act of combining two or more images on-screen at the same time. This can be as simple as superimposing a title card on top of an image or as complex as mixing multiple layers with special effects, transparency, and motion. The end result is a composite shot.*

Most professional editors have a big "box" of tools, each one suited for a different job. Knowing which tool is right for which job is one of the things that differentiates a pro from a novice—but this kind of knowledge comes only from experience. If you're still learning, be patient: Read books like this, and exchange ideas with more seasoned editors via user groups, online forums, and so on. You'll learn a lot.

Most important, edit everything you can get your hands on. Nothing can teach you better than actually doing the job. The beauty of the new technology is that it's easier (and cheaper) than ever to gain experience by actually producing video projects. If you've got some downtime between paying gigs, go ahead and put together a project to keep you busy. Try doing a public service announcement for a nonprofit you admire or a music video for a friend's band. Every hour you spend editing will make you a better editor. You will hone your craft, develop a personal style, and of course, add clips to your résumé and reel.

Know Your Audience

You can't edit well if you don't know your audience. Editing a film aimed at teenage girls will be very different than editing one targeted at middle-aged businessmen. A good editor never forgets who will be watching the film, and she uses that knowledge as the basis for every decision she makes. Hopefully, the writer, director, and production crew were aware of this, too, as they carried out their roles, but you, the editor, are the final gatekeeper, the ultimate arbiter of how to best communicate the film's message.

Still, don't presume that you can guess what your audience wants. Nothing turns an audience off quicker than a film that feels patronizing or "targeted." To learn what viewers want, find some and ask them. For instance, if you're making a film meant for single working mothers, ask your friends if they know someone in that demographic. Then quiz her about what television shows she watches and what kinds of movies she tends to see. You'll probably be surprised at what you find. Are you making a show that's supposed to be exciting for kids? Great! Go out and find some kids, ask the same questions, and listen to their answers. If possible, show your sample viewers a *rough cut* of your film and invite specific feedback.

This kind of legwork is what separates great editors from merely good ones: A few hours of research may be all it takes to turn your show from predictable to hip.

> **ROUGH CUT** *An interim cut of the show, usually containing incomplete sound, place-holders for special effects shots that aren't done yet, and some editing areas that require further work.*

Get Involved Early

It's your job to cut the movie and make it look as good as you can, but this can be tough if you have no control over what got shot in the first place. Is this an unfair predicament? Of course, but try telling that to your producer after the film bombs.

> **COVERAGE** *Refers to the number and variety of shots and angles that were filmed during production in addition to the "master shot." Good coverage means you have lots of editing choices; poor coverage means you have only one or two choices for cutting each scene.*

Smart editors get involved in the production as early as possible so they can ensure that adequate *coverage* is shot. Sometimes coverage is so bad that you simply can't cut the scene without changing its structure. On smaller productions, the producer and director may not have the foresight or budget to bring in an editor before finalizing their *shot lists,* but it's very much in your interest—and theirs—for you to look over those shot lists and (if necessary) talk with the writer, producer, and director before production begins.

> **SHOT LIST** *Breakdown of how a scene will be filmed, shot by shot. May be supplemented by a matching series of shot sketches known as a storyboard.*

> **INSERT** *A close-up of an object or detail within a scene.*

What should you look for? Every scene should be covered from multiple angles: long shots, close-ups, reverse angles (see Chapter 2, "Film Language"). Action sequences require even more coverage than static scenes. Objects that play an important role in the scene should be captured in *inserts,* and emotional content should be emphasized with close-ups of the actors' faces. Always insist on *cutaways* for every scene. And remind the audio recordist to record room tone for every location and mic position.

> **CUTAWAY** *A shot of a neutral element from the location that's not part of the current shot but is part of the current scene. For a scene that takes place at the beach, a classic cutaway would be a shot of seagulls flying.*

Another thing to watch out for is scene transitions. What's the editing plan to get out of one scene and into the next? If this is overlooked during production, the editor will have to scrounge up something for a suitable bridge.

Also, the earlier you get involved, the more opportunity you'll have to become familiar with the story and the details of the footage.

If you can swing it, it's great to be physically present on set during filming. Here's why:

- You may get ideas for cutaways or additional coverage once you see the actual location.

- If time is running short on set, shots are often dropped or combined. Sometimes that's OK, but it will end up being *your* problem if the crew fails to get adequate coverage or if the *DP* hurriedly places a shot on the wrong side of the *axis*.

> **DP** *Short for director of photography.*
>
> **AXIS** *An imaginary line based on the eyeline of the on-camera subject.*

Thirty seconds on set can save you many hours of post-production agony.

Sometimes it's nice for an editor to come onto a job completely "clean"—without any knowledge of, or attachment to, what occurred during production. For instance, someone who suffered through an 18-hour production day when the rave scene was shot may have a harder time trimming it. A totally mercenary editor can cut more ruthlessly and may make a better final program.

Meet the Team

If at all possible, take time to discuss the film with the writer and director before you start editing. You want to fully understand where the story originated and how it's been interpreted before you got involved. You will need to work closely with the director to find out if he wants to highlight or downplay certain script elements. This will provide valuable clues about how to approach the editing process.

For instance, in *Want* I intended it to seem as though the moon was watching over the main character, so throughout the film we continually returned to high-angle shots to simulate the moon's point of view. Regardless of what was photographed, the choice and placement of these shots was an editing decision. Another example would be the director asking the editor to use a certain sound effect every time a particular character or location is seen.

The relationship between the editor and the director is one of the most crucial associations in the production. Some directors spend many hours in the editing room, looking over the editor's shoulder and taking an active role in the editing process. Others assume that the editor has done her homework and leave it to her to get the job done. In either case, good communication with your director will result in a clear editorial vision that illuminates the project in its best light. A bad relationship may lead to a situation where the directorial vision and the editing style are so incompatible that they compete, confusing or distracting the audience and diluting the impact of the film.

Consider a music video I edited for the band Roadkill Jim. When they handed me the footage I wasn't given any specific instructions, so I followed my interpretation of the languid song and chose a slow pacing for the verse sequences and a choppy *jump cut* style for the chorus. The problem was that because the director had chosen to shoot the verse sequences with a hand-held camera, these shots had an unsettling feel that contrasted unpleasantly with my choice of pacing. Predictably, the director hated what I had done, and I wound up having to re-edit much of the piece. Better communication up front would have prevented me from going down a dead end and disappointing the director.

> **JUMP CUT** *Any cut or transition that breaks the continuity of time, space, or screen direction—deliberately or accidentally—or where the action doesn't match across the edit point.*

Working With the Director

The director is responsible for the overall look and feel of the program. Your job is to implement that look and feel, while stepping around the land mines inherent in the footage. In order for the decisions made during production and the decisions made in post-production to match stylistically, it is imperative that the editor understand and share the director's vision.

Unfortunately, many directors don't know anything about editing. The first thing you should do is buy them a copy of this book. OK, lend them yours—but make sure they read it. A director doesn't have to be able to use Final Cut Pro, but the more familiar she is with the details of the editor's job, the more effective your communication will be. Often the best directors have a background in editing and are fluent in the language and grammar of film.

I hate to say this, but I'm surprised how often I find myself working with incompetent directors. I think film directing is easier to screw up than most jobs. That's because a) it's very difficult to learn to direct in a classroom setting, b) there's no way to get experience directing except by directing, and c) it's tough to get a directing job unless you've had experience. These problems are frequently amplified by insecure directors' tendency to overcompensate for lack of ability with attitude.

For the most part, directors demonstrate their incompetence by not knowing what they want. The only solution to this is to *tell* them what they want—and to make them think they came up with the idea themselves. This is most easily accomplished by offering them a couple of options, carefully devised to guide them toward choosing the one you think is best.

Editing Room Protocol

Different people work differently. You need to figure out what your own preferences are so you can do your best work—and then make sure everyone understands how you want your editing room to run. Sometimes a director will look over your shoulder throughout the editing process. Other times she will leave you alone as long as you turn in a daily or weekly report. Which model makes you most comfortable? Do you enjoy the collaborative nature of having the director in the room, or does that destroy your concentration?

Make sure you find out how often you are supposed to turn in work to the director and producer. Different plans may be appropriate depending on the length of the program.

Create a Realistic Schedule

One of the biggest mistakes an editor can make is underestimating how long a project will take—and underbidding the price. The fact is, it can be very difficult to guess how long a film will take to edit, especially since so many factors that affect the schedule are beyond your control. Still, unless you help your producer and director set realistic expectations, you may be in for an unpleasant experience.

This may seem like an intrusion of business advice into the middle of what's supposed to be a creative manual, but in the film industry, creativity and business are inextricably connected. Depending on various factors, it can take anywhere from one day to one week to complete editing one minute of film. Coming up with an accurate overall estimate will mean the difference between a good edit and a sloppy rush job.

> **FINE CUT**   Sometimes called picture lock, this is the final edit of the picture.

Also keep the 80/20 rule in mind: The last 20 percent of the process invariably takes 80 percent of the time. You may complete a rough cut quickly, but that doesn't necessarily mean the *fine cut* will be equally fast.

Here are some of the factors that will impact your editing schedule.

The Footage

Before you come up with an estimate for editing time, take a look at the footage. Ideally, you should screen some of that footage before taking the job in the first place. What you mostly need to find out is how much coverage was shot. A show with very little coverage means fewer choices for you when it's time to build a sequence. Also, you want to check whether the camera angles match and the quality of the production sound is usable.

> **PICKUPS**   Additional shots requested by the editor, to be collected after principal photography is complete.
>
> **ADR**   Short for "automatic dialogue replacement," also known as looping. This is the process by which actors in a sound studio re-record dialogue while watching playback of a loop of the shot so they can match lip movements on-screen. ADR is frequently used to replace poor production sound or to change the delivery of a line.

The Budget

Is there enough money for reshoots? *Pickups*? *ADR*? *Foley* and proper sound design? How about *color correction*? How flexible is the budget for *post*? All of this will impact your schedule.

> **FOLEY**   *The art of re-creating incidental sound effects (such as footsteps) in the sound studio, in synchronization with the images on-screen. The term is named after Jack Foley, one of the first sound designers.*
>
> **COLOR CORRECTION**   *Part of finishing a show is fine-tuning the color matching for every shot.*

The Vision

How clear is the director's vision? Does the footage serve that vision? How well do you understand it? If the director's vision isn't clear at the start, you may need to re-edit a show multiple times while you and he try to figure out what it is. This will impact not only how long the project takes but also your satisfaction in editing it.

The Schedule

Of course, someone on the producer's staff has already decided how long the project will take to edit, and she will expect you to work within her schedule. While it is not *impossible* for someone to estimate correctly, in my experience most estimates fall somewhere between overly optimistic and wildly unrealistic. Shows that are budgeted for three weeks' editing time often take four weeks, and sometimes as many as six.

> **ASSEMBLY**   *The first rough cut of a show, which contains all the material in approximately the correct position but not yet edited for style or pacing.*

It's important to be clear on exactly what you are expected to deliver in the allotted time. An *assembly*? A rough cut? A fine cut? *Sound mix*? Sometimes dates are flexible; sometimes the schedule is locked down because of a commitment made by the producers. You need to know which is the case before you start, because as soon as you sign on this will be *your* problem.

> **SOUND MIX** *This is the final stage of post-production, after the picture is locked. It involves mixing the sound from many individual tracks into the final, balanced track that will be distributed with the film.*

How Much Should You Charge?

Sometimes you will sign on for an hourly rate; other times you'll be asked to bid for the job on the basis of a one-time project fee. In most cases, you should try to bill hourly. Otherwise you're going to wind up working a few 20-hour days at your own expense as the schedule draws to a close.

> **Sample Schedules**
>
> *Here is a sampling of rough estimates for how long a typical project is likely to take from start to finish. Of course, projects with special needs, like complex visual effects or sound design, can blow these estimates.*
> - *90-minute feature narrative film: 6 to 12 months*
> - *60-minute feature documentary film: 9 to 18 months*
> - *60-minute TV movie: 3 months*
> - *10-minute corporate training video: 4 weeks*
> - *4-minute music video: 8 to 10 weeks*
> - *4-minute film trailer: 3 to 12 weeks*
> - *30-second TV commercial: 3 to 6 weeks*
> - *1-second motion graphics title sequence : 3 to 6 weeks*

Read the Script

The most important thing an editor can do to prepare for a job is to become intimately familiar with the processes and creative decisions that preceded her work—starting with the script. The better you know your script, the easier it will be to create an editing style that's consistent with the larger vision of the production.

A good editor should know the script as thoroughly as the writer does—not just the structure of the story and the sequence of events but themes, tone, and style. Is the story about human relationships, or does it explore an inner psychological state? Is it comic? Contemplative? Suspenseful? Understanding the big picture will help you to resolve smaller editing problems as they arise.

View the Footage

You also need to become deeply familiar with all the *footage* available to you. Every shot, every *take*. The better you know the footage, the better you'll be able to edit it. Perhaps there's a two-second shot from scene 31 you can steal to complete an editing sequence in scene 18. Or perhaps there's a moment after the director called "Cut" but before the camera operator stopped shooting when the actor let her guard down and gave a genuine expression that's exactly what will sell scene 91.

I'll repeat this, because it's supremely important: *You need to review every take of every shot.* It's tempting to simply scan through the takes that the director circled on the shot list or camera log—meaning he thought they were "good"—but again and again I've found that there may be a magical moment, say, at the beginning of an aborted take, that might make all the difference when you construct the final sequence.

> **TAKE**   *Refers to a single iteration of a scene or shot, as in take 1, take 2, and so on.*

Final Cut Pro has very powerful tools for marking and cataloguing your media (see Chapter 4, "Preparing to Edit"). Use them! Watch the footage again and again. All of it. Catalogue it, make comments about the shots, and note the things that stand out. If you follow this advice you will find that you have the entire body of footage in your head and at your fingertips when you are editing. And that's exactly what you need.

Budget Time for Sound Design

Remember that audio creates more than half the impact of your program. Three kinds of sound are combined to create the final audio track: dialogue, sound effects, and music. Often these will take up dozens of discrete tracks. Thankfully, Final Cut Pro has unlimited audio tracks available to you (see Chapter 7, "Cutting the Track").

The process of assembling and editing audio can become very complex, and large productions typically hire two or three specialized sound editors to help you out— along with a post-production supervisor to boss you around. One sound editor will cut dialogue while another edits the sound effects tracks.

The music supervisor will secure rights to copyright-protected materials and hire a composer, if needed, to write an original score. A third editor, the music editor, may be responsible for editing the music and incorporating it into the final sound mix.

On smaller productions, many of these jobs are handled by fewer people, but ultimately you, as editor, will be responsible for bringing together dialogue, sound effects, and music for the final sound mix. For any film that will be dubbed, or distributed in foreign languages, you will be required to provide an M & E (music and effects) track, which is a separate version of the final mix with everything except the dialogue.

Coordinating Special Effects Production

Similarly, in most big-budget productions, special visual effects will be created and edited by a separate team. The visual effects supervisor will oversee the production of the shots, working with a crew that can range from a team of artists designing models at a digital workstation to an entire production crew responsible for shooting plates, making mattes, building models, filming motion control sequences, and so on.

It's critical for the visual effects team to operate in very close coordination with editorial, since the results of each team's work will affect the other. The editor needs to know the precise length and placement of the special effects shots, and the effects team needs to return *comps* as quickly as possible so the editor can see how they integrate into her scenes. This process often takes several rounds of back and forth to complete successfully.

> **COMPS** Short for "composites," rough versions of completed special effects sequences.

The Art of the Possible

It's essential to understand the realities of your production. Learn to factor budgetary constraints, time constraints, length of the show, and client control into your editing decisions. For instance, sure, the show might be better if you ran the whole thing through the *Cinelook* filter and remixed the sound at a Dolby Surround mixing stage—but before you start making editing decisions based on those expectations, be sure you have the time to do it and the money to pay for it.

> **CINELOOK** Cinelook, Filmlook, and Magic Bullet are all post-production processes that manipulate color balance, frame rate, and aspect ratio to make content shot on video appear as if it were shot on film. Filmlook and Magic Bullet require you to send your video to a facility for processing, but Cinelook is a plug-in that works with Final Cut Pro or Adobe After Effects.

Another example: Don't rely on special effects if the producer doesn't have the money to do them right. And yet another: It might be better to trim the car chase scene so the show will fit into the 47-minute required length for your desired TV slot, even though everyone referred to it as "the money shot."

A mediocre show that's finished is infinitely better than a brilliant one that never gets completed. Thousands of projects are abandoned every year.

Finally, it's important to know where your responsibilities begin and end. If your director or client has final say over your creative decisions, you need to understand that fact before you pull your hair out over creative differences. She has her reasons, and if you don't like 'em…go out and make your own film!

CHOOSING THE SHOT

One of the most important parts of the editor's job is to discard unusable footage. A typical production shoots between 20 and 100 times more footage than the editor will use in the final program. (This is what filmmakers mean when they refer to a 20:1 or 100:1 *shooting ratio*.) That means the editor must eliminate (in the former case) 19 minutes of footage for every minute she uses. How do you decide what to toss?

> **SHOOTING RATIO** *A comparison of footage shot to finished film. Shooting ratios may range from 5:1 on a typical low-budget industrial or training film to 100:1 or more on a TV commercial or big-budget feature.*

Usually you'll have *heads and tails* that inflate the shooting ratio a little. Depending on the nature of the production, you may have lots of different shots of each scene (coverage), you may have lots of takes of each shot, or you may have both.

> **HEADS AND TAILS** *Extra footage at the beginning and end of a shot.*

How do you tell a good shot from a bad one? Here are some criteria professional editors use to make the cut.

Composition

An editor has to be able to recognize the elements of good composition. Composition refers to the arrangement of objects within the frame, and the elements therein include both positive and negative space (**Figure 1.1**).

Figure 1.1 "Positive space" refers to the areas in the image containing subject matter, and "negative space" refers to the areas without it. Positive and negative space can also be thought of as areas of light and darkness. Good composition requires an appropriate balance between positive and negative space. This image contains a large amount of negative space at one side, which contributes to the dramatic impact of the shot.

To some extent defining "good" composition and "bad" composition is an aesthetic exercise involving subjective elements like personal taste—and a good editor should be able to recognize not just her own taste but the varied tastes of her varied audiences. Nonetheless, you can use several quantifiable technical criteria to help eliminate badly composed shots.

Headroom

Good composition requires adequate negative space framing a subject's head. Look for shots with a small but comfortable buffer between the subject's head and the edge of the frame. If the buffer space is too small, the subject will appear cramped or contained. If the buffer space is too large, the subject will appear to be floating loosely in his environment. Both errors make the viewer feel uncomfortable.

There are only two exceptions to this rule:

- Extreme close-ups where it's OK to cut off the top of the head in order to see the jaw move.

- Wide shots where showing the subject in the context of the environment requires placing him far from the edges of the frame (**Figure 1.2**).

Figure 1.2 The images above show proper headroom: The subjects are clearly visible without any wasted space.

The pictures above show incorrect headroom. The image on the left has too much empty space above the subject, and the image on the right cuts off the face of one of the two subjects.

The images above illustrate exceptions to the headroom rule. On the left, this wide shot captures the subject as a silhouette against the surf. The "excessive" space above the subject's head is desirable because it helps to show the environment and the subject's place in it. Tight close-ups typically cut off the top of the subject's head in order to reveal jaw movement, as illustrated on the right.

Noseroom (AKA Facespace)

Look for shots with adequate room between the subject and the edge of the frame *in the direction she's facing.* If the subject is too close to the edge of the frame, the audience can't see what she's looking at. This is unsettling and distracts viewers from the subject herself, focusing their attention on the space just offscreen where the subject is looking. This effect becomes amplified when you take into account the various rules and guidelines regarding screen direction, and whether a subject should be looking screen-right or screen-left (**Figure 1.3**). (See the section on screen direction in Chapter 2.)

Figure 1.3 The image on the left shows good noseroom: Since the subject is on the right side of the frame, looking left, the composition provides a comfortable amount of space between her and the edge of frame. The image on the right shows poor noseroom: The subject is on the right side of frame, looking directly into the right frame edge. This unsettles the audience because they can't see what she's looking at. That's true for the first picture as well, but at least in that composition the frame edge is a comfortable distance away.

Also, pay attention to how the character is centered in the frame—which may be significant both in terms of the shot's emotional impact and in identifying the correct reverse shot when dealing with point of view (see the sections on reverse and point-of-view shots in Chapter 2). This will be even more pronounced when working in a wide-screen format like 16:9 or 1:1.85.

Point of Focus

One of the editor's key tasks is to guide the audience's attention, not just in terms of how the main story is told from the beginning to the end of the film, but in each shot along the way. You need to choose shots with a clear point of focus. That could be a character, an object, a conflict, or an action.

For instance, a *two-shot* (that's any shot with two people in it; see the section on two-shots in Chapter 2) where one or both figures' head- and noseroom are compromised in order to see both of them, or where one subject is bouncing in and out of the frame, is very distracting. The viewer doesn't know where the point of focus is and loses interest in the narrative (**Figure 1.4**).

Figure 1.4 This shot is badly composed because it doesn't provide a clear point of focus for the viewer. Both characters are partially cut off. This could have been corrected by moving farther away from the subjects or panning to one or the other.

Distracting Background Elements

Shots in which an object appears to be sticking out of the back of someone's head (**Figure 1.5**) or a highly legible sign or brightly colored object is creating a distraction in the background are badly composed. The objects tend to draw attention away from the subject. Sometimes the distracting element might be a light stand, a *grip,* a mic boom, the boom operator, or maybe just his shadow. Pay special attention to reflections and shadows. Nothing spoils a shot like the camera operator's shadow falling on the subject.

Figure 1.5 While in some cases you can overlook distracting background elements, at other times they are just too glaring. This framing gives the actor an impressive hairstyle that I suspect neither she nor the set stylist intended.

It's general practice in dramatic films to hide the tools of film creation as much as possible. Some formats, such as documentary or reality-based programs, will tolerate revealing these elements.

> **GRIP** *The technical crew on a film shoot is usually separated into two categories, based on whether they handle electrical equipment or nonelectrical equipment. A grip handles nonelectrical equipment.*

Lighting Problems

Badly lit shots can diffuse the viewer's point of focus or destroy it altogether. At worst, they can be so distracting they are unusable.

But perfect lighting is not crucial—although it helps to be able to see the subject. The most important consideration is how well the lighting in a given shot matches the shots around it. If, in a single scene, you cut from a brightly lit shot to a dimly lit one, you pull the viewer's attention away from the subject and toward the construction of the film itself. Scenes that are under- or overexposed can play convincingly as long as all the shots in the sequence are consistent. Pickups can be problematic in this regard, because they are often shot at a different time from the sequence into which they'll be cut and may display different lighting characteristics.

> **LENS FLARE** *A spot of haze or discoloration created when a light source shines directly into a camera lens.*

In general, look out for *lens flares,* backlit subjects, and shots with conflicting key light. If the key light is coming from the left in the master shot and the right in the single, it won't match (see the sections on master and single shots in Chapter 2).

> **KEY LIGHT** *The primary source of light in a scene.*

Audio Problems

Audio that sounds inconsistent across different shots in the same scene is even worse than inconsistent lighting. Visuals convey information, so as long you can see what's going on, the picture will be understood. Audio tends to convey emotional tone, so we're much more sensitive to subtle inconsistencies in the audio. Fortunately, many audio problems can be repaired in post, but this is often expensive and sometimes quite difficult.

You may be able to steal better-matching audio from another take. This is generally easier to pull off in a long shot than a close-up, and it also depends on how consistently the *talent* delivered the lines. Sometimes you can get away with mixing the track with a fair amount of room tone to mask the mismatch or run music or other sound elements over the entire sequence to achieve the same result. As a last resort, you can ADR the production sound, although this can result in artificial-sounding audio. Even the most talented actors sometimes have trouble re-creating the same emotional tone they achieved during filming.

TALENT *Film-biz talk for actors.*

Check It Out on the Big Screen

Never make a final editing decision about anything until you view the sequence in the same format the audience will see. Problems that seem insignificant (or even invisible) on your 13-inch editing monitor can explode into disaster when projected 20 feet tall.

For instance, timing and performances work very differently at different scales, so you should hold off locking down a sequence until you've seen it at full scale. You'll want to pace your scene a little more slowly if the film is going to be projected in a theater and a little more quickly for shows intended for videotape release.

If your final presentation mode will be VHS videotape, don't finalize your edit until you see what happens to contrast and detail when your high-resolution masters are dubbed down to VHS. Perhaps that shot with borderline exposure problems will become unacceptably murky after it goes through the transfer process. Better to find out before 10,000 tapes have been duplicated.

PERFORMANCE: CHOOSING THE TAKE

The editor is responsible for choosing the performances that best communicate the purpose of the scene—and of the whole piece. Often the director will be involved in these decisions, but if you're lucky, he won't be there all the time.

In most cases someone on set will have kept a *camera log*. Sometimes the best takes will be circled, or flagged with Good, Better, Best indicators. Having this information is invaluable, especially when the director has already provided her recommendations. But don't rely on the log alone; the editor's eye may discern problems that everyone else has missed.

> **CAMERA LOG** *A detailed journal, made on set during production, recording essential information that will enable the camera crew to re-create the shot if necessary: the camera's f-stop, focal length, position, and so on. It also usually includes information for the editor, such as length of shots, where they are on the film or tape, and comments on the content of the shot.*

Watch Every Take

Occasionally a flaw that seemed fatal on the set proves to be subtle, unnoticeable, or easily fixable in the editing room. Unfortunately, most of the time the reverse is true—and what was chosen as the "best take" on the set has a glaring lens flare or some audio problem that went unnoticed at the time. Sometimes, the "best take" may not match *continuity* with the "best take" of another shot. In that case the editor must make a trade-off between maintaining continuity and choosing the best performance.

> **CONTINUITY** *In order to make a seamless edit between two shots, it's important that both shots match up in as many ways as possible: props, key lighting, focal length, speed of motion in the frame, screen direction, room tone, and so on. If all the elements match, the shots maintain continuity.*

In fact, often the best take is really a combination of several takes. Since you're likely to be cutting back and forth between shots, you can use the beginning of one take, the middle of another, and the end of a third. A shot described on the camera log as aborted or unacceptable may actually have been perfectly successful—until the moment when the light fell over. There's no reason not to use the beginning of that take.

Ultimately, it is up to you to make the best film you can with the footage available to you. The better you know every foot of that footage, the more likely you are to make the wisest choices. You should see every frame of film or tape, and you should see it more than once.

What constitutes a good take? Usually it's a combination of what happens in front of the camera and what happens behind it. Sometimes a mediocre performance can be transformed into a great take by a stellar camera movement. Sometimes the camera operator may reframe subtly at just the right time, accidentally anticipating the actor's movement within the frame. Each take is different and offers different opportunities to a good editor.

Style and How to Get It

Style is a pretty abstract thing. I use the word to describe a filmmaker's aesthetic approach to the material. Style explains why one editor might choose to edit rhythmically while another prefers a bumpier cutting style and a third uses a technique like jumpcutting (see the section on jumpcutting in Chapter 2). Style is why one director might select wide-angle lenses for a scene or shoot from a crane. Stylistic issues apply equally to audio, lighting, casting, and the script. Although style may seem subtle and of less concern than the content of your program, it can make the difference between a pretty good program and a great one.

Ask Orson Welles, Federico Fellini, or George Lucas. Style is everything.

Editing With Style

The key to good style is twofold: First, consistency. Second, appropriateness.

Consistency

In some ways, stylistic consistency is far more important than specific decisions about whether to cut fast or slow, hand-hold the camera, or play a whole scene in a low-angle wide shot. Consistent style may not necessarily be "good," but inconsistent style is always bad. Not only is inconsistency aesthetically unappealing, it interferes with communicating your program's message.

So...select an approach and stick with it. Simply being aware of having consciously *selected* a style will often be enough to remind you to make editing decisions consistent with that style.

Appropriateness

Next comes appropriateness. Editing style must complement the content of the film in a way that creates something greater than the sum of its parts.

For example, on my film *Want* I needed to show two different worlds in which the main character lives: the glamorous public world where he works, shops, eats, and drives; and the darker, personal world where he carries out private activities and makes emotional contacts. The DP and I called the two worlds Glamland and Underworld, and we set up a list of stylistic elements for each one: Glamland shots were made from a crane or a tripod, Underworld shots were hand-held or shot from a monopod; Glamland scenes were lit warmly and evenly, Underworld shots were lit with shadowed areas and a cooler look; Glamland used bright colors, while Underworld was muted and monochromatic.

We went through the entire script and identified where each scene fit along the continuum between Glamland and Underworld. This way, during production all we had to do was glance at our chart once per scene to know exactly what the intended style was to be.

In the end, our stylistic vision informed everything about the film, from the costume designs to camera placement and dramatic direction for the scenes. The end result was, I like to think, a film that has a clear and poignant style.

Where Does Style Come From?

Style starts with the script. Good writing always has style, and good script writing is no exception. At the simplest level you can look at what genre a script is: Comedy? Thriller? Western? Romantic comedy? Genres like these come with their own traditional styles, elements that an audience will expect. For instance, a thriller drops clues early on that will lure the audience into trying to solve the mystery.

To get an idea of how this works, look at some of your favorite genre films and try to figure out what types of scenes carry the weight of the film. Are the themes conveyed through dialogue or through actions? What are the rhythms of the script, the pacing of the cutting?

At every stage of a film production, as creative film workers do their jobs they are implementing visual and dramatic style. For instance, the art department sets production style through set design and dressing, costuming and makeup. Although this is most obvious in period dramas, where these elements are more pronounced, you'll see this process at work even in modern comedies.

The DP creates visual style by selecting camera position, movement, angle, and lighting design. For instance, Jim Jarmusch's *Stranger Than Paradise* used a unique photographic and editorial style by filming every scene in a static long shot and editing as sparsely as possible. Even the location manager has a big impact when she chooses a particular house or outdoor setting to film a scene.

On set with the actors, a good director will shape performances to serve the overall style of the piece. For instance, in the film *Raising Arizona,* the Coen brothers chose an acting style that was broad and exaggerated. For *The Remains of the Day,* James Ivory elected one that was understated and subtle.

During post-production, a talented editor will make countless choices about key elements like pacing and storytelling structure that will impact the final style of the film. Also, sound design is created almost entirely during post, including choices about music, special effects cues, even the equalization characteristics of the primary audio track. These days you may be responsible for color correction and visual effects as well. All of these elements will influence the show's style. Pay attention to the stylistic choices made earlier in the process, and make an effort to understand and complement them.

Developing a Personal Style

Everyone likes to think they have style, and the truth is, they do. Every filmmaker has a unique signature, whether she likes it or not. The question is: Is it aesthetically appealing or provocative, or is it just hard to watch? The more easily you can identify and understand other filmmakers' styles, the more clearly you will be able to identify and understand your own—and make the best of it.

A good craftsperson can mimic others' styles and still have a clear sense of his own. But it takes practice to achieve this kind of mastery. When painters train, they paint copies of masterpieces to understand how they were created. When musicians learn their instruments, they begin by reproducing music composed and recorded by others. Even craftspeople like woodworkers start by reproducing existing designs. It's strange to me that many beginning filmmakers jump right into their own film projects without ever taking this step.

In fact, one of the best ways to understand the aesthetic elements that make up cinematic style is to attempt to copy that style from an existing piece of work. Pick a scene from your favorite movie, TV commercial, or music video. Of course, since film is such a complex medium with so many elements, it may not be possible for you to faithfully reproduce your favorite TV show. But you can make a start.

Pay close attention to the elements that contribute to the finished film: What is the nature of the script or concept? What are the key elements of the art direction (color schemes, arrangement of props and sets, costumes), lighting design, and so on?

Notice the camera choices: Does the camera move a lot? If so, is the movement smooth or jerky? Are the camera angles extremely high or low? Is the camera generally close to the subject or far away? Do visual elements seem compressed because a long focal length lens was used? What medium was the film shot on?

Innumerable factors go into style, but since this is a book about editing and post-production, let's focus on editing: How long does each shot last? Does the editor generally use shots that are uniform in length, or is the editing arrhythmic with long and short shots intermixed? Are the edit points marked by cuts or dissolves? How often does the editor repeat shots? Does the film use traditional cutting patterns, or are the basic editing rules bent or broken? Does the editor favor jump cuts, or does he preserve continuity? Are camera angles consistent, or do they change from shot to shot? What can you say about the sound design? Most feature films use 48 to 128 discrete tracks throughout the film. How many different tracks can you identify (dialogue, sound effects, room tone, music, and so on)?

Once you've identified all the elements that contribute to cinematic style in the show you've chosen, go out and try to reproduce them. See how closely you can replicate the style. Try this a couple of times. What better way to master the tools of your trade? These days the tools of production are cheap enough that you have no excuse *not* to practice your craft—before you put your heart and your pocketbook (or your client's heart and pocketbook) into a real project.

Breaking the Rules

Genre guidelines and traditional styles are rules that can be most striking when they're broken. Let's go back to my Glamland versus Underworld example: At one point in the film, Trey (our main character) is starting to slip out of normal life into his inner psychological obsessions. To illustrate this, we shot one scene twice: first in the Glamland style, and then the Underworld style. I wanted to maximize the impact of the different styles, so I cut the whole sequence using Glamland takes—except for one shot, where I cut to a close-up of Trey from the Underworld footage. The effect of breaking my own stylistic guidelines was to emphasize the rules themselves, which accentuated the emotional content of the scene. The visual style reverberated with the content, engaging the audience in a more significant way than either element could have managed alone.

Interview: BRIAN BERDAN

Brian Berdan began his career with an apprenticeship on David Lynch's *Blue Velvet*. Since then he's worked with a variety of directors, including Oliver Stone and Peter Bogdanovich, and edited films with a wide diversity of style. His credits include *Grosse Pointe Blank, Natural Born Killers,* and *Smoke Signals.* When we spoke, he was working on Mark Pellington's *The Mothman Prophecies.*

Michael Wohl: How important is it for you to watch the dailies?

Brian Berdan: Lately directors haven't been very regimented about watching dailies every night. Part of it's because we have videotapes, and they say, "I'll see it back at the hotel." I like looking at dailies totally raw, never going to the set. That way I'm the first audience member to see something. I make little notes, and then I go back through the footage again and make selects. Just anything that's interesting: A flash frame, a smile… Then I build this huge "selects reel," and from there I'll just start refining.

How do you approach transitions between scenes?

On this one, we're coming up with all kinds of cool transitions after the fact. For instance, we had a place where we had a great transition, but the order of the scenes didn't work, so we had to give up that beautiful transition. Rarely have I been on a show where they had meticulously planned out cut points. One exception was Smoke Signals. *Chris Eyre had worked out some cool transitions for the flashbacks and flashforwards. It was very easy; put slot B into tab A and off you go. That's fun when they work, but I also like just finding things that fit together randomly or graphically.*

Have you ever looked at a sequence and said, "What the hell am I going to do with this?"

In Natural Born Killers, *there's a scene in the jail with Juliette Lewis and Tom Sizemore, and they'd shot all kinds of great coverage—black and white, blown-out color, normal color—but they'd spent so much effort making all these cool shots that I didn't have any really good performances from any one take. So I did a series of five jump cut close-ups on Tom Sizemore. Each one was in a different format. That turned what was a problem into a solution.*

Do you like a director sitting there with you in the editing room, or do you prefer to be left alone?

I prefer someone who leaves me alone. I like him to get a fresh look at it when I show it for the first time. If I've completely struck out on a scene, we'll go through dailies again and get our heads together on what he likes about a particular performance. But then I've got to go back and approach it by myself again. You need to concentrate, and if there's too much back and forth on every little thing, you lose your concentration. Editing to me is more subconscious. It's like sculpting with clay, and as you play with it, it keeps dripping and moving, and you're inspired by the way it drips.

CHAPTER TWO
Film Language

Before you can speak the language of film fluently, you need to understand its rules. What are the nouns? What are the verbs? How about punctuation? How do you combine all these "parts of speech" to construct meaningful sentences?

The metaphor works for film because film *is* a language, and the editor—even more than the director or cinematographer—must be a poet. The editor must choose the most compressed, economical, and precise forms of expression she can, while conveying a theme through the many different dimensions that this unique medium affords. As in any language, combining sentences creates meaning and carries themes.

PARTS OF SPEECH

Bear with me as I extend this metaphor a bit. It will prove very helpful in understanding how to edit. Think of shots as nouns and the transitions between shots as verbs. You might say that in cinematic language, sentences are constructed in a noun-verb-noun-verb arrangement and are punctuated with fades, freeze frames, and other graphical elements.

Types of Shots: Size of Subject

You can organize and differentiate between different types of shots in several ways. I will start with the most common: size of subject in the frame. This is where you'll finally find out what all those odd abbreviations (CU, LS, and so on) really mean.

Extreme Close-up (ECU, BCU, XCU)

An *extreme close-up,* sometimes known as a big close-up (BCU) or abbreviated XCU (for those who can't spell), is a shot in which the subject exceeds the boundaries of the frame. The actual framing may vary: In one instance an ECU might show a single eyeball. In another it might frame a tight shot of a face. An ECU might also show a single chip on a computer circuit board or a finger dialing a telephone. In all these cases, it's understood that the subject is bigger than the particular detail being shown (**Figure 2.1**).

Figure 2.1 An extreme close-up (ECU) is any shot where the subject extends beyond the boundaries of the frame.

The ECU creates tension and intensity, since it brings the viewer and the subject closer than we ordinarily get in a real conversation. It is often used to reveal a character's inner psychological space, or sometimes her thoughts and memories.

Close-up (CU)

The *close-up* (sometimes called a "tight shot") is one of the most frequently used shots. Most often it frames a person's face and cuts off midneck, showing the face or the entire head (**Figure 2.2**). Editors use the close-up for capturing subtle emotional movements of the face. It's a very intimate shot and should be used when you need to establish a personal connection with the subject. Think of this shot as simulating the distance a friend or family member might stand from the subject; a mere acquaintance would rarely get this close.

Part of the reason we feel we "know" movie stars so well is because we're used to seeing them so closely—more closely, in fact, than many of the real people in our lives. Sometimes a close-up is intended to force intimacy; some editors use it to make the audience feel connected with, or sympathetic to, a character.

The close-up can also be used to show an inanimate object. In this case, the camera moves close enough so the object fills the frame comfortably.

Figure 2.2 A close-up (CU) is a shot in which the subject fills the frame. In the case of a human, the subject is usually the person's head.

Medium Close-up (MCU)

As its name suggests, a *medium close-up* is a slightly wider shot than a close-up. Usually it frames the head and upper torso, cutting off midchest (**Figure 2.3**). If the close-up suggests familial intimacy, the MCU feels more like the social distance an acquaintance or business associate might enjoy. It gets close enough to read facial expressions but holds a polite distance from the subject. It is also wide enough to reveal a bit of the environment surrounding the subject.

Figure 2.3 The medium close-up (MCU) simulates the distance we'd stand from someone with whom we're having a casual conversation. The MCU on the right allows us to see both subjects comfortably while focusing mainly on their faces.

Medium Shot (MS)

A *medium shot* frames the subject from the waist up (**Figure 2.4**). It is, as the name implies, a happy medium between a close-up (which emphasizes facial activity) and a long shot (which favors the environment). Since it allows the subject enough room to move around inside the frame, it is ideal for active subjects. Emotionally, as you might expect, the MS is slightly ambivalent. Although it is less intimate than a close-up, it still favors a single subject and clearly directs the viewer's attention.

Figure 2.4 The medium shot (MS) gives us a sense of the subject's environment. In the shot on the left, we can see that Rich's office has big windows overlooking the city. The scene on the right is obviously taking place in a laundromat.

Long Shot (LS, FS)

The *long shot* (sometimes known as a full shot) can be framed various ways. When dealing with a human subject, the camera might be set back just far enough to include the whole figure. However, an LS may also place the camera even farther back, so we can see that person walking around. In either case, while the point of focus of the shot is the human being, the environment is clearly visible as well (**Figure 2.5**).

Figure 2.5 The long shot (LS) shows the entire human figure. While it allows us to clearly identify which character we're looking at, the environment is an equally important element.

For the most part the LS is used to show action, not convey emotion. We rarely interact with people from this far away, so this shot suggests a more objective point of view than the closer shots. Since it can't capture the details of facial expression, the LS relies on a broader context, placing the subject in relation to his environment and the people around him. When the subject is an inanimate object, an LS or FS usually frames the object in its entirety, showing it in its environment.

Wide Shot (WS)

The *wide shot* focuses primarily on the environment. In a WS the camera is far away from the action and captures roughly what might be witnessed with the naked eye (**Figure 2.6**). The human subjects in a WS are no longer the point of the shot, even if their activity is. For example, a WS might show a firehouse with the fire truck exiting. This shot provides information and context we need to make sense of the actions and events occurring in the sequence. Although a WS usually interrupts the story's flow, audiences have become familiar with such shots and stay with the narrative when they occur.

Figure 2.6 The wide shot (WS) shifts our focus from the characters in the shot to their environment.

Extreme Long Shot (ELS, EWS, XLS)

The *extreme long shot* (sometimes called an extreme wide shot) covers a vast area. Like the LS and WS, this shot supplies context—but not just for a specific action or event. Usually editors use an ELS to provide broad context for the entire story line of the film. It can supply a temporal context as well as a geographical one. For instance, an ELS might show a vast, sandy desert with the hero's caravan seen as a tiny speck of black in one corner. Or it could hover over a cloverleaf on the Los Angeles freeway with the protagonist's car caught in an endless traffic jam (**Figure 2.7**).

Extending our grammatical metaphor, you can think of an ELS as a $10 word: a shot that lets the editor deliver a great deal of information and impact with a single edit.

Figure 2.7 The extreme long shot (ELS) not only gives the filmmaker an opportunity to show the subject and his environment but also provides a sense of the larger context of the sequence, or even the entire film. The image on the left emphasizes the feeling of loss by placing a tiny figure amid ruins decaying around him. The image on the right, from *Want,* shows Trey futilely throwing rocks at the giant TV billboard, a miniature Don Quixote tilting at the digital windmill.

Body Language (the Rule of Four T's)

This isn't a shot but rather a way of thinking about shots. I find handy, and I suspect you will, too.

When I was interning at that video production company in the late eighties, a crafty camera operator named Stanley took me under his wing. I thought of Stanley more as a craftsperson than an artist, but he was very skilled at what he did. One of the lessons he taught me was a handy rule of thumb for recognizing a properly framed shot of a single person. He called it the Rule of Four T's: Tonsils, Tits, Testicles, Toes. (Stanley wasn't the most politically correct crewperson I ever worked with, but he sure knew how to take great pictures.) Any framing *between* these points was bad composition, he said. Stanley's rules of composition were more practical than aesthetic: In fact, these four points capture the basic categories of human body language.

T One

Obviously, this refers to a close-up, but Stanley's point is that when you place the bottom frameline at midneck, you achieve a clean shot of the face—including the jaw, which moves downward. This shot captures facial expression and movement very well.

T Two

This refers to a medium close-up, and what differentiates it from the tonsils shot is that it includes the subject's upper torso. In this shot you can see not just facial expression but also neck and shoulder movement. If you pay attention you'll discover that neck and shoulder movements are full of subtle variations that add inflection to speech. Stanley considered composing a shot framed at the collarbone wasteful, since it doesn't capture any more detail than the tonsils shot and is farther away.

T Three

I would call this a medium shot, but Stanley chose to put the bottom frameline slightly lower than hip-level. This enables you to capture the movement of the subject's spine and pelvis—the next significant element of human body language. A shot that cuts off at the waist captures some spinal movement but loses some, too—especially when the subject is standing. This shot is also good framing for two people, because you can read posture much more clearly if you can see their pelvises—and much of the unspoken body language between two people is conveyed in their posture. (Are they squared off to one another, leaning away, touching?)

T Four

This is Stanley's name for a long shot. It enables us to see the full range of human motion. Cutting off a subject at the knee (or midthigh, or midcalf, for that matter) provides no significant advantage over a medium shot, but framing to include legs and feet lets us see how the subject is standing. (I have a theory that our society's odd footwear fetish is rooted in our unconscious habit of sizing each other up by glancing at the feet to assess firmness of posture.) Are both feet firmly planted? Is the person shifting from one foot to the other?

The real lesson behind Stanley's division of the human body is that compositional aesthetics are based in practical considerations.

Types of Shots: Camera Angle

Subject size is only one way of organizing shots and understanding their function in film language. Another way to identify a shot is by the camera angle.

By default, the camera is usually placed at or near average human eye level. Sometimes it may be adjusted to simulate a character's point of view while sitting and so on. When a shot takes an angle that's notably different from average human eye level, that angle becomes the name of the shot. These names apply to shots of any subject size.

High-Angle Shot (hi<)

The *high-angle shot* is filmed with the camera above the subject and looking down. When it's a WS or an ELS, it suggests a kind of omniscience that may provide context for an event. When used for closer shots, it tends to make the subject appear inferior or weak (**Figure 2.8**).

Choosing this type of shot is one way to guide the audience's opinion of a character. However, if the angle is too extreme it draws attention to itself, and rather than conveying a subtle emotional judgment, it will suggest a psychological distortion that might, for example, indicate the subject is in dire conflict.

Figure 2.8 A high-angle shot like the one on the left will give the audience an "omniscient" view of an event, especially when the angle is not too extreme. The high angle of the image on the right is much more radical, simulating the giant billboard's POV of Trey. This angle was chosen to reciprocate the angle of Trey's eyeline, as well as to diminish him in size.

Low-Angle Shot (lo<)

A *low-angle shot,* filmed with the camera below the subject and shooting up, has the opposite effect of the high-angle one (**Figure 2.9**). In tight shots, a lower angle tends to accentuate the feeling of being immersed in the action. It's less common to use a low-angle LS, unless you're looking at the bottom of a boat.

Low angles are often used to make an object or person appear intimidating or powerful. As with the high angle, the more extreme the low angle, the more exaggerated the effect becomes. Cutting back and forth between slightly high- and low-angle shots in a dialogue sequence is an effective way to guide viewers toward understanding the power relationship between two people.

Both high and low angles should be motivated in some way. Using an extremely low-angle shot with no justification for why we're seeing the action from that perspective runs the risk of distracting the viewer.

For instance, if you simply drop in a low-angle shot of your main character and then continue cutting from normal angles, the viewer may be distracted. However, if you follow the low-angle shot with a reverse angle of the character's dog (thereby letting the viewer know that the low-angle shot was from the point of view of the dog), everyone is happy. (For more information on this "shot–reverse shot" technique, as well as point-of-view shots, see "Reverse Shot" and "Point-of-View Shot," later in this chapter.)

 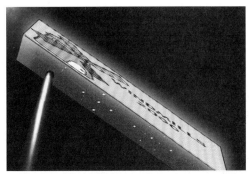

Figure 2.9 Low-angle shots like these can make a character appear more powerful or can simulate a subject's POV.

Camera Angle and Gender

When you're trying to make subjects look as attractive as possible, it's traditional to photograph women from a slightly high angle and men from a slightly low angle. I believe this is because men are typically taller than women, and these are the natural angles from which we look at each other. Still, it's interesting to note how this subtle power relationship influences audiences. One of the benefits you'll gain from making a more active analysis of the film and television shows you watch is a sharpened ability to see what filmmakers are trying to communicate to us and how our cultural stereotypes are subliminally reinforced or challenged.

Dutch Angle

The term *Dutch* or *Dutched* refers to a shot in which the horizon is tilted (**Figure 2.10**). A Dutch angle literally puts the audience off balance to create tension and anxiety. If the angle is too extreme (sometimes called gonked), the effect can be comical. One interesting shot we used repeatedly in *Want* was a "rolling Dutch," where the camera was rocked from left to right. We used this effect to convey Trey's ambivalence and his inability to make a decision.

Figure 2.10 The more you "Dutch" the angle, the more disoriented the subject appears—and the more disoriented the audience feels. We used this shot in *Want* for the moment when Trey finds out his father has died.

Types of Shots: Camera Movement

Camera movement adds significant impact to a shot. But it's important to understand when to use moving shots and when to stick to static ones. When the camera is moving, the audience is moving, too. This produces a definite sense of exhilaration, but it can make the viewer miss details.

Editors must be efficiency experts. If you can get your point across with a fast, simple cut rather than a long, luxurious camera move, it's usually good practice to choose the cut. Using a move may add dynamism to a dull scene, but if you use moving shots gratuitously, they draw attention to themselves and break your storytelling flow.

A moving shot must provide new information with every new framing. Famous, elaborate moving shots, such as the opening crane shot in Welles's *Touch of Evil* or the seemingly endless tracking shot through the restaurant in Scorsese's *GoodFellas,* are effective because they continually provide new information, so there is no need for a cut.

It is your job as an editor to make these decisions. The best advice I can give you is to make your choices deliberately and consciously. Moving shots should follow the Rule of Motivation: If you don't know why you are choosing a moving shot, don't use it.

Pan and Tilt

A human head can turn (or *pan;* short for "panoramic") from left to right, and it can *tilt* up and down. That's why shots in which the camera pans (**Figure 2.11**) and tilts (**Figure 2.12**) feel quite natural to the viewer. The trick is to use a pan or tilt only when there's something to pan or tilt *to*. In and of itself, a pan across a room is a completely dead shot unless there's something worth seeing at the beginning and the end. These shots look even better if there's something to lead our vision across the space—for example, a bird flying by. You can use a pan or tilt to drive the action of a sequence (and the audience's point of focus) from one place to another.

Figure 2.11 This pan follows the barrel of a gun from the shooter to his victim. You can see in the diagram how the camera is pivoting on a single point, as if the viewer were turning his head.

Figure 2.12 This shot tilts up from the proposal Rich is reviewing to show his face as he delivers his first lines. As the diagram illustrates, the camera's pivot simulates the effect of nodding your head.

For example, a tilt from a cop standing in an alleyway scratching his head to a jewel thief climbing the fire escape above him is a much more compelling editing choice than simply cutting from the cop to the thief. The tilt provides information about the proximity of the two, as well as showing us that the thief is escaping at exactly the same time that the cop is looking for him.

A less glamorous, but more practical, example would be a sequence showing an assembly line at an auto factory. Cutting between stations on the line would show the different tasks and might communicate the order in which they occur, but a pan from one station to the next, following the movement of the conveyor belt, will give a much better understanding of how the pieces make up the whole.

Tracking Shot

Tracking shots, dolly shots, crab shots (named after the "crab dolly"), and truck shots are various synonyms for shots that begin in one physical location and move along the ground to another. You can use a tracking shot to immerse the viewer in a location in a way that you can't achieve with a static camera. Because humans can walk around, too, simple tracking shots can be very organic and pleasant to watch (**Figure 2.13**).

Using a moving shot is like taking your viewer on a physical ride—complete with the possibility of motion sickness. This is one of the most compelling ways to guide your viewer's point of focus. However, just like pans and tilts, dolly shots should follow the Rule of Motivation: If you don't have a deliberate reason for choosing a dolly shot, don't use one.

Follow Shot

When a tracking shot is used to move along with a subject (for instance, a car-to-car shot), it is often called a *follow shot.* This is simply a special kind of tracking shot, but it is exempt from the Rule of Motivation. As long as the viewer is moving along with the subject at a constant velocity, you can edit this tracking shot just as you would a static shot.

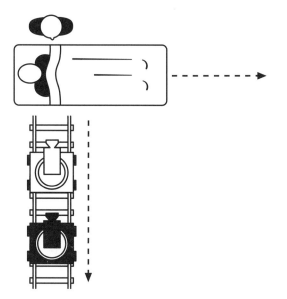

Figure 2.13 This shot, from *Want,* is a tracking move straight back from Trey after he identifies his father's body. It begins with a pedestal move that raises the camera from Gene's face to Trey, and then pulls backward until Trey becomes a tiny figure in the frame. To emphasize how Trey withdraws into himself at this moment, we removed the gurney and nurse from the corridor before the track-back could reveal them. In this way they seem to vanish. The camera setup is shown in the diagram.

Crane Shot

A *crane shot* moves freely in three-dimensional space, and since it can make the viewer feel as if she's flying, it's quite exhilarating (**Figure 2.14**). Modern dollies usually have an arm (called a jib) that facilitates some complex camera movements, but the impact of a crane is significantly different from that of a simple dolly shot.

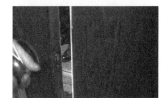

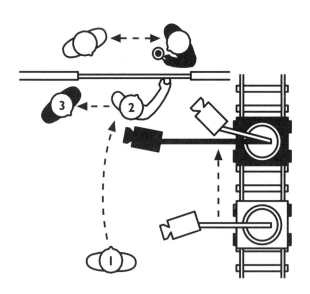

Figure 2.14 This crane shot follows Bruce as he approaches a window and sees a woman dancing outside. The camera moves down to a tight close-up on the doorknob as Bruce opens the door. As it swings open, we move back up, revealing that the woman has now become a man drinking tea. Frightened, Bruce slams the door shut and turns away. Using a crane allowed us to create a single fluid shot that elevated the suspense and emphasized the bizarre transformation of the dancer. Also, moving into a tight CU on the doorknob gave the dancer and tea drinker time to switch places. The camera setup is shown in the diagram.

Humans can walk around, but they can't levitate into the air or dip their heads down to ground level while walking. Thus the crane shot is the first type of camera movement we've discussed that is outside the range of normal human activity. For this reason, a crane shot is much more likely to pull a viewer out of the narrative than any of the previous shots. On the other hand, the impact and excitement of a successful crane shot is unparalleled. It conveys a godlike omniscience that's often exploited in action flicks or romance films.

Pedestal Shot

Many camera dollies include a hydraulically controlled pedestal that raises or lowers the camera position. If you combine a dolly move with a pedestal move, you end up with something pretty close to a crane shot, only without the complication and expense of a crane. By itself, a pedestal move is a "natural" movement, since humans can kneel and stand up. When you combine it with a dolly move, however, it seems less natural.

Zoom Shot

It's hard to find a DV camera that doesn't have a zoom lens. A *zoom shot* involves changing the focal length of the lens while the shot is rolling to make the subject seem larger or smaller in the frame. This is similar to moving closer in or farther away with a dolly, but the visual effect is quite different (**Figure 2.15**).

When you physically move the camera closer to a subject, the relationship between the subject and the background changes in an organic way—similar to what you'd see in real life if you walked closer to an object. On the other hand, when you zoom in, the background is compressed in a way that our eyes cannot simulate. This odd visual effect can distract the viewer.

Figure 2.15 The image on the left shows the final frame of a zoom-in. The image on the right shows the final frame of a dolly-in. Notice the difference in the size of the windmill in the background.

Most instructors lecture on the evils of the zoom shot, but I think it has its place. By pulling the subject out of natural space, a zoom shot can create a psychological connection between the viewer and the subject. This technique is often employed in melodramatic shows like soap operas.

Sometimes a zoom can be combined with a dolly move. If you zoom out and dolly in at the same time (a technique popularized by Alfred Hitchcock in *Vertigo)*, you can create a sense of diving into someone's head (or out of it). If the zoom complements the dolly (zoom in/dolly in), it amplifies the dolly movement and disorients the viewer. At times this is desirable.

Hand-Held Shot

With new lightweight camcorders, it's easier than ever to shoot while holding a camera in your hand. This means you can take a camera places you could never get to with a bigger, heavier camera and explore nonstandard angles. The disadvantage of hand-holding is the same one I described earlier in terms of crane and zoom shots: the unnatural-movement problem.

Since our eyes are not mounted at the end of our arms, the types of movement our arm can make with a camera do not match up very comfortably with the types of movement we expect to see with our heads stuck on our necks. One of the biggest problems is simply the speed at which your arm can move around. Watching footage that was shot with a wildly swinging camera feels weird and is hard on the eyes.

You may notice that professional DV cameras are still the same size as their older Betacam cousins. This is partly because a professional videographer uses the weight and inertia of the large camera (which still rests comfortably on her shoulder) to restrict her movement—which creates smoother, more pleasing shots. The instability of a hand-held shot invariably puts the audience on edge psychologically. This effect can be felt even in shots that waver only slightly. We can detect movement in the frame at very subtle levels.

Types of Shots: As the Editor Sees Them

Now that we've considered shots in terms of subject size, camera angle, and camera movement, here's another useful way to think of them: by their function to the editor.

Master Shot

A *master shot* is framed to capture all of the action in a scene and usually runs from the beginning of the scene to the end. Typically, a master is a wide shot, but it doesn't have to be. The term is useful to the editor because you know that you can cut back to it at any point during the scene (**Figure 2.16**).

Figure 2.16 These master shots show all of the people who will appear in each scene, as well as placing them in their environment. In both cases, these masters were used as the first shot in the scene.

A master shot is often the simplest way to start a sequence: Tell the audience where the events are happening through a master WS, then move in and use tighter shots to put across the emotional content of the scene. Of course, this convention has been so overused that some modern editors do everything they can to avoid opening a sequence with a master shot. Just remember to learn and understand the rules before you start breaking them.

Single Shot

A *single* is simply any shot of one person (**Figure 2.17**). Most of the time a single will be a close-up, but it could be a medium shot as long as only one character is clearly the subject. Often the term is used to differentiate a shot with one character in it from, say, an *over-the-shoulder* shot or a two-shot. For instance, if you were talking about getting coverage for a dialogue scene, you might call for "a wide master, an MCU over-the-shoulder shot of each player, and a single CU of each player."

Figure 2.17 A single can be as close as the CU on the left or as wide as the high-angle MS on the right. Note that in the shot on the left, even though there is technically more than one person in the shot, it's still considered a single since the figure in the foreground is clearly the focus of the shot.

Over-the-Shoulder Shot (OS, OTS)

Over-the-shoulder, or OS, refers to a shot in which two people are facing one another—one in the foreground with his back to the camera, the other facing the camera (**Figure 2.18**). An OS shot could be an MS, an MCU, or a CU. The tighter the shot, the more obscured and out of focus the foreground character will be.

Figure 2.18 Most often, the over-the-shoulder (OS) shot is a medium close-up (MCU), as in the example on the left. But it can be tighter, or wider like the MS on the right. Typically, the tighter the OS shot, the more obscured and out of focus the foreground figure is.

An OS shot has a very different psychological effect from a single. It shows the two players in relation to one another, whereas a single focuses on the emotional state of the individual subject. Typical syntax for an over-the-shoulder shot would be: CU Trey OS Ben. This means that Trey is the subject of the close-up, shot from over Ben's shoulder.

Note: "OS" is also sometimes used to mean "offscreen," as in "Rich laughs OS." Context will dictate which meaning is implied. Typically, "offscreen" refers to sound, while "over the shoulder" refers to image.

Reverse Shot

A *reverse shot* (or "reverse angle") is a relative term for any shot taken from the opposite angle of the previous shot. It often serves to explain the source of the preceding shot—such as a high-angle shot of a college quad following a low-angle shot of the bell tower. It can also be used in the simple case of reciprocal OS shots (as in "Follow the OS of Trey with a reverse of Dana") (**Figure 2.19**).

Figure 2.19 A reverse shot is a reciprocal angle of the shot that preceded it. Here are two examples.

Point-of-View (POV) Shot

A *point-of-view shot* lets us look through a character's eyes and shows us exactly what she's seeing. If she's in a conversation with her brother, for instance, a POV shot might show the brother speaking directly into the camera lens.

A POV shot is a common way to justify a strange angle—for instance, a shot peeking out from behind a wall or the extreme high- or low-angle shots described earlier in this chapter. Standard editing technique calls for bracketing a POV shot with a matching reverse single to indicate whose POV it is (**Figure 2.20**). So in the bell tower example above, if the low-angle shot of the tower was intended to be a character's POV, you would follow it with a shot of someone in the quad looking up at the tower.

Figure 2.20 The point-of-view (POV) shot is commonly used in conjunction with a reverse shot. Here, the shot on the left is Trey's POV, showing what he sees when he peeks out from behind the curtain. The shot on the right is the reverse, which reveals whose POV it is.

Reaction Shot (RXN)

A *reaction shot* reveals how a character reacts to something that just happened. This term refers less to the content of the shot than to its emotional purpose in terms of editing.

Frequently, an RXN will be a single cut right after another single, and most often it's a shot without dialogue.

For instance (**Figure 2.21**):

1.   WS Rich and Trey in restaurant.

2.   CU Rich describing how much money Trey can make.

3.   RXN shot of Trey.

4.   CU Rich continuing his sales pitch.

Figure 2.21 In this dialogue sequence, shot 3 is the reaction shot.

Alternatively, a reaction shot can be a single following some event. For instance, after an LS of the marketplace in which a bomb goes off, you would cut to an RXN of the mother hearing the explosion and turning to see what happened (**Figure 2.22**).

Figure 2.22 The reaction shot in frame 6 gives the explosion emotional impact.

Two-Shot

A *two-shot* is any shot with two characters in it. It could be an MS, an MCU, or a CU (**Figure 2.23**). An OS shot is a kind of two-shot, although it's rarely identified as such. Often it is more important for the editor to know how many players are in a given shot than to know how large they may be in the frame.

Figure 2.23 A shot with two people in the frame is called a two-shot.

Group Shot

A group shot is simply any shot that shows a group of people. It could be as wide as an LS or as tight as an MS (**Figure 2.24**). Here again, the content of the shot is often more important to the editor than the size of the characters in the frame. Sometimes people will describe a shot based on the number of people in it. You might hear terms like "three-shot" or even "six-shot," although this is usually relevant only when everyone involved knows specifically *which* three or six people are in the shot.

Figure 2.24 Any shot that shows three or more people is called a group shot. You could also call the picture on the right a three-shot.

Cutaway

A cutaway is a shot of any subject that's *not* part of the current shot but *is* part of the current scene. The editor can use a cutaway to show passage of time or just to break away from alternating shots of the characters without interrupting continuity of place. Cutaways provide atmospheric context and contrast.

For example:

1. MCU Trey sits on beach.
2. LS OS Trey looks at girls on beach.
3. MS girl playing.
4. CUTAWAY CU seagulls flying.
5. MS Trey walking away.

In this case, the cutaway indicates the passing of time without breaking continuity of place. A cutaway allows the editor to take the viewer's focus away from the subject at hand or to change focus within the same locale (**Figure 2.25**).

Figure 2.25 In this 5-shot sequence, shot 4 (the seagulls) is the cutaway. The seagulls are presumably part of the environment of the previous shots but do not necessarily appear in any other shot.

Insert

An insert functions much like a cutaway, but the term refers to a tight shot of a subject or object that's already present in the current shot. By definition, an insert must be tighter than the shot preceding it.

For example:

1.   Master FS Trey, Gene, and Starr in restaurant.

2.   Two-shot Gene and Starr as she reaches for wineglass.

3.   INSERT wineglass as Starr picks it up.

4.   CU Trey RXN shot.

In this case, the insert draws attention to the wineglass. Rather than disrupting the action of the scene, it focuses viewers' attention on a particular item. It's typically followed by some kind of RXN shot to give it emotional context (**Figure 2.26**).

Figure 2.26 In this sequence, shot 3 (the wineglasses) is the insert. Shot 4 is the reaction shot that shows how Trey feels about Gene and Starr getting drunk.

Voice-Over

A *voice-over* is an audio-only shot. It may be narration or speech from another context, overlaid on a scene to provide commentary, context, or a special point of view. Don't forget audio when thinking about the editing options available to you. Often you can perform an audio "insert" or "cutaway" without changing the visual focus.

Music

Music is one of the most important ways of adding emphasis to a film sequence. Using different music can create wildly different effects when it's laid over the same sequence of visuals. Music is the principal tool you will use to tip off the viewer to a scene's emotional context. Comedy can turn tragic and suspense can be rendered frivolous if you pick the wrong music.

Flashy Shots

Now and then you may find a single shot that achieves multiple purposes. Sometimes it's a moving shot that changes subject or point of view. Alternatively, it might be a static shot where many things come and go in the frame or happen simultaneously on different planes in three-dimensional space.

But be careful. If a shot is too complex, it will draw attention to itself and may need to be cut into pieces to avoid distracting the viewer.

Slow Motion and Other Visual Effects

Your editorial lexicon can include a variety of shots that were not achieved in the camera but can be created during post. Digitally enhanced shots range from something as simple as a cropped shot to something as complex as a multilayered composition with elements *rotoscoped* into the scene.

> **ROTOSCOPING** *The process of painting digitally on the individual frames of the film. It's used primarily for cleaning up mistakes or removing the wires from a model shot.*

With even a modest desktop editing system like Final Cut Pro, you have a huge library of options at your fingertips that allow you to modify pre-existing shots or develop new shots from scratch.

Types of Cuts and Transitions

Now for some verbs!

As I mentioned at the beginning of this chapter, if you think of shots as nouns, the basic building blocks of cinematic sentences, then the transitions the editor uses to move from one shot to the next can be thought of as verbs.

There are really only a few ways to make a transition from one shot (and its point of focus) to another. The simplest way is just to cut from one shot to the next: Stop the first shot and start the second. But you can accomplish even a simple cut in many different ways. The editor is always drawing the viewer along, guiding the point of focus so skillfully it seems effortless, while carefully maintaining the precise sequence of thoughts, emotions, and reactions the director desires.

Continuity Cut

Most cuts within a scene should be continuous. That means action that begins in one shot should continue in the next with flawless continuity of time, space, and screen direction. (I'll get to screen direction shortly.)

The simplest example of this is a door that starts to open in one shot and finishes opening in the next. This could be a cut from a CU to a WS, or it could be one MS cutting to another MS from a complementary angle. In every case it would be a successful continuity cut only if the door appeared to open with a natural, fluid movement across the boundary between the two shots. Fluid movement between shots is one of the most critical elements in convincing your audience of the reality of the film (**Figure 2.27**).

Figure 2.27 The action in this edit will appear continuous across the cut point.

The more smoothly space and time seem to run across an *edit point,* the more invisibly you can guide the focus of the scene. Of course, most often the shots you are cutting between were not actually shot at the same time, so the action may not match perfectly. For instance, the door may be opening fast in one shot and slowly in another. Compensating for inconsistencies like this is a huge part of the editor's job, and as you read on, you'll learn many ways to accomplish this.

Split Edits

Creating seamless audio continuity across shot boundaries is even more important than maintaining visual continuity. While you see only 25 or 30 frames per second of visual information, you hear 48,000 samples of audio. Even a tiny discontinuity on the soundtrack will be far more jarring than a visual error.

One of the most common techniques editors use to create seamless continuity of sound is to overlap the audio from the shot that's ending with the start of the picture in the following shot. For instance, if Dana is speaking in shot 1, and you want to cut to her companion Lindsey listening in the next shot, you would probably cut to the image of Lindsey before Dana finishes her dialogue. The sound from shot 1 would continue over the image of shot 2.

Generally, any edit where audio and video are cut at different points is called a *split edit*. How many frames of audio you overlap depends on the content of the shots and their length. When the sound of the first clip overlaps the image of the second, it's called an L cut. When the sound of the second overlaps the image of the first, it's called a J cut (**Figure 2.28**). I find myself using the latter ten-to-one over the former, but that may just be a question of personal style.

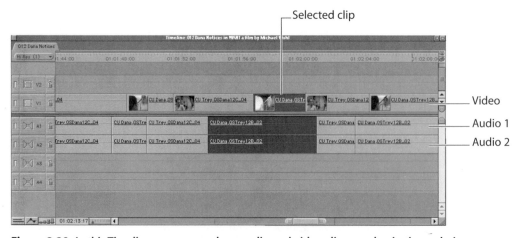

Figure 2.28 In this Timeline, you can see how audio and video clips overlap in time relative to one another. The lower tracks represent the audio, while the V1 channel above represents the video. The selected clip begins with a J cut (where the audio clip begins before its corresponding video clip) and ends with an L cut. In the L cut, the audio extends past the end of the corresponding picture.

A typical dialogue scene should be cut entirely with L and J cuts. Otherwise the scene feels jumpy and unnatural. Most action sequences also employ L or J cuts to tie the events together. Sometimes you can even use L or J cuts to take the viewer from the end of one sequence to the beginning of another or to bridge two locations into a single event.

If you look at mainstream media, nearly every cut will have overlapping audio except for changes in location or event. Final Cut Pro has a couple of features designed specifically to help you perform split edits (see the section on split edits in Chapter 6, "Advanced Editing").

Incidentally, you can also use room tone to help the soundtrack feel seamless (see the section on room tone in Chapter 7, "Cutting the Track").

Jump Cut

A jump cut is any cut or transition that breaks the continuity of time, space, or screen direction—deliberately or accidentally—or where the action doesn't match across the edit point. This is true even if the jump cut is disguised to appear continuous.

Jump cuts used to be considered unacceptable mistakes. Jean-Luc Godard's *Breathless* (1960) was the first time jumpcutting was used extensively in a narrative film. Godard employed it to show the isolation of his two characters, even though they were sharing the same physical space. In recent years, jump cuts have become a fashionable way to draw attention to the act of film creation and celebrate the artifice of the medium.

Since jump cuts force the audience to reconstruct the time or space that has been "jumped," they can be used to disorient or agitate the viewer. Jump cuts are also wonderfully effective, when used selectively amidst a mostly conventional editing palette, to simulate moments of confusion or disconnection.

Jumpcutting is an art. I find that compositional choices become more critical than ever in a jump cut, because once you remove the artificial continuity of the scene, what you're mostly left with is two juxtaposed images that draw attention to themselves. If the goal is anti-continuity, then you should be careful to create compositional opposition: Cut from opposite Dutch angles or break screen direction. And take time to experiment: You may find that by rearranging the order of a jump cut sequence, you can achieve very different emotional results (**Figure 2.29**).

Figure 2.29 This is a sequence of jump cuts focusing on Trey as he practices asking his co-worker for a date. The first few images illustrate good contrast in composition, primarily thanks to alternating screen direction. The last few shots rely on the actor's gestures to create contrast across the edit points. Our goal was to show Trey getting more and more frustrated. While the performance conveys most of this, we accentuated the effect by using a telephoto lens for the earlier shots and a wide angle for the latter ones.

Unwanted jump cuts are more troublesome. You will create an unwanted jump cut by cutting between two camera angles that are too similar, even if the action across the cut is entirely continuous. In general, a shot should be 30 percent or 30 degrees different from the previous shot. That means either 30 degrees to the left or right, 30 degrees higher or lower angle, 30 percent tighter or wider, and so on.

Scene Cut

A *scene cut* takes the viewer from the end of one scene to the beginning of another. Traditionally, transitions between scenes were marked by some sort of punctuation, like a dip-to-black. These days, modern style favors "hard cutting" from one scene to the next. The effect is a more forceful transition—especially if the audio is also hard cut rather than overlapped. Using this technique, you don't give the audience quite enough time to digest the final images of the previous scene before they must begin taking in all the new information associated with a new location and a new event.

A nice technique to make scene cuts work is to let a graphic or compositional element carry the viewer past the cut. For example: If the last shot in scene 1 is a round car tire, a good beginning shot for scene 2 might be a globe of roughly the same size spinning in approximately the same place in the frame. This provides visual continuity and makes a smooth bridge between the scenes (**Figure 2.30**).

Figure 2.30 A good scene cut matches a graphical element from the ending frame of the outgoing scene with one in the first frame of the incoming scene. In this case, we cut from the park adjoining Kachina's apartment to a CU of her CD collection. The strong vertical lines create a visual bridge between the scenes.

Crosscutting

Crosscutting, also known as intercutting, is one of the oldest editing techniques in film. It refers to the process of showing two events that are taking place in two different locations at the same time by alternating shots from each of the events.

While crosscutting usually depicts events that are taking place at the same time, it can also be used for other purposes, such as a scene where someone is remembering an event intercut with footage of the event itself.

Crosscutting is essential in editing a chase sequence where you cut between the pursuer and the pursued, usually alternating shots from the two sequences faster and faster until the pursuer converges on the pursued and the crosscutting evolves into a single scene. This is one of the most common editing structures in film language. By showing the audience two events at the same time, you allow viewers to not only observe those events but draw some conclusions about the relationship between them.

Usually, crosscutting involves intercutting two complete sequences. For instance, you might cut a western like this:

1. ELS outlaw in desert.

2. CU outlaw smokes and throws his cigarette butt to the ground.

3. ECU INSERT cigarette butt.

4. LS sheriff riding through desert.

5. CU sheriff's face. He sees something on the ground. He stops his horse.

6. ECU INSERT same cigarette butt.

7. CU sheriff's face lights up.

8. MS outlaw pitching tent near a campfire.

9. ECU cigarette pack as outlaw takes one out.

In this example, the story of the outlaw could have been shown continuously by simply using shots 1 through 3 and shots 8 and 9, but by intercutting the sheriff's story we set up suspense. Now the audience not only knows that the outlaw is being followed but that since the sheriff has spotted the cigarette butt, he will probably catch the outlaw.

Note: The edits between shots 3 and 4 and shots 7 and 8 are scene cuts. All the others are probably continuity cuts.

Cross-Dissolve

A *cross-dissolve* (also known as a dissolve, cross-fade, or mix) is a transition between shots where frames are superimposed, "mixing" the images for the duration of the transition (**Figures 2.31** and **2.32**).

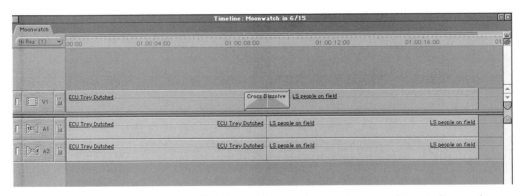

Figure 2.31 Final Cut Pro represents dissolves with icons that overlap two adjacent clips on the same track.

Figure 2.32 Image 1, an ECU of Trey, is dissolved with image 2, a wide overhead shot of a crowd gathering on a field. The frames in the middle show the images overlapping.

The most common use of a mix is to suggest the passage of time. This is why a cross-dissolve is often a good choice for scene cuts where time passes between the scenes.

Cross-dissolves can be particularly effective when you use them to bridge what would ordinarily seem like a series of jump cuts: shots from the same angle with the subject moving in the frame. If you use cross-dissolves instead of cuts, the viewer will accept that the jump cuts are actually taking place with long periods of time between them. For instance, imagine a sequence in which someone is hiding in a room. A series of high-angle shots shows him washing dishes, then pacing the floor, then reading, then banging his fist against the wall. If you use cuts, they may seem jarring; if you use dissolves, the shots just show that time is passing.

Cross-dissolves offer the editor an opportunity to create beautiful and powerful filmic images, especially on longer dissolves. When planning a mix, think carefully about composition and how the two images will overlap spatially. You can mix any two images, but when the images work together compositionally, they can have a profound impact.

> **Make Sure You Have Extra Media**
>
> *An important technical point: If you're considering using a cross-dissolve, remember that both shots need to have extra media on either side of the cut point equal to half the length of the dissolve.*
>
> *For instance, if you want to place a one-second dissolve between two shots, there must be half a second (15 frames of NTSC video) of good frames before and after the cut point on the incoming clip and the outgoing clip. If a slate or a light-leak appears within those 15 lead-in or lead-out frames in either shot, it will become visible once the effect is applied, making the dissolve unusable.*

> **SLATE** *Also known as a clapboard, this tool is primarily used to identify a shot. On productions where the sound and picture are recorded on separate media, clapping the top bar gives a "sync" point that allows the editor to line up the separate recordings in post. The Final Cut Pro icon and box art show a typical slate.*

Soft Cut

A very short dissolve that lasts between three and five frames is often called a *soft cut* because its effect falls halfway between that of a hard cut and a cross-dissolve. You've probably seen soft cuts used in documentaries as an elegant way to disguise the jump cuts that occur when you trim a long interview down to watchable length.

At one time, to bridge those gaps you would have had to cut away to a reaction, a graphic, or an insert in order to avoid a jump cut that might unsettle your audience. But as viewers have gotten more accustomed to seeing jump cuts in creative shows, editors working in more conservative genres have been able to introduce techniques like the soft cut. The soft cut is less gentle than a full-on cutaway but less disorienting than a flat-out jump cut.

Lap Dissolve

At the other end of the spectrum we find the *lap dissolve*—a cross-dissolve that lasts longer than 2 seconds; in fact, it may last 15 or 30 seconds. This effect is more like superimposing the two images and has a very different impact than a shorter dissolve.

A dissolve that lasts this long puts the two images up for some kind of comparison. A resourceful editor might employ this effect as an alternative to a scene cut to show a character moving from one world to another and to illustrate the differences between those worlds. Or she might aim for the same effect as a crosscut sequence. Alternatively, a lap dissolve can lead the viewer to compare two events or perspectives within a scene.

The long duration of a lap dissolve gives the audience time to contemplate the situation or circumstances. Sometimes such dissolves can be used sequentially, with one following another, sometimes leaving three or more images on-screen simultaneously. The opening scene of *Apocalypse Now* is one of the most elegant and elaborate uses of continuous lap dissolves, showing two worlds at once (the outer world of the Vietnam War and the inner world of the story's protagonist) and creating a correlation between them that captures the essence of the entire film. Simultaneously, the sequence begins unfolding the plot without feeling expository or didactic.

Other Effects

Tools like Final Cut Pro place a vast selection of special visual effects at your disposal—effects you can use for transitions between scenes (and occasionally between shots). For the most part, they fall into three categories:

- wipes (including iris effects).

- 2-D effects, such as pushes or slides.

- 3-D simulations, such as cubes turning or pages peeling.

There are also countless combinations and variations, everything from the famous Toaster wipes to custom-shaped dissolves based on a corporate logo.

Traditionally, editors have scorned these effects with reactionary zeal. I suspect this is because they are relatively new, relatively unfamiliar, and break the rule of the invisible edit. In general, wipes and effect transitions make no effort to hide the contrivance of an edit. On the contrary, they draw attention to it. Essentially, they say, "Hey! You're watching a movie, and movies are *fake,* and by the way, this is a scene change!"

Wipes were initially used in feature films. Nowadays, ironically enough, they are most likely to be found in corporate or educational shows, which are ostensibly more "factual" than fiction films—where they are rarely used anymore.

One notable exception is the *Star Wars* series, where all the scene cuts were made with wipes of various shapes. This was done as an affectionate nod to the early days of filmmaking and to emphasize the fairytale nature of the story.

Composite Shots

Any time two shots are visible at once—whether it's a picture-in-picture effect used in a news show or a *process shot* of a computer-generated dinosaur chasing real children—that's a *composite* shot. Technically, this type of effect isn't considered a "verbal" transition between shots, but it serves to compare or contrast two or more shots, creating the same effect that transitions do.

PROCESS SHOT *An old-school film term for compositing. On film, if two images are to be optically combined, an additional lab "process" is required.*

Superimposition

The editor creates a superimposition when he displays two or more shots at the same time, each one layered on top of the others. The effect is similar to that of a lap dissolve but lasts for the entire duration of the shots.

Supering two shots does not provide a gradual movement from one event to another but shows a static view of the events together. So while a lap dissolve could be used to show a transition between two different worlds, a superimposition might illustrate two worlds coexisting.

SUPERING *Short for "superimposing."*

Supering is also frequently used for titles and *lower thirds*.

> **LOWER THIRD** *When you superimpose a title or other graphic element over the bottom third of the screen to identify the person speaking in an interview, it's called a lower third.*

Split Screen

Split screen offers a very different way to show multiple images simultaneously. Although it violates the invisible-edit dictum, much like the jump cut, it's finding its way into narrative fiction filmmaking. Even so, split screen can be employed more freely in non-narrative projects (**Figure 2.33**).

Figure 2.33 Split screens can have a hard edge like the example on the left or a soft edge like the example on the right.

It is commonly used in telephone sequences where two characters in different locations are talking to each other. You can also see many creative examples of inventive split screen in Darren Aronofsky's *Requiem for a Dream;* my favorite is where two characters are in the same physical location (lying on a bed together) but emotionally separated by their drug addictions. Director Brian DePalma has often demonstrated his mastery of split-screen storytelling as a form of high-tension crosscutting, particularly in early films like *Sisters* and *Phantom of the Paradise.*

In Mike Figgis's *Timecode,* the entire film was shown in a four-up split screen, where four events were going on simultaneously. This was possible because those events were carefully timed so that usually just one of them drew the audience's primary focus. When the events competed for attention, the audio was mixed to let the audience know where to look.

In general, if you're planning to use split screens in your show, you should communicate that fact to the director before the scene is shot. That way she can weight the composition to one side or the other so the joined image will show both subjects.

Split-screen shots can be divided by a hard edge, a soft edge, or even a colored border. This choice further affects the impact of the shot.

> **TIP:** *Any time you put more than one image on the screen simultaneously, arrange your timing so viewers' point of focus is deliberately shifted from one image to the other. One way to accomplish this is by controlling which clip's audio is heard on the soundtrack.*

Rack Focus

Rack focus means the camera operator shifts (or racks) the focus from one character or object to another within a single shot, bringing the audience's point of focus with it (**Figure 2.34**). Since this is a single, self-contained shot, it seems as if it would be a noun rather than a verb. But it does the job of a verb by redirecting the viewer's attention—just as an edit does. Sometimes a camera move can accomplish this same effect.

Figure 2.34 The rack focus effect shifts the viewer's attention without the need for a cut or camera move. Here, focus moves from Trey waiting in the car to the negotiation going on in the office.

Punctuation

There are only a handful of standard ways to begin and end film sequences. Typically, they involve showing some amount of black, which is the film language equivalent of a comma or period.

Fade-to-Black, Dip-to-Black

The most common way to end a sequence is to gradually mix the last shot with black. A dissolve (or fade) is used because it conveys the sense that time continues within the world of the film, even though the viewer is no longer seeing it. Like a cross-dissolve, the duration of the fade-to-black can vary. The most common length is probably between one-half and two seconds (**Figure 2.35**).

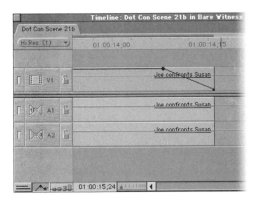 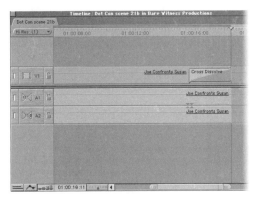

Figure 2.35 You can perform a fade-to-black either by *keyframing* a clip's Opacity graph, as shown on the left, or by applying a cross-dissolve at the end of the last clip, effectively dissolving from the clip to nothing, as shown on the right.

KEYFRAMING *Any time you tell Final Cut Pro to make changes (such as fading to black) over time, you must provide different values at different points in time. These markers are called* keyframes, *and the act of defining them is called* keyframing.

Fading to black usually means the show or sequence is over. If the image remains black for only a moment, it's a scene change and is called a dip-to-black. Occasionally you may want to fade or dip to white or some other color, although both alternatives break the rules of the invisible edit.

Why doesn't fading or dipping to black break that rule? Because on the most basic level, a fade-to-black is an organic and familiar transition that exists naturally in our world. We all experience fading to black every day: slowly, as the day turns to night, and more quickly, when we close our eyes.

Fade-Up-From-Black

Matching the fade-to-black is the fade-up. Think of this as a capital letter that marks the beginning of every cinematic sentence. Again, a mix is used to convey the sense that the world you are about to view has been in existence long before you got there (**Figure 2.36**).

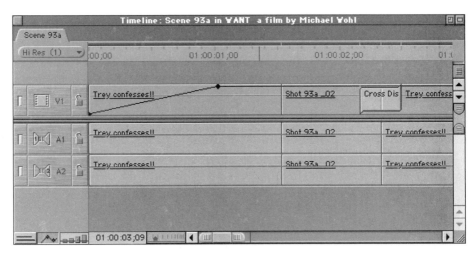

Figure 2.36 Fading up from black is the opposite of fading down to black. Use either the transition effect or the *rubber band control* illustrated here.

> **RUBBER BAND CONTROL** *One way to set keyframing. You click and drag a line that represents various values over time—and it stretches like a rubber band.*

Cut-to-Black and Punch-Up-From-Black

One alternative to the fade-up-from- and fade-down-to-black is simply to cut. This creates a much more abrupt transition, akin to waking with a start and popping your eyes wide open—or being bopped on the head and knocked unconscious. It's a great way to grab the viewer's attention and demand that she direct her point of focus to the image you're presenting. Because of this, it makes sense to punch to or cut from a close-up; a fade fits more naturally with a wider shot.

Freeze Frame

If you want to contradict the implied consistency of the world within the film, one good way to do that is to end a scene—or the entire film—on a freeze frame. Eventually you will probably fade the freeze frame to black, but in the meantime, halting the flow of images is a very powerful effect, forcing the viewer to stay in that final moment.

This punctuation is best used when trying to leave the characters, and the viewer, in the midst of some kind of dilemma. That's why it often occurs at the end of

"Part 1," leaving you anxious to see the completion of the frozen event in "Part 2." You can rarely get away with this in narrative fiction, but it is excellent for training or educational shows because it keeps the viewer psychologically engaged with the conflict, rather than offering the "happily ever after" closure of the more conventional fade-to-black.

Establishing Shot (Locator Shot)

An *establishing shot* (sometimes called a locator shot) shows the environment in which the events to follow take place and indicates to the viewer that a story (or sequence) is beginning. Usually it provides just enough visual context to make sense of the scene.

You'll see this technique employed tirelessly in TV sitcoms. One exterior shot of the *Cheers* pub and you never need to see the outside of the set again. *Third Rock From the Sun* cleverly replaced the standard locator shot with a shot of planet Earth from space. This made fun of the formula by showing a valid locator without actually providing any information.

An establishing shot is not always a wide shot, although that's the standard convention. It might even be an insert, a detail that will later prove critical to the story. In any case, you will rarely create a sequence without using some kind of establishing shot to get your audience's attention and let them know that a new part of the story is about to begin.

Final Frame

Choose your final shot carefully; it's the image viewers will walk away with. It is quite possibly the most important shot in the show, as it is being asked to carry the weight of everything that came before. A powerful ending shot can spin a movie into an entirely new context, or it can summarize and clarify the message your show carries.

RULES OF FILM GRAMMAR

Now that we've gone over the basic elements (nouns, verbs, punctuation) that make up the language of film, I'd like to take you through a few rules and general guidelines governing how editors use them. This is essentially the grammar of film language.

While the language is still growing and evolving, quite a few of the basic rules have remained surprisingly consistent over the years. In most cases, these rules are aimed at maintaining the invisibility of the edit. If you break them, you will create jump cuts or other violations of the invisible edit that will bounce your viewer out of the story you're telling and change her point of focus so she's watching the filmmaking process itself.

New Shot = New Information

The most basic question facing the editor is when to make an edit. And the basic answer is: Edit only when there's new information to be shown. If there's no new information, don't cut.

This rule even helps you figure out which shot to choose next. Just ask yourself what new information is relevant. It could be as simple as one character's reaction to another character or to an event. It might be as specific as a change of angle that reveals a gun hidden in a character's coat.

This doesn't mean that the new information needs to be revealed exactly at the cut point. As with an L-cut, you can offset the shift in the viewer's point of interest from the cut point itself, thus hiding the edit more effectively.

For example, imagine a scene where a boxer has just lost a match. His wife is begging him to leave the sport, while he's insisting that his injuries are insignificant. In the final shot, we cut to the boxer just before he storms off and leaves the room. After he exits, we see a bloodstain left behind on the wall where he was leaning. The new information is the bloodstain, but we don't see it at the cut point. Revealing this information midshot (after the boxer exits the frame) is more powerful than cutting to it in a new shot.

Screen Direction

A good editor is constantly aware of screen direction. Screen direction simply refers to the direction (left or right) that a subject is facing, or moving, in the frame. The simplest way to illustrate this is to consider how a moving object appears as it moves across multiple shots. If the object is moving left to right in shot 1, it must continue to move left to right in shot 2 (**Figure 2.37**).

This is vitally important in sequences like chase scenes or races, where the audience needs to understand that one party is following another or which horse is ahead (**Figure 2.38**).

Figure 2.37 These shots show correct screen direction. If the bicycle in the second image were heading right to left, its motion would not appear continuous in time and space.

Figure 2.38 In this chase sequence, Jane is planning to jump off the Golden Gate Bridge and Anna is determined to stop her. After an establishing shot to set the location (not shown), the scene begins with a CU of Jane walking toward the bridge. The next shot films Anna walking in the same direction (right to left), which makes it clear that she is following Jane. A wider shot of Jane shows that she is now on the bridge, and the next shot captures Anna beginning to run. As long as her legs are moving in the correct direction, we know she's part of the chase. The last shot shows Jane holding the stuffed animal that will prove to be the linchpin of the scene.

Screen direction is equally critical when two or more people are talking to one another (**Figure 2.39**). If one character is shown facing toward the left side of the frame, the person she's talking to should be facing frame-right. This also applies to which side of the frame the character is on. If the subject is on the right side of the frame in shot 1, then he should *still* be on the right side of the frame in shot 2, even though it's a reverse.

Figure 2.39 In this sequence, Trey remains on the left side of the screen and Dana on the right.

Never Cross the Line (the 180° Rule)

To make sure that all your shots have the correct screen direction, draw an imaginary line between the actors' eyelines (or between an actor's eyes and whatever he's looking at) and take all your shots from the same side of "the line" (or axis) (**Figure 2.40**). A shot made from the other side of the axis will result in the actors appearing to be on the wrong side of the frame. If you violate this rule, a viewer watching the scene will think that the actors have switched places—a hugely disorienting effect.

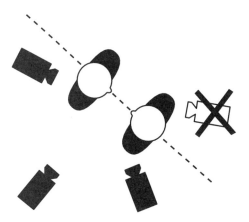

Figure 2.40 Draw an imaginary line between the eyes of the subjects. All the shots taken from one side will have proper screen direction. If you take a shot from the other side, the characters will appear to switch sides, confusing the audience.

While it's the production team's responsibility to avoid errors of this sort during shooting, it's not always as clear-cut as the simple case I just described. Sometimes multiple eyelines are going on simultaneously. Sometimes the eyeline shifts during the course of the action. Sometimes one shot is made on Monday and the reverse isn't shot until Thursday.

Regardless of why mistakes happen, it is the editor's job to prevent errors in screen direction from making it into the finished film. Several common solutions can get you across to the other side of the line if necessary. One is to use a shot that's directly *on* the line: one where the eyeline is directly at the camera (**Figure 2.41**). Another is to use a moving shot that crosses the line during the shot (**Figure 2.42**). From that point on, you can use shots from the other side of the line.

Figure 2.41 This sequence begins with Pete Peters (at the podium) on the right side of the frame looking left. Shot 2, the reaction shot of Trey, confirms this (since he is looking the opposite direction). In shot 3 we show a neutral angle in which Peters is dead center in the frame. After that we are free to move to the other side of the line, as in the fourth shot, where Pete is looking left to right.

Figure 2.42 In this sequence Kip Ruthburn is addressing the workers of Hot Tot Dot Com. It begins with a shot of him looking right to left and a reverse shot of the workers looking left to right, watching him. The camera dollies around in front of him until he's looking left to right. In order for the workers' reactions to match, they must now be looking right to left, as Tess, the office manager, is doing in shot 5.

In desperate cases you can flop a shot (**Figure 2.43**). But this is difficult to pull off, because even if there are no obvious errors (like a sign with the writing backward, or a car with its steering wheel on the wrong side), people usually look "funny" when reversed. We are not symmetrical beings, and although you can often get away with one shot like this, cutting back and forth between a flopped shot and a normal shot of the same subject may not work.

> **FLOP** *A digital effect where the image is reversed left to right.*

Figure 2.43 Any shot can be flopped to change its screen direction, but beware of things that give the trick away. Who knows, maybe Trey drives a British car?

In Final Cut Pro, flopping a shot is as easy as choosing the Flop filter from the Effects menu and applying it to a clip (**Figure 2.44**). (See the section on filter effects in Chapter 8, "Special Effects.")

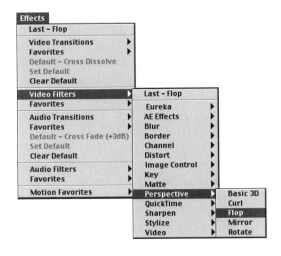

Figure 2.44 To flop a shot in Final Cut Pro, choose the Flop filter from the Perspective submenu of the Video Filters section of the Effects menu.

You can intentionally disrupt screen direction to create a specific effect. For instance, if two people in conversation are facing the same direction, one is talking to the other's back. You can use this to show a power relationship (**Figure 2.45**).

You can also show two people conversing while facing away from each other, conveying conflict between the characters. This is harder to achieve than you might think, because in an edited sequence, intercutting subjects who are looking in opposite directions usually gives the impression that they're facing each other.

Figure 2.45 In this scene, Dawn has picked up her brother from prison. Throughout the long bus ride home, they almost never look at each other.

This is an optico-psychological gestalt effect and has to do with noseroom. If the shots are composed with proper noseroom (see the section on noseroom in Chapter 1, "The Editor's Job"), the people appear to be looking at one another. If, on the other hand, the shots are composed with insufficient noseroom (that is, with the subjects seeming to face directly into the frame edge), intercutting them creates the effect that they are indeed looking away from one another. This can be sold even better if the eyelines don't match (**Figure 2.46**).

Screen direction is not neutral. Subjects moving (or facing) right to left have a very different psychological effect than those moving (or facing) left to right. In some ways this may be cultural, based on the fact that we read words left to right and tend to read pictures similarly: The left comes before the right. I've long been curious whether people in cultures where writing is read right to left (as with Hebrew) have different interpretations of our movies.

Left-to-right orientation impacts composition in subtle but interesting ways. Things on the left tend to read as though they have a certain amount of cause over the elements (or effects) on the right. This is not an absolute rule, but it tends to be what audiences unconsciously expect.

Figure 2.46 In the first two images, the characters seem to be looking at one another. In the second two, they don't. Composition and eyeline differentiate the two sequences.

You can use this effect to your advantage. If you want to show something moving harmoniously in flow with the story, or the universe, use left-to-right movement. If you want to show something creating conflict, or stopping the flow, use right-to-left movement. In static shots, positioning the agent of change on the right side of the frame (opposite to the expectation) can create tension and conflict (**Figure 2.47**).

Figure 2.47 This shot illustrates how the right side of the frame can be used very effectively to show an obstacle facing a character. To emphasize the significance of this barrier for the man, we placed it in bright light and left the subject in dark silhouette.

Cut on Action

One of the best ways to hide an edit is to place it in the middle of action. If the action is continuous across the two shots, the shot change will go virtually unnoticed. This is why editors are always making mental notes about shots with doors closing or people making hand movements. Any clear action in the frame that pulls the viewer's focus is a potential cut point. Of course, it requires a second shot containing the completion of the same action. This is why it's so critical for actors to match their actions exactly across different shots and multiple takes.

Pay attention to the films you watch, and you'll see that most edits occur on some kind of action. An edit between two static shots will draw unwelcome attention to itself. If you're forced to make such a cut, use audio to bridge the shots.

Match Your Shots

When cutting back and forth between two shots, as in a dialogue sequence, it's best to use shots that match each other in focal length and frame size. Intercutting between a CU and an MS creates a jarring effect that keeps the viewer from falling into the dramatic flow of the scene.

Take this example from a dialogue scene. (I won't transcribe the dialogue itself.)

1. Establishing LS, busy restaurant.

2. MS two-shot of couple at table.

3. MCU Max OS Julie.

4. MCU Julie OS Max.

5. MCU Max OS Julie.

6. ECU INSERT engagement ring.

7. CU Julie.

8. CU Max.

9. CU Julie.

10. CU Max.

11. MS two-shot of couple at table as waiter arrives with check.

12. MCU Max OS Julie.

13. MCU Julie OS Max.

14. LS Max and Julie exit restaurant.

Notice that in this sequence I match MCUs to MCUs and CUs to CUs. Using the insert to make the transition from MCUs to CUs isn't strictly required, but it serves to make the transition more subtle. Likewise, when I want to pull back out to the MCUs (after the intimate dialogue is done), I bridge it by cutting back to my master shot, which, in this case, is a two-shot of Max and Julie at the table. That cut is additionally motivated by the new information of the waiter arriving.

It is also critical to choose shots with matching focal length. Ideally, this will be handled in production, but as the editor you're going to have to deal with the results if someone screws up. If one CU was shot from 5 feet away with a wide-angle lens and the other was shot from 25 feet away using a telephoto, the shots will match so poorly that you'll find it hard to maintain the illusion that they were taken in the same place (**Figure 2.48**).

Figure 2.48 These shots are both close-ups, but they were filmed with different focal lengths. Trying to cut back and forth between the two shots would be disruptive to your scene.

In such a situation, if this is the only footage available to you, I suggest using especially long J and L cuts to accentuate the connectedness of the shots. I would also recommend cutting as little as possible. Once you settle on a shot, the audience will forget the rough juxtaposition of the last edit—but every time you cut, you'll reintroduce that disorientation. It may be better to stick with an OS shot even if the subject talking is facing away from the camera than to cut back and forth between mismatched singles. At least the OS is a two-shot and shows the two people in physical proximity.

Cut Moving to Moving, Still to Still

Avoid cutting from a moving shot to a still shot, or you will find yourself drawing attention to the edit instead of the content. If you use a moving shot of an object and cut to a static shot of the same object, it reads as a sort of unwanted jump cut—even if continuity is maintained. For example, if you had a dolly shot that circled around the outside of a dinner table and a tripod shot of one of the people eating, these shots would not cut well.

Moving shots can be cut against other moving shots, but ideally you should let a moving shot come to a standstill before cutting to a static shot. If you have no choice because of limited coverage, try to bridge the transition from moving shot to still shot with an extreme angle. For instance, in the dining room scene I just described, you might cut from the dolly shot to an ECU of a plate of food or an extreme high-angle overhead shot. In this way, you are creating a dramatic visual change that overshadows the distraction of the moving-versus-still-shot problem.

This rule has a few exceptions. One occurs when the movement is motivated by the subject. In other words, it's OK to cut between the moving POV of a child on a merry-go-round and the static POV of his father watching from the solid ground. Another exception involves cutting from a moving shot to a shot that *seems* static only because it is moving at the same speed as the subject (a follow shot). For instance, you can cut from a tracking shot of a moving car to a "static" shot of the driver in the moving car; continuity is maintained because the second shot is really moving, even though the subject is static in the frame.

Find a Compositional Link

If at all possible, every edit should contain a compositional link between the two shots. Sometimes the shots will give you this automatically: For instance, two OS shots will usually provide reciprocal angles and match compositionally (**Figure 2.49**).

Or sometimes you can find a graphical element in the first shot that matches a graphical element in the second shot, like the example I mentioned earlier in this chapter: matching a round car tire in shot 1 with a spinning globe in shot 2.

Visual continuity is usually lower priority than contextual continuity, but it really enhances an edit to have a matching visual component to soften the transition. This is particularly critical in scene cuts and dissolves.

Figure 2.49 Reciprocal shots like these naturally provide a compositional link between shots.

Manipulating Time

When you're editing a scene, you don't always aim at capturing a precise re-creation of reality. Sometimes your goal is to *enhance* reality, to create a fictional world that's most appropriate for carrying your themes.

This is particularly true when it comes to time. Film is a time-based medium, which means that the fluent manipulation of time becomes a critical element for successful editing. Except in rare cases (like the shoot-out at the end of Fred Zinnemann's *High Noon),* film time is a lot more compressed than real time.

Think about it. Let's say you need to go to a police station to give a deposition about your crazy neighbor who is building a nuclear submarine in his backyard and plotting to take over the world.

You step out your door, turn around, and lock it (which takes five seconds). You walk to your car (:20), get out your keys (:10), open the door (:05), sit down (:05), put on your seat belt (:05), start the car (:05), put it in gear, and pull out of your driveway (:20). You drive to the police station (5:00). Once you arrive, you have to park and walk into the building (1:00). Then, after waiting in line (3:00), you get to talk to the detective and explain about the suspicious periscope peeking over the fence (5:00).

You get the idea.

This sequence could take over 15 minutes of real time, but if you were editing it for a film you would probably cut it down to 90 seconds, maybe less. It's not just that the details are so familiar that they're boring to watch, but that real life simply takes a long time. Even in the so-called reality shows that are so popular on television, gobs of time are edited out to allow viewers to focus on the bits that actually tell a story. This is what makes film more interesting (and more exciting) than real life: It's compressed.

Let's say that the director who is shooting the story about you and your neighbor abridges this sequence to take just 75 seconds. She then shoots three sequences:

1. You leaving your house.

2. You arriving at the station.

3. You greeting the detective and giving the deposition.

She will probably end up shooting at least 7 to 10 minutes of footage. In reality, coverage and multiple takes could triple that total. The editor is responsible for taking that 10 (or 30) minutes and whittling it down to the 75 seconds that will play in the final film. If you are that editor, you will need to decide which individual moments, or beats, best capture the whole event.

Here's just one sample solution:

1. You lock your door at home (:03).

2. Your foot hits the parking lot pavement as you exit your car at the police station. The shot tilts up to show the doorway as you walk toward it (:05).

3. The handshake as the detective greets you (:02).

4. The detective's fingers press the record button on his tape recorder (:02).

5. You take a sip of water before you begin (:03).

6. A sequence of simple two-shots and singles shows you telling your story and the detective listening.

This last sequence (6) probably comprises 12 to 15 shots (1:00). Most of them just show faces (CU or OS shots), but a good editor might include a cutaway to the tape recorder, or the clock on the wall, or your foot tapping nervously. All the cutaways emphasize the emotional undercurrents of the scene and its physical circumstances.

Even within a simple conversation, a good editor will often find himself manipulating time, adding or removing pauses between lines, or removing lines altogether to create a natural-sounding conversation—while keeping the lines clean enough so viewers can follow them. This is a real art. In reality, most conversations have dead spaces where no one is talking—or sometimes, as soon as one person starts talking, several others overlap her. In a crowd everyone might be speaking at once. If your intention is to direct the viewer's attention to the dialogue, you have to make sure that the content of what is being said is audible, even while you maintain enough overlap so the conversation feels natural.

Finally, beware: While compressing time can improve the pacing and rhythm of the scene, it is considered bad form to alter the timing of an actor's performance without the director's approval. Presumably the director would have said something during the shoot if he wanted the actor's pacing to be much faster—or slower.

Respect Silence

Not every moment should be filled with dialogue. The most powerful moments are often those that occur during silence: reactions, thoughts, emotions. These are the elements that really tell the story. Give them space to work.

Set the Pace

Pacing makes a huge impact on how a film works—and for the most part the editor is responsible for setting it. Pacing can vary widely. Some stories need to be slow, languid, or contemplative; others want to flash by quickly, packed with dense editing sequences. Pacing is generally determined by the themes and intentions of the entire show, as well as the special dramatic requirements of any given scene.

Slow pacing doesn't mean you're wasting screen time. No matter how hard you look, you probably won't be able to find any "dead time" in a well-edited film— even one with a languid pace. Every frame will be working to tell the story.

Fast pacing doesn't mean overwhelming the viewer, either. No matter how much information you cram into every second, the emotional content of the scene must be paramount.

Most of the time the director will let you know what sort of pacing he expects. However, you will be primarily responsible for bringing that pacing to life, moment to moment, as you tell your story. As an editor, you are perpetually guiding the viewer, and you must feed her new information at just the right pace to keep her engaged. This is why it's critical not only to know the subject and intention of the piece but also to know your audience.

STORYTELLING

Put it all together and…you're telling a story. All films are stories—even documentaries and industrial films. Humans pass on information to one another through storytelling.

Over time, storytelling media have changed from oral histories to writing, and then to multimedia, while storytelling styles have exploded into many different formats. Humans are programmed to understand certain communication patterns best. The patterns can be subtle, and an inventive storyteller will find room for endless creativity in using language. Nevertheless, to communicate successfully, a good editor needs to learn the elements that make up a story.

At its most basic level, a story is a vehicle for exchanging information. According to the classic definition, a story is a sequence of events that follows characters in conflict in context. The typical story also has a beginning, a middle, and an end.

Stuff Happens

A chronicle, an account, a version, a history, a legend, a saga, a myth, a fable, a parable. This is the story of story. Stuff happens, and in order to explain it to someone else, the storyteller breaks it down into smaller chunks and communicates it. The receiver reassembles the chunks and understands the whole. As the story is passed from one source to another, as in a game of telephone, the chunks may be modified, simplified, forgotten, and reinvented—but each time, meaning is derived.

You can break down events into smaller events, and break those down in turn, until you're looking at a single human event, or *therblig*.

> **THERBLIG**   This term was coined by Frank and Lillian Gilbreth, behavioral scientists whose analysis of human behavior made huge contributions to the technological advances of the 20th century. It refers to the most basic mechanical action a human can make. The Gilbreths came up with 17 or so unique therbligs. Note that "therblig" is Gilbreth spelled backward (almost).

"Well, I <u>said</u>, 'Walter, *you're* the one!' And he <u>gasped</u>, and <u>sat</u> down, and <u>looked</u> at me…"

Four therbligs occurred in that sequence.

When an editor sits down to cut a film, she is handed an enormous pile of individual therbligs, often shot completely out of natural sequence. What an editor does all day long is to assemble one therblig after another, one element after another, shot by shot by shot. She arranges them one way, and then another way, until finally a coherent story begins to emerge.

Characters in Conflict in Context

Who, what, where, when, why, and how? These are the elements that comprise a story. You know that list by heart, because we all use those questions every day in daily life to understand the world around us: We think in stories. In film, these elements are represented by individual shots. Every shot has a point of focus: one or more vital bits of information it can communicate to the viewer. A good editor must be able to look at a shot and understand which bits of information it contains and which questions it answers.

How you deal with characters, conflict, and context has a huge impact on how you tell your story. It conveys the sense of theme and meaning in your work. And it answers the most important question: *Why?*

Stuff Happens to Characters (Who?)

Humans are most interested in stories about humans. Even a show about animals or objects requires a degree of anthropomorphizing in order to help the viewer make sense of the event. Sequences without a character quickly lose an audience's interest. Which shots in your sequence are about characters?

Event = Conflict (What? How?)

Without some kind of contrast or opposition, an event does not occur—at least not on-screen. Conflict can take many forms, but the editor creates meaning by contrasting ideas or images. What are the opposing or contrasting elements of this event? What shots can you use to represent them?

For example, let's say your story is about a divorcing couple. What are the elements of the conflict? Primarily, you have the two parties: husband and wife. Each time you juxtapose separate singles of each party, you emphasize the conflict. This may be obvious when they are in conversation, but you can make the point even more subtly by contrasting a shot of the wife having coffee with her new lover and the husband at home with their child.

Events Take Place in a Context (Where? When? With Whom?)

You can't construct meaning from these story elements without context. Nor can you prevent context from affecting the events in the story, although you can shape *how* the context affects events through your editing choices.

For example, let's expand our divorce story and set it in the midst of the Colombian civil war. Your editing choices will determine how the external conflict contrasts with or reflects the domestic story. You might align the husband with the government forces by linking them with similar music or grouping shots together so every time we see the husband, he is preceded by a shot of tanks in the streets.

Another interesting way you might align the two elements is by screen direction. If you make sure that the government forces are always moving left to right, and the revolutionaries are always moving right to left, you can borrow those directions and show the husband and wife moving in similar ways. Although this effect would be subtle, it might be effective in communicating the correlation between the political struggle and the personal one.

On the other hand, sequences that contain too *much* context may seem overly expository and disengage the viewer; just because a scene is set in the Musée D'Orsay in Paris doesn't mean you have to show every Monet and Renoir in its collection.

Ask yourself which shots in your sequence show the context. What would happen if you eliminated those shots or rearranged their order? Perhaps choosing one painting of a calm, beautiful meadow and inserting it in the midst of the heated argument will serve not only to identify the location as the Musée D'Orsay but also to emphasize the conflict between the characters by contrasting it with the serene image.

Don't get stuck thinking that context simply means location. A shot of a Model T Ford or a particular costume can be used to convey a specific time period. A close shot of a child laughing and playing in a playground might serve to flavor the emotional context of a scene.

Two Cool Rules

There are two important rules of storytelling, and both are derived from the rules of the world we live in.

Cause and Effect

Rule #1 is based on the rules of physics: For every action, there is an equal and opposite reaction. The order in which you present events to your viewers implies cause and effect. Every good editor must understand this essential insight for arranging shots.

For instance, if you follow a shot of a dead soldier with a shot of his comrade saving a baby, you may be implying that the death of the soldier inspired his comrade's bravery.

On the other hand, if you show the comrade saving the baby followed by a shot of the dead soldier, you may be suggesting that saving the baby required sacrificing the soldier.

In most stories, many events are going on simultaneously. When you tell a story on-screen, you instill meaning by the choices you make in arranging how those events will be presented to the viewer. Even a simple conversation contains actions and reactions. Precisely when you choose to cut to a reaction shot indicates what the character is reacting to—right down to the word.

Timing Is Everything

Rule #2 has to do with timing. Good storytelling is all about good timing. You probably know people who tell wonderful stories and others who can't tell a joke to save their life. The difference often lies in knowing how much time to spend telling each piece of the story.

For instance, if you spend too long describing every detail of the heroine's clothing, the audience will lose interest in what she's doing. And if you rush past her escape from the castle too quickly, you'll disappoint the audience and lose its interest again.

Timing is the most difficult editing skill to teach, because it's very personal and often unique to each event. The only overall rule is this: Stay on a shot exactly as long as is necessary to communicate the information it contains—not a frame less and not a frame more.

Storytelling Structure: Secrets Revealed

Well-told stories have an effect on us. We are moved in a way that's nearly incomparable and largely indescribable. Sharing stories is as vital to us as love. This is one reason we are drawn to filmmaking, to writing novels, to storytelling. But even if the final effect seems magical, we can still deconstruct a story and learn how that powerful effect is created.

And almost every time, the secret that's revealed is *structure.* The order in which events occur as a tale unfolds is fundamental to affecting an audience. And since the editor determines the order of events in a film, down to the tiniest detail, she is the one who ultimately tells the story and makes it work.

You can find some excellent theoretical writing on story construction, notably Joseph Campbell's *The Power of Myth* and *The Hero with a Thousand Faces.* If you find those useful, take a look at *The Writer's Journey* by Christopher Vogler, an interesting work that applies Campbell's theories to the art of screenwriting. All three books will help you understand storytelling structure. While these books focus primarily on overall structure, they provide useful insights on how to organize smaller events and even how best to set the specific order and timing of shots.

Interview: CURTISS CLAYTON

Curtiss Clayton has edited a wonderful collection of independent films, including many of Gus Van Sant's best pictures. His credits include *Drugstore Cowboy* and *My Own Private Idaho* (both by Van Sant), Vincent Gallo's *Buffalo '66,* Bill Duke's *A Rage in Harlem,* and Jonathan Kaplan's *Brokedown Palace.* At the time of this interview, he had just completed the delightfully stylish *Made,* directed by Jon Favreau.

Michael Wohl: Do you have any advice for beginning editors?

Curtiss Clayton: Anyone who wants to study editing seriously should study the fundamentals and not have an attitude about it, like, "I don't need these rules. These are just hindering my creativity." Concepts of screen direction, matching, the axis, the stage line, creating that illusion of a three-dimensional space…all that stuff is really important.

You also need to know how the sound and image work together, how important the sound is, how to manipulate the sound to create the illusion of continuity and seamlessness, especially applied to a cut that might not work visually. There are a bunch of weapons in your arsenal that you can employ if you take the time. It's like studying your multiplication tables: It's necessary. You can do anything you want. The questions are: Does it look good, is it going to be clear, and can you follow it?

Why did you choose a career in editing?

When I was in film school I didn't like the fact that as the cameraman, or in some of the other crew positions, you had this intense experience on the set, you finished shooting, and then you were done. Some time later you'd go to see the finished film, and very often it was not what you thought you were working on. That's one reason why I think actors are so frustrated in Hollywood and why so many want to be directors. As the editor, you participate in the ultimate form of the film, deciding what it's finally going to look like.

Are you aware of having a unique editing style?

Generally a particular aesthetic is already built into the shooting. Style is 80 percent determined by how a film is shot. You're in trouble if you have to impose some sort of style that's not inherent in what the film material already is.

How has the new technology changed the way you work?

It's fantastic. You don't need to spend nearly as much time searching your material; that's the best part about it. You have random access to any shot in the whole library of images, whereas before you'd be thinking of a moment you remembered from the dailies, and you'd have to go to that scene on the shelf, and take down the box, and there would be maybe five takes, and you'd have to wind through all of them looking for what you wanted. It's like, "Roll down through take one, then roll down through take two…" Now, you just click your mouse a couple times and it's instantaneous. That's the most wonderful thing about the new technology. It's like the difference between silent film and talkies.

CHAPTER THREE
Editing Patterns

Good editors rely on a library of "standard" editing patterns that serve them as guidelines for approaching each particular type of show. After all, no one has time to reinvent the wheel every time she sits down to edit a sequence.

I know you think that you are a unique snowflake, with a personal vision so fresh and insightful that every editing choice you make will be both original and stunningly beautiful. But remember that an average hour of film contains as many as 1,000 edits, and under that kind of pressure even the most resilient snowflake is likely to melt eventually. There is nothing wrong with standing on the slushpile of editors who have come before you and following the tried-and-true editing patterns they have established.

I use the term "pattern" to refer to a sequence of shot types and associated editing strategies that create a consistent effect on screen, regardless of the specific content of the shots. These formulas won't help you convey the deeper themes of your show, but they provide valuable guidelines to save you time and help you choose the most effective shot type to use next. To extend the grammatical metaphor from the last chapter, you can think of these patterns as common idioms in the film language.

Naturally, some turns of phrase become overused and clichéd as time passes, and innovative editors are always creating new ways of presenting even the most familiar types of stories. Moreover, each show and each editor is unique; a good editor will impart his own style even when using one of these standard patterns, and of course the specific choice of shots will be unique for every show. In this way the language is continually evolving.

This chapter is a collection of different types of sequences (dialogue, action, comedy, documentary, and so on), with examples and guidelines for how to cut each one most effectively using a traditional editing pattern.

EDITING WITH COMMON PATTERNS

Before we discuss editing patterns for specific genres, let's consider patterns that are so basic they cut across genre lines. You'll find yourself using these structures again and again in common editing situations.

Starting a Scene

Every scene has to start somewhere—but getting started is often the hardest part. The most common way to start any scene is with the basic once-upon-a-time film "sentence" that goes, LS MS CU. The LS can be any establishing shot that introduces the characters in an environment. Cutting to an MS moves your viewer closer to the subject. Finally, you settle into a close shot, where you can show the details of what's going on (**Figure 3.1**).

Figure 3.1 In this typical scene opening, we begin with a master LS showing Gene and his entourage. Next, we cut to an MS so we can see who's talking; the audio is of Gene reading an astrological chart. Finally, we move into an MCU of Gene, framed so we can see Trey approaching in the background.

This convention is one of the most basic editing patterns you can find. You can apply it at the beginning of a scene, or at the beginning of a new event within a scene. It's even appropriate, used in reverse, to end a sequence.

Changing Locations

One of the most common ways editors create smooth transitions between locations is by using the exit-entrance pattern. Here, a shot of someone exiting a frame is cut to match a shot of the same person entering the next frame. This relies on the shots maintaining correct *screen direction,* although in some cases you can flop one of the shots if it doesn't match (**Figure 3.2**).

Figure 3.2 Here, in shot 2, we see Trey exiting frame-right and, in shot 3, entering frame-left. Keeping him partially in frame across the cut point maintains continuity of time even though the location has changed.

To make this transition seamless, cut out of the outgoing shot a few frames before the subject actually exits, and cut into the incoming shot a few frames after he enters. Because the subject stays on-screen, his motion appears continuous and provides a smooth transition, even though you may be cutting between two locations.

Show Time Passing as You Change Locations

You can vary this technique to link scenes where you want to show time passing during the transition. Simply let the subject exit the frame completely in the outgoing shot, wait a few frames, then cut into the incoming shot a few frames before the subject arrives. This requires you to decide how many frames should be shown after the exit and before the entrance. If you wait too long, the viewer's focus will change from the character himself to the surroundings the character has just left behind. Typically, you want an equal number of "empty" frames at the end of the first shot and the beginning of the second.

Shot–Reverse Shot

When a scene features a live person, the audience will watch her eyes to see what she's thinking or feeling. If the subject is looking at something offscreen, the audience will want to know what she's looking at. This is the basis for one of the most common phrases in film language, the shot–reverse shot. "Reverse" refers to any shot that shows the opposite of the previous shot.

Cut Between Two Characters

If you need to cut back and forth between two participants in a conversation, you'll probably use the shot–reverse shot pattern. For instance, when actor 1 looks at actor 2, the editor will cut to show what he's looking at (the other actor). Then, when the second actor looks back at the first, the editor cuts back to the first shot. The actor's look can give you a great clue as to when to make your cut.

Show Offscreen Action

You can also use the shot–reverse shot pattern to edit a scene where the subject is looking at something offscreen.

Let's say a man is sitting next to the window in a café, writing in a journal. At some point, he looks up and glances at something going on offscreen, outside the window of the café. Don't wait too long to show the thing he's looking at, or you will confuse and upset your audience. You can hint at what's going on with offscreen sound or a CU revealing his emotional state, but eventually you've *got* to show what the heck he's looking at.

Narrative patterns and expectations are so powerful that even now, gentle reader, you are probably wondering what that man is looking at. If I wait too long to tell you, you will get frustrated and perhaps forget the point of this lesson. The longer the editor waits to reveal the answer, the more tension he creates in his viewer—which can be effective, if you know when to release the tension. If you wait too long, it just comes across as bad editing. In some situations, you can get away with not revealing the object of your subject's attention: for instance, if the thing he's looking at is a secret that will be revealed later. (Oh. The man in the café was looking at Alfred Hitchcock, making his customary personal appearance carrying a French horn.)

Montage

Although in French, *montage* is the general term for editing, in English, editors generally use it to mean an extended sequence of short images that are tied together thematically but break the rules of continuity of time and space.

Montages are used widely across all types of projects. They can often solve the problem of how to show a large, complicated event in the shortest period of time. A well-executed montage is like a poem, communicating deep feelings with an impressive economy of words. The art of montage is to find the fewest (and most meaningful) images that will convey the essence of the entire event.

Montages frequently use cross-dissolves rather than cuts to transition between shots, and most editors choose to back them with music or voice-over rather than *sync sound*.

> **SYNC SOUND** Audio that's synchronized with the image. For instance, the sync sound for a wine-tasting sequence might include the clink of glasses being set on the counter and the tasters' discussion of the grassy overtones of the Sauvignon Blanc.

Show Time Passing

The most clichéd montage, which illustrates the passage of time, usually intercuts pages blowing off a calendar (or hands spinning on a clock face) with shots of pertinent action involving the characters, such as a prisoner sitting in his cell or snapshots of children growing up.

You probably don't want to repeat the cliché, so you need to find a unique way to convey the passing of time: maybe hair growing or leaves turning gold. Try to find something that fits with the story. In one time-passage montage I cut for a training video about gas station attendants, we showed candy wrappers accumulating in the trash can.

Compress Complex Processes

You can use a montage to simplify complicated procedures. For instance, imagine a story about an auto company designing a new car. Once the drama of the design team's decisions is played out, the actual construction of the cars might be edited into a montage showing various operations taking place on the assembly line. This way, a process that might take several hours or days in real time can be condensed into a few seconds.

Recap and Review

A montage can be very handy for presenting a recap or review. Typically, if you were cutting an educational or informational video, you would place a montage of memorable frames from the film at the end of a section (or the whole show), joined with dissolves or cuts.

Occasionally a dramatic film will use this technique to recap key events in a brief montage at the end. This can give the whole film a broader context. A good example is Woody Allen's *Annie Hall*. At the end of the film, Allen's character, Alvy Singer, is reminiscing about his failed relationship with Annie Hall. Allen shows us a montage of the highlights of the relationship. It wouldn't work if he included shots that we had not seen already. The point is to remind us of the emotions associated with each scene in the movie. The montage brings the scenes together to make a larger point about the bittersweet nature of relationships.

Contrast Counts

In many ways, building a montage is a lot like creating a sequence for an experimental film or music video. Since the rules of continuity are suspended, creating a memorable montage depends almost exclusively on the visual and emotional contrasts of the images you bring together.

Start by collecting the shots you intend to use. Of course, you will want to choose shots that are appropriate to the subject at hand. Usually, you won't need to include more than one angle of any one scene or detail. For instance, in the assembly line montage I mentioned, one shot of each machine would probably be enough. Choose shots that best illustrate the procedure or event taking place, and always look for the most visually striking shot.

Next, experiment with ways to assemble the shots. The order of shots in your montage is seldom critical, so try rearranging them in different ways for the best visual effect. Continuity doesn't matter, so what you're left with is the visual effect of bringing two adjacent shots together.

Composition Counts

Remember one of the rules we discussed for jumpcutting and scene changes, neither of which depends on continuity: Pay close attention to the composition of the shots. How do they compare? How do they cut together visually? Look at the positive and negative space of the different shots. Adjacent images should contrast with each other. If the shots are too similar, the cut may be missed or misread as an accidental jump cut.

These issues can affect your shot selection as well as the order in which you assemble the shots. In the assembly line montage, for instance, you might choose only ECUs of the various moving parts on the machines (assuming they look different enough to be visually entertaining). Alternately, you could cut back and forth between ECUs and LSs.

Ideally, you can apply these same rules to the emotional content of the shots in a montage. If a prisoner goes through a range of feelings while in solitary confinement, don't worry about continuity or showing subtle changes from one state to another. Cut from a shot of him crying to one of him calm, then show him screaming, then catatonic. The juxtaposition of contrasting emotional content will heighten the impact of the sequence.

WORKING WITH NARRATIVE STRUCTURE

While you might think that narrative editing patterns and storytelling techniques are mainly pertinent to fictional feature films, you can apply the same insights and strategies to almost all types of film editing. You will find yourself drawing on storytelling techniques whether you're editing informational corporate communications pieces or educational projects. Basic storytelling is also essential to good documentary filmmaking. In fact, the only place where narrative conventions go out the window is in abstract cinema, which these days is found mainly in advertising, music videos, and experimental art films.

Some of the most frequently used editing patterns and techniques involve dialogue scenes and action sequences. If you can master dialogue editing and the art of the *continuity cut* in action scenes, you'll find that 80 percent of your editing will be some variation on these techniques.

> **CONTINUITY CUT** *Any cut that preserves continuity of action, space, time, and screen direction across the edit point.*

Editing Dialogue Sequences

The dialogue sequence is the centerpiece of all narrative filmmaking and supplies some of the most common editing patterns. Whenever two or more people are speaking, the editor can fall back on standard patterns for editing the sequence.

The primary goal in almost any dialogue sequence is to allow the content of the dialogue to get across to the viewer. However, there is usually much more going on in a scene than just the words being spoken: the body language of actors, the reactions of the listeners, the environment in which they exist, and all the other elements that contribute to the story.

It's also important to understand dramatic timing in order to create a naturalistic effect when cutting dialogue that may have been recorded at different times (see the section on manipulating time in Chapter 2, "Film Language").

Cut Audio First

In most dialogue sequences, you will want to create naturalistic conversational timing. One way to make this a lot easier is to cut your *track* before you start worrying about the picture.

> **TRACK** *Film editors refer to all the sound elements as "the track." It's short for "soundtrack."*

Once you've captured all the clips you need for the dialogue scene, you'll find them in Final Cut Pro's Browser window. Review the shots one by one to find the best ones, and start building the sequence. For starters, don't worry too much about what the clips look like. Choose the shots that will allow you to create the most fluid and seamless audio track.

You'll probably need to play with your clips quite a bit, making minute adjustments before you find the right timing to create a seamless, natural-sounding conversation. You may have to alter the pacing by adding gaps between words or phrases or editing out fractional seconds of the clip. You'll often need to overlap your audio clips to make the dialogue overlap as it does in actual conversation. Since you're not paying much attention to the images yet, you can concentrate on fine-tuning the audio. Use Final Cut Pro's Timeline tools to move the clips in one direction or another, fade them in and out, and so on, to create just the right overlap (**Figure 3.3**).

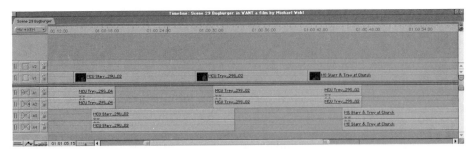

Figure 3.3 The audio on tracks A3 and A4 is from MCU Starr 29U_02. By overlapping this clip with the audio clips on tracks A1 and A2, the editor can condense time—giving the impression that the characters' dialogue is overlapping.

Once you've built the audio track, you should be able to close your eyes and hear a natural-sounding conversation. You'll probably continue to refine the audio as you cut your picture, but the better you build the audio in the first place, the easier it will be to choose your visuals.

Do It by the Numbers

*In Final Cut Pro you can move Timeline items forward or backward by specific numbers of frames, simply by selecting the item in the Timeline and typing +5 or –3 or however many frames you want to move the item. Just the thing for fine-tuning an audio track. You'll quickly get the feel of how long "+5 frames" is on-screen, and learn how many frames to move items to make the timing to your liking (**Figure 3.4**). (I'll elaborate on all these techniques in greater detail in Chapters 4, "Preparing to Edit," and 6, "Advanced Editing.")*

The pop-up window gives visual feedback so you can see what you're typing.

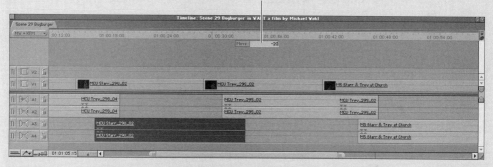

Figure 3.4 Any time an item in the Timeline is selected, simply typing ⊞ or ⊟ initiates the Move function. Hitting Enter or Return performs the edit.

*You can also drag items around in the Timeline, but this is far less precise than the technique described above. Depending on how zoomed in your view is, the same tiny drag might move the clip ten frames or ten seconds (**Figure 3.5**).*

Figure 3.5 Clicking and dragging any Timeline item allows you to move it, but this is far less precise than typing in a numerical entry. In a pinch, you can move one frame at a time by holding down ⌘ while you drag.

Sometimes there may be a mistake in either the picture or the track that threatens to ruin the shot. It's much easier to replace audio (through Foley, ADR, or stealing good audio from another shot) than it is to replace images (which could require a reshoot). So you will generally overlook an audio error to use a great-looking shot but will almost never overlook a visual error.

For example, pretend you're editing an imaginary wedding scene in one of *The Godfather* movies. Your goal at this stage is to create the best audio track you can. You have two takes of the CU of Michael Corleone giving a toast to the newlyweds. In take 1, there's a fabulous flash of light refracting through his upraised glass—but an overflying plane ruined the audio. In the second take, there's no flash but the dialogue is perfect. Make an exception and lay in take 1. You can fix the audio by using the track from take 2 or another take in the sequence; in the worst case, add the shot to the ADR list.

> **TIP:** *If the actors turned in good performances, you may be able to use their pauses and phrasing to guide your pacing, but most often, when you're matching shots from various takes and different setups, you'll have to set dialogue pacing on your own. The current fashion is for film editors to create somewhat accelerated speech. What might sound natural in real life or onstage often feels too slow or "stagey" when played on film.*

Dialogue for Two

The simplest dialogue sequences involve two people, and they come with their own sets of editing patterns.

Establish a Physical Relationship

When you cut a dialogue sequence involving two people, it's important to begin with a two-shot to establish the characters' physical relationship. If you can't make it the first shot of the sequence, try to show it as early in the sequence as possible. If too much time passes entirely in singles, the audience will lose the sense of connection between the characters.

Your choice for the two-shot can be an establishing shot or long shot that places the characters in their environment, or it might be a tighter MS that simply serves to show the characters' proximity. This critical two-shot also provides an opportunity to reveal the physical dynamic of the discussion. Are the protagonists facing away from each other? Across a table? Side by side? Once you establish this in the two-shot, the screen direction in the singles will continue to communicate the relationship. Another common two-shot is the over-the-shoulder shot; sometimes you can edit almost an entire dialogue sequence between two people just using OS shots.

Once the physical relationship has been established through the two-shot, you can cut back and forth between the two players using singles, but you should adhere to the basic grammatical rules of matching shots—that is, cutting MS to MS, CU to CU, and so on (see the section on matching shots in Chapter 2).

Cut in Close for Pivotal Moments

You can emphasize the key moment of a sequence with an effective editing pattern. Typically, you'll begin a dialogue sequence in wider shots, perhaps MCU over-the-shoulder (OS) shots. Then, at the pivotal moment of the scene, you can switch to single close-ups (CUs). This focuses attention on the subjects' emotional state.

Once the key moment is over, you can back out of the CUs in order to close the sequence comfortably. You might switch back to MCUs, jump back out to an MS, or try something even wider. Usually, the scene is pretty much over after its climax, so there won't be too many shots after the CUs anyway.

For instance, in a critical scene from *Want,* Trey goes to his mother to seek help after he's been fired from his job. The sequence opens with a long shot (LS) of her living room as Trey sits down. They exchange a line or two of small talk, which is covered in matching MCUs. When Trey tells her about getting fired, the sequence cuts into a CU and matches it with a CU of the mother as she responds. Once Trey realizes that she is unable to comprehend his problem, his delusional defense mechanism kicks in. To convey that, the sequence cuts back to the wider master to show the whole set: Trey looks on, horrified, as stagehands come in and disassemble the set of his mother's living room while she watches TV, oblivious (**Figure 3.6**).

Figure 3.6 The close-ups (shots 4 and 5) focus attention on the key emotional content of the scene. Once the crucial moment is over, we cut back to a long shot.

Follow the Reactions

Once you get the hang of it, cutting dialogue scenes is fairly easy. The only trick is understanding when to make the cuts. One good way to figure that out is to follow the characters' reactions.

People's feelings are far more important to the audience than their moving lips. Your protagonists' reactions to what others say tell a much more important story than the words themselves. Rather than simply cutting back and forth to focus on the character who's speaking, you should edit to show important reactions.

For example, in the sequence above, as soon as Trey begins his confession about the job, both he and the audience are wondering how Mom is going to take it.

His whole line is: "Mom… I'm not working there any more. I quit… Well, actually I got fired…"

I might have stayed on him for the entire line, but instead, as soon as he says, "Mom…" I cut to her reaction and the rest of his line is heard offscreen. This works nicely because when he calls her name, he elicits her eye contact—which gives us a physical action to cut on (her looking up). Even more important, it allows us to see her reaction as he stumbles through his line. Because her next line is still part of her reaction, I stay on her until she finishes the line. Then I cut back to Trey to show *his* reaction to *her.*

Use Split Edits

As I've already said several times, successful dialogue editing requires offsetting your audio and video cuts. This technique carries the viewer past dialogue cuts so smoothly she never notices them. Almost every editor uses lots of split edits when editing conversations. Those are edits where the audio and video begin and end at different times. In fact, in most dialogue sequences you see, *every* cut is an L or J cut (**Figure 3.7**). (See the section on split edits in Chapter 2.)

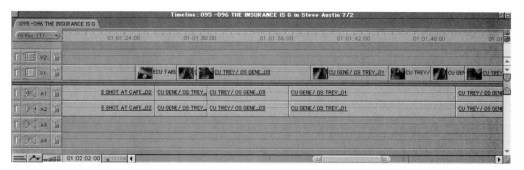

Figure 3.7 Most dialogue scenes look something like this in Final Cut Pro. Note that nearly every cut is a split edit.

Don't Cut on Pauses

It's tempting to make your cuts exactly on the beginnings or endings of phrases. Resist the temptation. These cuts become painfully apparent, especially when you're taking the audio from different shots. Since your goal is usually to make your cuts invisible, avoid cutting at these natural pauses.

Better yet, you can turn one of these "natural pause" edits into an invisible L or J edit after laying down the basic shots by rolling the video edit forward or backward so it doesn't coincide with the audio cut point (see the section on the roll edit in Chapter 6).

> **ROLLING** *Moving an edit point forward or backward in time by lengthening one clip while shortening another.*

Find the Best Performance

To make your dialogue scenes as effective as possible, you should use the best performances for every line in the show. This brings sequences to life and keeps the dramatic action at a high level.

A lazy editor cutting a two-person dialogue scene may pick one take of each shot (e.g., two matching CUs) and simply cut back and forth between them for the duration of the scene. This is easy, but it runs the risk of missing a gem hiding in another take. Every time you cut, you have the opportunity to go to a new take (unless continuity problems make that impossible). The only thing to watch out for is that sometimes the energy in a particular take will be so consistent that dropping in a moment from another take can destroy its subtle continuity.

In any case, a skilled editor will look at all the footage and mark every good line reading for possible use.

Three or More People

Editing an effective dialogue sequence with three or more people forces you to vary some of the rules for working with two people.

Use Group Shots

Since group scenes involve more camera angles, it's important to use shots that show more than one person at a time. This reinforces the physical relationships between the participants and keeps the viewer from becoming confused. Using too many singles in a row can destroy the sense of physical space in the room.

Follow the Dominant Character's Eyeline

You already know how important it is to stay on the same side of the axis when you're editing (see the section on the 180° rule in Chapter 2). However, group dialogue scenes can be a real nightmare in terms of keeping track of the axis. Because eyelines are continually changing as people move and interact, staying on one side of the line can become a real challenge.

One way to solve this puzzle is to identify the character who is dominant and guides the conversation. Then simply follow that person's eyeline and treat it as the axis—until it changes.

Avoid Confusing Two-Shots

Another thing to watch out for, though, is creating screen direction problems by using two successive two-shots of the same person in different positions (**Figure 3.8**). Imagine a scene of three people talking. Even without crossing the line, it would be easy to make one of the characters switch frame location by cutting the wrong two-shots together.

The way to overcome this is by interjecting a single into the series, or cutting out to a wider shot before going to another two-shot (**Figure 3.9**).

Figure 3.8 Notice how player 2 is on the left side of the frame in shot 1 and on the right side of the frame in shot 2. This violates continuity of screen direction even though the camera has not crossed the axis.

Figure 3.9 The sequence can be remedied by inserting a WS or CU between the two offending shots.

Editing a Soliloquy

Editors encounter many film sequences showing a single person talking or thinking. This is almost always a scene illustrating a character's inner conflict.

One of the most common techniques you can use to make this kind of scene dramatic and exciting is to cut back and forth from LS to CU of the same subject (**Figure 3.10**). This allows the audience to contrast the subject's thoughts (in CUs) with an objective view of his situation (in LSs), and it has the added benefit of avoiding jump cuts.

Figure 3.10 Alternating tight shots and wider shots is an effective way to cut a scene of one person alone, thinking. Here, Trey is preparing to face his family after his father's death.

On the other hand, if jumpcutting doesn't bother you, try using jump cuts of the subject doing different things or different angles of the same action. These jump cuts might be a series of CUs, a series of LSs, or a mix of both. This has the effect of adding tension to the sequence, forcing the viewer to participate in the subject's conflict.

There may be a voice-over monologue or some other audio element that can help you figure out how to cut the sequence. For instance, if an astronaut is describing his ordeal in a crippled landing module, he might list the specific things he did to save his life. In the editing room, you could choose to jump cut between the different actions he describes. This narration then becomes a clear guide for what to show and when to show it.

EDITING ACTION SEQUENCES

Any narrative sequence that is not a dialogue sequence is an action sequence. An action sequence can be as simple as a single person walking down a hallway— or as complex as a huge war scene, with people running in all directions and multiple events going on simultaneously. In either case, the basic rules are fairly simple.

At its simplest, action is movement, and in general, the more movement in a shot, the more exciting it is. This has been taken to an extreme in popular action films, where almost every shot is filled with moving objects; indeed, the basic premise of some films involves a fast-moving vehicle like a helicopter, bus, or train. To raise the excitement level even more, many action films employ shots where the camera seems to fly through the air with dizzying speed, moving along with a bullet, an arrow, or a falling bomb.

Even if you're not shooting a high-speed chase, camera movement can add excitement to otherwise boring scenes. For instance, you can raise the suspense level of a shot of a static object simply by employing slow, smooth camera moves around it.

Unfortunately, many filmmakers abuse these concepts and shoot every scene in the movie with moving cameras—even when there isn't any call for it in the story. While this does add drama and tension, it has the cumulative effect of diluting the impact of truly dramatic scenes and numbing audiences into a shallow engagement that evaporates the second the credits begin to roll.

Preserve Continuity

The first thing to think about as you begin editing an action scene is creating a sequence of events that makes sense in a chronological time frame. The key to this is maintaining continuity across cuts: Actions that begin in one shot and continue in the next should feel continuous.

The simplest example is someone walking through a doorway. If the first shot ends with the door one-third open, the next shot should begin with the door one-third open. If instead the second shot begins with the door all the way open, or opened just a crack, there will be an overlap of action and the edit will be a jump cut (**Figure 3.11**).

To convince the viewer that the action is continuous across the cut, the match in door position and the speed at which the door moves must be fairly precise. Of course, in reality the action is not continuous. The first shot may have been shot on Tuesday at 3 p.m., and the reverse inside the room may have been picked up a week later at 10 a.m., but in the story the action is supposed to be continuous, and your job is to stitch it together so it appears that way.

This is true of any action, no matter how big or small. Someone getting thrown through a plate glass window should be the same percentage of the way through the window across the edits—accounting for momentum.

Figure 3.11 In the first series, continuity is preserved because at the edit point, the door is partway open in both shots.

In the second series, the door has opened too wide in the first shot and creates a jump cut.

Preserve Momentum

Creating a smooth, invisible continuity cut in an action sequence requires some understanding of basic physics, particularly the concept of momentum. Fortunately, you don't need to explain the underlying theories mathematically as long as you understand them. A good editor always accounts for the velocity at which an object is moving when she is editing. Since video runs somewhere between 20 and 30 frames per second (fps), you need to allow for how far a fast-moving object will travel in the short time between two frames when you make a cut.

For instance, in our plate glass window example, the person being hurled through the window might be just hitting the pane when you cut out of shot 1, but shot 2 must begin at a point where he is already a few inches through the glass. If you were working in PAL (which runs at 25 fps), he would move a bit farther in between frames than he would if you were working in NTSC (30 fps) (**Figure 3.12**).

> **TIP:** When switching video formats, editors who've grown accustomed to one format (PAL or NTSC) go through an adjustment period during which they are likely to make timing mistakes.

Obviously, allowing for one single frame's worth of momentum entails a very subtle adjustment, but if you fail to make it the action won't feel right and the audience will notice.

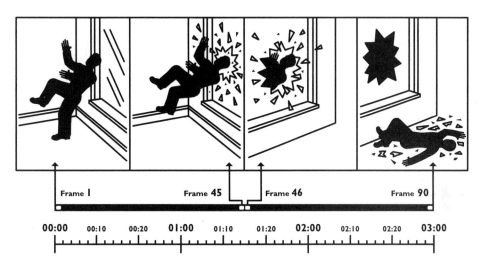

Figure 3.12 As time progresses, the man moves farther through the window. In this example, it takes him three seconds from the beginning of the motion until he lands on the ground. Because he's moving so quickly, you can't cut during this motion without accounting for his momentum.

If you have to cut between shots where the velocity of the movement is inconsistent (in shot 1 the actor slams the door shut, and in shot 2 he closes the door delicately), you will have great difficulty matching the momentum. In this situation, you should experiment, frame by frame, evaluating what might make the smoothest motion across the cut. In dire circumstances you can modify the speed of one clip digitally, or avoid the problem altogether by using a cutaway.

Cut on Action

This is one of the most basic action-editing rules: If you have the same action in two different shots, and you are trying to cut between them, and you want the cut to be as invisible as possible, you can hide the cut by doing it while movement is occurring within the frame. In other words, cut on action.

If the viewer's attention is focused on movement within the frame, and you present that movement continuously across the cut, the viewer will pay attention to the moving object and won't notice the cut (or the perspective change it forces). You can also use this technique to shift point of view without drawing attention to the edit.

For example, rather than running shot 1 until the subject has opened the door, stepped through, and closed the door behind her, and then cutting to shot 2, in which the subject is already inside the room, cut while the door is in motion. Then the audience won't notice that there were two shots, two camera positions, and an editor who joined them together.

Cutting on Action Adds Excitement

In addition to masking the edit point, cutting on action adds dynamism. For instance, in the plate glass window example, it would be much more exciting to cut while the person is in midair than wait until he lands outside.

You can tell the same story many ways. For instance, if you don't want to actually break the plate glass window, you can take one shot from inside (of the subject hurtling toward the window) and another shot from outside (showing him landing on the ground with glass shards falling around him). With proper timing and a sound effect of glass breaking, the audience will think it has just seen the character plunge through a plate glass window—and you will have told your story. Probably more safely and more cheaply, too.

Of course, this version sacrifices the excitement of seeing the violent shattering of glass. In our first example (cutting with the subject in midair), we maximize the impact by showing it twice, from two angles.

Building Tension

Action sequences depend on building tension. A good editor can create tension in a number of ways.

Use Crosscutting

One very common way to build tension is through crosscutting—that is, cutting back and forth between multiple events that are occurring simultaneously (see the section on crosscutting in Chapter 2). Each time you cut from one event to the next, as in the outlaw sequence I described in Chapter 2, you force the viewer to try to complete the action of the event left behind. This keeps the brain busy (thinking of two things at once), which causes a tense mental and emotional state.

Sync Up On the Easy Spot

*One of the best ways to ensure accurate continuity of movement across shots is to first make your cut on a spot that's easy to identify in both shots, such as the moment the door cracks open (**Figure 3.13**). Then roll the edit forward to some point where the door is in the process of opening, and make the actual cut there (**Figure 3.14**). (See the section on the roll edit in Chapter 6.)*

If the door is opening at the same speed in the two shots, no matter where you roll the edit to, it will be a successful continuity cut.

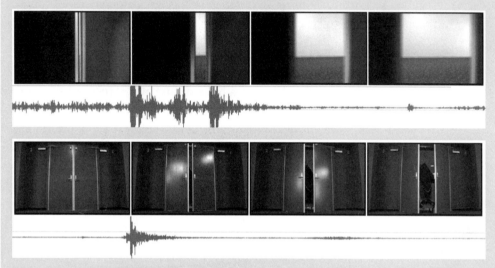

Figure 3.13 Find a point that's simple to identify in both shots. The moment the door opens is especially handy because the sound of the door opening is easy to locate.

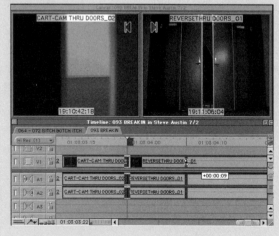

Figure 3.14 Rolling the edit forward allows you to move the cut point so it occurs midmotion. Experiment to find the best place for the cut.

Speed Up the Cutting

Another way to build tension is to speed up the cutting. By shortening each shot, you force the audience to absorb more information in less time. Before viewers can figure out what's going on, you cut to a new shot and compel them to start taking in new information. In real life, when you are forced to take in too much information, your stress level rises and you slip into a heightened state. This is why many people turn down their car radios when trying to maneuver in fast-moving traffic. You can evoke a similarly tense state for your viewers through editing. As you overload their ability to keep track, you cause an actual physiological reaction.

Raise Tension With Close-Ups

Editing a sequence using tight close-ups has a similar effect. Just as crosscutting, or cutting quickly, forces the viewer to construct the surrounding time, using tighter shots makes the viewer construct the surrounding space. Cutting into a tight CU (especially without an establishing shot to let the viewer know what the context is) requires the viewer to construct the environment in order to understand what she is watching. Cutting from ECU to ECU without showing any context makes it even harder for the audience to understand the larger circumstances. This creates stress and serves to heighten the tension of the scene.

For instance, let's say we're at the climax of a movie about a sailing race. The two main rivals are in the final leg, and we want to create a tense atmosphere to give the audience a sense of the adrenaline rush the racers are experiencing.

The most straightforward way to cover the scene would involve close-ups of the key personnel, full shots of each boat capturing the crew hard at work, and wide shots showing the two boats and their relative progress. However, in order to raise the tension of the scene, I would probably cut one close shot after another and limit the number of wide shots that reveal the racers' relative positions. After all, most of the crew members are so engaged in their jobs that they don't have time to look at the competing vessel, and not knowing who's ahead is part of what causes the tension we're seeking to evoke.

The chaos created by cutting tight close-ups back and forth amidst the many actions going on simultaneously is an effective way to keep the viewer engaged—as if she were on the boat herself.

1. WS two sailboats cutting through the bay. One boat suddenly begins to tack.

2. ECU captain's face screaming orders.

3. ECU sailor 1's hands reeling in the main sheet.

4. ECU tell-tales on sail beginning to flop.

5. ECU sailor 3's face grimacing.

6. ECU captain screaming.

7. ECU tell-tales straightening out.

8. MCU several sailors stacked in perspective, all working frantically.

9. ECU sailors' hands.

10. ECU captain's eyes looking toward the other ship.

11. Reverse POV (LS) showing the other vessel rounding the final marker.

> ### Sex, Violence, and Responsibility
>
> *It's amazing (and slightly creepy) that a skillful film editor can create involuntary physical reactions in the audience. This is one reason film is such a powerful medium. Similarly, the simple act of viewing images of sex and violence has a visceral impact on us. I won't enter the battle about whether or not it changes our behavior, but it is inarguable that films can cause a physical reaction in their audiences.*
>
> *By learning which shots to choose, how long to run them, and in what order to arrange them to affect the audience most powerfully, you are acquiring a type of mind control. Never underestimate the power of the film medium or your responsibility in wielding that power.*

Use Setup to Create Suspense

The setup is a common pattern that editors use quite often in action or suspense sequences. It creates an expectation in the audience by showing a subject or object that implies some expected result.

Imagine the following sequence:

1. LS woman and her child shopping for fruit at a stall in a public market.

2. MS mother walks away to another stall, leaving boy behind.

3. MCU man carrying a suitcase approaches the marketplace.

4. LS man approaches shopping cart where boy is.

5. MCU mother is engaged in a conversation with another vendor.

6. ELS explosion in the square.

7. MCU mother looks to where her son was.

8. LS (reverse: mother's POV) cart is gone amid debris and chaos.

9. CU mother screams.

The setup is shots 2 and 3. These shots create most of the tension in the scene.

When the woman walks off, leaving her son behind in shot 2, the audience becomes aware of the boy's vulnerability. The next thing we see, in shot 3, is the agent of conflict, the suicide bomber. The fact that the shot is a CU draws the audience's attention to the character and gives him extra significance. If we had skipped shot 2, we wouldn't know where the suicide bomber is headed when we see him in shots 3 and 4. If we had skipped shot 3, the impact of the man walking into the market would have no meaning until the bomb went off, and there would be no suspense.

Don't Forget the Payoff

Every setup should have a payoff, or the viewer will feel cheated and angry. The emotional payoff of this scene happens in shot 9, when we see the mother's reaction to the bomb blast.

As the editor, you have the ability to guide the emotional dynamics of the scene. For instance, you could have told this event entirely through shots 4 and 6: A man walks into a market and sets off a bomb. But when you include the woman and her son, even if we never see them again, you provide a human point of view that draws in the audience and intensifies the scene's emotional impact.

The Cliff-hanger

In the section on storytelling in Chapter 2, I discussed the importance of cause and effect and how you can manipulate these editing elements to control the flow of your story. One familiar cause-and-effect technique is the cliff-hanger, which involves ending a sequence with a "cause" shot but not providing the resulting effect. Since humans are programmed with a need to know the outcome of uncertain situations, good storytelling (and therefore good editing) can use cliff-hangers and payoff shots to powerful effect. If you need to maintain viewers' interest across commercial interruptions (or summer reruns), the cliff-hanger is one great way to do it.

The cliff-hanger is used tirelessly in soap operas and other episodic television programs to keep viewers hooked from episode to episode. However, this technique is equally effective if you need to interrupt an educational program to summarize a section with graphics, or send your viewers off to their workbooks.

By all means, go ahead and experiment with how long you can separate the cliff-hanger and the payoff. The more intensely you have engaged your viewers, the longer you can leave them hanging.

> *TIP: An adept editor can stack up several "cause" shots before paying any of them off, playing on viewers' anticipation level to keep suspense and interest dialed to the maximum. Because most humans can keep track of about five things at the same time, you will need to pay off a cliff-hanger that's been hanging for a while in order to introduce a new one. Superb editors know how to create a payoff that resolves multiple cliff-hangers simultaneously.*

Work With the Writer to Accentuate the Cliff-hanger

All this may sound like the writer's job to you, but an editor has to understand these techniques, too—which is why editors frequently make good screenwriters.

For instance, imagine a scenario in which a villain plans to take over the world by implanting microchips in people when they drink the coffee sold in her ubiquitous chain stores. Our hero walks unsuspectingly into one of the coffee shops and orders a mocha. By ending the scene on the shot where he orders the drink, we create cliff-hanger 1.

The villain has a deadly allergy to chocolate, alleviated only by a shot of epinephrine she keeps in her purse. In the next scene, an argument with one of her store managers, she drops her purse, and we end the scene with a tight shot of the serum falling out of the purse and rolling under the table—creating cliff-hanger 2.

The writer has created the story elements that generate the cliff-hangers, but by ending the scenes on these specific shots, the editor builds the suspense and compels the reaction in the viewers. Best of all, the editor can resolve both cliff-hangers in a single shot, as illustrated in the following sequence.

1. LS villain walks out of the back room and orders a latte.

2. MS hero picks up a newspaper.

3. CU coffee jerk making hero's mocha.

4. ECU the chocolate as it's poured in.

5. MS villain pacing, dreaming of world domination.

6. ECU espresso machine inserting microchip into mocha.

7. MCU hero, reading the paper.

8. CU coffee jerk makes latte for villain.

9. ECU newspaper story about chocolate allergies.

10. MCU villain yells at coffee jerk, "I'm late! Hurry up!"

11. MCU coffee jerk puts two identical-looking drinks on the counter.

12. ECU one of the coffees marked as a mocha.

13. MS hero and villain collide as they reach the drink counter.

14. CU villain accidentally takes mocha, leaving clean drink for the hero.

Good suspense requires holding off, or suspending, the resolution as long as possible without destroying momentum. If you feel confident that the audience will stay involved, you can stretch the suspense even further by introducing extraneous shots—for instance, the coffee jerk chatting with a co-worker. In any case, the repeated references to chocolate and the microchip remind the audience of what they are anticipating and accentuate the suspense. If we left out those reinforcing shots, the power of the sequence would be reduced.

Finally, shot 14 succeeds in resolving both cliff-hangers simultaneously. Alternately, you could cut the scene so we don't know who got which drink, and you could continue intercutting shots of the two players drinking their coffees, further suspending the resolution—but resolving both cliff-hangers in a single shot is far more elegant.

Manipulating Cause and Effect

Action sequences depend on proper manipulation of cause and effect to create tension and drama. When an editor chooses the order in which shots and sequences appear in a film, she is controlling the chronological flow in which the viewer will experience events. This in turn translates into meaning for the audience (see the section on storytelling in Chapter 2).

For instance, if there is a cause (say, a hand grenade with the pin pulled) with an obvious effect (an explosion), one quick shot of the grenade is all you need to make the audience anticipate the explosion. Thereafter, your viewers will be waiting anxiously for the explosion, and that expectation will flavor every shot in between the CU of the grenade and the eventual explosion.

Consider this cutting sequence:

1. LS soldier outside the enemy barracks.

2. MS enemies inside playing poker.

3. MCU soldier pulls the pin from a grenade and throws it through the barracks window.

4. CU grenade lands softly on a cot, not making a sound.

5. MS poker players oblivious.

6. MCU soldier covering his ears, anticipating the explosion.

7. MS poker players.

Even looking at this shot list, you are probably anticipating the coming explosion. But without those preceding shots of the live grenade, the same shots of the poker players would have a totally different meaning. You can increase the tension even further by cutting back to the grenade once more before it explodes.

The impact that any one shot has on the images that follow it is a kind of cause and effect. For instance, in the sequence above, you might cut to a framed family picture belonging to one of the poker players. In and of itself, that shot is virtually devoid of meaning—but here, combined with the previous grenade shot, it creates sympathy for the doomed men.

Similarly, if you never show the faces of the poker players, your audience will probably feel little sorrow when the grenade goes off. But if you spend just a few seconds showing the soldiers' camaraderie and pleasure in playing the card game, the scene takes on an entirely different emotional meaning.

The precise placement of cause-and-effect shots is critical to building tension. Like other timing issues, this requires a certain learned ability to judge when, and for how long, to show these shots for maximum effect. As a beginning editor, you can always fall back on trial and error to get it right.

Cutting the Shoot-out

The shoot-out, a familiar element of many action sequences, comes with its own set of standard editing patterns. You can use them with equal success in hand-to-hand combat or a courtroom drama where the subjects are shooting each other with words. Oddly enough, the shoot-out is actually a variant on a dialogue sequence—so the basic rules about cutting for reactions, and copious use of L and J cuts, remain in effect.

Don't Forget the Witness

One unique element of the shoot-out is the presence of a witness. In fact, you'll rarely run across a shoot-out without a witness. The witness provides an opportunity for cutaways and adds additional tension to the scene.

For instance, consider this sequence:

1. ECU villain draws his gun.

2. CU witness observes the action.

3. MCU sheriff leaves his office, laughing with his partner.

4. LS (witness's POV) of sheriff. Gunshot rings out. Sheriff ducks.

5. CU sheriff pulls out his gun. (Continuous action as he ducks.)

6. MCU villain hides behind a post.

7. MCU sheriff warns villain to drop his gun.

8. MCU villain rejects the sheriff's offer and fires his gun.

9. MCU sheriff dodges bullet and shoots back.

10. CU witness watches in horror.

11. CU villain shoots again.

12. ECU sheriff gets hit (in the arm, of course).

13. MS villain runs across the square.

14. CU sheriff fires.

15. CU witness reacts as we hear the villain exclaim.

16. MS villain slain on ground. Sheriff and crowd gather.

You'll note that this sequence closely resembles the cutting pattern for a conversation. The basic pattern goes like this: We exchange MCUs of the two participants until the scene escalates, then transition to CUs for the key moments, bridged by a cutaway to the witness (shot 10). Once the climax is over, we retreat to a wider shot to put the conflict in a larger perspective.

In this case, I used the witness's reaction to avoid showing the actual moment of death. While most audiences these days seem to have an unquenchable appetite for violence, I feel that the approach taken here actually will have a more lasting emotional impact. Sure, showing the bullet striking the villain would have a powerful physical effect, but the deeper emotion would be sacrificed for the physical gross-out factor. Choosing to show the impact the death has on the witness provides a concrete emotional reaction with which the viewer can identify and empathize.

Effective Chase Sequences

Chase sequences are another of the basic building blocks of action films. Like most action sequences, the chase is based on a familiar editing technique: crosscutting.

Build Your Chase by Guiding Screen Direction

The key to crosscutting an effective chase sequence lies in manipulating proper screen direction.

Typically, party A will be chasing party B, and you can crosscut between them indefinitely—as long as they continue traveling left to right, or vice versa (**Figure 3.15**). If you intercut even a single shot that shows one party moving in the opposite direction, you'll destroy the flow of the scene.

Figure 3.15 If you want to show that one party is chasing another, it's vital for both of them to be facing and moving in the same direction.

Indeed, one way you know that the chase sequence is over is when the screen direction changes. If you plan it right, that change can give the audience an important clue about the outcome of the chase.

For example, take a story about an adopted woman searching for her birth mother. Throughout the film, the two have been traveling in the same screen direction. Finally, as the film nears its climax (when the two will meet), the editor might choose to change the mother's screen direction. Although the effect will be subtle, the audience will unconsciously sense a change in the dynamic between the two parties—and know that something important is about to happen.

This same technique (changing a character's screen direction) is often employed to set up the supervillain's "one wrong move," which allows the hero to catch him. It's a way to tip off the audience that there's been a change in the flow of events and that a confrontation is imminent.

Use Chase Patterns for Romantic Comedy

You can use the same chase-sequence editing patterns in circumstances far beyond the basic car or helicopter chase. Romantic comedies, for instance, frequently turn on a subtle chase of sorts, where screen direction plays just as important a role.

Even though the characters in a romantic comedy may not be chasing one another physically, repeated shots of them traveling or facing in the same direction indicate that an emotional chase is going on. Editors of romantic comedies often cut conversations in which the romantic duo are facing in the same direction. This is ostensibly motivated by the story or context, but the effect is to let the audience know that one is pursuing the other or that one is avoiding the other.

You can mark the turning point from avoidance to affection in a subtle way by inserting a shot of one of the parties suddenly facing the opposite direction (so she is now looking toward the romantic interest). This indicates an emotional change, and even though the audience isn't consciously aware of the editorial trick, the point will be made.

Editing Fight and Battle Sequences

In action films, fights and battle sequences are almost as common as chases. You can think of a fight or battle sequence as simply a group of simultaneous shoot-outs, but using standard patterns and techniques will help you make them exciting.

> **TIP:** During a complicated battle scene, it's easy to lose track of who's on which side and exactly what's going on. You can make the sequence play more effectively if you include snippets of dialogue or breaks in the action to give the viewer a chance to catch his breath and make sense of what's going on.

Provide Context With Long Shots

In order to convey a larger context and tie the various melees together, it helps to intercut occasional long shots that contain complex intraframe action (that is, lots of stuff going on in the frame). This helps the viewer maintain his orientation in the midst of all the confusion.

Expand the Duration of Key Action

Creative editors accentuate action by expanding the duration of stunts and impacts (for instance, a blow, a fall, an explosion, or a bullet hitting its target) by duplicating some of the action in both the outgoing and incoming shots. This gives you the opportunity to extend the viewing time of exciting moments. The technique involves making an ordinary continuity cut over the point of action, but rather than placing the edit points so the action appears continuous, you overlap the action so it occurs in both shots. The more time you overlap, the more stylized the effect.

This is commonly employed in explosions. Actual explosions happen in a split second, but to maximize their impact, editors usually show the blast two or more times from different angles. For instance, if an explosion lasts five seconds, you might include the first four seconds in your first shot and the last four seconds in the second shot. Seconds 2 through 4 would be duplicated and appear in both shots.

Technically this breaks continuity, but it has become widely accepted. This may be because the excitement caused by the violent image distracts the audience and they ignore the temporal discontinuity, or perhaps it's because most viewers have never seen a real-life explosion, so they actually think explosions take 10 or 15 seconds to occur.

Countdown to Climax: Speed Up the Cutting

As a film, or even a sequence, comes to its climax, the editor will normally want to raise the excitement and tension. The most common way to accomplish this is by increasing the speed of the cutting. Sequences will grow shorter as the film nears its end, and individual shots will get shorter within each sequence. Interrupting this process with a lengthy shot, or a sequence that goes on for a long time, dissipates the tension and disrupts the audience's anticipation of the climax.

> **TIP:** If you're building excitement by speeding up the cutting, and you need to include a critical event that will take a long time to show, you can break the long event into smaller pieces and keep those smaller pieces moving along briskly by crosscutting them, thereby compressing time.

As your story reaches its climax and you are crosscutting between two events, typically the crosscutting should get faster, the sequences you are intercutting should get shorter, and you will end by intercutting shot for shot between the two separate events. Finally, the way you pay that off is to make the events converge so the crosscutting dissolves (figuratively) into a single scene.

1. MS serial killer prepares to load gun (:10).

2. MCU his victim squirms (:05).

3. MCU killer grins (:05).

4. ELS cop caught in traffic jam (:05).

5. MS cop beats fist on dashboard (:05).

6. CU cop curses (:05).

7. MCU killer loads gun (:05).

8. CU victim cries (:05).

9. WS cop breaks out of traffic (:05).

10. LS cop car screams down the street (:05).

11. CU killer cocks gun (:03).

12. MS cop breaks down door of house (:03).

13. ECU killer's trigger finger tightens (:02).

14. CU cop runs down hall (:02).

15. MS cop breaks into room OS killer (:05).

In this example, shots 1 through 3 are from scene 1 and last 20 seconds. Shots 4 through 6 are from scene 2 and last 15 seconds. Shots 7 and 8 are back to scene 1 again, lasting 10 seconds, and shots 9 and 10 are from scene 2, also lasting only 10 seconds. From here on we begin intercutting the two scenes shot for shot, until finally, in shot 15, the two scenes are joined by the OS shot. At this point the scene would likely play out in a typical shoot-out pattern, with the victim acting as the witness (see "Cutting the Shoot-out," earlier in this chapter).

Notice that while the sequences are getting shorter and shorter, the shots themselves also get shorter until shot 15. In addition, the angles of the shots get increasingly tighter, adding one more element of tension.

Cool It Down

After the climax, traditional storytelling calls for a resolution, a relatively quiet moment when the characters and the audience get an opportunity to think about and understand the impact of the preceding events. This is an essential element of narrative structure. Don't fail to provide this period of reflection and resolution or you will leave your audience in an uncomfortable state. While the script probably includes a scene to serve this important purpose, it is your job as the editor to adjust your pacing and cutting style to support this emotional effect. Generally that will mean slowing the editing, using longer shots, and avoiding moving-camera shots.

In the example of the serial killer, once the killer is apprehended, good structure dictates a scene in which the victim will get a moment to reflect on his ordeal. But even if the writer has neglected to put that scene in the script, you can look for a shot of the victim walking alone, outside. Maybe it was filmed as part of the scene where she was abducted, but placed here it will seem to be taking place after the ordeal and provide the reflection time missing in the script. If a shot like that isn't available, you could try ending the "shoot-out" with a long, static single of the victim, which will again serve to allow some reflection on the events that just took place.

CUTTING FOR COMEDY

You can cut an action scene many different ways, and the same shots can create tension or comedy depending on how you arrange them. Certain editors have a knack for comic timing; others are better suited to drama or action.

Create Laughter With Surprise

One of the main elements that makes comedy funny is surprise. You can create surprise in the editing room by setting up expectations and then breaking them— another way of manipulating cause and effect.

In our hand grenade example, once you build up the expectation that the grenade is about to go off, the audience will be anxiously awaiting the explosion. If you cut back to the grenade again and again, and it never explodes, the audience will eventually catch on that it is actually a dud—and laugh.

Funnier the Second Time Around

Another key element you can use to great comic effect is repetition. Imagine another version of the grenade sequence:

1. LS soldier outside the enemy barracks.

2. MS enemies inside playing poker.

3. MCU soldier pulls the pin from a grenade and throws it through the barracks window.

4. CU grenade rolls under the poker table.

5. MS poker players oblivious.

6. MCU soldier covers his ears, anticipating the explosion.

7. ECU grenade.

8. MCU soldier.

9. ECU grenade.

10. MS poker players.

11. MCU soldier anticipating explosion.

Now imagine how the audience would react if the soldier pulled out another grenade and went through the whole sequence again, and the second grenade was also a dud. It would be funny. If he did it a third time it would be *really* funny. Eventually, through a little artful editing, there might be 100 grenades piled up under the card table, the poker players would still be oblivious, and the audience would be rolling on the floor. The repetition of the joke is what makes it funny.

Remember the classic comedy maxim: Tell them what you're going to do, do it, and then tell them that you did it. With the right editing, you can get three laughs out of every joke.

> **TIP:** It's generally a bad idea to use the exact same shot more than once in a dramatic film. If the viewer notices, it will pull him out of the narrative and draw attention to the form. In comedy, however, you have tremendous leeway with rules like that. Sometimes, reusing the same exact shot again and again can be terrifically funny.
>
> For example, when the jewel thieves are sneaking through a museum, you might cut to a shot of a guard sitting in front of a bank of security monitors—fast asleep! Each time the thieves penetrate another security barrier, you can cut back to the sleeping security guard. Repeating the exact shot emphasizes the uselessness of the guard.

DOCUMENTARY PATTERNS

While most documentaries follow the basic rules of narrative editing, including cause and effect, chronological passage of time, and other familiar storytelling strategies, some of the editing patterns and techniques you'll see in documentaries differ quite a bit from those used in narrative or dramatic films.

For one thing, while most film projects begin with a script, often the "script" for a documentary is created after some (or all) of the footage is shot. Sometimes that script creation comes out of a collaboration between the editor and the director. To build the script, the two of you will need to sit down and go through the footage together before you start editing. Otherwise you may waste your time venturing down some path that is ultimately not going to be part of the film.

Documentaries take all forms and shapes. Some contain sequences that might feel like (and be cut like) straightforward action scenes or, at the other extreme, abstract passages that resemble an experimental film.

A great recent example of a documentary that does both is Errol Morris's *Mr. Death,* a film about Fred A. Leuchter, Jr., a manufacturer of capital punishment devices who became a Nazi apologist and Holocaust denier. One sequence in the film shows how Leuchter designed and built a gallows for the state of Tennessee. The sequence could be a scene from any dramatic film, since it includes extensive coverage and uses traditional narrative editing techniques. But another scene is an abstract vision of Leuchter encased in a huge, weird, bubble-like machine. There is no dialogue in this sequence, and the editing is rhythmic and poetic. No effort is made to explain the "story" of this sequence, nor what the images mean.

Cutting documentaries is a bit like putting together a jigsaw puzzle without looking at the picture on the box. One thing working in your favor is that there's more than one right answer. It's a kind of treasure hunt. Often the magic moments happen unexpectedly, when image and sound come together to make an emotional impact beyond your expectations.

Cutting Interviews

Most documentaries use interviews to tell their stories—and cutting interview footage is a very different task than cutting dialogue. Depending on how the project was produced, you may be working with pre-scripted Q&A sequences that have obvious beginning and end points. More often you will have to wade through lengthy interviews hunting for verbal nuggets that summarize or illustrate the points you're looking for. Unlike with dramatic footage, where you will probably have multiple takes to choose from, with rare exceptions you will get only one take of any given "answer" in interview footage.

Usually, the first pass I make on documentary footage is to collect all the interesting bits of the interviews and store them as subclips (see the section on marking subclips in Chapter 5, "Basic Editing"). Once I've collected all the good stuff, I go through it with the director and decide what to use. Then I lay down all those selected chunks end to end, ignoring jump cuts and any visual concerns.

Finally, I fine-tune the timing of the soundtrack, rearranging sections, trimming unneeded bits, finding what sections go best with others, and essentially creating the structure that will serve as the basis for the show. Only when this audio edit is complete do I go back and begin inserting cutaways and other shots to correct visual problems and bridge jump cuts.

Use Ripple Delete to Eliminate Pauses

Time and again you will find yourself working with an interview that includes pauses or mistakes you want to eliminate. One quick and easy way to accomplish this is to use the Ripple Delete function in Final Cut Pro. This tool eliminates clips, or sections of clips, from a sequence without leaving gaps.

First, drop the entire section you want to use into Final Cut Pro's Timeline (**Figure 3.16**).

Then play the sequence, and set your In and Out points at the beginning and end of the section you wish to eliminate (**Figure 3.17**).

Finally, select Ripple Delete from the Sequence menu—or hit Shift-Delete from the keyboard. The area between the In and Out points is eliminated, and the gap will be closed (**Figure 3.18**).

Beware! Ripple Delete works first on selected items, so if something in your Timeline is selected, Final Cut Pro will delete the selected item rather than the material between the In and Out points. In general, it's a good idea to get in the habit of hitting ⌘-D (deselect all) before you use Ripple Delete.

Figure 3.16 Place the whole clip in the Timeline.

Figure 3.17 Set In and Out points at the beginning and end of the section you want to eliminate.

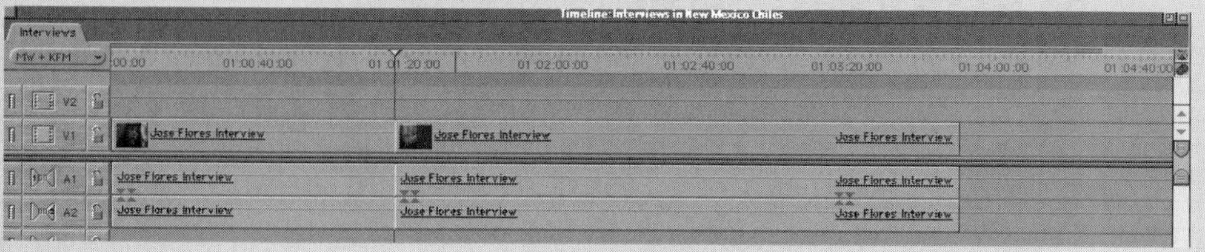

Figure 3.18 Ripple Delete will remove the section and close the gap automatically.

Editing Narration

Another element you'll often find in documentary projects is off-camera narration. Narration is usually recorded after the basic picture is complete, so the writer and narrator can adjust the length of the narration to the existing edit. Sometimes it's done as a sort of scripted interview. In that case, you'll have the advantage of multiple takes and different line readings, but you should edit the footage pretty much the same way you'd handle interview footage: Lay down the tracks, cut for audio first, then go back and clean up the picture.

Working With B-roll

B-roll is a catchall term used to describe the footage that is neither interview nor narration. Most commonly, this will be footage illustrating whatever the narrator or interviewee is talking about, but it may also be anything from establishing-type shots of environments relevant to the commentary to dramatic reenactments, photos, or contextual illustrations.

Variety Is the Spice

While the talking heads who make up your A-roll deliver the bulk of information to be conveyed, you will create the flavor of your piece by the B-roll elements you employ. There's no limit to the type of images you can choose to spice up your documentary, and using a variety of element types will be more palatable to the audience than repeating the same stuff again and again.

For example, *Reason to Fear,* a recent documentary about a Native American on death row, employed nearly ten types of B-roll elements. The filmmakers went to the location of the alleged crime and filmed all the locations, street signs, and buildings that were described in the courtroom testimony. They also included photographs of the people involved, the alleged murder, and the aftermath of the crime, as well as historical photos, lithographs, and illustrations of Native Americans and their plight during the American expansion. Finally, they created maps, diagrams, and charts that provided a factual context for the testimony and helped to explain the specific details of the case. All of these elements were woven together to illustrate and punctuate the interviews that made up the spine of the piece.

In using a rich variety of B-roll elements like these, the filmmakers kept the audience interested by continually supplying new types of material to supplement the interviews that otherwise might have seemed like dry legalese.

Provide Creative Solutions

Sometimes the B-roll will hold carefully planned shots intended for use with specific interview sequences, but more often it will be a jumble of random material that you'll have to sift through to discover the usable moments. In many cases, your editorial creativity can find brilliant ways to put some of the stuff you find there to work.

For instance, your B-roll will probably become your cutaway footage. You can use it to cover up a jump cut in the interview or break up a long passage of talking heads.

If you're lucky, the B-roll footage will show exactly what the audio is talking about. For example, a documentary on chile peppers might have a section of narration explaining how and where they are grown. Ideally, the B-roll would include shots of fields full of growing chiles, a map depicting regions where chiles are grown, and some shots of workers harvesting the fruit in the fields.

However, in many cases you'll find yourself in a sticky situation where, for instance, the narration refers to the medical benefits of eating chiles, and you don't have any footage of a hospital, or anything even vaguely medical, on the B-roll. Here's your chance to get creative with your interpretation of the script. Look for a shot of a healthy-looking family eating some chile rellenos, or even some shots of food being prepared. In the worst case, you can always just cut back to the talking head or request a pickup shot or a graphic.

Look for Imaginative Images

Sometimes you can create a thematic link that might not even have been present in the narration by choosing the right B-roll clip. For example, let's say the narrator is talking about how genetic engineering of chiles has reduced the available varieties and potency of the fruit. Your first thought might be to show a supermarket shelf with limited choices, a literal image of the point in the text. However, you might venture further afield and use a shot of a family farmer selling his farm. In this way, you will have enriched the subject by illustrating another kind of impact caused by genetic engineering and mass production: the impact on family farming. This is especially powerful because you are increasing the amount of information communicated without making the sequence feel too dense.

Go Back to the B-roll

The more carefully you log and catalogue your B-roll footage, the likelier you'll be to find the right shot for some problem spot in your notes. But if not, don't be afraid to go back to the B-roll in a pinch. There could be gold there you overlooked on your first run-through.

Typically I wade through all the B-roll footage available to me and note interesting or useful shots. But inevitably, at some later point, when I'm staring at a section of interview requiring an illustration I don't have, I'll dive back into the mass of B-roll clips and find some great five-second nugget that I overlooked entirely on my first pass through the footage. And it will be perfect.

Use Keywords

*Final Cut Pro has a powerful search engine built into the Browser (**Figure 3.19**). The more information you provide when you name your B-roll clips (or create subclips), the easier it will be for you to find those clips later. Use one of the Comment fields in the Browser window to enter keywords you can search on (**Figure 3.20**). It's important to use consistent spelling, though, or when you search for "chile," you won't find the clips where you spelled it "chili" or "chilli."*

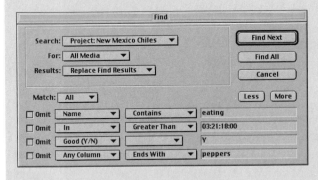

Figure 3.19 Final Cut Pro's Find tool (⌘-F) can search on as many as eight criteria.

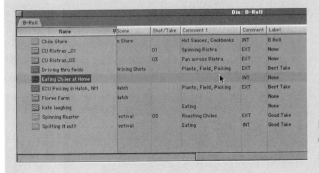

Figure 3.20 Choose any one of the Comment columns to enter useful information about your shot.

You can make it easier to enter the same exact text into the Comment field for each subclip by using the Shortcut menu (accessed by pressing Ctrl *and clicking on the Comment field), which will let you select an entry from a pop-up list of previous entries in that column (**Figure 3.21**).*

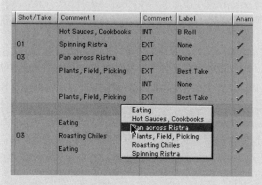

Figure 3.21 Each time you enter text in a given column, it is added to a list you can access via the Shortcut menu. To bring up the Shortcut menu, Ctrl -click on the field you wish to modify.

The more information you provide when you're logging clips and subclips, the better. What shot type is it? CU? LS? What's the subject? What details might be helpful when you're searching for just the right clip four months from now? Don't skimp. Remember, you may not be the one doing the search. It might be your assistant, or even the director.

*If you plan to dedicate one of your Comment columns to keywords, you can change the name of the column by using the Shortcut menu on the column header and selecting Edit Heading (**Figure 3.22**).*

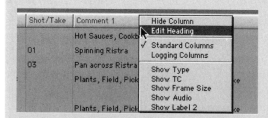

Figure 3.22 The Shortcut menu for the column headers allows you to change the name of any of the four Comment fields.

EDITING FOR CORPORATE COMMUNICATIONS

Corporate communications include in-house training videos, video press releases (sometimes called EPKs, short for "electronic press kits"), messages to stockholders, product demonstrations, and so on.

In many ways, corporate video (sometimes called industrial video) is situated halfway between narrative and documentary work, and sometimes may seem the best of both worlds. Corporate videos are like pre-scripted documentaries. The B-roll footage is usually meticulously planned out, with adequate coverage to ensure that the subject is successfully captured. (No more hunting for just the right shot!) Interviews are usually scripted and may well include multiple takes so you'll have a choice of shots to use. Best of all, corporate videos are frequently well funded. Of course, on the downside, they often lack the excitement and soul of true narrative or documentary films.

Corporate videos usually center around a narration or scripted interviews, so building your initial framework is similar to the recipe for documentary cutting described earlier.

Eliminate Graphic Overload

Corporate clients often worry that their points will not be made clearly with moving footage alone and want you to reinforce every point with a title card or chart. Sometimes you can find a way to incorporate at least some of the graphics the client wants without boring your audience to tears, but at times you'll have to dig in your heels and try to talk the client out of it.

If you find yourself faced with a plethora of graphics, such as charts, bulleted text, logos, and so on, which must somehow be incorporated into the video, watch out! Too many interruptions can drive the viewer crazy and make it impossible for her to lose herself in the material.

Still, as the editor it's your job to make everyone—the viewer and the client—happy. Sometimes you can accomplish this as easily as superimposing the graphics on top of your B-roll shots. Beware, though: It's possible to make the screen so dense with information that neither the text nor the video will hold the viewer's interest or keep information flowing.

TIP: One of the most common problems for beginners working with titles and graphics is not knowing how long to leave them on-screen. Sometimes the script will tell you, but you can always double-check by having two or three people watch and raise their hands when they have had adequate time to read the text on-screen. Keeping text on-screen too long runs the risk of making viewers lose interest. The basic rule of thumb is three seconds for every line of text.

EDITING EXPERIMENTAL VIDEO

The film medium is capable of communicating in much more subtle and stylized ways than what we see in most Hollywood blockbusters or high school sex-education films. Moreover, every editor loves to experiment with variations on how to cut images together, looking for new ways to convey a mood or feeling through a creative arrangement of image and sound. At one time experimental filmmaking was relegated to an obscure, marginalized area categorized as avant-garde or underground cinema. To extend the language metaphor, you might consider this film genre akin to poetry.

Experimental filmmakers like Stan Brakhage, Andy Warhol, Flavio Kampah, and many others have made countless incredible films that ignore traditional editing structures. Sometimes these experiments work brilliantly, communicating unusual feelings, ideas, and themes with terrific power. Other times they are too obscure or random to make much of a mark on their audience.

Just as the French New Wave of the 1960s introduced jumpcutting as a viable story-telling technique, a new generation of "experimental" editors has introduced countless innovations to contemporary editing that were previously considered bad or wrong. These include *ramping;* mixing different types of media, such as film and video, or color and black and white; rapid cutting that sometimes shortens shots until they're just a few frames long; holding shots on-screen for unusually long times; layering multiple images on top of one another (see the section on composite shots in Chapter 2); and most significantly, a fundamental disregard for continuity of time and space. This last innovation is perhaps the most important, because it flouts most of the basic rules of editing.

RAMPING   Manipulating the playback speed of a clip so that it varies over time. For example, a shot can begin at normal speed, slow down smoothly to a few frames a second, then speed up to a superfast playback rate that's three or four times the normal speed.

Experimentalists Join the Mainstream

Thanks to MTV, so-called experimental filmmaking has moved into the commercial mainstream. As long as you intercut your images with an occasional shot of someone holding a guitar, anything goes in the music video genre. At the same time (perhaps because of the popularity of MTV and its ilk), television commercials are striving to differentiate themselves and appeal to younger audiences by employing some of the most outrageous, experimental cinematic techniques in highly polished (and very expensive) 30-second spots.

As audiences have grown more sophisticated, experimental editing techniques have begun cropping up in mainstream feature films as well. A recent example is Darren Aronofsky's *Requiem for a Dream,* edited by Jay Rabinowitz. *Requiem,* a film about drug addiction, uses a series of ECUs, cut very quickly, each time the characters take drugs. The sequence is repeated almost shot for shot many times throughout the film. These sequences are intensely poetic, unfettered by ordinary limitations of visual cause and effect, continuity of time and space, or traditional narrative structure. The film also uses split screens (not just vertically but horizontally as well), slow motion and fast motion effects, and many other creative techniques seldom seen in narrative drama.

If you've got the opportunity and interest in experimenting, there are some useful guidelines to help you decide where to venture.

Emphasize Mood Over Plot

Going back to music video for a moment, the goal of most of these short films is simply to complement the emotional tone of the song. To do that, filmmakers are willing to abandon virtually all the traditional rules and grammar of film language— including the basic concept of continuity. Add a three-to-four-minute time limit, and the filmmaker must accelerate the amount of information he delivers and simultaneously loosen the bonds of traditional narrative structure.

This has created a stylistic revolution in film editing, the key to which is mood over plot. Of course, most shows are still based on the rules and techniques described in this book—but exceptions are becoming far more common.

Oliver Stone's *Natural Born Killers* and David Lynch's *Lost Highway* are wonderful examples of how these new "MTV" techniques can be applied to traditional narrative cinema to create stunning (and disturbing) visual poems. Both films provide amazing insight into the new age of film editing. *Killers* was shot on more than six types of media (video, 8mm, 35mm, and so on), but the shots are intercut with no concern whatsoever for the dislocation such editing forces on the audience. *Highway* makes seemingly random jumps in time and space that are so disorienting they can only be compared to waking up in someone else's dream world. The striking similarity between both of these films (and others like them) is that they emphasize the emotional tone of the scene at the expense of the basic continuity that is the spine of traditional editing.

Editing Hints

Given the intrinsically radical nature of experimental filmmaking, there are far fewer rules and patterns to worry about. Still, here are some general editing guidelines you may find useful.

Ask yourself: What is the emotional tone of the scene? What images can you use to convey that tone? What special effect might help to communicate it to your audience? Because the palette of effects at your fingertips is so incredibly broad, part of the challenge is deciding which ones are appropriate to play with.

If you're interested in distorting the linearity of time, try rearranging cause and effect, as editor Dody Dorn did with Christopher Nolan's film *Memento*. In that film the entire movie is told backward, reversed sequence for sequence from ordinary chronology.

If you want to draw attention to the filmmaking process itself, you can use visual devices like *wipes* for transitions, or paint on the frames themselves. Alternatively, you can try a minimalist approach, like the Dogme 95 filmmakers who shoot everything hand-held, refuse to use any music that wasn't played when shooting, and strive to create a more raw, real film experience in reaction to the controlled nature of mainstream cinema.

Whatever approach you take, don't try to put all the effects available to you into the same scene. Just as with mixing paint in kindergarten, if you combine too many elements, it becomes a dull brown mess.

Interview: HERVÉ SCHNEID

Hervé Schneid is responsible for editing some of the most striking films to come out of France over the last ten years, including *Delicatessen* and *The City of Lost Children* (both co-directed by Jean-Pierre Jeunet and Marc Caro). In addition, he has cut films for directors like Mike Figgis *(The Browning Version)* and Sally Potter *(The Tango Lesson, The Man Who Cried)*. His most recent film at the time of this interview was Jeunet's *Amilie from Montmartre*.

Michael Wohl: What do you do on an average working day?

Hervé Schneid: It depends on the day. I split the editing of a film into three or four stages. The first would be choosing shots, and then making the first cut scene by scene. I like to take a day for choosing, then I let it rest in my head without even thinking about it, then I cut it a day or two later.

When the first cut is finished, you can look at the film as a whole and discover the internal life that it has taken without asking you. It's alive, so it goes in directions that you didn't think of, and you discover this when you look at the complete project. It's a very interesting moment, very depressing sometimes, but I feel reassured to know that at least the film exists already.

How do you decide which films to work on?

By reading the script or knowing the director. With some directors I don't even need to read the script. It takes such a long time to work on a film, and if you don't make a good decision you're stuck for half a year or even a whole year.

What do you like about working on the computer?

A movie has no physical existence, so I love the idea that now, with this tool, everything is digital. It's ones and zeros and it's the same as the final result: You can't really define it. It's something in the air you can't touch.

Do have any advice for an editor who's just starting out?

First you should be brave. Each film is a challenge, and you have to look for perfection each time. So you should make sure that you are trying everything that you can, finding all options, finding the right line and not deviating. Also, listen to the unsaid. The interesting part of making a film is to listen to what is not said, to see what is in the frames, what is said without saying it.

What's your least favorite part of editing?

I hate that it's so tough not to smoke while cutting a film.

That's a very French answer. At least it's not dangerous like it was when the film was flammable...

Well, it is dangerous. After all, the film is not important, it's your health that's important. The film is just a film at the end of the day. My philosophy is not to make films which are going to be important, or even which are going to be successful. The important thing is to have pleasure doing the films you've chosen. I think that is very important. That's your life you are spending in the cutting room.

CHAPTER FOUR

Preparing to Edit

I know you're desperate to get started. You're sick of all the theories and patterns and definitions and tips. You're ready to start chopping up film.

Well, hang on, we're almost there.

You can't edit anything until you've got footage to cut, so before we can get into the nitty-gritty nuts and bolts of editing, you have to get some footage into your computer. And to do that, you have to log and organize it.

Much of this chapter is going to be about how to use various features of Final Cut Pro, but I'm not just rewriting the manual. I'm going to point out the most effective, efficient, and powerful ways to use these features—inside stuff that I've learned from long experience. And I'm also going to let you know which features to ignore for now.

THE ASSISTANT EDITOR'S GUIDE TO FINAL CUT PRO

Typically, editors start out as assistant editors—and it's assistant editors who do most of the work of getting the raw footage into, and the final program out of, the editing system. If you're going to be working as an assistant editor on a Final Cut Pro project, you'll need to learn every detail in this chapter top to bottom.

If you are a high-powered editor who always has an assistant by your side, you can just rip this chapter out of the book and hand it over to him. But if you're a one-woman or a one-man show, and you are your own assistant editor (as is the case with many Final Cut Pro editors), you need to read this chapter yourself. Now.

Log It or Lose It

Editing begins with *logging:* the process of cataloguing your footage and preparing your original source tapes for *capture.*

> **CAPTURE** *Transferring audio and video from your original videotapes to your computer's hard disk.*

Logging is the first time you get to review your footage. This is when you'll make your first set of decisions about what stays in and what gets tossed out of your show. If you think of editing as a process of eliminating all but the most essential frames, then logging is the first and coarsest pass. This is where you can eliminate aborted takes, wasted tape before and after the action of the take, and any shots or scenes that just don't work in the show.

Why Bother?

Logging can be tedious. Typically, it takes between two and three times as long as the running time of the footage you're logging. That doesn't include the actual capturing time, either, which takes an additional 1.2 to 1.5 times the length of the footage. For instance, we shot roughly 60 hours of footage for *Want.* Logging it took about 150 hours. Capturing it took another 75 hours.

Because logging involves looking at (and eliminating) a lot of the junk, it may feel like a waste of your time—and it's common to let an assistant editor complete the process. This has advantages and disadvantages. The main advantage is that by dividing the work, you can get it done faster; you can begin editing logged scenes while additional footage is still being catalogued.

The disadvantage is that you lose a great opportunity to get better acquainted with your footage. Familiarity with every frame of your film is one of the keys to good editing. The more times you view your footage, the better. That minute of "garbage" recorded when the camera operator was *rolling out the tape* might hold the key to a problematic transition or sequence somewhere else in the film.

> **ROLLING OUT THE TAPE** *To make sure they don't run out of tape in the middle of a shot, videographers commonly swap a new tape into the camera two to five minutes before the current tape runs out. However, since editing software like Final Cut Pro requires at least three to five seconds of recorded footage after the last Out point, it's good practice to record a few moments of "junk" after the last shot on the tape so the very last recorded frames aren't ones you intend to use. Filming that junk is called rolling out the tape.*

One nice thing about logging is that you don't have to do it in the studio. Since you aren't actually capturing footage yet, you don't need access to the hard disk space required for your editing station. You can log footage on a laptop, on an airplane, or at the beach (**Figure 4.1**).

Figure 4.1 Does anyone really bring his laptop to the beach?

Collect All the Information You Can

The more information you collect during the logging process, the easier your job will be when you sit down to edit the film. Final Cut Pro is designed to help you compile a great deal of information while logging and recall it efficiently during the editing process.

What Information Should You Collect?

Ask yourself: What kind of information will help you recall the contents of a clip six months from now?

Start with the categories described in Chapter 2 ("Film Language"). Who or what is the subject of the shot? What is the shot type (CU, MS, LS)? Is it a moving shot? How long does it run? What scene is the shot associated with? When was it shot? What take number is it? Is there anything technically wrong with it (focus problems, audio noise, lens flares, and so on)? What were the director's comments about the shot? If you like, you can even include a transcription of the shot's dialogue.

Different footage requires different kinds of logging information. For instance, footage for a dramatic show typically needs the scene and take number, any comments the director made on the set, and any problems recorded at the time of production (such as the sound of an airplane flying by). A short description of the shot might be nice, but if the editor is working from storyboards or a detailed shot list, it may be unnecessary. B-roll footage from a documentary might benefit from much more detailed descriptions of the shots, but information like a take number wouldn't apply.

> **TIP:** Avoid cryptic descriptions or abbreviations when logging footage. This kind of shorthand can be especially awkward if an assistant is logging footage that the editor hasn't seen. If the editor has to spend hours scouring through the original footage before she can figure out that "L-CTrkTrukDrvTckt_03" means "Long shot to close-up tracking shot of truck driver getting a ticket, take 3," the assistant who came up with the clever abbreviation isn't likely to be working for that editor again.
>
> Unfortunately, Final Cut Pro and the Mac Classic OS both limit the length of filenames, so some abbreviation is inevitable. But you have lots of comment fields and description columns to use in addition to the clip name.

Check the Camera Log

Hopefully, you have access to a camera log or *continuity report* that identifies exactly what was recorded on the tape: timecode numbers, shot names or numbers, take numbers, and some comments about each shot. The log may include additional information as well, such as the focal length and exposure setting of the camera (useful if something needs to be reshot). Transfer all of these details into Final Cut Pro.

> **CONTINUITY REPORT** Similar to a camera log, this report is made during production and lists every shot and every take in the order in which they appear on the tape. It focuses on continuity elements within the shots: props, costumes, makeup, gestures, and blocking.

You may also have access to a shot list, a breakdown of how a scene is supposed to be filmed, shot by shot. Though some crews may deviate from the plan, this is still valuable information to have.

These documents are the only clues you'll get to understanding what is on the tapes—aside from information gathered via your eyes and ears.

Log It All

I strongly recommend cataloguing every inch of tape on your source reels. You don't have to capture it all; in fact, if you have limited disk space (and who doesn't?), you won't want to capture more than you absolutely need. But you should log all of it. You never know what you'll want to use.

For instance, if you logged only the *circle takes* of a particular scene, and it later turns out that one of those shots is problematic, going back to find another take will mean relogging the tape. Since you don't want to have to log a tape more than once, do yourself a favor and log everything the first time.

> **CIRCLE TAKES** At the end of the shooting day (or the next morning), the crew usually gathers to watch the dailies. The director will identify the takes she prefers, and an assistant will circle her choices in the camera log. (In the old days, economy dictated that only the circled takes would be printed onto film for editing.)

You should even log the junk *between* takes. If you look at the clip list later, you should be able to account for every minute on the tape.

For instance, let's say at some point the camera was accidentally turned on between two shots, wasting two minutes of tape. Obviously, the editor won't be using this footage, but if months later he's looking at the takes from that particular scene and discovers a two-minute gap in the timecode, he may suspect that a take or shot is missing—and send you back to the source tapes to check it out. If you logged that segment of tape as a garbage shot in the first place, you'll be able to avoid wasting everyone's time.

> **DAILIES** To make sure that the scenes have been photographed successfully, each day's work is reviewed either at the end of a day or the next morning (to allow some sleep after a long or late shooting day or, if you're shooting on film, to give the lab time to print the film). These screenings are called rushes or dailies.

Scenes, Shots, and Takes

The terms "scene," "shot," and "take" can be confusing when you're new to filmmaking. Let's see if we can straighten out the jargon.

In the most generic sense, scene *refers to an edited series of shots of related events taking place in a single location—for instance, "the bank robbery scene." During production, a scene is usually identified by a number based on the order in which it appears in the script or occasionally by the order in which it is shot.*

Shot refers to each of the individual camera angles used in the scene. Every time the camera frames a different angle or image of the events being filmed, it is a new shot.

Take refers to a single iteration of any given shot—take 1, take 2, and so on.

Figure 4.2 A typical slate has one slot for the scene number and one for the take number, and that's that.

*To further confuse matters, most Hollywood productions identify shots by referring to the scene number. For example, successive shots in scene 5 would be called scene 5a, 5b, 5c, and so on. Furthermore, takes are sometimes referred to as shots. This is why a typical film slate has only two blank slots: one for a scene number (which is actually the shot name) and another for a take number (**Figure 4.2**).*

LOGGING WITH FINAL CUT PRO

Log and Capture Window

At first glance, the Log and Capture window can be intimidating. It certainly seems to require a lot of information! However, once you learn to use this tool, it will speed your logging process considerably.

The Basics

Like most features in Final Cut Pro, the Log and Capture window includes a huge number of options you don't need right away. You can get by just fine with a very limited subset of logging capabilities.

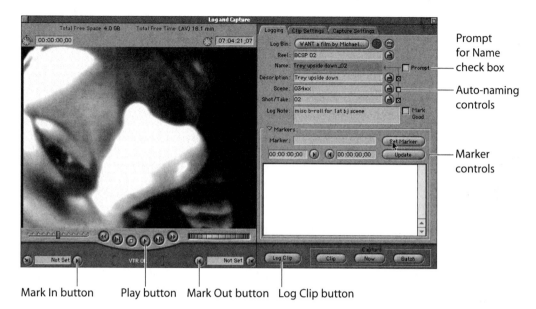

Prompt
for Name
check box

Auto-naming
controls

Marker
controls

Mark In button   Play button   Mark Out button   Log Clip button

Figure 4.3 The Log and Capture window is accessible by selecting Log and Capture from the File menu or typing ⌘-8. Any time you want to move footage from your tape into your computer, you will use this window.

At the most basic level, you can log a clip if you can tell Final Cut Pro just three things:

- the clip's starting time (its In point).

- the clip's ending time (its Out point).

- the clip's name.

> ***IN AND OUT POINTS*** *When you're working with a clip, Final Cut Pro allows you to set special markers identifying the frames that begin and end each shot you want to use. These markers are known as In and Out points.*

When it comes time to log, four basic steps will do the job:

1. Play your tape, using the (Spacebar) to start and stop playback, until you find the clip you want to log.

2. Use (I) and (O) to mark the In and Out points, thus marking the precise segment of the tape you wish to log.

3. Hit (F2), or click the Log Clip button to enter the clip into the database.

4. Type in a name for the clip in the dialog box that appears, or accept the name generated by Final Cut Pro's auto-naming feature.

That's it! Once you've learned those steps, you're ready to log and capture your footage. All the other controls are gravy.

I find the on-screen controls too small to use effectively, especially since you need them so often—so I recommend memorizing and using these four keyboard shortcuts.

Required Fields

As you can see, the Log and Capture window contains more than ten fields waiting for input. How do you know which fields to use for each clip?

Only four fields are required: Reel, Clip In and Out points, and Name.

Provide Meaningful Reel Numbers

It's critically important to enter a reel number (or name) when you log shows with source footage that spans more than one tape. In fact, Final Cut Pro won't allow you to log a clip without entering something in the Reel field.

Be sure to enter meaningful information in the Reel field. Final Cut Pro doesn't care whether you enter text or a number, but whatever you enter into that field is the only thing that will tell you which tape to put into the deck when you do the capture later.

Always include something that's actually written on the outside of the tape. While you may remember which tape is which over the first few weeks of a project, who knows what you'll remember when you need to revisit the film months or years down the road?

It's equally important to be sure that all clips from the same tape are entered with exactly the same reel name. Final Cut Pro will treat Tape 2 and Tape 002 as different tapes. To assist you in making the names identical, the Shortcut menu will pop up a list of all the reel names you've already used in a given project. Rather than retyping a reel name from memory, select it from the pop-up menu to ensure that syntax and capitalization are identical (**Figure 4.4**).

Figure 4.4 The Shortcut menu provides a list of all the reel names used in the current project. Access it by Ctrl-clicking the Reel field.

Setting In and Out Points

I've already described how to set the In and Out points. But how do you know *where* to set them?

Breathing Room

Always overestimate. Set your In early and set your Out late. Once your clip is captured, you don't want to have to go back and look at the tape again. If an assistant is logging, the editor may never even know that something exists on the tape if it was cut off during logging.

Also, transitions and other effects sometimes require additional frames beyond the footage you mark between your In and Out points—another reason to provide a little slop on either side of each clip.

When to Add Handles

At the point when you actually capture the logged footage, you have the option of adding *handles* to extend the shots slightly. This is one way of ensuring you capture enough extra footage before and after each shot to allow room for transitions and other effects.

> **HANDLES** Extra footage before and after the selected In and Out points. Final Cut Pro can add handles automatically during capture.

You can set the default length for your handles in the Batch Capture dialog box (**Figure 4.5**). Handle length will be applied uniformly to the beginning and end of every captured clip. Usually editors set this value to one or two seconds.

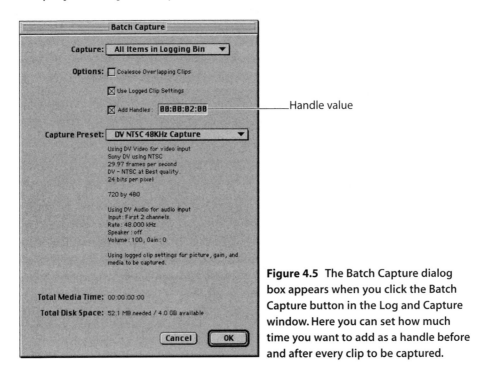

Handle value

Figure 4.5 The Batch Capture dialog box appears when you click the Batch Capture button in the Log and Capture window. Here you can set how much time you want to add as a handle before and after every clip to be captured.

Using handles ensures that you get a little room to maneuver within each clip, but it's a pretty generalized way to address this problem. If you set your In and Out points thoughtfully in the first place, you can customize the amount of elbow-room you leave yourself shot by shot—and may not need to add handles at the time of capture.

It's a good idea to decide whether or not you intend to use handles before you begin logging. If you do plan to use them, then you can set In and Out points for the beginning and end of the action in each shot. For example, set the In just as the director calls "Action!" and the Out right as she says "Cut!" The handles will provide the slop you may require later. If you don't intend to use handles, you should set your In and Out points earlier (perhaps as soon as the camera begins rolling) and later (when the camera stops rolling).

The only problem with using handles is that Final Cut Pro requires at least three to five seconds of *pre- and post-roll* before and after each clip it attempts to capture. This means that you cannot safely set an In point earlier than five seconds into the tape or an Out point later than five seconds before the end of the timecode on the tape. Since most people log a tape right up to the last frame, adding a handle may reset the Out point for your last clip off the end of the tape—which will generate an error when you attempt to capture the clip.

> **PRE- AND POST-ROLL** *In order for Final Cut Pro to capture clips accurately, the deck needs at least a few seconds before the clip gets up to speed—and a few seconds after the clip ends so Final Cut Pro can close the file properly. Different decks require different amounts of pre- and post-roll; you can set the values in the General Preferences window.*

What's in a Name?

Because naming your clips is so important, Final Cut Pro provides quite a few powerful features to help you do it.

Keep Names Short

I warned earlier about using cryptic names for your clips, but sometimes you won't have any choice. The problem is that the name you give your clip is carried over to name the actual file on disk. And thanks to the Mac Classic operating system's antiquated 32-character limit on filenames, that means you can't exceed 32 characters when you name your clips.

To make matters worse, Final Cut Pro reserves 6 of those characters, leaving you only 26 characters to work with. Why? To accommodate another of the Classic OS's limitations: the 2GB file-size limit. When you capture a clip that needs more than 2GB (easy to do, since 2GB stores only ten minutes of DV), Final Cut Pro creates a reference movie that points to a linked array of 2GB files. Each of these files is given a custom extension: AV-001, AV-002, and so on.

Fortunately, we can look forward to relief for both of these problems when an OS X version of Final Cut Pro is released.

No Dupes, Please

It's very important to avoid creating duplicate names when you're logging your clips. Final Cut Pro allows you to have multiple items with the same name in the Browser, but because your clip names will become filenames, they must all be unique.

This may sound easy, but when you start logging shots for a long project, you'll be surprised how often you're tempted to use the same clip name, such as CU Trey_01 or LS Sailboat. Fortunately, Final Cut Pro has a screening mechanism that warns you during capture if you attempt to create a duplicate filename. But at that point you won't know which clip is which, so it's much better to avoid the problem in the first place. Use some piece of information unique to the shot, such as a description of the scene it was in (CU Trey Hockey Game_01) or, with more generically named footage, the date or some other detail to help differentiate the clip (Feb2 LS Sailboat BootWaves).

When to Use Auto-naming

For certain types of footage, where the names of clips are going to be very repetitive or follow numerical patterns based on scene and shot names, you should use Final Cut Pro's auto-naming features to generate clip names. This capability is designed to name and number your clips automatically, based on the information you type into the fields below the Name field (**Figure 4.6**). The tiny check boxes beside each field indicate whether that field will become part of the clip name. If you leave a box unchecked, that information is still recorded with the clip but will not become part of the clip name.

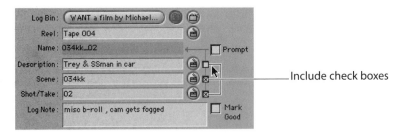

Figure 4.6 The clip name is based on the text in the fields below. Check the boxes next to the fields you wish to include. You cannot type directly into the Name field.

In the simplest case, you can just use the Description field to name your clips. Every time you log a clip, the field is incremented with a number or letter. This prevents you from logging clips with duplicate filenames.

For instance, let's say you're logging a tape of nature footage taken in Yosemite National Park. The first thing on the tape is a long shot of Yosemite Falls from the valley floor. The shot runs for 20 seconds, and then zooms into a CU of three struggling hikers climbing an adjacent trail. You type Waterfall Hikers Zoom into the Description field and log the clip by pressing F2.

Once the clip has been logged, the Description field automatically increments to Waterfall Hikers Zoom1 (**Figure 4.7**). Assuming the next shot on the tape is another take of the zoom, all you need to do is set new In and Out points and press F2 again—and the second shot will be automatically logged as Waterfall Hikers Zoom1. No retyping required.

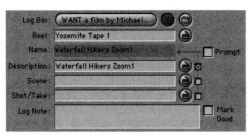

Figure 4.7 The Description field becomes the name of the clip. Each time you log another clip, this field automatically increments the previous shot's name so the current one has a unique name or number.

Using Multiple Fields

If you check any boxes to include additional fields in the clip name, the information will be separated with an underscore. Use the Description and Shot/Take fields when you plan to have multiple takes of each shot.

For example, imagine the next section of the Yosemite tape shows a series of CU shots of the hikers. Since you know ahead of time that this series exists (from the camera log, or from having been at the location), go ahead and type CU Hikers into the Description field and 01 into the Shot/Take field (**Figure 4.8**). After you log the first clip by pressing F2, the Description field remains unchanged, but the Shot/Take field changes to 02. Each time you log a clip, the last-used field will be incremented; the others are left alone.

Figure 4.8 The checked fields make up the name of the clip separated by an underscore. Each time you log the clip, the last-used field is incremented.

If you're working with footage that was shot using the traditional Hollywood naming scheme, you will have scene numbers and take numbers for each shot. In this case, you can ignore the Description field, and just use the Scene and Shot/Take fields (**Figure 4.9**). Or you can use all three fields to provide a description plus the scene and take information (**Figure 4.10**).

Figure 4.9 Footage named in traditional Hollywood style has only a scene number and a take number. In this case, use just those two fields. Be sure to check the correct Include check boxes to reflect the fields you are using.

Figure 4.10 You can add a description to the shot to help the editor identify what the subject is.

Alternately, if you have distinct scene, shot, and take numbers, you can use the Description field for your scene number, the Scene field for the shot number, and the Shot/Take field for the take number (**Figure 4.11**). This is great for footage coming from corporate or industrial shoots, where scene names tend to be discrete from shot numbers.

Figure 4.11 If your shots have unique scene names, shot numbers, and take numbers, you can use all three fields to hold the different bits of information.

Using Manual Incrementing

All these auto-naming and auto-incrementing features really come in handy. Even a small reduction in steps will save you loads of time and hassle, given the huge number of shots you have to log in any project. Using the auto-naming utilities also assures that your clips are uniformly named, which makes them easier to sort on and search for.

But wait, there's more! You may have noticed a little button, the one with a picture of a slate on it, next to each of these naming fields. This is the Manual Increment button (called the Slate button in the documentation). Clicking it adds a number (or letter) to the end of whichever field you clicked next to.

This is great if you want to increment the scene number. Let's say you're working in the Hollywood naming scheme and the last shot you logged was scene 44a, take 4. The next shot is take 1 of scene 44b. You can increment the scene number from 44a to 44b by clicking the Manual Increment button once (**Figure 4.12**). This not only changes the value in the Scene field, but it resets the Shot/Take field back to 01! It's a great time-saver when you're working with clips that are constantly incrementing, such as footage from dramatic or scripted shows.

Figure 4.12 Clicking the Manual Increment button increases the number or letter in the corresponding field and automatically resets the fields below it.

TIP: If you Option-click the Manual Increment button, it clears the field entirely.

Why All These Fields?

There's no reason you can't simply type the scene, shot, and take numbers right into the Description field. But by breaking down the information into individual fields, you will be able to sort and search on any one of these fields later.

For instance, if you want to find all the shots from scene 21, you can perform a Find All in the Browser, search only in the Scene column, and look only for clips with the number 21. Once you do that, you can collect all those clips into a single bin, and sort based on shot number or take number. For simple projects with only a hundred or so clips, this degree of control may not be absolutely necessary. But on a larger project like a feature film, with thousands of individual shots, file management at this level is fundamental to the editing process.

How to Log Short Clips

Ideally, you will be able to log your clips without stopping the tape—but when you find yourself logging clips that are less than 30 seconds long, you will hardly have time to name them and enter your comments before they've passed and the next clip has begun. You may find yourself racing against the tape or constantly stopping and starting playback to give yourself a chance to fill in the fields in the Logging tab.

This is the time to turn on the Prompt for Name feature by checking the Prompt check box on the Logging tab (**Figure 4.13**). When this option is enabled, clicking the Log Clip button (or hitting ⌐F2⌐) automatically pauses the tape and opens the Log Clip dialog box, which will prompt you for a name (**Figure 4.14**). Once you dismiss the dialog, the tape will begin playing again, and you can move on to setting the next clip's In and Out points.

Figure 4.13 If the Prompt box is checked, every time you click the Log Clip button (or type ⌐F2⌐), the Log Clip dialog box will open, asking you to name the clip you are about to log.

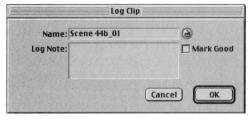

Figure 4.14 The Log Clip dialog box includes the Log Note field and the Mark Good check box to allow you to provide additional information about each shot.

TIP: The Log Clip dialog contains a Manual Increment button (the one with the little slate). If you want to increment the shot name (trees, trees1, trees2) just click that button, and the clip name will be updated without any further typing on your part.

How to Log Long Clips

Logging longer shots allows you plenty of time to type in a name, comments, and whatever other information you require while the tape is rolling. If your shots are mostly longer than 30 seconds, you may be able to log the entire tape without ever stopping it.

To work this way, uncheck the Prompt check box (see Figure 4.13). Then, while the tape rolls, set your desired In point and enter the name and any other information you want to supply in the fields in the Logging tab. When the shot ends, mark the Out point on the fly and log the clip. The fields you've chosen to fill in are captured and stored with the clip. Playback will not be interrupted, and you can begin logging the next clip immediately.

> **TIP:** Back up your project file! All the information you enter during logging is stored in that file. (It is not stored with the media files when you capture.) With a copy of the project file (and your source tapes), you can re-create your whole project—any time, anywhere.

ENTERING ADDITIONAL INFORMATION

Experienced editors have learned the hard way that the more information you record during logging, the happier you will be later. Final Cut Pro makes it easy to add all types of additional information while logging.

Use the Log Note Field for Longer Notes

Now that you've got the clip-naming process figured out, you're probably disappointed that Final Cut Pro cuts you off after only 26 characters. If you want to record more detailed or elaborate information, you'll have to put it somewhere else.

The Log Note field is your best bet. You can comfortably view two lines of notes in this field (and you can type as much text as you want for searching purposes). Be sure to enter the log note *before* logging the clip. Unlike the other fields, the Log Note field is cleared every time you log a clip.

If you want to use the same note repeatedly, you can access previous notes from the Shortcut menu by Ctrl-clicking the Log Note field. You might use this to enter frequent comments like "Director liked this take," "Aborted take," or "Traffic noise."

Using the Shortcut menu minimizes repetitive typing and assures the uniformity of your log notes (**Figure 4.15**).

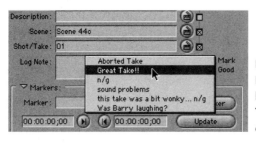

Figure 4.15 The Shortcut menu on the Log Note field pops up a list of the other log notes used in the current project. This way you can reuse comments that occur frequently.

Set Markers While Logging

Final Cut Pro provides yet another cool feature to make logging easier: the ability to set *markers* while logging.

> **MARKER** *A placeholder or bookmark you can use to identify a specific frame (or a range of time) within a clip or sequence.*

Markers are among the most valuable tools available to you as a digital editor (see the section on working with markers in Chapter 5, "Basic Editing"). The ability to set them while logging is unique to Final Cut Pro.

It's probably too time-consuming to bother setting markers for short clips while you're logging, but placing markers in longer clips is a fine way to point out both positive and negative things that occur during the clip. For instance, you might identify a lens flare, a flaw in the performance, a mic boom in the shot, or the duration of an airplane sound that interferes with your audio. You can use markers to identify the frames where a character is speaking in a clip that includes long portions of silence, or note a good performance of a particular line.

Here's how to set markers while logging: Twiddle open the Markers revealer in the Logging tab (**Figure 4.16**). (If you're not going to be using markers, you can close this up to avoid the clutter and distraction it creates.) You can set marker In and marker Out points using the buttons you'll find there (shortcuts are ⌃ for In and Option-⌃ for Out), and name the marker by typing in the Marker field. Out points are required only if you want the marker to have duration; if you don't set one, the marker will simply identify a single frame in the clip.

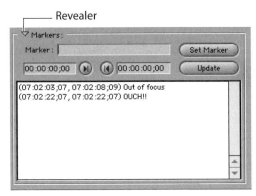

Figure 4.16 The Logging tab contains a set of controls for adding markers to your clips. These controls can be hidden or shown depending on the state of the revealer widget.

Once you've set your desired marker In and Out point and typed in a name, clicking the Set Marker button adds the marker to the list box. You can stack up as many markers as you want in the list or delete existing ones. You can change markers any time you like by selecting them in the list; making changes to the In point, Out point, or name; and clicking the Update button.

Create Subclips on the Fly

Because markers turn into subclips, you can easily create subclips from longer clips, on the fly, while logging. Let's say the script calls for an insert of a hand opening a door. When the crew shot the scene, rather than stopping and starting the camera for different takes, they simply ran the action four or five times during one shot. When you log this footage, keep the clip all together as one shot, and use markers to set In and Out points for each door opening. Once you capture the clip, your markers can be accessed directly as subclips in the Browser (see "Subclips in Disguise" in Chapter 5) (**Figure 4.17**).

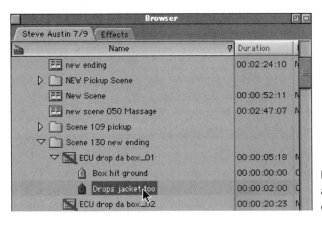

Figure 4.17 Double-clicking a marker in the Browser opens it up as a subclip.

Good, Better, Best

The Mark Good check box in the Log and Capture window (**Figure 4.18**) is simply another piece of information you can store with a clip you're logging. The original idea was that this would be akin to marking a circle take. You can check this box to identify good clips you will probably want to find later. Once all your clips are logged, you can do a search to find all clips that have the Mark Good check box checked, and use that list to decide which clips to capture—or just to jog your memory on which takes you liked while logging.

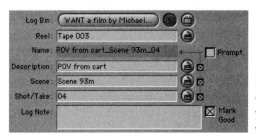

Figure 4.18 The Mark Good check box can be used to mark clips you like. Later you can search on the Good column in the Browser to find them.

Of course, you don't *have* to use this check box just to mark good takes. I always wanted this feature to pop up a menu that would let me choose Good, Better, or Best—since most of the time I don't know which is the circle take until I've seen them all.

So, weirdly enough, I generally use the Mark Good check box to mark shots that are unquestionably *bad*. For example, I use it to mark the junk in between shots, or takes that were aborted, or footage of the crew goofing around. Then I know what I *don't* want to capture.

Apple finally addressed the Good-Better-Best concept in Final Cut Pro 2, but in a somewhat awkward way. This version offers a Label Category option for every item in the Browser, allowing you to assign a label to each clip that you can search and sort on later.

The default labels are Good Take, Best Take, Interview, B-Roll, and Junk—but the label names are fully customizable in the Preferences window. Each label has a color associated with it (also customizable). Once you get used to the colors, you can quickly distinguish clips in the Browser by the color of their icons. This color also shows up on the clip when it's edited in the Timeline, which can be helpful when you're glancing at a long show and trying to identify a particular clip to which you previously assigned a label.

The only problem is that you can't actually apply any of these labels in the Log and Capture window (where you really want to). To use the labels, you must first log the clip. Then you can bring the Browser window forward, select the clip, and change the value in the Label column (**Figure 4.19**).

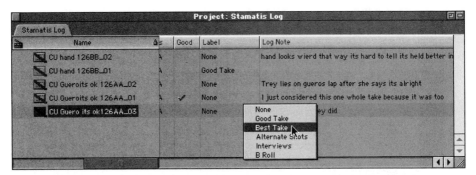

Figure 4.19 You can set a label for each clip you log, but you can only do it in the Browser window after the clip is logged. Ctrl -click the Label column and assign the label of your choice.

Add Additional Information in Browser Columns

You can use other Browser columns to add additional information to your clips— but as with the Label Category option, you have to log the clip first.

There are four comment fields you can use to catalogue things like shot type, day/night, script day, shooting day, camera focal length, *f*-stop, and so on. To use any of these columns you must first log the clip, then open the Browser and type directly into the column you want to use. All of the columns support the Recent Items pop-up list I described for the Reel and Log Note fields; Ctrl -clicking a column opens up a list of all the values previously used in that column (**Figure 4.20**).

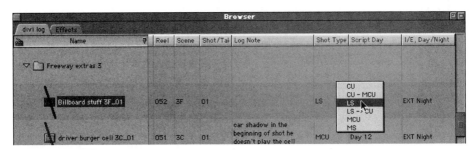

Figure 4.20 Ctrl -clicking any of the comment fields in the Browser will pop up a list of all the comments previously entered in that field for the current project.

SPEED LOGGING

I've already described a number of things that Final Cut Pro does automatically to assist you in naming the clips you're logging, but it gets even better. Check this out:

If you log a clip by pressing F2 without setting an Out point, Final Cut Pro simply sets the Out point at the exact moment you press the key. And whenever you log a clip, Final Cut Pro resets the In point for the *next* clip immediately following the Out point for the clip you just logged.

These two features make it possible for you to log clips with a single keystroke.

Here's how:

1. Insert a tape, and enter a reel number and name for the first clip.

2. Set your first In point at the beginning of the first shot, and let the tape roll.

3. When you get to the point where you'd like to end the first clip, instead of setting an Out point, simply hit F2. That sets the Out point and logs the clip.

4. Final Cut Pro automatically increments the clip name, resets the In point, and the tape continues to play. At the next scene break, simply hit F2 again.

5. Continue this process until you reach the end of the tape.

If the takes are long enough, you should even have time to enter comments in the Log Note field, change the clip name, and so on. When we developed this method of one-key logging, we informally dubbed it "speed logging." It's a bit too complicated to explain on a marketing sheet, but it's a great feature for the serious user to know about, as it can save you lots of time.

AUTO SCENE DETECTION

If you still hate the idea of spending hours and hours logging your tapes, you may be curious about a spiffy new feature in Final Cut Pro 2 called Auto Scene Detection. To use it, capture your entire tape as one single clip, then select the clip and choose Auto Scene Detection from the Tools menu.

Final Cut Pro then goes through the clip and adds a marker for every time you stopped and started the camera while recording. (This works on any tape shot with any DV camera. The memory chip included on the more expensive DV tapes is not required.) Each marker can be double-clicked in the Browser and opened as a subclip.

This feature will identify only moments when the camera stopped and started. This may or may not have much relation to where your clip boundaries should actually be. It certainly won't tell you when the director called "Action!" or "Cut!" And it's not going to name your clips in any useful way (unless Marker 31 makes your heart beat faster). For professionally shot footage, you will probably not find Auto Scene Detection terribly useful.

One additional disadvantage is that working this way assumes you are going to capture every second of footage on all your tapes, which will eat up huge amounts of unnecessary disk space.

That said, for certain applications it may be great. For instance, if you're logging footage shot by an amateur videographer on a safari in Africa, just knowing where the camera started and stopped may be useful. Provided he didn't let the camera roll endlessly on every animal he saw or accidentally record ten bouncy minutes of the jeep ride through a dirty window.

Working With Timecode

One of our goals when designing Final Cut Pro was to make migration from older tools as painless as possible. We wanted people familiar with Avid, Media 100, or even traditional linear editing systems to feel comfortable with Final Cut Pro right away. This had a major influence on our decisions about what to name various features and what keyboard shortcuts to implement.

One important example is the way we designed Final Cut Pro to work with timecode. Linear video editing systems were operated almost entirely from a numeric keypad. Editors got very handy at typing in timecode numbers and learning to add and subtract frames in base 30 (for NTSC) or 25 (for PAL).

Although it seems tricky at first, once you learn to think in timecode, you will be able to edit more quickly and more accurately. The more advanced you get, the more you will think only in terms of frames and timecode, and you will probably find yourself editing by typing numbers into your keyboard just as the editors on those older systems did—and less by dragging things around or clicking buttons.

To start you on the path toward timecode enlightenment, here are some of the basic rules and concepts about how to use timecode in Final Cut Pro. Don't panic—it may initially seem mind-boggling, but you'll get it eventually.

Timecode contains eight digits, separated by colons: 00:00:00:00 (hours:minutes:seconds:frames).

If you're going to enter all eight digits, you can forget the punctuation: 18102118 will be interpreted as 18:10:21:18.

continues on next page

Working With Timecode *continued*

OK, but this is real life, and most of the time you aren't interested in the hours column, or even the minutes column. Most of the edits you'll be making will involve a few seconds or a few frames. That's why we arranged for Final Cut Pro to accept less than eight digits. In fact, it will read right to left in two-digit increments.

For example, if you enter 01:23, Final Cut Pro will interpret it as 00:00:01:23.

A colon with no number after it is interpreted as a placeholder for 00. So...

If you enter 11:, Final Cut Pro will interpret it as 00:00:11:00.

If you enter 11::05, Final Cut Pro will interpret it as 00:11:00:05.

Similarly, you can enter math commands such as –5 or +10. These apply to the current timecode following the same conventions:

If the current timecode is 02:20:55:10...

-5 subtracts 5 frames, and the current timecode becomes 02:20:55:05.

Or

+10: adds 10 seconds, and the current timecode becomes 02.21:05:10.

You can use a period or a comma instead of the colon, and you can also omit leading zeros.

So you might type +10.5. which would be read as 00:10:05:00 and bring our timecode from 02:20:55:10 to 02:31:00:10.

In case all that isn't enough, you can also enter simple frame values like +125, which means "add 125 frames." In NTSC timebase, that would equal 4 seconds and 5 frames. This is an easier way for some editors to think. You can even combine these methods:

-2.50 would subtract 3 seconds and 20 frames. The -2. means subtract 2 seconds, and the 50 is interpreted as 50 frames, or 1 second, 20 frames.

At any point while working in Final Cut Pro, you can simply type in a timecode number, even without clicking a field. Final Cut Pro will recognize what it is and apply it to the most likely place based on the current context.

*If the Viewer is active, timecode entry will move the playhead forward or backward. You do not need to actually click the Current Position field, although doing so accomplishes the same thing. Typing an absolute timecode number (01:21:10:15 or just 10:15) will move the playhead to that absolute position. Typing in a mathematical statement (+16, -200, and so on) will move the playhead forward or backward as requested (**Figure 4.21**). The Log and Capture window works the same way: Changing the value modifies the Current Position field to shuttle the tape and cue it up to the requested timecode frame.*

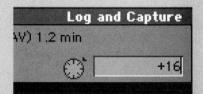

Figure 4.21 Direct timecode entry in either the Viewer or Log and Capture window will apply the timecode to the Current Position field and move the playhead (in the Viewer) or the tape itself (in the Log and Capture window).

If you wish to change a clip's duration in either the Viewer or the Log and Capture window, hit ⟨Tab⟩
*before entering your timecode. This will highlight the Duration field in the upper left corner of the
window. You can type in a new absolute value or use math in this field, too. For example, if the current
clip duration is 00:10:00:05, entering* ⟨Tab⟩ *-10. would highlight the Duration field and shave off 10
seconds by changing the Out point to make the new duration 00:09:50:05 (**Figure 4.22**).*

Figure 4.22 You can modify a clip's duration by clicking the Duration field (also
accessible by hitting ⟨Tab⟩). Making changes there will modify the Out point to
result in the desired duration.

*Entering timecode numbers when the Timeline or Canvas
is active initiates a wide variety of editing operations
depending on the current state (see the sidebar "Just Type
a Number" in Chapter 6, "Advanced Editing").*

*If the timecode value you want is sitting in a nearby
window, you can actually drag it from one timecode field
to another by holding down* ⟨Option⟩ *as you drag (**Figure
4.23**). You might do this while logging to move the tape
to the In point. By dragging the timecode from the In
point into the Current Position field, you will make the
tape shuttle to that timecode, lining your tape up on the
current In point.*

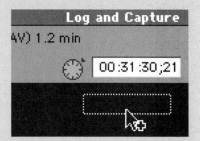

Figure 4.23 You can drag a timecode value from one field to another
by holding down ⟨Option⟩ when you
begin to drag.

Drop Frame Versus Non-Drop Frame

NTSC timecode comes in two flavors: drop frame (DF) and non-drop frame (NDF). Don't be fooled by the name. No frames are ever dropped. These are just different ways of counting the frames. Non-drop frame timecode counts every frame consecutively, and every 30th frame marks a new second. Because NTSC video actually plays at only 29.97 frames per second, this method of counting is not a very good way to tell how long a program will be.

For example, if you ran a stopwatch, a show measuring exactly 1 hour in NDF timecode would actually last 1 hour, 3 seconds, and 18 frames!

So who cares? Broadcasters. Problems arise when television stations are creating broadcast schedules that must be precise lengths. That's why they invented drop frame timecode.

With drop frame, every so often frame numbers are skipped so when the edit machine says the program is 01:00:00:00, it is actually 1 hour long on the clock. No frames are dropped, but some numbers are skipped so the count remains true to real time. It's exactly the same concept as leap year, only instead of skipping the 29th of February 3 out of every 4 years (except every 100 years), DF timecode skips frames 00 and 01 every minute (except every 10 minutes). That means if you want to look at frame 1800 (1 minute), the counter would read 00:01:00:02 even though in NDF, it would read 01:00:00:00. You can tell DF and NDF apart by the punctuation used. DF is always identified with a semicolon instead of a colon between the seconds and frames: 00:00:00;00.

NTSC DV is always recorded in drop frame timecode.

LOGGING OUTSIDE OF FINAL CUT PRO

Logging doesn't require having the hard disk space to capture the logged footage. A logging station can be a minimally configured iMac or laptop. As long as you can run Final Cut Pro and connect to your source deck, you can record all of the logging information you need. Then, you can transfer your information to a computer with big hard drives and capture away.

Log From a Window Dub

Because timecode is not program specific, you can actually log your tapes using any software program, on any system, and transfer that data to Final Cut Pro for capturing. Sometimes tapes will even be logged by hand, perhaps by watching a *window dub*. In that case, all you'll have will be a handwritten list of In points, Out points, clip names, and comments.

WINDOW DUB *Some video decks can display timecode numbers in a window right on top of the video image, so you can see the exact timecode number for any given frame on the TV monitor. This is known as BITC—short for burned-in timecode, and pronounced "bit-see." A dub made with that window visible is called a window dub. This makes it possible to record timecode values even from a nonprofessional tape format like VHS (**Figure 4.24**).*

Figure 4.24 When timecode is printed on top of a video image, it's called BITC.

Import Batch Lists

Final Cut Pro can import and process batch lists of logging information from any program as long as it's stored as Tab-delimited text. You can even type the details from a hand-written list into a spreadsheet if you know what you're doing. You can use as many or as few of the Browser columns as you choose.

To enable Final Cut Pro to read the file, you must take one additional step. Before importing the file, you must modify it in a text editor, or a spreadsheet program like Excel, and add one new record at the beginning of the file with the exact Browser column headers that correspond with the fields in the data file (**Figure 4.25**).

	A	B	C	D	E	F	G
1	In	Out	Name	Take	Reel	Comment 1	
2	01:18:24:02	01:20:14:28	CU Reggie_01	01	001	Good perf, bad audio	
3	01:21:42:10	01:22:10:20	CU Reggie_02	02	001	n/g	
4	01:22:31:05	01:22:55:13	CU Reggie_03	03	001	Good	
5	01:23:18:02	01:24:45:10	Lions in Cage		001	roar!	
6	01:25:10:21	01:26:58:00	Baby Gorilla	01	001	swings for a few minutes and	
7	02:35:15:20	02:37:18:12	Momma Rilla	01	002	Kids in f/g	
8	02:39:40:41	02:42:12:05	Momma Rilla2	02	002	No kids, good	
9	02:48:18:01	02:50:01:29	Killer Koala	01	002	draws blood, at end of shot, n	
10	02:55:10:05	02:56:21:10	Meekrats		002	Lots of good moments	
11	03:10:21:04	03:12:14:18	Reggie in Gift shop		003	Spot On	
12	03:12:20:12	03:14:01:00	Pegnuins 1	01	003	Above water	
13	03:14:45:20	03:14:50:10	Penguins 2	02	003	Above water	
14	03:15:31:10	03:16:33:06	Penguins 3	03	003	Below water	

Figure 4.25 Add one record at the head of the list identifying the Browser columns you want the corresponding data to go into. You can use as many or as few columns as you like. Final Cut Pro will use that first record to identify which data goes into what column.

You can also work the other way around. If you prefer to log your footage in Final Cut Pro and edit on some other system, go wild. Final Cut Pro exports batch lists that you can import into an Avid or another system and use to capture and edit on that system. Beware, though: You are probably limited to essential information: reel number, In point, Out point, clip name, and possibly one comment.

Incidentally, making a batch list is also a great way to create a fail-safe backup of your Final Cut Pro project file. Even if those files are corrupted somehow, or it's ten years from now, Apple is out of business, and Final Cut Pro is so antiquated you've moved on to some new editing program, you will still have a reliable way to access the data gained during that long, painful logging process. Add an *EDL* of your finished show, and you can rebuild it on any system at all.

> **EDL** *An edit decision list (EDL) is a text file containing the bare minimum of pertinent information to allow you to re-create your sequence. These files are commonly used to transfer projects from one editing system to another, such as from Avid to Final Cut Pro (or vice versa).*

TROUBLESHOOTING

Stuff happens. Sometimes you are totally screwed, but now and then there are solutions to help you resolve the problem.

Repairing Broken Timecode

It's fairly easy to end up with a tape with a timecode break in it. All it takes is removing your tape from the camera before you finish using it, or shuttling it around in the camera, and failing to resume recording *exactly* where you left off. Either of these moves will cause a timecode break.

Final Cut Pro doesn't like timecode breaks and will give you an error if you attempt to capture over an area in your tape that contains a break. In some cases this means you won't be able to capture the clip at all.

If you find yourself in this situation, the solution is to dub the tape onto a new DV tape in one continuous pass. The dub will have consistent timecode all the way through.

Correcting for Insufficient Pre- and Post-roll

Final Cut Pro may give you a similar error message if you attempt to capture a shot at the beginning or end of the tape and there's not enough pre- or post-roll for the deck to cue up.

If a shot that you absolutely must have lies on the very beginning or end of a tape, and Final Cut Pro won't let you capture it because it doesn't have adequate pre- or post-roll, follow the same procedure: Just dub it onto a new tape, ensuring that this time there's ample room around it, and capture from the new tape.

Fixing an Incorrect Reel Number

Whenever you put a new tape into your deck, Final Cut Pro will remind you that you really ought to set a new reel number for it. Even so, if you're thinking about how to solve some esoteric editing problem (or what to buy your husband for his birthday), sometimes you'll OK the dialog box and continue working without ever changing the reel number. Usually you realize this only when you look up in horror to see 15 clips already logged with the incorrect reel number (**Figure 4.26**). A useful, undocumented feature in Final Cut Pro can easily remedy this. You can multiselect a bunch of clips in the Browser and change all their reel numbers simultaneously by changing the reel number of any one of the group.

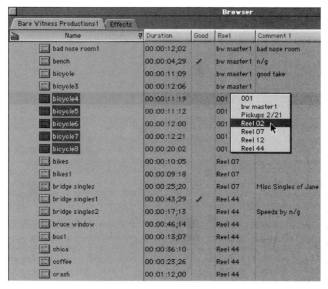

Figure 4.26 If you need to change the reel number for a group of clips, select the group and change any one. All the other clips will update as well.

Interview: *STEVEN MIRRIONE*

Steven Mirrione has cut an interesting variety of projects, alternating big-budget studio pictures with smaller independent films. There's an arresting intensity to all of his work, from Doug Liman's *Swingers* to Steven Soderbergh's *Traffic*. At the time of this interview he was just finishing Soderbergh's latest, a remake of *Ocean's Eleven* (originally made in 1960 with Frank Sinatra, Dean Martin, and Angie Dickinson).

Michael Wohl: Can you describe your overall editing process?

Steven Mirrione: I begin with watching the dailies. I don't take very detailed notes, but when I'm watching, if there's a particularly interesting moment, or something I think I might forget, I'll write it down. "Look what that actor did there," or "Look how the camera reveals that." And then, maybe there's a moment where I know, "OK, this is a pivotal part of the scene." And so I'll either go forward or backward from there, and shape the whole scene around that moment.

What happens after the rough cut?

A film gets created in layers. First you're dealing with the arcs of the individual scenes, then the arc of three scenes together, then the arc of the entire movie. That's why it takes so long to edit a movie. It's not because it takes six months to get it to where you can see it from beginning to end, it's because once it's all together, that's when you can finally start to do the work of the movie instead of the individual scenes.

Do you read the script before you start editing?

Absolutely, otherwise I would be completely lost. But scripts have a tendency to be slightly overwritten. It's the nature of the beast. A writer has to communicate what's going on in people's heads somehow. And a lot of times that comes out through dialogue. When it gets performed, however, suddenly words are coming out of their mouth that don't seem natural because you can see so much in a look or an expression.

That's exactly what happened at the end of Traffic, when Michael Douglas is giving that speech. That speech was twice as long as what's in the movie, and what happened was the way he delivered it, you could feel all the things that the script had him saying in the second half of the speech. A lot of times you end up cutting lines of dialogue, or huge sections of stuff, because an actor did something more efficiently with the way he raised his eyebrows or moved his head. Something as simple as that can make three paragraphs of dialogue completely unnecessary.

How does the budget affect your editing style?

Well, on a movie like Oceans Eleven, we shoot it, we cut it, we do a preview screening. There's money in the budget to say, "Okay, there's this whole section here that we really can't fix editorially; let's go back and do some re-shooting." You can't do that with an indie film. You either get it or you don't and you just have to make everything work.

CHAPTER FIVE
Basic Editing

All right. You're ready. You've committed to memory all the definitions, theories, patterns, and procedures in Chapters 1, 2, 3, and 4. You've looked at every frame of your footage and logged all the good stuff. There's plenty of fresh coffee. You've already spent your first paycheck.

Let's do it.

IF IT WERE EASY, EVERYONE WOULD DO IT

If I haven't made it clear by now that editing is a very complex task, let me state that fact explicitly here. When you sit down at the editing console, you have to bear in mind all of the rules and ideas presented in the earlier chapters—more or less simultaneously. For every shot you look at, you must pay close attention to the visual content, the audio content, the emotional and thematic content, and the compositional characteristics. What's worse, you must be acutely aware of all these things not just for one clip but for *two* clips: the ones on both sides of each edit point.

Is your brain tired yet? Sorry, there's more. Don't forget to think about the impact of the juxtaposition of the two images and tracks. For continuity cuts you must be aware of the three-dimensional space and time within the frame and how the two images maintain or destroy their seeming reality. Remember to maintain screen direction, continuity of motion and action within the frame, and... The list goes on and on.

Most important, film is a time-based medium—and to edit successfully, you need to find the flow of the show. You can't possibly do any of this (let alone *all* of this) if you're constantly being interrupted by your software.

Grooving With Your Software

As a matter of fact, the most important thing your video-editing software can do is stay the hell out of the way so you can focus on the complex business of editing your project as brilliantly as possible. Anything that interferes with the process of translating ideas from your brain into your show is an obstacle, not a tool.

Novices at digital video editing often have a hard time understanding the critical differences between various editing platforms. In a magazine ad, the bullet lists of features offered by Adobe Premiere, Avid Media Composer, Discreet Edit, and Final Cut Pro look very similar. But real life in the editing room is more than bullet points, and as far as I'm concerned, Final Cut Pro is the best editing software you can use. Why? Good workflow.

Software should be like an extension of your body. The best analogy I can make is to a musical instrument. Once you've learned how to hold the bow or vibrate the reed, you can translate your thoughts and ideas directly into music, and eventually you aren't thinking about the individual steps required to produce the sound. The instrument disappears.

Similarly, once you master the basic controls of Final Cut Pro, you will be able to groove with the software in a way where the user interface seems to disappear, and you can simply translate your thoughts and ideas into sequences of images and sounds on the screen. We've all known a mechanic with a favorite wrench. Our goal in building Final Cut Pro was to create a tool that earned the love of the editors who used it.

Some of the things that make Final Cut Pro stand out become apparent only after you've worked with it for a while. For one thing, it has very few dialog boxes to slow you down. In general, software hits you with a dialog box when it doesn't know what to do next. ("Excuse me, where should I save this file?") By definition, this interrupts the workflow. Some such disruptions are inevitable, but as much as possible Final Cut will avoid annoying you when it doesn't have to.

Modal software is another obstacle to smooth workflow. In order to perform a specific task, modal software forces you to stop working and switch into a different mode—usually via a menu or keyboard shortcut. For instance, many video-editing applications force users to switch modes from working with clips to working with sequences, or from making an edit to applying a filter. Final Cut Pro avoids this distracting process.

Nonetheless, for all its elegant simplicity, Final Cut Pro is a sophisticated tool, and consequently it offers so many choices about how to perform basic editing functions that it can be daunting to a new user.

For instance, the software lets you perform your basic edit (putting a clip in a sequence) in just about any way you can imagine. You can drag a clip from the Browser to the Timeline or the Canvas. You can open a clip in the Viewer and drag it from there. You can use a keyboard shortcut or you can click a button on the screen. And then, for each of those methods, you have seven additional permutations to choose from to determine exactly *how* you want the edit to be executed (Insert, Overwrite, and so on). And while there is no right way or wrong way, there *are* reasons to make different choices depending on the circumstances of the edit.

And now the good news. Final Cut Pro was designed in a way that enables you to use the simpler features without needing to know anything about the advanced ones. However, this requires some discipline.

So here's some important advice: Don't go poking around in all the menus or clicking around all the different tabs in each window. Stick to a few basic operations as shown in this chapter, and learn them before you try to absorb everything that the software can do. The key to working successfully with whatever tool you choose is to figure out which of its features you'll be using all the time, learn them well, and ignore the rest of the bells and whistles for now.

In this chapter, I'll highlight the most important controls, give you a few hints about the ones you should ignore, and offer some tips about when to choose one particular editing method over another.

WORKING WITH CLIPS

Once you've captured and catalogued all your clips, you're ready to begin editing—and at this stage, that means assembling sequences. Depending on the type of show you're building, you may go about this in different ways. But the first thing you need to know is how to select and extract the precise parts of those clips you want to include in your sequence.

Marking Clips

Every clip should have some "slop"—unnecessary frames surrounding the section you'll eventually select to use in the show. Before you move a clip from the Browser into a sequence, you should open it in the Viewer and mark the precise section you want to use (**Figure 5.1**). Identify this segment by setting In and Out points at the start and end of the section.

Figure 5.1 View your clips in the Viewer before editing them into a sequence.

 The left side of this pill-shaped button will set your In point, and the right side will set your Out point.

Use the Keyboard, Not the Mouse

Software designers don't always get everything they want. One of my biggest complaints about the user interface for Final Cut Pro is that the most commonly used buttons are way too small. Using the mouse to place the pointer right on top of small controls requires fine motor skill movements with lots of repetition. This leads to fatigue and may cause repetitive stress injury.

Fortunately, Final Cut Pro has keyboard shortcuts for almost every command in the program. For the sake of your health, please learn them and use them. (See the Keyboard Shortcuts table later in this chapter for a list of the ones you'll use all the time.)

The first controls you should learn are the basic playback and marking controls you'll use to move around inside the clip and mark the In and Out points. Fortunately, these are easy to remember.

The (Spacebar) starts and stops playback; to play backward, hold down (Shift) while pressing the (Spacebar).

Set your In point by hitting ⓘ. Set your Out point by hitting ⓞ.

For more precise playback control, you can use ⓙ, ⓚ, and ⓛ. The arrangement of these keys is not accidental. By placing your hand over this area of your keyboard, you'll have one-finger access to all the most important controls (**Figure 5.2**).

Figure 5.2 The keyboard layout is designed so you can move around inside a clip and set markers without ever having to take your hand off the keyboard. The most common controls are literally right at your fingertips.

ⓙ plays backward, ⓚ pauses playback, and ⓛ plays forward. Tapping ⓙ or ⓛ multiple times will play faster and faster. Holding down both ⓙ and ⓚ, or ⓚ and ⓛ, will play at half speed.

ⓘ sets your In point and ⓞ sets your Out point. (Option)-ⓘ or (Option)-ⓞ will clear those points. (Shift)-ⓘ or (Shift)-ⓞ moves your playhead to that point.

Hitting ⓜ adds a marker at the current position.

Mark It While It's Playing

To make accurate decisions about where your In and Out points should be placed, set them while the video is playing at regular speed—as opposed to *jogging* (**Figure 5.3**) or *shuttling* (**Figure 5.4**) through the clip. This is critical if you want to understand the proper timing of the clip.

Figure 5.3 The Jog wheel plays the clip forward or backward, frame by frame, when you roll it left or right. ⬅ and ➡ on your keyboard do the same thing.

Figure 5.4 The Shuttle control plays the clip forward and backward at variable speeds. The farther you drag the handle from center, the faster the clip plays.

> ***JOGGING*** *A way of moving through a clip frame by frame, using the Jog wheel or* ⬅ *and* ➡ *to go forward or backward one frame at a time.*
>
> ***SHUTTLING*** *A way of moving through a clip at variable speed by using the Shuttle control. Hitting the play keys* J *and* L *multiple times serves as the keyboard equivalent.*

You can set the In and Out points as many times as you like while you're working on a clip, but since there can be only one In and one Out point in any given clip, only the last one sticks.

Mark It Like a Pro

With hundreds (or thousands) of In and Out points to set in a show, the faster and more smoothly you can place them, the better off you'll be. Here's how a professional editor marks a clip:

1. Double-click the clip in the Browser to open it in the Viewer window.

2. Hit L to begin playback.

3. Hold your finger over I, and keep tapping it until the action is just about to begin.

4. Stop tapping it when the section you want to use begins.

The last tap sets the In point for the clip.

The better you know the footage, the better you'll know when to start the shot. But even so, it's easy to wait too long. You can set the In and Out points while playing backward, too, so if you miss the beginning of the action, tap J for backward play and reset your In point to the correct spot. Then resume forward play and prepare to set your Out point.

Many editors will tap O constantly as the clip plays, especially as it nears the end point. That way, when the right spot rolls by, they just stop tapping and the point is marked.

Find the Rhythm

Pay attention to the pace of your tapping for an early clue about the editing rhythm and pacing of a scene. I try to tap in a regular, rhythmic pattern. If I find myself tapping in a dance club groove of 180 beats per minute (bpm), I know the scene is going to require fast cutting to match the rhythm inherent in the shot. If I'm tapping at a leisurely 30 bpm (about the rhythm of a Frank Sinatra standard), I can prepare for longer shots and less frequent edits.

Typically, action shots inspire faster tapping, and dialogue shots call for slower tapping, but sometimes you'll be surprised. On one show I was cutting about occupational safety, I was so bored by the narrator that I found myself tapping [O] faster and faster while listening to his droning instructions. Although a conservative and slow editing pace seemed most appropriate for the show, I realized that my viewers would probably find the narrator's voice just as mind-numbing as I did—so I sped up the editing pace and offset some of the impact of that soporific narration.

Tapping has the added benefit of working off the effects of drinking too much coffee during the editing session, but if you want to preserve your fingertips and the springiness of your keyboard, you can simply hold down [I] or [O] and let it up at the spot you want to mark. (Too much tapping can be hard on your hands and wrists.)

Marking Subclips

Sometimes a clip will contain more than one section you want to use. In those cases, you can create subclips and have access to all the good sections.

For example, you may have several shots in one clip. This happens frequently with documentary B-rolls. Let's say you're working on a documentary about high schools, and the camera crew captured lots of snippets of kids in the hallway between classes. When you were logging the footage, you grabbed big chunks of the reel to sort out later, rather than chopping them up into loads of tiny clips. Now it's time to sort them out.

Or maybe you have several takes of the same shot all wrapped into one clip. This happens frequently when the camera crew is shooting a short action like a button being pushed or a handshake. They'll film the action several times in one take, and the series of actions winds up getting logged as one clip.

Or sometimes lazy assistant editors (with access to unlimited disk space) will log and capture the whole tape as one huge clip. I don't recommend this. It saves time during logging, but you'll just have that much more junk to wade through and eliminate once you begin editing. It also means that you're not watching the footage very closely. However, if you end up having to work with one of these huge clips, you can use the subclip controls to break it up into bite-size pieces.

How to Mark Subclips

Marking subclips is very much like logging footage, except it happens after the clips have already been captured. Begin by marking the clip as described above. Once you've set the In and Out points, select Make Subclip from the Modify menu (**Figure 5.5**) or hit ⌘-Ⓤ. As soon as you do this, a new item with a new icon appears in the Browser at the same location as the parent clip.

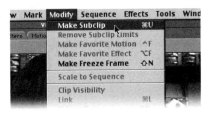

Figure 5.5 Make Subclip is found under the Modify menu. The keyboard shortcut is ⌘-Ⓤ.

Final Cut assumes that the first thing you want to do with your new subclip is rename it, and it brings the Browser window forward with the Name field automatically selected so you can type a descriptive name for your subclip (**Figure 5.6**). Unlike filenames, subclip names can be as long as you want. (I think the limit is 32,768 characters, but who's counting?) The contents of the various Browser columns such as Comment fields and Log Notes are copied from the parent clip (or *master clip*) to the new subclip, but once the subclip is created, you can change the contents of any column without affecting the master clip. This enables you to search and sort your subclips more easily throughout the editing process.

MASTER CLIP *The clip from which a subclip was generated.*

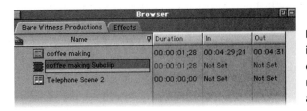

Figure 5.6 When a new subclip is created, the Browser window comes forward so you can name your new clip. Note that a subclip has a special icon.

Creating a subclip does not make a new file on your hard disk; it merely makes a new reference to the file from which the master clip came. Once created, subclips can be treated exactly like any other clip—including using them to generate more subclips.

Use the Go to Master Clip Command

One nice feature of subclips is that you can get back to the parent clip at any time by using the Go to Master Clip command from the Go To submenu of the Mark menu (**Figure 5.7**), or by pressing (Shift)-(F) on the keyboard. This can be helpful if you're editing a subclip and realize you need it to be a few frames longer to allow room for a transition or speed effect. With the Go to Master Clip command, you can jump back to the master clip and have access to all the original frames.

Another way to add frames to the subclip is to use the Remove Subclip Limits command from the Modify menu. This resets the In and Out points of the sub-clip to those of the parent clip. Beware, though: This change is permanent.

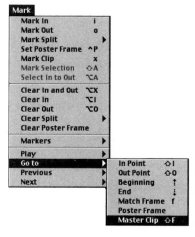

Figure 5.7 Go to Master Clip can be found in the Go To submenu under the Mark menu. The keyboard equivalent is (Shift)-(F).

TIP: *Some of Final Cut Pro's file management features don't work very well with subclips. This includes exporting EDLs, the Reconnect function, recapturing files, and using the Media Manager. Every once in a while the link to the master clip can be lost—in which case the program will mistake the subclip for a proper clip. Although these problems aren't widespread, if you are relying on EDLs or any of these other features, to be absolutely safe I recommend avoiding the use of subclips.*

WORKING WITH MARKERS

As I mentioned in Chapter 4, "Preparing to Edit," markers are one of the most valuable and versatile tools available to you as an editor. Final Cut Pro's markers are very robust, and once you begin working with them, you will continually find new uses for them.

Marking a Moment in Time

You'll recall that at its simplest, a marker is just a placeholder or bookmark you can attach to a given frame of your clip or sequence. When a clip has a marker attached to it, that marker sticks around even when the clip is edited into a sequence. Although there is no functional difference, markers attached to a clip are called clip markers and markers attached to a sequence are called sequence markers. You can place as many markers as you like in any clip or sequence.

Set a marker by clicking the Add Marker button on the Viewer or Canvas (**Figure 5.8**), selecting Add from the Markers submenu of the Mark menu (**Figure 5.9**), or using a keyboard shortcut. You can use either Ⓜ or ⓐ (the one on the upper left corner of your keyboard next to ⓵) to add a marker to the current frame in either the Viewer or the Canvas. All markers can be set while the video is playing forward, backward, and at high or slow speeds (as is true for In and Out points, which are just special kinds of markers).

Add Marker

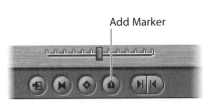

Figure 5.8 Clicking the Add Marker button adds a marker at the current position. The keyboard equivalent is to type Ⓜ or ⓐ. If you are already parked on a marker, this button will open the Edit Marker dialog box.

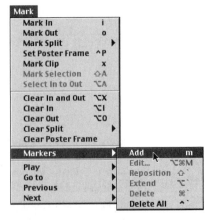

Figure 5.9 You can also create a marker by choosing Add from the Marker submenu of the Mark menu.

Markers will be applied to the current selection. If you have a clip selected in the Timeline, and you set a marker over that clip, the marker will go into the clip (**Figure 5.10**). If the clip isn't selected, the marker will go into the Timeline itself (**Figure 5.11**).

Figure 5.10 If a clip is selected in the Timeline, adding a marker will place it in the selected clip.

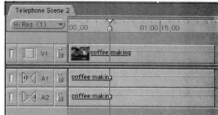

Figure 5.11 If no clip is selected, the marker will be applied to the sequence.

What Do Markers Look Like?

Markers are visible in every window in the program. In the Viewer and Canvas *Scrubber areas,* markers appear as little pink flags (**Figure 5.12**). When the playhead parks on a frame identified by a marker, the flag turns yellow and the Viewer or Canvas displays the name of the marker overlaid on the video image.

SCRUBBER AREA *A graphic representation of the length of the clip or sequence. The playhead, In and Out points, and markers are all indicated.*

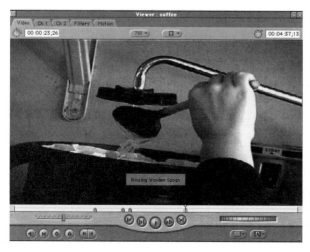

Figure 5.12 In the Viewer or Canvas windows, markers show up as small flags. Names and comments do not appear while footage is playing.

In the Timeline, clip markers appear as flags on the clips themselves, and sequence markers appear in the ruler at the top of the window (see Figures 5.10 and 5.11). The Canvas will display the marker name only when parked on a sequence marker.

Even the Browser shows markers. A clip with a marker attached will appear in the Browser with a revealer (or "twiddle"). Activating the twiddle will display a list of markers and their names (**Figure 5.13**).

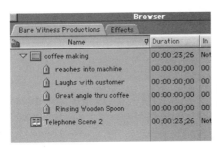

Figure 5.13 If a clip has markers attached to it, the Browser will display a revealer next to the Clip icon. Twiddling it open reveals a list of all the markers in the clip.

What's Worth Marking? And When?

I use markers to identify many different things: stuff I like; stuff I don't like; areas that need further work; areas that are complete; sound cues I want to use as sync or snap points. And sometimes I just use them to make notes to myself or my assistant (when I'm lucky enough to *have* an assistant).

Set Markers While Logging Clips

You can save yourself lots of time if you set markers while you're logging clips (see the section on setting markers in Chapter 4). I use them to mark areas that are probable cut points or areas that are clearly unusable in the midst of a good clip.

For example, if I were logging footage of highway traffic filmed from the back of a truck, I might make one long clip for the entire time the camera was rolling. But then I'd use markers to identify when the camera zoomed in or out to frame specific cars, a section where the camera went out of focus for a few moments, a spot where a passing driver's face was recognizable (which I couldn't use, since I wouldn't have a release from the driver), and a particularly great moment when a motorcycle split the lanes of traffic and screamed past the lens. Once the clip was logged and captured, all of these important moments would be identified and visible whenever I viewed the clip.

Use Markers as Reminders

There's a limit to how many things you can hold in your mind at the same time, but you can use markers to leave little reminders for yourself.

I often use markers to hold my place in a sequence or make a note about something I need to fix while I go off and tweak something else. Many times when I'm playing a sequence after making some adjustment, I'll be struck with new ideas, or I'll see edit points that need work. Since I can do only one thing at a time, I usually drop a few markers in at the trouble spots so I'll be able to remember the things I want to work on.

Use Markers as a Third Hand

Working with just In and Out points is like having only two hands. And while two hands are good enough most of the time, sometimes we all wish we had a third one. Markers can give us that extra advantage.

For example, one sequence in *Want* features Ben and Trey dreaming about ideas for start-up businesses while driving along the highway. At one point Ben looks out the window and sees a billboard that gives him an idea.

Whenever I edit a sequence, I'm constantly using my In and Out points to identify where my next edit is going to be (see the section on three-point editing later in this chapter). In this case, I wanted to drop in the cutaway of the billboard at just the right moment to match Ben's eyeline when he looks out the car window, and I wanted to cut back to the car on a particular line of Trey's. (There are my In and Out points.)

Since the billboard was a moving shot, and the words on the ad would be most easily legible at a particular instant, I used a marker in the cutaway clip to flag the sweet spot for reading the billboard. I wanted that spot to hit the Timeline at just the instant when Ben's eyes light up as he gets his idea, so I used another marker to identify *that* point in the Timeline **(Figure 5.14)**. Lining up the two markers in the Timeline enabled me to create the perfect effect.

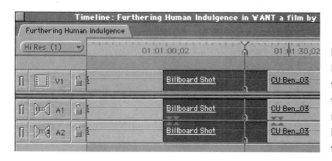

Figure 5.14 In this example I used a marker in the clip to identify the best frame of the cutaway and a second marker in the sequence itself to highlight where the cutaway should go.

Use Markers for Making Split Edits

Markers can be very helpful when planning L or J cuts (see the section on split edits in Chapter 2, "Film Language"). You can mark the spot where you want audio or video to begin or end separately from the primary In and Out points.

> **TIP:** *Clips move around in the Timeline while you're editing. If you want to mark an important moment in a sequence, think twice about whether you want to use a clip marker or a sequence marker. A sequence marker will stick to an exact location in time, regardless of which clip it happens to land on. A clip marker will stick with the clip and move with it as you edit the sequence.*

Name Markers Wisely

Three weeks from now, you probably won't remember what "Marker 27" or "Here" means. Use a name that will remind you why you marked this spot in the first place. Good marker names should be very specific: "License plate visible," "Good match for Trey's POV," or "Soft focus" will be much more useful than "Here."

To name a marker, park on the frame where the marker is located and open the Edit Marker dialog box (**Figure 5.15**). You can access this dialog box by clicking on the Add Marker button again (the first click sets the marker; the second click opens the Edit Marker window) or typing Ⓜ or Ⓒ on the keyboard. Note that a marker can have both a name and a comment. Both will be displayed in the Viewer or Canvas overlay.

Figure 5.15 The Edit Marker dialog box lets you modify all the parameters of a marker or simply delete it.

Mark a Range of Time

You may have noticed the Duration field in the Edit Marker dialog box and wondered what it was for. Few beginners realize that markers can have duration, but this is a feature that professional editors use all the time.

Not only can you mark a moment of time, you can use a single marker to denote a whole range of time. Rather than simply indicating when the motorcyclist begins his ride between the lanes, you can mark the whole ride, from the moment we first see him until he passes the lens.

This compounds the usefulness of markers because now each marker has its own In and Out point. Not only can the marker serve as your third hand, one marker can actually be a second *pair* of hands.

Deleting Markers

Once a marker has served its purpose, delete it. Having a bunch of markers that are no longer relevant will clutter up your workspace and may confuse you the next time you want to create a new marker. Even if you're pretty sure you can tell the new ones from the old ones (and if you didn't give them all descriptive, custom names you'll be regretting it now!), sorting out extraneous markers will distract you and slow you down.

There are three ways to delete a marker:

- Park on it and choose Delete from the Marker section of the Mark menu.

- Option-click the Set Marker button.

- Press ⌘-`.

You can also delete all the markers in a clip or sequence by choosing Delete All from the Markers submenu of the Mark menu or pressing Ctrl-`.

Navigating With Markers

Once you begin using markers, you'll want to find them quickly. Here's how the pros do it.

Using the Previous and Next Marker Controls

You can move your playhead quickly from marker to marker within a clip or sequence using the Previous and Next Marker controls. You'll find them on the Mark menu, or you can use the keyboard shortcuts Shift-M (next marker) and Option-M (previous marker).

A third technique is to use ↑ and ↓ while holding down Shift; this stops at all markers. (Ordinarily, you can use ↑ and ↓ to navigate through your sequence, but unless you hold down Shift, you will stop only at edit points and the In and Out markers.)

> **TIP:** *Make sure to check your selection before trying to navigate to markers in the Timeline. If a clip is selected, markers in that clip will be included when you go to the next or previous marker. If the clip isn't selected, those markers will be ignored.*

Jumping to Markers

Another handy way to navigate between markers is by using the Shortcut menu on the Current Position field in the Viewer or Canvas (**Figure 5.16**). All the markers in the clip or sequence will be listed at the bottom of the menu. Clicking a marker name will take your playhead right to that spot. This shortcut is also available on the ruler in the Timeline and on the rulers in the Filter and Motion tabs.

Figure 5.16 All the markers in a clip or sequence are listed in the Shortcut menu, which can be accessed by Ctrl -clicking on the Current Position field in the upper right corner of the window. Selecting one of the marker names will jump your playhead right to that spot.

To access clip markers within a sequence, open the Shortcut menu on any clip in the Timeline. All visible markers will be listed at the bottom of that menu as well (**Figure 5.17**).

Figure 5.17 Within a sequence, clip markers can be accessed via the Shortcut menu on the clip itself. Selecting one of the marker names will move the playhead right to the marker.

I find these features especially helpful when I'm cleaning up the rough cut of a long show. First I watch the whole show and set markers at the areas where I know I want to make changes. Then, using one of these navigation shortcuts, I can jump right to the spots I want to fix. Once each spot is clean, I delete the marker and go on to the next one.

Searching for Markers

Although Final Cut Pro's Search feature is quite robust in the Browser, searching for something in a sequence is far less flexible. You can look only for clip names, timecode values, and, yes, markers (**Figure 5.18**). You can search for text in both the Name and Comment field of the marker, and the Find dialog will take you right to that spot.

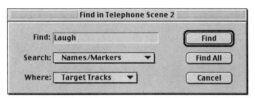

Figure 5.18 The Sequence Find tool allows you to search for clip names, timecode values, marker names, and comments.

TIP: Final Cut's Sequence Find tool only searches forward from the playhead and doesn't wrap around to the beginning of the sequence when it's through. Therefore, it's usually a good idea to hit Home *to bring you to the beginning of the sequence before performing a Timeline find.*

Snapping to Markers

One of the most useful things about markers is that they can be sticky. When you enable *snapping* in the Timeline, both clip and sequence markers will act as snap points.

> **SNAPPING** *A Timeline state. When snapping is turned on, certain items attract and grab other objects (such as clip edges, edit points, In and Out points, the playhead, keyframes, and markers) that are dragged nearby.*

You can toggle snapping on and off by hitting N or clicking the Snapping indicator in the Timeline window (**Figure 5.19**). When you drag a clip with markers into a sequence, the markers are visible to be used as snap points during the drag (**Figure 5.20**).

—Snapping indicator

Figure 5.19 The Snapping indicator, possibly the tiniest control in Final Cut Pro, lights up green when snapping is enabled and dims to gray when it's disabled. Clicking on the control will toggle the snapping state, but it's much easier to use the keyboard shortcut by typing N. This shortcut works even while the mouse button is pressed, so you can toggle snapping on and off while you are dragging to help you complete your drag.

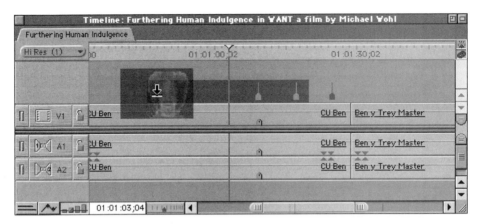

Figure 5.20 Dragging a clip that has markers attached will display those markers as the clip is dragged into a sequence. This can be very helpful for lining up important frames in your shots.

Reposition Marker

Since markers behave a lot like In or Out points, you would expect to be able to set a marker by tapping a key until just the right moment occurs, the same way I described for setting In and Out points earlier. And you'd be almost right. It just takes one additional key.

For example, if you notice an audio glitch in a clip, you might want to identify it with a marker to be cleaned up later. So you play the sequence, and (just as if you were setting an In or Out point), you begin tapping ` as you approach the spot where the glitch should be. You stop when you hear the glitch. Unfortunately, since markers work slightly differently than In and Out points, you have just set 30 or 40 new markers, one for each time you tapped the key.

But hey, don't worry. Final Cut Pro has a special feature just for this situation. It's called Reposition Marker. You access it by holding down (Shift) while you tap the ` key. Then, instead of setting a new marker each time you tap, it sets just one marker and moves it along until you stop tapping.

Extend Marker

Since markers can have duration, you can set In and Out points for the marker that are separate from the In and Out points for the whole clip. And you're probably going to want to set them on the fly. Use the Extend Marker command to set a marker's Out point; the keyboard shortcut Option -⟨`⟩ lets you set it on the fly. For example, imagine you're making a video about earthquake safety. You've shot a re-enactment of an earthquake, and during the shot the actors all reacted to an imaginary earthquake. The camera operator even shook the camera to further the effect, but now you need to add a rumbling sound to really sell it.

You've already set In and Out points for the clip identifying the whole scene and dropped it into a sequence. Now you play the sequence back, and at the first frame where the camera begins to shake, you hit ⟨`⟩ or M to set the marker. It will be stamped wherever the playhead is at the moment you hit the key. When the shaking is all done, hit Option -⟨`⟩, and the marker will be extended to that point, covering the entire duration of the earthquake. Now, when you drop in your sound effect, you know exactly where to lay it (**Figure 5.21**).

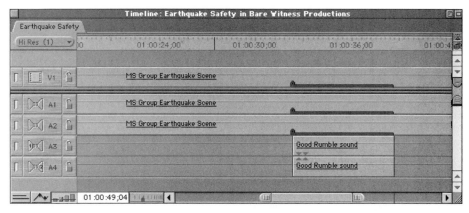

Figure 5.21 When you've set duration for a marker, its flag grows a tail that extends the length of the marker. Both ends will act as snap points. In this case, I can use the extended marker to help me lay in a sound effect for the earthquake safety video.

Subclips in Disguise

One interesting (and little-known) fact about markers is that they are actually sub-clips in disguise. When you twiddle open a clip in the Browser, the markers will be listed below the clip. If you double-click on one of the markers, it will open in the Viewer as a subclip. (If the marker has no specified duration, the subclip will begin at the marker point and extend until the end of the master clip.) You can drag the marker and drop it right into a sequence, or even another bin, and it will act exactly like a subclip.

Thanks to this feature, if you understand how to set extended markers (markers with duration) as explained previously, you can use markers as an alternate way of creating subclips.

This is one reason for setting your markers while logging; you get the benefit of a single large file, but the subclips you need for editing are right there when you open up the clip.

Mark Music Beats

Here's another nifty trick you can do with markers. Often when editors are cutting a program to music, they need to arrange the edits to fall right on the beat. Someday, I hope, Final Cut Pro will have a feature that automatically detects the beats in the music, but until then, you can use markers to make a pretty close approximation.

Play back the music clip, rest your finger right above ⌐, and tap along with the beat. If your rhythm isn't great, you may need to delete all the markers (⌐Ctrl⌐-⌐) once or twice, but eventually your markers will hit right on the beat. Now, drop this clip into your sequence and voilà! You've got automatic snap points to help you decide where to make your edits (**Figure 5.22**).

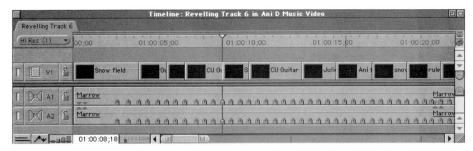

Figure 5.22 By tapping ⌐ in time to the music, you can add markers on every beat. These can be helpful if you are trying to make your cuts to the beat of a song. Remember, every marker is a snap point you can use to align your edits.

BUILDING SEQUENCES

Assembling clips into sequences is the most primal act of editing—and Final Cut Pro provides nearly 20 ways to do it. While this might seem overwhelming, once you understand when to use each method (and which ones you can forget altogether), this level of versatility will prove invaluable.

Final Cut Pro is a *source/record* editor. Clips to be edited are "loaded" into the Viewer the way traditional tapes were loaded into a source deck to be played back. Then, bit by bit, sections of the clips are copied from the Viewer to the Canvas (Final Cut Pro's version of the record deck).

> **SOURCE/RECORD** *Traditional videotape-based editing systems comprised two tape decks: one to play back the source tapes, and one to record the master sequence. This model has carried over into the digital realm, even though tape decks are no longer required.*

Just as with the tape-based systems, Final Cut Pro is nondestructive. On the old systems, content was copied from the source tapes to the master, leaving the source tapes unmodified. Similarly, in Final Cut Pro, the clips you load into the Viewer are not modified when you edit them into the Canvas.

Three-Point Editing

Before we delve too deeply into the nuances of the different types of edits, and when you should choose one over another, we need to discuss the nature of *three-point editing*.

Every edit you make has four points (**Figure 5.23**):

- the starting point of the source clip (the Viewer In point).
- the ending point of the source clip (the Viewer Out point).
- where the clip will begin in the sequence (the Canvas In point).
- where the clip will end in the sequence (the Canvas Out point).

If you supply three of the four points, the computer can figure out the fourth. (No rocket science required: If a clip starts at 0:00 and ends at 4:00, it's four seconds long—and no matter where you drop it into the sequence, it's still going to last four seconds. Therefore, if you begin it at 5:00 into the sequence, the computer can calculate that it will end at 9:00.)

> **TIP:** *If no In or Out point is specified in the sequence, the current playhead position is considered to be the In point. Because of this, if you're laying down clips one after another, or if you're placing the first clip in the sequence, no In point is required in the sequence.*

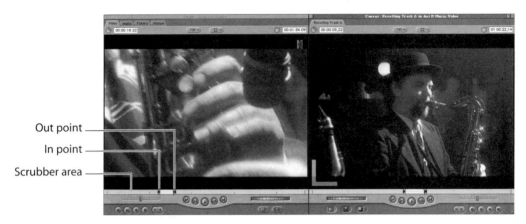

Out point
In point
Scrubber area

Figure 5.23 You can set In and Out points in both the Viewer and Canvas windows. The Scrubber area indicates how much media is available outside of the In and Out points.

Which Points Should You Provide?

You will want to choose different sets of three points for different circumstances.

Assembling Clips End to End

If you're assembling a number of clips end to end, as you might for a montage or a rough assembly, you are not going to be too worried about the sequence Out point. You will choose the clips you want to use, set In and Out points in the Viewer, and lay them into the sequence one by one (**Figure 5.24**). The three points you provide will be source In, source Out, and record In.

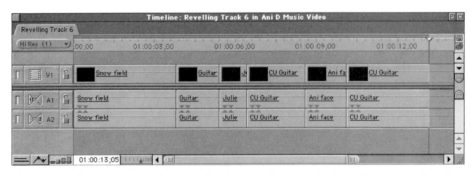

Figure 5.24 If you're assembling one clip after another, you don't need to worry about In or Out points in the sequence. Each clip will begin where the last one ended by default.

B-roll Editing

If you are laying down a long clip like an interview, and you're planning to go back and edit B-roll elements into the sequence, you'll use a combination of these approaches for choosing which of the four points you need to provide.

For the long clip (the interview), choose the source In and Out, and drop it into the sequence (**Figure 5.25**). Then, go back and listen to the interview. Find a section where you want to use a B-roll shot and mark a record In and Out point in the sequence (**Figure 5.26**). Let's say you mark an area five seconds long. When you find the B-roll shot and load it into the Viewer, you need only choose either a source In or a source Out point for the new clip. Either way, Final Cut Pro already knows it's going to be five seconds long.

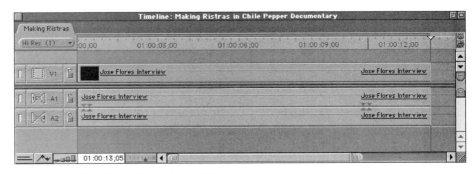

Figure 5.25 First, lay the interview clip into the sequence.

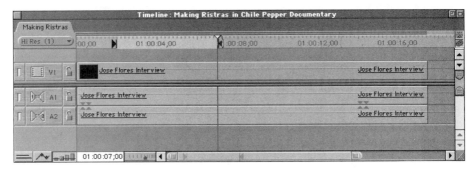

Figure 5.26 Next, set an In and Out point in the sequence where you would like the B-roll shot to appear when you perform your next edit.

You'll know whether to set the In or the Out depending on the footage. If the narrator is describing how to tie a ristra (an ornamental display of dried chiles) and your B-roll footage shows a man tying one, you may want to find the exact frame where he finishes and holds the ristra up to the camera. If you mark this as your source Out point, the shot will automatically begin five seconds earlier.

If it's more important for the B-roll shot to show how to start the ristra, then rather than defining the Out point, you should identify the In point and let the computer calculate when the shot should end.

If you must show the entire B-roll shot from beginning to end, from first twist to final knot, you can define both the source In and Out points—but then you'll have to give up one of the record points defined in the Canvas. You cannot stuff a 20-second source clip into a 5-second slot in your sequence. (Unless you speed up the clip, but we'll get to that later. See the section on fit to fill in Chapter 8, "Special Effects").

If you provide all four points, Final Cut Pro will ignore the source Out point.

> **TIP:** If no In or Out point is specified in the source clip, the first frame of the clip will be used as the In point. And if no Out point is specified in the Canvas (so there's no fixed duration), the entire source clip will be used.

Dialogue and Action Scenes

If you're laying down clips for a dialogue or action sequence, you'll probably use a combination of these types of edits. I usually begin with one angle (shot 1) and lay down more of it than I plan to use (**Figure 5.27**).

If I know I'm going to be cutting back to this shot later, I define two points in the Canvas (In and Out) and find an appropriate point (In or Out) in the source clip (**Figure 5.28**). Note that the frame I'm choosing in the Viewer should match continuity with the action in the Canvas. This way I will maintain continuity when I perform the edit.

If I don't plan to cut right back to shot 1, I'll pick two source points in the Viewer and set the Out point long, providing a little slop (**Figure 5.29**). Notice that the edit point still needs to be a continuity cut.

Figure 5.27 For dialogue and action sequences, I begin with one clip, adding enough extra space at the end to allow me to choose the edit point for the next shot.

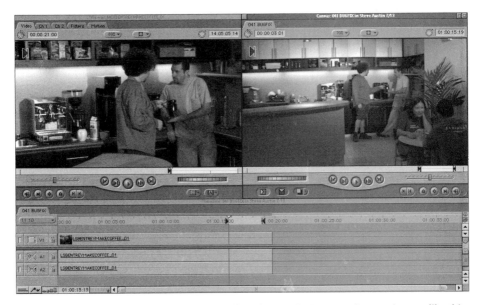

Figure 5.28 If I'm planning to return to this first shot again, I set my three points up like this: two record points in the Canvas and one source point in the Viewer. Ideally, both sides of the clip (two edits) will be continuity cuts. It may not be possible to match continuity on both sides in one operation; in that case I'll focus on the first edit and clean up the second one later.

Figure 5.29 If I'm not planning to cut back to the first clip, or I know that it's too hard to match continuity for both edits in one shot, I'll pick the source In and Out I want in the Viewer and just choose one record point in the sequence. I usually add a little slop at the end of the first clip, since I know I'll need to create another continuity cut with the next edit.

Picking the Right Editing Style

When you drag an item onto the Canvas, the semi-transparent Edit Overlay appears. It provides targets for the seven different types of edits available to you (**Figure 5.30**).

Figure 5.30 The Edit Overlay lets you make a decision about which edit type you want to apply *after* you've begun dragging your clip.

Overwrite Edits

Most edits you perform will be overwrite edits. This means that the footage you drag into the Canvas will replace the shots that were there before, just like pasting text onto a selection in a word processor. Since this is the most common type of edit, if you drag and drop a clip into the Canvas without using the Edit Overlay, the edit type defaults to overwrite. (Or you can simply press F10.) On the old videotape editing systems, all edits were overwrites. That was just the way it worked.

Choose Target Tracks

If you want to overwrite just the video, or just the audio, you must target the tracks to which you want the edit to apply (**Figure 5.31**). To do this, click the Film or Speaker icons to enable or disable a particular track. Alternately, you can click the Lock icon to lock tracks, which prevents edits from affecting those tracks. Keeping tabs on your target tracks complicates the decisions you must make for every edit you perform, but it'll soon become second nature.

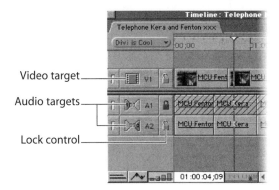

Figure 5.31 You'll find several important controls at the head of every track in the Timeline. The Film icon (for video) and the Speaker icon (for audio) enable you to select which tracks will be targeted in the next operation. If they're targeted, they light up yellow; if they're not targeted, they remain gray. If a track is not targeted for a given edit, the edit will ignore that track. This is one way of performing an audio-only or a video-only edit. Clicking the Lock control prevents all editing on the locked track. Locking a targeted track serves the same purpose as turning off targeting, because locked tracks cannot receive edits.

When you drag a clip onto the Canvas, the Edit Overlay displays the current target tracks to remind you what you're about to do (**Figure 5.32**). In the interview about ristra making I described, when laying in the B-roll clip you would make sure the audio was untargeted so the sound from the interview would not be overwritten and would continue playing underneath the B-roll image (**Figure 5.33**).

— Target track indicator

Figure 5.32 The Edit Overlay shows you your current track targets, so while you're dragging you will be sure you're getting what you want. In this example, both audio tracks are set to "None," indicating that this is a video-only edit.

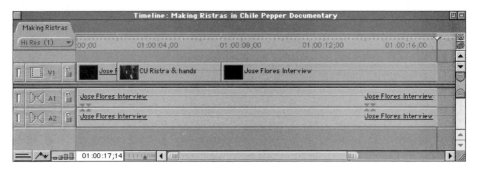

Figure 5.33 The overwrite edit "writes over" clips where the edit is applied. This is a video-only edit, so the interview can still be heard even while the B-roll image is displayed.

You can also use track targeting to help arrange your clips on multiple tracks. For example, if you designated tracks A5 and A6 exclusively for sound effects elements, you would target only those tracks every time you were about to edit a sound effect into the sequence.

Insert Edits

The second most common edit type is the insert edit. You can perform one by dragging your clip to the Insert target on the Edit Overlay or by pressing F9. An insert edit will *ripple* everything in the sequence forward in time (**Figure 5.34**). Remember: *When you perform an insert edit, your show gets longer.*

> **RIPPLE** *The act of pushing all the items in a sequence forward or backward in time to make room for new material. However long the new material is, that duration ripples through the entire sequence like a wave traveling down a rope.*

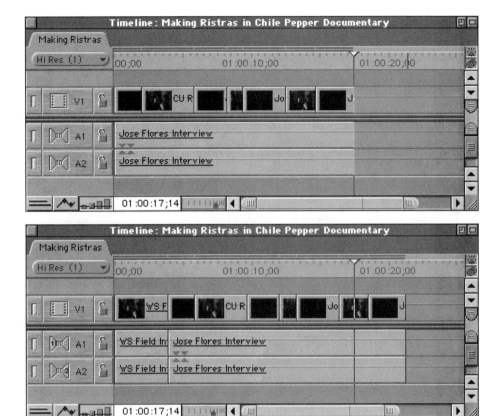

Figure 5.34 The insert edit pushes down everything in the sequence and makes it longer. Here, a shot was added at the head of the sequence.

Insert edits aren't possible on videotape-based editing systems, since you can't slide the entire contents of a sequence down the length of the videotape. However, when editors are physically cutting actual film, the insert edit is the only type of edit available. Every time you splice in a new piece of film, the reel gets longer.

Use Insert Edit for Adding a New Opening

The insert is a great edit to use when you're adding a clip to the head of a sequence—for instance, if you decide to add an establishing shot in front of shots you've already edited together (as shown in Figure 5.34 above).

Not for Video- or Audio-Only Edits

Don't use an insert edit if you plan to do a video-only or audio-only edit. The insert edit can knock clips out of sync *downstream* (**Figure 5.35**). Although Final Cut Pro will alert you that clips are out of sync and provides tools to fix the problem, it's easier to avoid the situation altogether.

> **DOWNSTREAM** *Events or clips that exist later in the sequence from the point where you're working are described as downstream. Events or clips that exist earlier in the sequence from the point where you're working are upstream.*

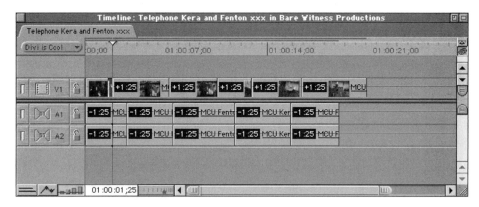

Figure 5.35 Any rippling operation has the potential to knock downstream clips out of sync. Final Cut Pro will usually warn you before allowing you to proceed with operations that will do this. Whenever a clip is out of sync, a bright red Out of Sync indicator appears. Not only does it tell you the clip is out of sync, it even tells you by how many frames. Ctrl -click the Out of Sync indicator to display options for resolving the problem.

When to Use Overwrite or Insert Edits With Transition

Both the overwrite edit and the insert edit can be performed with an automatic transition effect (such as a dissolve or wipe) built in. Final Cut Pro will apply whatever default transition you have previously selected from the Effects menu.

Although you won't use this function often, in some cases it can be helpful. For instance, it would be perfect for building a montage where you wanted every shot to be mixed together with a 50-frame dissolve.

To use the automatic transition feature, drag each shot onto the Insert or Overwrite with Transition target in the Edit Overlay. If you prefer to use a keyboard short-cut, hold down `Shift` when hitting the corresponding Function key (`Shift`-`F9` or `Shift`-`F10`).

Deleting Clips

Getting clips out of a sequence is just as important as putting them in. You might want to remove a clip or two to shorten a montage sequence that's running too long or speed up a dialogue scene by getting rid of the last exchange. You may want to remove a small section of a clip to create a better continuity cut or slice out just a piece of audio or video.

As with everything else in Final Cut Pro, there are many ways to delete clips. The key is knowing when to use which method.

Lift

The lift is the default type of deletion. To execute a lift, simply press `Delete`. Like an overwrite edit, a lift doesn't change the position of any surrounding clips; it simply removes the selected item and leaves a *gap* in its place. The length of the sequence will be unaffected.

> **GAP** *Final Cut Pro-speak for any empty space in a sequence. If you play across areas of gap, you'll either see black video or hear silent audio, depending on which tracks contain the gap.*

I use the Lift command to remove something when I'm not quite sure what to do next. Eventually I'll fill the gap with something, or remove it altogether, but lifting a section of the sequence allows me the luxury of delaying that decision.

> **TIP:** *Final Cut Pro will let you jump from gap to gap by hitting* `Shift`-`G` *to move to the next gap and* `Option`-`G` *to move to the previous gap.*

Lift is also a good way to remove an item from only one track of a particular sequence. Let's say you've got a dialogue shot where the audio was recorded on channel 2 only, but for some reason it was captured with both audio tracks (see the section on audio shapes in Chapter 7, "Cutting the Track"). Whenever you edit this clip into a sequence, you're carrying around an extra track of audio that's unnecessary. If you want to delete that one track, select it (using `Option` to tem-porarily override *linking*) and lift it from the sequence (**Figure 5.36**).

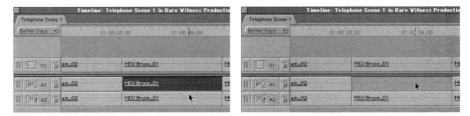

Figure 5.36 In order to remove a single track of audio, select it and choose Lift from the Sequence menu.

LINKING *Final Cut Pro links clips that should normally remain in sync (such as stereo audio tracks or clips originating from the same file). If you edit a linked clip, the other clips to which it is linked are affected, too. A Timeline state called linked selection (**Figure 5.37**) controls whether selecting items in the Timeline observes linking or ignores it. Deactivating linked selection makes it easier for clips to get out of sync but permits finer control of individual elements. Whatever the current state,* ⟨Shift⟩-⟨L⟩ *toggles it.*

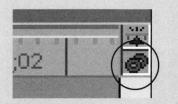

Fig 5.37 The Linked Selection control lights up green when it is active and dims to gray when it's disabled. The shortcut ⟨Shift⟩-⟨L⟩ toggles the state.

Another common use for the Lift command is to remove a clip on track V2 (such as a lower third graphic) without affecting the clips on the other tracks.

Ripple Delete

Ripple Delete (sometimes called extract) is the reverse of an insert edit. To execute a ripple delete, simply press ⟨Shift⟩-⟨Delete⟩ from the keyboard. This removes the selected elements from the sequence and automatically closes the gap. It's akin to removing a piece of film from a reel and splicing together the remaining pieces; the entire sequence gets shorter. However, Final Cut Pro will not be able to close the gap if edits on another track will be affected (**Figure 5.38**).

I generally use Ripple Delete if I've got a sequence with a bunch of clips stacked end to end and I want to remove one or more of them to shorten the show. In this case (since my intention is to make the program shorter), I know before I start that I intend to close the gap. So Ripple Delete is the perfect tool: It deletes the clip, selects the resulting gap, and deletes that, too, all in one step.

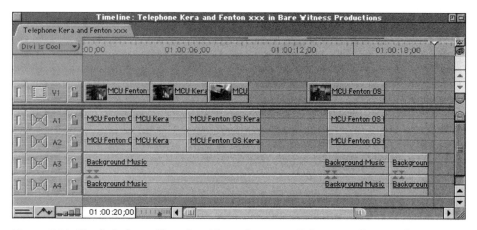

Figure 5.38 Ripple Delete will not be able to close gaps if there are clips on other tracks that are in the way. Here, although I deleted the clip from V1, A1, and A2, the edits on A3 and A4 prevented the gap from closing.

Remember that this operation (like all the delete functions) is not limited to clip boundaries. You can delete an area from within a single clip or across the borders of multiple clips. This is perfect for removing passages of dead space in an interview or even in a dialogue sequence.

For example: Recently, I began editing a scene from a Bare Witness project called *Telephone,* and I saw that the dialogue between two characters, Bruce and Rain, was a little redundant:

Rain: I've got this weird condition called hammertoe.

Bruce: Hammertoe? I've never heard of such a thing. Are you making this up?

Rain: No. It's serious, too. I've got to go to Mexico to get it treated. There's a clinic that specializes in holistic medicine. So I need to borrow some money to treat my hammertoe.

Bruce: Are you kidding me? It's called hammertoe? And you need to borrow money from me?

Rain: It's just fifteen hundred dollars...

During production we thought that the more times the actors said "hammertoe" the funnier the scene would be, but in the editing room the repetition seemed to slow the scene down. So I decided to remove the end of Rain's second line and the beginning of Bruce's second line to condense the sequence (**Figure 5.39**).

I set my In and Out points to mark the section I wanted to remove and used the Ripple Delete function to execute the edit (**Figure 5.40**).

> **TIP:** You can use the In and Out points to identify a particular section of a sequence, but for some operations you may need an actual selection. You can convert an area between the In and Out points (called the marked area) to a selection using the Select In to Out control located in the Mark menu, or through the keyboard shortcut Option-A. You can do the reverse (convert a selection to an In and Out) via the reverse control: Mark Selection (also under the Mark menu) or by hitting Shift-A.

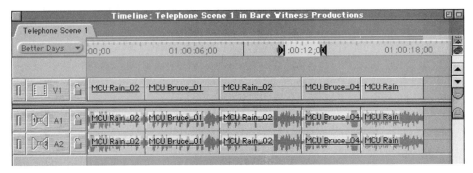

Fig 5.39 In this scene I wanted to remove the end of clip 3 and the beginning of clip 4, so I set my In and Out points to mark that area.

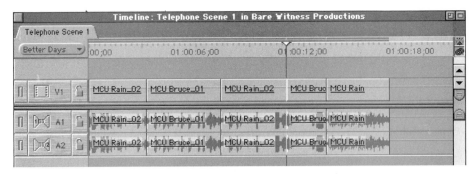

Fig 5.40 If nothing is selected, Ripple Delete will apply to the current In and Out points. In one step I eliminated parts of each clip and tightened the scene.

Ordinarily, when you're dragging items around in the Timeline, Final Cut Pro defaults to selecting whole clips. If you want to select a section of a clip, you can use the Range Selection tool, which allows you to grab areas not confined by edit points (**Figure 5.41**).

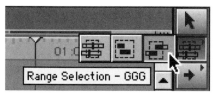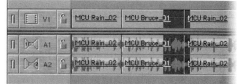

Figure 5.41 The Range Selection tool allows you to select any area of the Timeline regardless of clip boundaries.

Ripple Delete is best used on simple sequences. When you're working with a lot of tracks, it can become confusing, and you may end up knocking clips out of sync. Still, for simple cases it's a handy way to do several operations in one step.

Copy/Paste

Another common type of edit is the cut/copy/paste edit. These familiar commands will work on any selection you make in your Timeline. By default, Cut performs a lift, but it stores the selection on the clipboard so you can paste it somewhere else. Paste performs an overwrite edit on the target tracks at the current playhead position.

When would you use Cut and Paste instead of more customized editing tools? Sometimes you know a clip isn't working in its current location, and you want to find a new home for it in the sequence. For instance, say you're doing a show about Galileo, and you've got a great lithograph of a young Galileo with a filter applied. You tried laying it into the introduction, but it just didn't fit—and you aren't sure where it should go. Rather than deleting it, cut it—so it will hang out on the clipboard until you find a new place to put it. Then, when you find that perfect spot, rather than searching for your original clip, just hit Paste and there it is.

> **TIP:** You can choose to paste clips as an insert edit by pressing Shift-V. This works exactly like a normal paste, but instead of performing an overwrite edit, it does an insert.

Replace, Fit to Fill, Superimpose

Ninety percent of your edits will be some combination of the styles we've just discussed. However, Final Cut Pro offers three other edit types: replace, fit to fill, and superimpose. I'll cover the replace edit in Chapter 6, "Advanced Editing." The other two will be described in Chapter 8, "Special Effects." As a beginner, you should ignore all of them. You will be able to edit quite successfully using just Overwrite and Insert.

Drag and Drop Versus Keyboard Entry

You can perform any of the edits we've discussed by dragging a clip onto the Canvas and dropping it onto the corresponding target in the Edit Overlay. You'll also find buttons on the Canvas (**Figure 5.42**) that will perform the corresponding edit on the clip currently in the Viewer—and for every button, there is a keyboard equivalent.

Figure 5.42 One more way to perform edits is by pressing one of the buttons on the Canvas. Holding down the arrow on the third button will bring up a pop-up with the remaining edit styles.

When dragging clips directly into the Timeline, you can choose between executing an insert or an overwrite edit depending on where you drop the selection. Each Timeline track has a top and a bottom section (**Figure 5.43**). Dropping the clip in the top third will perform an insert edit, and dropping it in the bottom two-thirds will perform an overwrite edit.

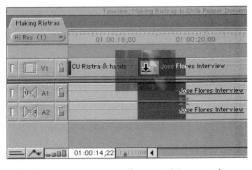

Figure 5.43 The top third of the track is for Insert, and when your mouse rolls over this area, the cursor turns into a right-facing arrow indicating that you will be pushing things downstream. When you roll over the larger bottom section, the cursor turns into a downward-facing arrow, indicating that the edit operation will place the clips right here (Overwrite). The clip highlight also changes from a hollow shadow for Insert to a solid shadow for Overwrite.

I am a big proponent of learning keyboard shortcuts. I've already mentioned the detrimental effect of repetitive mouse movements, but another, equally convincing reason is that it's much faster to hit a key on the keyboard than it is to click on an on-screen object and drag it around. The faster you can work, the more editing will feel like playing a musical instrument—and the less it will feel like filling out a tax form.

Still, as a beginner, you can start out applying all of these editing techniques with your mouse. As you discover which tasks you repeat thousands of times, you'll begin to learn the shortcuts that will make your editing experience easier, quicker, and healthier.

Keyboard Shortcuts

While the *Final Cut Pro 2 User's Manual* has an excellent and comprehensive chart of every keyboard shortcut in the program, I thought it would be helpful to summarize some of the ones you'll use most often (particularly those listed in this chapter), plus a few bonus ones you may find helpful:

PLAYBACK/NAVIGATION

Play Forward	Spacebar or L
Reverse Play	Shift-Spacebar or J
Slow Forward Play	L-K
Slow Backward Play	J-K
Fast Forward Play	LL, LLL, LLLL
Fast Backward Play	JJ, JJJ, JJJJ
Stop/Pause	Spacebar or K
1 Frame Forward	→
1 Second Forward	Shift-→
1 Frame Backward	←
1 Second Backward	Shift-←
Next Edit	↓ or Shift-E
Previous Edit	↑ or Option-E
Go to Beginning of Clip or Sequence	Home
Go to End of Clip or Sequence	End or Shift-Home
Play Around Current Position	\
Play In to Out	Shift-\
Play From Current to Out	Shift-P

SUBCLIPS

Make Subclip	⌘-U
Go to Master Clip	Shift-F

TIMELINE STATES

Snapping Toggle	N
Linked Selection Toggle	Shift-L
Zoom In on Timeline	Option-+
Zoom Out on Timeline	Option-− (minus sign)
Zoom Fit to Window	Shift-Z

MARKING CLIPS

Mark In	I
Mark Out	O
Clear In	Option-I
Clear Out	Option-O
Clear In and Out	Option-X
Go to In	Shift-I
Go to Out	Shift-O
Select In to Out	Option-A
Mark Selection	Shift-A

MARKERS

Set Marker	M or `
Edit Marker	M or ` (when parked on marker)
Delete Marker	⌘-`
Delete All Markers	Ctrl-`
Reposition Marker	Shift-`
Extend Marker	Option-`
Go to Next Marker	Shift-M
Go to Previous Marker	Option-M

COMMON TOOLS

Arrow/Selection Tool	A
Razor Blade Tool	B
Track Select Tool	T
Range Selection Tool	G G G

PERFORMING COMMON EDITS

Insert Edit	`F9`
Insert Edit With Transition	`Shift`-`F9`
Overwrite Edit	`F10`
Overwrite Edit With Transition	`Shift`-`F10`
Lift	`Delete`
Ripple Delete	`Shift`-`Delete`
Cut	`⌘`-`X`
Copy	`⌘`-`C`
Paste	`⌘`-`V`
Paste Insert	`Shift`-`V`

TRANSITIONS

Apply Default Transition	`⌘`-`T`
Set Alignment to Begin On	`Option`-`1`
Set Alignment to Center On	`Option`-`2`
Set Alignment to End On	`Option`-`3`

TIMELINE EDITING

Getting your clips into the sequence isn't the end of the editing process, it's just the beginning. Most of your time will be spent fine-tuning the clips and edits in the Timeline. (Remember the 80/20 rule: The last 20 percent of the editing process invariably takes 80 percent of the time.)

Like everything else, you can manipulate your Timeline clips in countless ways. There is no right or wrong method, and as you gain proficiency in the program, you'll probably experiment with some of the more advanced features.

In this chapter I will show you how to do what I call "no-trim editing." That means most of your edits will be done by dragging things around in the Timeline, using a simplified set of tools and avoiding the complex trim operations that I'll introduce in Chapter 6.

By nature, no-trim editing is fairly slow. If you want to make an adjustment to a particular edit point, such as shortening one clip and lengthening a second, many steps are involved. But in a strange way, the thing I like most about no-trim editing is precisely its slow nature. Every step is broken up, and it's easy to follow exactly what's happening.

Minimize Your Video Track Count

You can stack up as many as 99 layers of video in a Final Cut Pro Timeline—but it's not always a good idea to do that. In fact, when you're doing basic editing, you should strive to keep your edits on as few tracks as possible. (The time you'll need all those tracks is when you're doing compositing, where you may want to layer many tracks together to create complex collages.)

> **TIP:** Final Cut Pro Timeline displays tracks in top-down order, just like the layers in Photoshop. Clips with higher track numbers will obscure clips on lower tracks.

Ideally, you should put all of your edits on video track 1. This makes it easier to work with transitions (see the section on transitions, further along in this chapter) as well as simplifying media-management tasks like recapturing, reconnecting, and working with EDLs. The more tracks you use, the more likely you are to encounter one of a few known bugs in these functions and run into trouble.

Swap Edit

One advantage to putting all of your clips on a single track is the swap edit. This edit will rearrange the order of your clips without leaving a gap in the Timeline.

For instance, let's say that you're editing a dialogue sequence, and at some point you want to show an insert of a stolen watch on a player's wrist. Your first idea might be to put it right after shot 6, when the opposite player (a cop) mentions the theft (**Figure 5.44**).

Figure 5.44 The watch insert begins between shots 6 and 7.

After reviewing the sequence a few times, it occurs to you that you can heighten the suspense if you can get the audience thinking about the stolen watch even before the cop mentions it. So you decide to move the insert earlier in time, between shots 4 and 5.

Using the Swap tool makes this operation simple. Select the watch shot and drag it to its new position between shots 4 and 5. Before you drop it, press and hold (Option). Notice that the cursor changes to a curved arrow. This is the Swap cursor. When you release the mouse button, the shot will be inserted in that new position, and the gap that would have been left where the shot used to be is automatically closed (**Figure 5.45**).

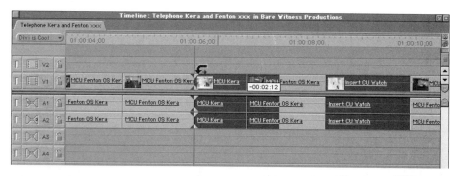

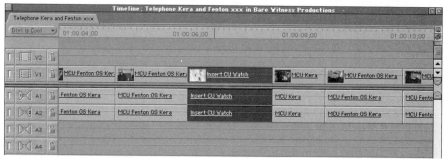

Figure 5.45 The Swap tool allows you to drag a clip to a different point in the sequence without generating gaps. The Swap tool is activated by hitting (Option) when dropping the clip.

> **TIP:** *Dragging in the Timeline while using* (Option) *has way too many functions associated with it. If you press the key, or let go of it, at the wrong time, you'll get an unexpected result. If you hold down* (Option) *before you select something, it acts to override the current linked selection state. Once the selection is made, you can let go of* (Option). *If you begin dragging a clip with* (Option) *down, you create a copy of that item instead of moving the original item. Finally, if you hold down* (Option) *right before releasing the mouse button, it will force an insert edit (as opposed to overwrite). Or in the case above, it will perform a swap edit.*

Editing on Two Tracks

There are exceptions to the one-video-track rule. Some editors find it easier to "read" the Timeline if they alternate clips like a checkerboard between video tracks 1 and 2 (**Figure 5.46**). This allows you to see that each clip has more media available to you beyond the In and Out point. However, sometimes it's hard to distinguish exactly where the actual edit point is.

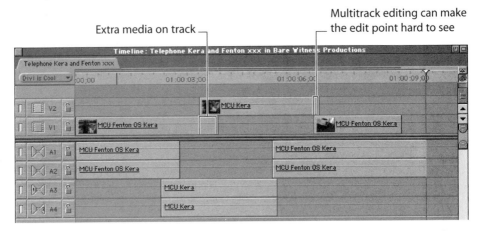

Figure 5.46 When you use multiple tracks, the visual representation of the clips' overlap can be useful.

Another benefit of placing alternating clips on multiple tracks is that it lets you try out a second shot, like a cutaway, without committing yourself to chopping up the main clip (**Figure 5.47**). If you don't like the positioning of the shot, you can move it back and forth on V2 until you're happy with its placement.

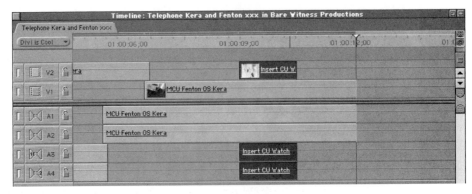

Figure 5.47 You can put a cutaway on V2 and move it around to decide the proper placement without having to modify the underlying clip.

Using the Razor Blade Tool

Beginning editors seem to take an immediate liking to the Razor Blade tool, which splits a clip into two pieces. For instance, you might use the tool to cut a hole in a clip on track 2 to let a clip on track 1 show through (**Figure 5.48**).

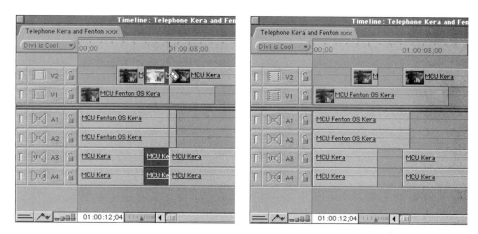

Figure 5.48 Using the Razor Blade tool, you can remove an area from V2 to allow clips on V1 to show through. This is a way of creating two edits (from V2 to V1, and then back from V1 to V2) at one time.

Assume you're cutting a dialogue scene and you want to trim a little space at the end of the first clip to tighten up the edit (**Figure 5.49**).

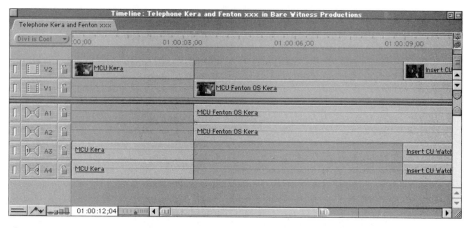

Figure 5.49 Making a simple edit in the no-trim model can take several steps. Here's the starting point. In this example, we want to shorten MCU Kera.

1. Select the Razor Blade tool by clicking on the Tool palette or hitting B on the keyboard.

2. Place the cursor over the end of clip 1 and click to break clip 1 into two pieces (**Figure 5.50**).

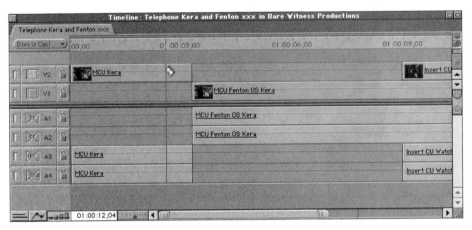

Figure 5.50 Start by using the Razor Blade tool to split the MCU Kera clip into two pieces.

3. Change tools back to the Arrow tool (click on the Tool palette or hit A on the keyboard).

4. Select the chopped piece of clip 1 and lift it by hitting Delete (**Figure 5.51**).

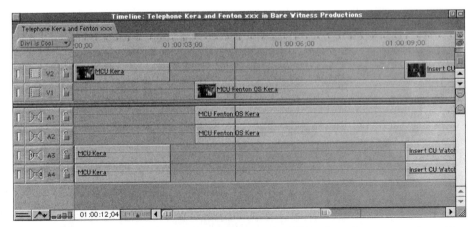

Figure 5.51 By selecting the trimmed section and then lifting it, we leave a gap that will show up as a black section of video and silent audio.

5. Select clip 2 and drag it upstream until it lines up with clip 1 (**Figure 5.52**).

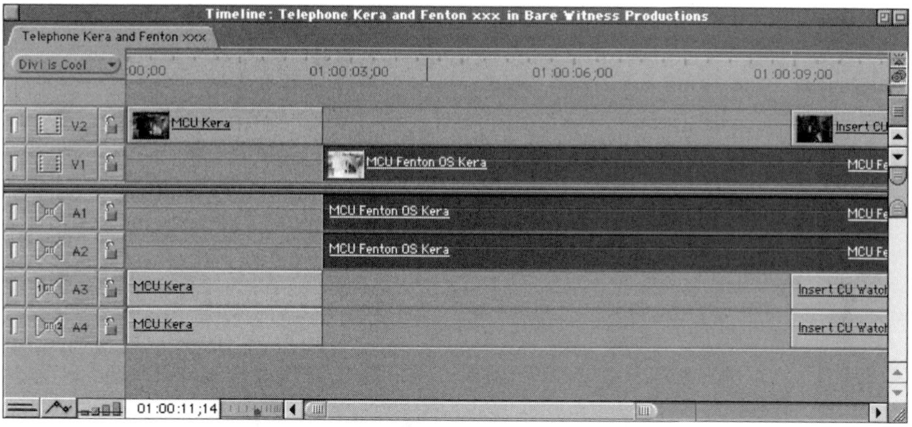

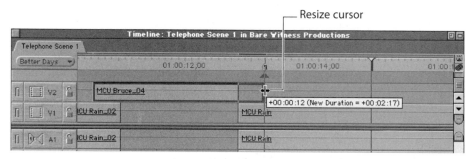

Figure 5.52 Finally, we select the second clip (MCU Fenton OS Kera) and drag it left until it aligns with the new Out point of MCU Kera.

Resize by Dragging

Instead of using the Razor Blade tool, you could just grab the edge of clip 1 and drag it to shorten it. When you grab a clip edge to change its duration, your cursor changes to the Resize tool (**Figure 5.53**). It's tempting to just drag clip edges to resize them, since it's so fast and easy, but it's not a very precise way to work.

Also, remember that you should try to make as many editing decisions as possible while playing the sequence. So if you want to use the Resize tool to change a clip's length, first play through the sequence and identify the new edit point with a marker. Then you can use the Resize tool to drag one of the clip edges, but now you will be dragging toward a specific location.

Resize cursor

Figure 5.53 The Resize tool appears when you drag the edges of clips in the Timeline to change their duration. Use a marker as a snapping guide when resizing a clip.

Select Track Tools

Another set of tools you'll find handy when working with clips on multiple tracks is the Select Track tools (**Figure 5.54**). They allow you to select all clips on a single track downstream from the current playhead position, all clips upstream, or all clips on multiple tracks. If, in the dialogue example we just discussed, there were a bunch of clips beyond clip 2, dragging clip 2 upstream to align it with the new ending of clip 1 would leave a gap after clip 2 (**Figure 5.55**). If instead you selected all clips downstream by using the Select Track Forward tool, when you dragged them to the left, no gap would remain (**Figure 5.56**).

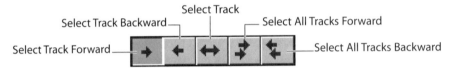

Figure 5.54 The Select Track tools are extremely helpful in the no-trim model. Once a track is selected, you can add tracks to the selection by holding ⟨Shift⟩.

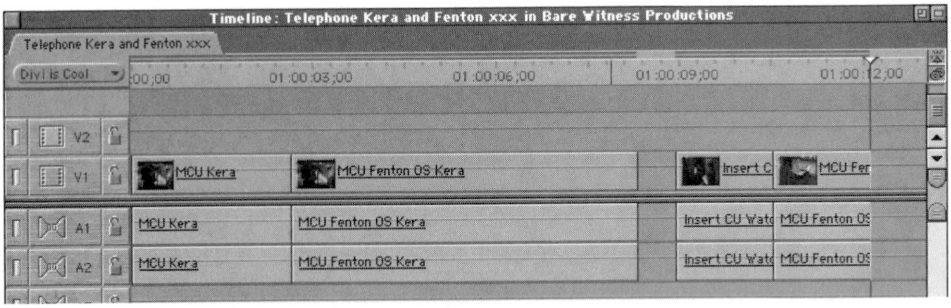

Figure 5.55 If we move only one clip at a time, we can leave a gap later in the sequence.

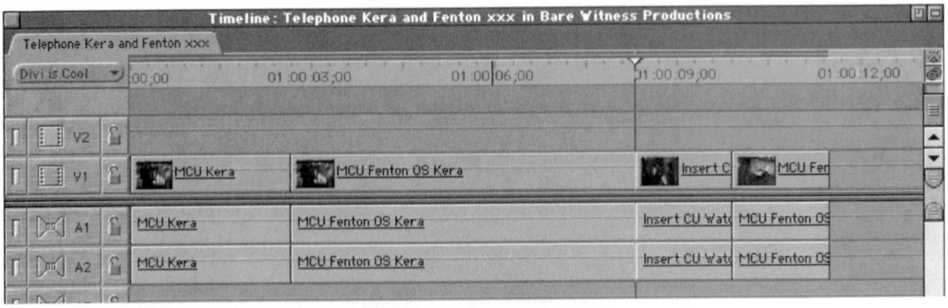

Figure 5.56 The Select Track tool enables you to select all the clips forward and move them all at once. This way you eliminate any gaps. Alternately, ripple-deleting the trimmed section would automatically move all the clips downstream.

Editing on the Fast Track

The disadvantage to the no-trim model is that besides requiring many steps, it is not precise. It's fairly easy to leave gaps when you are dragging clips around in the Timeline. This produces little black flashes or moments of silence between your edits. The Snapping control helps to prevent this, but it is still fairly common to create these kinds of errors when working this way.

Of course, once you learn some of Final Cut Pro's advanced tools, you can perform these same operations in fewer steps. For example, if the clips in the previous example were on one track instead of two, you could break clip 1 in two with the Razor Blade tool, and ripple-delete the extra piece (**Figure 5.57**). And the Ripple tool can perform that same edit in only one step (see the section on the ripple edit in Chapter 6).

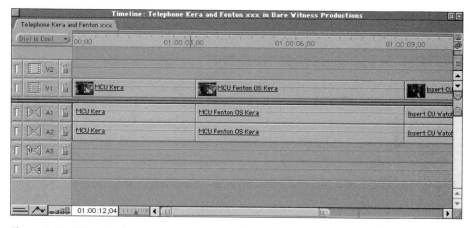

Figure 5.57 When all the clips are on one track, you can perform more complex operations with fewer steps.

TRANSITIONS

Every edit point is a transition from one shot to another, so in a way all cuts are transitions. If you want to use a special type of transition, such as a dissolve or wipe, you need to apply that transition to the edit point as an effect.

Transitions can be applied in a number of ways. If you like to drag and drop, you can select a transition from the Effects tab in the Browser (**Figure 5.58**) and drag it onto any edit point in your Timeline (**Figure 5.59**). If you're parked on an edit point, you can also drag and drop the effect onto the Canvas. Alternately, you can use the Effects menu and choose an effect from the Video Transitions submenu. The Effects menu and the Effects tab in the Browser are duplicates of one another. If you add or modify something in the Browser tab, it will be reflected in the menu.

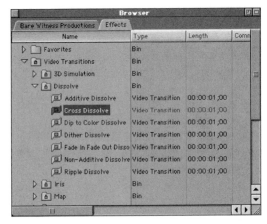

Figure 5.58 The Effects tab in the Browser lists all the effects available to you.

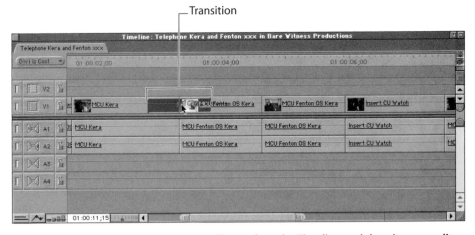

Figure 5.59 Drag a transition from the Effects tab to the Timeline and drop it on an edit point. You can also drag directly to the Canvas if the playhead is parked on an edit point.

You can apply a video transition from the Effects menu only if you are parked on an edit point. Otherwise, the effect names will be grayed out. You can also apply transitions only to clips that are on the same track. So if you're editing in the checkerboard pattern described earlier and you want to add a transition effect, you will first need to put the two clips together on the same track (**Figure 5.60**).

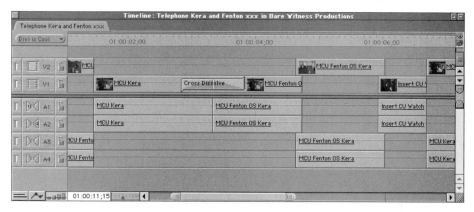

Figure 5.60 Applying a transition requires both clips to be on the same track. So even if you prefer to alternate clips between V1 and V2, when it comes time to add transitions, you'll need to move them onto the same track.

You can also apply transitions from the keyboard by hitting ⌘-T. This will apply the default transition to the edit point at the current playhead position on the currently targeted track. You can set the default transition by highlighting a transition in the Effects tab of the Browser and choosing Set Default from the Effects menu.

Make Sure You Have Enough Room

Transitions take place over time, so check to ensure that you've got adequate elbowroom to apply the transition. All transitions default to one second in length. That means that there must be at least half a second of extra footage on either side of the edit point, in both shots, to accommodate the effect (**Figure 5.61**). Once a transition is applied, you can change the duration of the effect either by dragging one edge of the Effect icon (**Figure 5.62**) or via the Shortcut menu (**Figure 5.63**). You will only be able to extend the duration as far as you have extra frames available in both of the underlying clips.

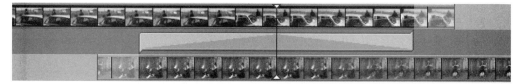

Figure 5.61 Every transition requires adequate "extra" media on both sides of the edit point in both clips to cover the entire duration of the effect. And those frames need to be free of obvious mistakes, such as a slate or a shaky camera move.

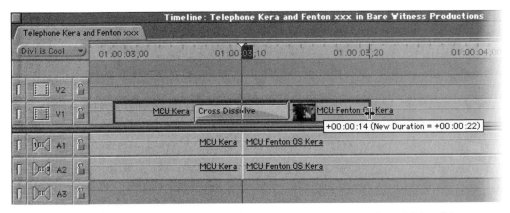

Figure 5.62 Transitions extend equally on both sides of the cut and require additional frames from both clips. You can extend the length of a transition by dragging one edge of it.

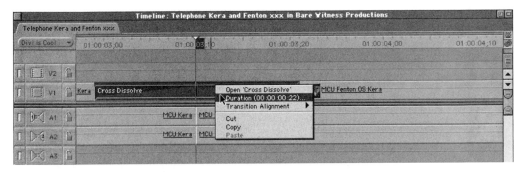

Figure 5.63 You can enter a duration for your transition numerically by selecting Duration from the Shortcut menu. To access the Shortcut menu, Ctrl-click the Transition icon.

Deciding Where Transitions Begin and End

There is a cut hiding underneath every transition, and that cut can fall in one of three places:

- at the beginning of the transition.
- at the center of the transition.
- at the end of the transition.

This is important to understand because it affects how the clips move around if you change the duration of the transition or if you trim the edit point underneath the transition.

Final Cut Pro's Transition icons give graphic feedback to indicate in which of the three locations the actual cut lies (**Figure 5.64**). You can choose which type to apply when you drag a transition from the Effects tab to the Timeline. The transition will snap to these three points, suggesting where you should drop it. After you drop it, you can change the alignment via the Shortcut menu for the transition or from the Transition Alignment submenu of the Sequence menu.

Figure 5.64 Transition icons show you whether they're set to begin on, center on, or end on the edit point. This state can be changed via the Shortcut menu.

If you have a centered transition and you change its duration from one second to two seconds, the transition will extend equally into both clips (as seen in Figure 5.62). In the case of a transition that ends on the cut, the transition will extend upstream only into the preceding clip. You still need to have an additional second of media in the second clip, but the new frames needed from the first clip are already there, so you don't have to worry about running out of media (**Figure 5.65**).

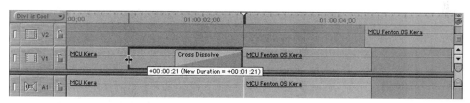

Figure 5.65 When you extend an end-on transition, it extends only in one direction.

Once you understand this concept, it can suggest how to use a transition when you don't have enough room in one of the clips. It will also help you construct well-composed dissolves as recommended in Chapter 2.

For example, in a music video I cut for Steve Lucky and the Rhumba Bums, there was a lap dissolve between the guitarist onstage and the dancers swinging on the dance floor. The clip of the dancers I wanted to use started right at the beginning of the shot, so I didn't have any extra frames before the action to accommodate the dissolve (**Figure 5.66**).

I wanted to line up the movement of the guitarist (who was bopping up and down as she played) with the beat of the dancers on the floor to make the dissolve match nicely.

Figure 5.66 In this shot of the dancers, I set my In point very close to the beginning of the media, as you can see in the Scrubber area.

First I made a *straight edit* lining up the guitarist's movement with those of the dancers (**Figure 5.67**). Then I dragged a one-second dissolve onto the edit and set it as a begin-on edit (**Figure 5.68**). This set the effect to begin on the edit point and extend into the clip of the dancers. I wasn't sure exactly how long I wanted the transition to last, so I dragged the edge of the transition downstream into the dancers clip, extending it by ten frames (**Figure 5.69**). Since there was plenty of room in the guitarist clip, I could comfortably extend it all I wanted to—even though there were no spare frames at the start of the dancers clip. I was adding frames only to the transition *after* the edit point.

STRAIGHT EDIT *A cut, as opposed to a dissolve or an L or J edit.*

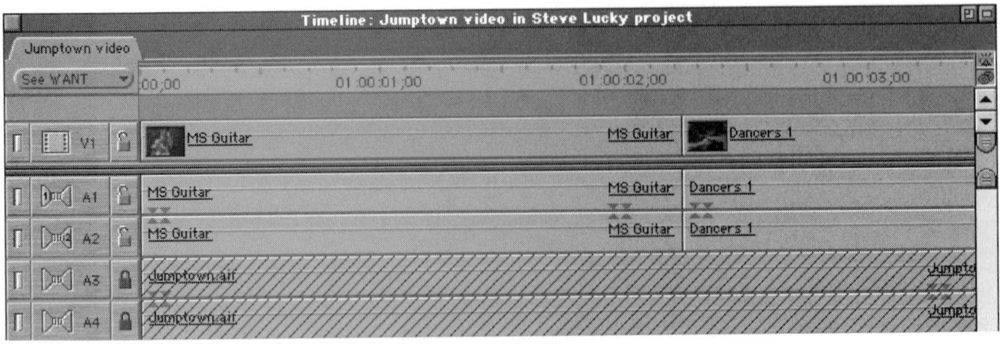

Figure 5.67 First I create a cut between the guitar shot and the dancers shot. Then I move the edit point to a place that reinforces the continuity of the music's rhythm.

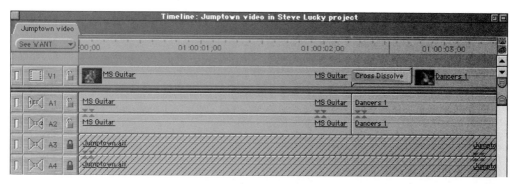

Figure 5.68 When I apply the transition, I set it to begin on the edit point. That way no additional frames are needed before the In point of the dancers shot.

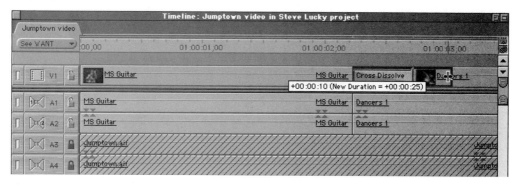

Figure 5.69 As I extend the transition, it moves only to the right (downstream), adding more frames from the guitar shot. Since my edit point was timed correctly, the guitarist's bopping will line up with the dancers' movements throughout the dissolve.

Change Effect Parameters

Use the Transition Editor if you want to change the parameters of an effect that has options—such as the number of bands in a band wipe, or the center point of an iris (**Figure 5.70**). Double-click the Transition icon in the Timeline to open the Transition Editor. You'll also find controls that let you adjust the start and end point of the transition and reverse the direction of the effect.

For example, you could set the iris wipe to begin one-third open by adjusting the starting percentage control. Or by using the Reverse control, you can create an effect where the transition starts as a point and expands to fill the screen. (Ordinarily, a wipe begins full screen and reduces to a point.) The Transition Editor can also be used to trim the contents of the clips underneath the transition (see the section on trimming under transitions in Chapter 6).

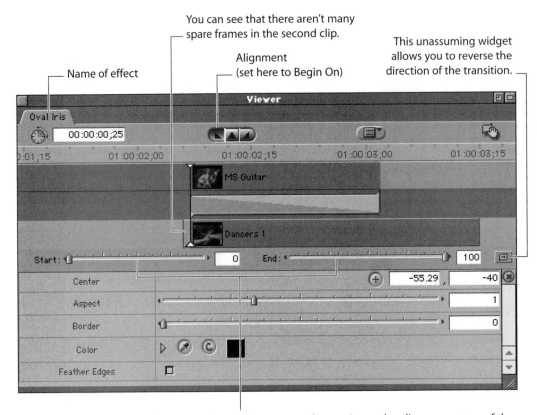

You can see that there aren't many spare frames in the second clip.

Alignment (set here to Begin On)

This unassuming widget allows you to reverse the direction of the transition.

Name of effect

These controls enable you to set the starting and ending percentage of the effect. If you set this to start at 50 percent, the iris would begin half open.

Figure 5.70 The Transition Editor gives you a view of the transition where you can see how the clips overlap and view the transition as a separate element. You can also set parameter controls like a border or the center point of this Oval Iris effect.

More Than Just Dissolves

Any transition other than a basic cross-dissolve draws attention to itself and will usually disrupt the narrative flow. But if your goal is to wake up your audience from the movie dream, by all means use some of the wackier effects.

For example, suppose you're making an educational video about bicycle safety that includes a mix of dramatic scenes, graphic charts, and narration. It's often a great idea to use a wipe or some other flashy effect to highlight the transitions out of the dramatic sections, because it lets the viewer know he should disengage from the story and prepare to view some different type of information.

Which type of effect should you choose? Think compositionally. In this case I might look for a wipe effect that resembled the shape of a bicycle, or maybe a clock wipe that could simulate a rolling bicycle wheel. Possibly I would find something suited to the particular images on-screen at the time of the effect. For instance, if the final shot of the dramatic sequence was a bicyclist cruising down a road and vanishing into the distance, I might amplify the effect by applying a zoom transition where the video image itself begins moving away to the vanishing point (**Figure 5.71**).

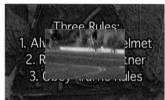

Figure 5.71 This zoom effect complements the footage of the biker riding off into the distance. I use it here to transition from the dramatic section of the video to a title card describing safety rules. During the dramatic section, all the edits were cuts.

One warning, though: As with fonts on a poster, it's best if you limit yourself to one or two effects and use them consistently throughout your show. Mixing dozens of effects dilutes the impact of any one of them. Also, flashy transitions are similar to exclamation points! If every sentence ends with an exclamation point, no one can understand which bits are more important than others! The more sparingly you use effects like these, the more powerful they will be.

Different Types of Dissolves

Even among basic dissolves you've got a lot to choose from (**Figure 5.72**). Your basic cross-dissolve will have highly varied effects depending upon how long it lasts (**Figure 5.73**).

Also, you can try an alternative, such as an additive dissolve that adds the numerical color values of the images together, so where bright areas overlap they become white. This works well for shorter transitions (less than a half second) and creates a kind of organic bright flash effect, but it may look decidedly inorganic on some images. Alternately, try a non-additive dissolve, which has the effect of dissolving the brighter areas of the frame before the darker areas (**Figure 5.74**). Both additive and non-additive dissolves are highly dependent on the specific composition of the shots being dissolved.

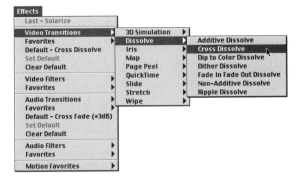

Figure 5.72 Final Cut Pro offers quite a few dissolves to choose from.

Figure 5.73 This image shows a normal cross-dissolve.

Figure 5.74 These images show an additive dissolve (left) and a non-additive dissolve (right). The results vary widely depending on the lightness and darkness values of the images being mixed.

You can also try a dip-to-color dissolve, in which, instead of the two images being cross-dissolved together, the first image fades out before the second one fades in. This allows you to create the common dip-to-black scene change with a single effect, rather than fading out one image and fading in the second with two effects. Note: In general, the default one-second duration is a little too quick for this effect, since it results in a half-second fade-out and a half-second fade-in.

You can also experiment with changing the color that's dipped to from the default black. Changing it to white is a nice way to create white flashes between shots (sometimes employed to simulate a flash camera going off, or for dramatic psychological impact). In this case, you're better off shortening the transition so the white frames look more like flashes than gradual lightening of the frame.

Choose any color you like to dip to—maybe blood red for a vampire thriller or the royal blue of your favorite corporate logo. If you are going to fade to a color other than black or white, try to pick a color that exists in the outgoing shot. If your subject is standing in front of a green chalkboard, and you set up the dissolve to dip to that exact color, it will make for a much more organic effect than if you choose a color that doesn't exist anywhere in the frame. (Final Cut Pro provides an Eyedropper control that lets you pick a color from your video image.)

Custom Transitions

By default, all transitions in Final Cut are one second long. This is a pretty good length for many applications, but some effects and some situations may require you to modify this default. Once you apply a transition, you can change the duration by dragging the edge of the transition, using the Shortcut menu, or opening the Transition Editor.

If you want to change the duration of the transition *before* you apply the effect, it's a little trickier. To do this you need to create a copy of the transition and place it in the Favorites folder (**Figure 5.75**).

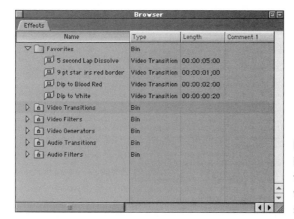

Figure 5.75 The Favorites folder is where you store any custom transitions that you create. These will stick around across editing sessions.

Suppose you want to make a soft cut transition that will be a five-frame dissolve. First drag the cross-dissolve transition into the Favorites folder, thereby making a copy of it (**Figure 5.76**). Now, modify the Length column and set the value to be 00:00:00:05. Then rename the effect "Soft Cut" (**Figure 5.77**). This effect is now available to you whenever you want it from the Favorites section of the Effects menu (**Figure 5.78**).

You can do this with as many effects as you want, and change much more than just the length of the effect. You can modify any parameter of the effect and store it as a favorite. Go ahead and create a venetian blind wipe with ten bands, or a star iris with seven points and a three-pixel purple border.

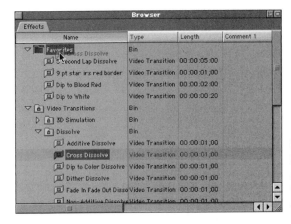

Figure 5.76 Create a new favorite by dragging a transition from another bin in the Effects window. You can also drag a transition from the Timeline to the Favorites bin.

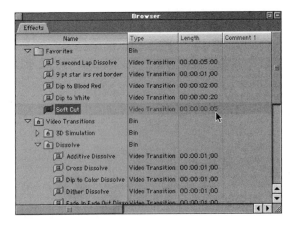

Figure 5.77 Make whatever changes you want to the effect in the Favorites folder. Change its duration, change its name, or change parameters in the Transition Editor. All the changes will be saved with the item in the Favorites bin.

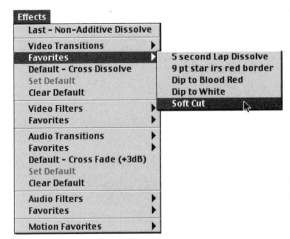

Figure 5.78 Any effects you move to the Favorites bin will also show up in the Favorites submenu of the Effects menu.

Making a Custom Default Transition

You can even designate one of these effects as your default transition if you like—which makes it the effect applied automatically when you choose Overwrite with Transition or use the ⌘-Ⓣ shortcut. The factory default transition is a one-second cross-dissolve. But you can set any effect as your default by selecting the icon in the Browser and choosing Set Default from the Effects menu. If you were doing a nature montage where all the transitions were two-second non-additive dissolves, you could make that your default—so rather than having to wade through the submenus to get to the effect you use all the time, it would be available instantly from the keyboard shortcut.

Transitions as Fades

You can apply transitions to the beginning or end of a sequence, creating the effect of transitioning to or from black (**Figure 5.79**). This is a quick and easy way to perform a fade-out or fade-in. As with any transition, if you apply it at the default center-on position, you are using frames from the clip that were previously hidden (before the In point or after the Out point). So I recommend setting the Out point of the clip to be the very last frame you want seen (as it will be almost completely faded out) and applying the transition at the end-on position. (Reverse the process for a fade-in.)

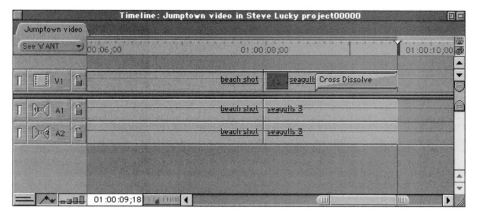

Figure 5.79 A dissolve applied to a clip at the end of a sequence is the same as a fade-out.

Effects applied to clips on Timeline tracks V2 or higher create a transition between the clip and transparency rather than a transition between the clip and black. This means if you're working in the no-trim model with two clips stacked up at the end of your sequence, and you apply a cross-dissolve to the clip on V2 to create a fade-out effect (**Figure 5.80**), you're going to be revealing the clip on V1 as the effect progresses.

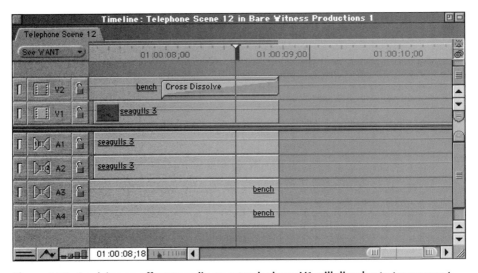

Figure 5.80 Applying an effect to a clip on a track above V1 will dissolve to transparent (not black). This means if a clip exists on a lower track, it will show through as the clip above becomes transparent. Sometimes this is desirable; other times it may not be.

If you line everything up properly, this is another way to create a dissolve between two clips, but it's far less precise than doing it as instructed at the beginning of the section on transitions—and with many effects (such as pushes, stretches, or slides), the second clip won't move along with the effect as intended.

Still, this does open up some interesting opportunities. You could conceivably create multiple transitions on multiple tracks that would all combine to create some whacked-out visual layering effect. Or, more likely, a big visual mess. Final Cut Pro places few limitations on what you can or cannot do. But just because something is possible doesn't mean you need to do it. In most cases, simple is elegant and elegant is better.

Let the content of your film speak to the audience without bombarding them with elements that distract them from that content. You can't save a show by adding too many effects.

Interview: VALDÍS ÓSKARSDÓTTIR

Valdís Óskarsdóttir is an Icelandic film editor who's been responsible for editing many of the Dogme 95 films, beginning with *The Celebration*. She also cut Harmony Korine's Dogme-like *Julien Donkey-Boy*, and brought that same sense of immediacy to Gus Van Sant's *Finding Forrester*.

Michael Wohl: What happens after you finish your first cut?

Valdís Óskarsdóttir: After the first cut, you start all over again. You watch the film, and usually the director gets depressed. I think I've never met any director who doesn't get kind of depressed or disappointed at that stage.

So what do you do?

You go home and watch TV, or you go and see a movie, or whatever. And then you come back, and you watch some scenes, and maybe there's a shot in there that you liked so much, and you know deep inside that you have to take it out, but you just have to keep it as long as you possibly can. It might take you five weeks to throw it out, but once you get a week off, you come back to the computer and you say, "Eeek, what was I thinking about?"

How do you know what's the best way to tell the story?

I don't know. I watch the tape before I go home in the evening, and then when I get back in the morning, I have it. I always have the feeling that the film itself, it is itself. It's your job to find that. And I don't think you can force things on stuff that isn't there. You always have to be true to your characters, to the story, and to the film. Those are the three obligations that you have.

What was it like working on The Celebration?

Well, with all the camera movements and everything, it was like playing because I could do whatever I wanted to do. There was no one who could come and say, "You can't do that. That's not allowed," or, "You can't cross the line, because people will get confused." We had 56 hours of material, and sometimes they had two, three, even four cameras on the same scene. And we had to put everything in order. So, after working for three weeks, we realized that if we were going to sit together and watch all the takes we would never finish the film. So we got a big room, and [director] Thomas [Vinterberg] would sit on the sofa with headphones and watch the raw material, and he'd write down which takes to use, and I was sitting at the computer and editing. It was kind of fun because if he had some doubts about something he could ask me, and if I had a question I could ask him.

What influences your editing style?

I learn something new with each film I edit. But I'm just as affected by what's outside— all the movies and music and books that I've read and paintings I've seen. I take all of that with me into the editing room and use it.

CHAPTER SIX

Advanced Editing

I previously likened film editing to solving a jigsaw puzzle, but a more accurate analogy might be playing a chess game in which every edit point is a move. You have dozens of possible choices, but whichever one you pick will affect all the decisions available from that moment onward. As you consider each move, you have to play out the consequent scenario at least a few moves ahead in order to make the best choice. And at all times, you must be able to take in the whole board and keep track of the big picture.

Fortunately, in editing, you have no opponent (except time, or perhaps your producer). Furthermore, Final Cut Pro provides you with up to 99 undos, so you can actually try out an idea and let it play for a few steps before you're stuck with it. And since Final Cut Pro is nondestructive, you can even save different versions of your sequences (or your entire show) and let the director make the final choice.

IN THE GROOVE

Once you find the heart of the scene, the edits flow like a surging stream of water. You're swept up by the current of the action, and your hands can hardly keep up with your ideas. These magical moments are what editors live for. When you're in that groove, you want to be able to work as quickly as possible—and Final Cut Pro is endowed with advanced tools to enable that seemingly effortless workflow.

Sure, you can use Final Cut Pro to create successful pieces without understanding more than a few of its features. But the longer you work with it, the more familiar it becomes, and the more you learn how to take advantage of some of its esoteric features. This chapter is just a sampling of Final Cut Pro's advanced capabilities—and how professional editors make use of them.

Flying Through the Edits

For example, there's a scene in *Want* where Trey and Ben sneak into their company's storeroom and steal a bunch of computers. Ben is nonchalant, but Trey is scared to death of getting caught. As I edited the sequence, I could see the whole scene in my head, shot after shot, all at once. To keep up with the flow of my ideas, I found myself flying along, creating continuity cuts on both sides of each shot. That means not just aligning the two frames on either side of one edit but actually lining up four frames at once (**Figure 6.1**).

Final Cut Pro made it easy.

Figure 6.1 While editing this sequence, I was creating continuity edits on both sides of each shot as I laid them in.

TRIMMING

The no-trim method I described in the last chapter works fine to get your scenes assembled, but it's far too slow to accommodate the kind of rapid-fire, high-powered editing that I just described. The trim tools are the key to fast editing. They enable you to control both sides of one edit point at the same time, or even modify two or more edits at once. And working fast is not only efficient, it's exhilarating.

You can define trimming as anything you do to your sequence after the initial clips have been laid down. While that's an accurate definition, under its terms, plenty of the slowpoke techniques I described in Chapter 5, "Basic Editing," would qualify as trimming. So let me refine the meaning here to refer specifically to the advanced techniques experienced editors use to edit quickly and confidently with Final Cut Pro's trim tools: *Roll, Ripple, Slip,* and *Slide.*

Roll Edit

The simplest trim operation is the roll edit. Rolling an edit shortens one clip while lengthening the other—with a single adjustment (**Figure 6.2**). It doesn't matter whether it's the outgoing clip (clip 1) getting shorter and the incoming clip (clip 2) getting longer or the other way around; the overall sequence length doesn't change.

I've already described some great uses for this tool, such as syncing continuity edits and creating split edits (see the sidebar "Sync Up on the Easy Spot" and the section on using split edits in Chapter 3, "Editing Patterns"). But the Roll tool has infinite applications.

Figure 6.2 A roll edit moves the edit point, shortening one clip while lengthening the adjacent one. It doesn't disturb the rest of the sequence.

Access the Roll tool by choosing it from the Tool palette (**Figure 6.3**) or typing Ⓡ on your keyboard. The Roll tool operates only on edit points. If you roll your cursor over the middle of a clip, you'll see an "x" next to the cursor (**Figure 6.4**). This helps you understand where and how to use the tool.

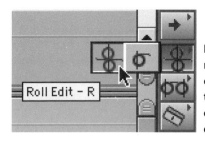

Figure 6.3 The Roll tool looks like a pair of film reels. The two reels are a reminder that you're changing both sides of the edit when you apply this tool. The Ripple tool (discussed later) has only one reel and correspondingly affects only one side of the edit.

Figure 6.4 The Roll tool works only on edit points. If your cursor is over an area where the tool won't work, a tiny "x" appears next to the Roll icon.

Once the Roll tool is activated, the simplest way to execute a roll is to click the tool on an edit point and drag (see Figure 6.2). A Tip window will appear indicating how many frames you're moving the edit. If you are zoomed out, dragging can be fairly imprecise. Holding down ⌘ helps in this situation by "gearing down" the effect of your drag and limiting movement to one frame at a time.

If you roll both the audio and video tracks of a particular edit point, you simply move the edit point, but if you roll either the audio or the video independently, you will create a split edit (**Figure 6.5**). If you are rolling an edit that includes sync sound elements, such as lips moving or a car door slamming, you probably need to roll both the audio and video to keep the picture and sound lined up.

I roll almost every edit point in every sequence back and forth a few times until I like the feel of the transition, sometimes creating splits, sometimes just fine-tuning the cut. I can't stress how often you'll use this tool once you get familiar with it.

> **TIP:** When you're making tiny frame-by-frame adjustments to an edit to create seamless continuity, keep moving the edit one frame at a time until it's clear that you've passed the sweet spot. Then back it off a frame or two until it feels just right.

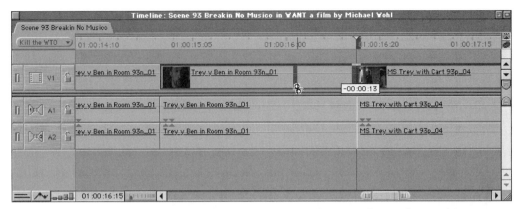

Figure 6.5 By rolling only the video clip, I can create a J cut that smooths out the transition across the two clips.

Canvas Feedback

Whenever you roll an edit in the Timeline, the Canvas temporarily turns into a special two-up display showing the two frames getting modified (**Figure 6.6**). This can be extremely helpful in deciding where to make your edit. As you drag the edit point back and forth, you can make decisions based on the content and the composition of the frames on either side of the edit point.

Figure 6.6 When rolling a clip, watch the Canvas window to see the frames that will become your new edit point.

Extend Edit

Because editors use the roll edit so frequently, there's a way to do it in one step. The Extend Edit command will roll the currently selected edit point to the playhead position (**Figure 6.7**).

Figure 6.7 You can roll an edit without using the Roll tool by using the Extend Edit command.

This has essentially the same effect as selecting the edit point with the Roll tool and dragging it to the new position, but can be done from the keyboard by hitting E. Professional editors tend to use this feature while playing the sequence.

For example, suppose you've got a sequence of kids in a zoo looking at gorillas. You rough in a couple of edits:

1. LS kids looking at gorillas.

2. MS gorillas.

3. MCU kids' faces.

But there's a problem with shot 3: The MCU of the kids is supposed to show them looking interested in the gorillas, but in the beginning of the shot one kid is staring at the ground, bored as a stick. After a moment he glances up and gets mildly interested to the point where he might pass as engaged, especially surrounded by the other excited kids.

You decide to fix the problem by extending the gorilla shot to cover up the undesirable frames of shot 3. (Who could complain about a few extra frames of gorillas?) Here's how you might use Extend Edit to accomplish that very quickly.

1. Select the edit point between shots 2 and 3.

2. Play the sequence.

3. At the moment where the kid stops looking bored, hit $\boxed{\text{E}}$.

That's it! No setting markers, no dragging, no calculating how many frames you want to trim. If you do this while playing, Final Cut Pro will even extend you the courtesy of backing up a few seconds and playing over the new edit point—all before you can say "Stop."

Extend Edit works in reverse, too, either by letting you extend the edit while playing backward, or by allowing you to position the playhead upstream from the selected edit and hitting $\boxed{\text{E}}$.

Delete Shots With Extend Edit

You can even extend your edit right past another edit point, completely eliminating a clip. This is another efficient, high-speed strategy.

Let's say you'd like to try the zoo scene without gorillas—you want to extend shot 1 (the LS of the kids looking) right past shot 2 (the gorilla shot) and past the bored kid in shot 3, so you'll end up with two shots of kids, no gorillas, and no bored kid.

Select the edit between shots 1 and 2, place the playhead at the right spot in shot 3, and perform an extend edit (**Figure 6.8**). This will eliminate the gorilla shot from the sequence entirely, along with the bored brat.

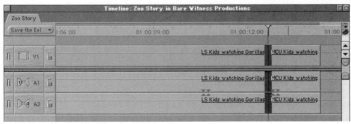

Figure 6.8 As long as there's enough media in the underlying clips, you can extend an edit as far as you like. In this example we completely overwrite the second shot.

Ripple Edit

The ripple edit modifies an edit point by changing the duration of only one of the clips involved. This changes the duration of your entire sequence. While you can roll in only two directions (forward and backward), you can ripple in four different ways (**Figure 6.9**). Rippling is one of the most powerful tools in Final Cut Pro, but it can wreak havoc by affecting clips on other tracks.

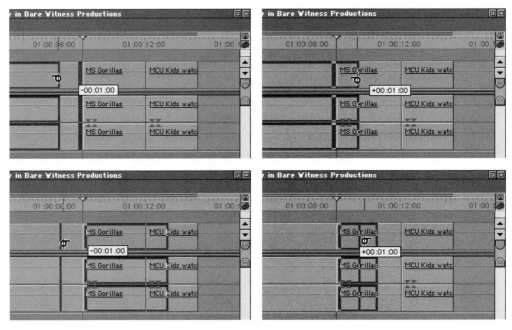

Figure 6.9 You can ripple either side of an edit point in either direction.

Even though a ripple edit modifies only one clip and a roll modifies two, the ripple is much tougher to keep track of in your head, since it actually modifies the whole sequence. Consequently, you should be a bit more careful with it than with a roll. Part of the problem is that some ripples create results that are the exact opposite of what you expected.

In general, changes to the outgoing clip are much more straightforward than changes to the incoming clip. To make the outgoing clip longer, you drag it to the right; to make it shorter, you drag it to the left—just as you would with a roll edit.

For example, let's go back to the kids and gorillas. Suppose you wanted to make shot 2 (the gorilla shot in the middle) longer without changing the duration of shot 3. You could simply type ⓇⓇ to bring up the Ripple tool, select the outgoing side of the edit, and drag it to the right. Shot 2 would get longer, shot 3 would remain the same, and everyone would be happy because you'd have more gorilla footage in your movie (**Figure 6.10**). However, you would not have solved the bored-kid problem.

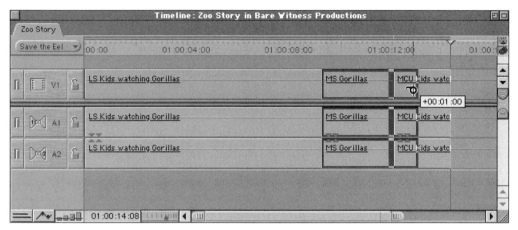

Figure 6.10 Everyone loves gorillas. To make shot 2 longer, select that side of the edit point and drag to the right. The duration of shot 3 will not be affected, but your overall sequence will be lengthened.

To do that, we must shorten shot 3. Select the incoming side of the edit with the Ripple tool, and drag it to the right. This is exactly what you would do if it were the only clip in the sequence, but the result can be confusing because it's the opposite of how the Roll tool works (**Figure 6.11**). You can watch the highlight on the back end of the clip to see how long the clip will be after the trim is done.

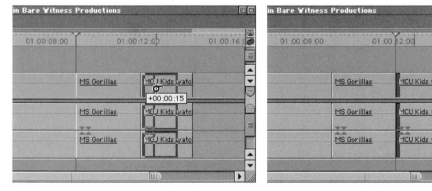

Figure 6.11 To shorten the incoming side of the edit, grab the right side of the edit point with the Ripple tool and drag to the right. Note the highlight around the back end of the clip, which indicates its new ending point.

If you want to make the incoming clip longer, drag it to the left (**Figure 6.12**). Watch the highlight to see how long the resulting clip will be.

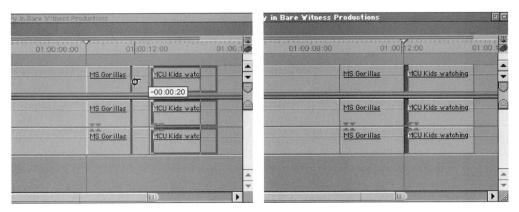

Figure 6.12 If you drag the incoming clip to the left, it gets longer—but the edit stays in the same position. The highlight on the back end of the clip indicates how long the clip will be following the edit.

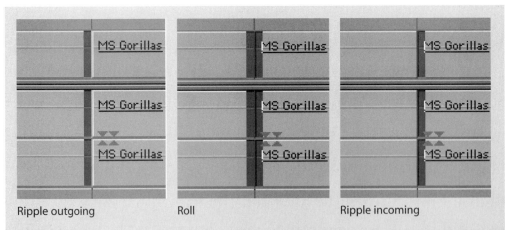

Ripple outgoing   Roll   Ripple incoming

Figure 6.13 The Timeline indicates which way an edit point is selected by displaying one of these three states.

Selecting Edits

*An edit point can be selected in one of three ways: as a roll, where operations will affect both sides of the edit; a ripple outgoing, where the outgoing clip will be affected, but the incoming clip is left alone; or a ripple incoming, the opposite of the last (**Figure 6.13**).*

continues on next page

Selecting Edits *continued*

Final Cut Pro includes so many different ways to select edits, it can make your head swim. The simplest method is to click on the edit with the Arrow tool or press ⓥ, which selects the nearest edit point to the playhead backward or forward. (If you're exactly halfway between two, it will select the one downstream.)

Selecting an edit with the Arrow tool will select both sides of the edit (making it a roll edit). You can also click on an edit with the Roll tool itself. If you click on an edit point with the Ripple tool, you must choose which side of the edit you wish to select, incoming or outgoing. The shortcut key ⓥ will select an edit as a roll—unless the Ripple tool is active, in which case it will select either incoming or outgoing, depending on which clip the playhead is currently parked on.

Once an edit is selected, you can toggle between the three types of selection (roll, ripple outgoing, ripple incoming) by using ⓤ.

*As if this weren't complicated enough already, Final Cut Pro provides one more way to select edits: a special tool called Edits Selection (**Figure 6.14**). Armed with this tool, you can select edits either by clicking on them or by dragging a marquee around a group of edits (**Figure 6.15**). Once edits are selected with the Edits Selection tool, the Trim Edit window will open automatically. This methodology exists only to accommodate migrating Avid users who are used to this exact behavior.*

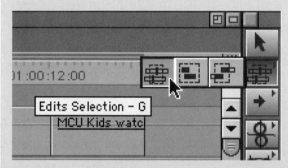

Figure 6.14 The Edits Selection tool can be accessed by pressing Ⓖ.

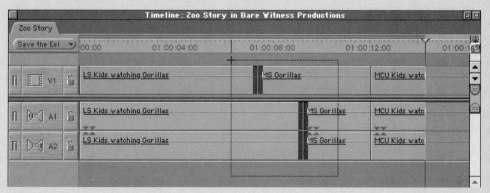

Figure 6.15 Use this tool to select edits by dragging a marquee or lasso around them. This allows you to select different edits on different tracks.

Check the Canvas

As with a roll, the Canvas provides feedback about your ripple edit. Since rippling an edit modifies only one frame, the Canvas shows only a one-up display. Use this to help determine which frame you want to set as your new edit point.

Just Type a Number

The more you edit, the more you'll find yourself thinking in frames. You'll be able to look at an edit and estimate just how many frames it needs to be adjusted. An experienced editor can easily identify even two- or three-frame errors. Does the edit feel smooth? If not, is the first clip too long? Too short? And by how many frames? How about the second clip? Or maybe the continuity seems fluid but the edit point occurs at the wrong instant in the action: after the door closes completely instead of midway through its motion.

Once you begin thinking in frame numbers, you will want to be able to tell the software precisely how to make these fine adjustments. Final Cut Pro permits numerical edits like these very easily.

Any time you type a number on the keyboard, or hit ⊞ or ⊟, Final Cut Pro understands that you want to perform a numerical edit. All you need to do is tell it what kind of trim you want to perform: a roll, ripple outgoing, or ripple incoming edit. The current selection defines what edit will be applied.

*For example, if you want to shorten the clip of the gorilla at the edit point where it begins, select the edit point as a ripple incoming (**Figure 6.16**) and just type +1.15. This will perform a ripple edit, shortening the clip by one and one half seconds. (The + is optional.) Why does entering a positive value make the incoming clip shorter? Because you are moving the edit point forward in time by that amount.*

continues on next page

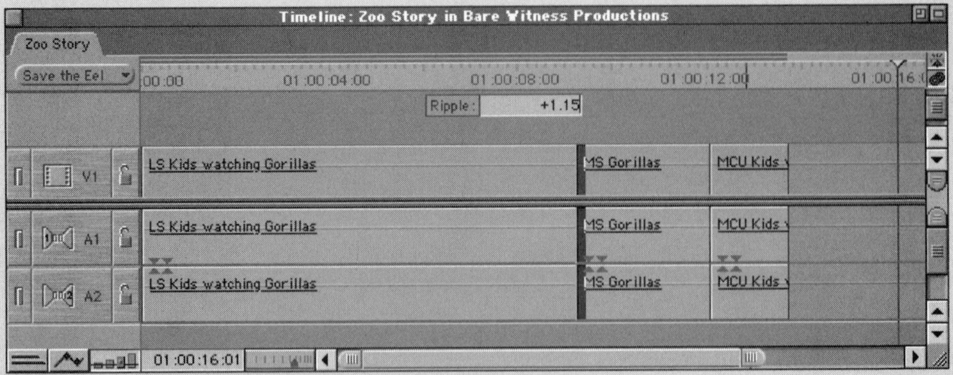

Figure 6.16 Select the edit you want to adjust numerically. The type of edit you select determines how the numerical entry will be applied. In this case, the edit is a ripple incoming. The pop-up window in the middle of the Timeline confirms what type of edit is being made.

Just Type a Number *continued*

*Whenever you begin a numerical edit, Final Cut Pro pops up a tiny window in the middle of the Timeline indicating what type of edit you are performing (see previous figure). If you want to perform a roll edit in order to make the adjacent shot longer while making this one shorter, simply select the edit as a roll (**Figure 6.17**).*

*If a clip is selected instead of an edit point, typing in numbers will move the clip by the number of frames entered. In this case, the pop-up will identify the operation as a move (**Figure 6.18**).*

continues on next page

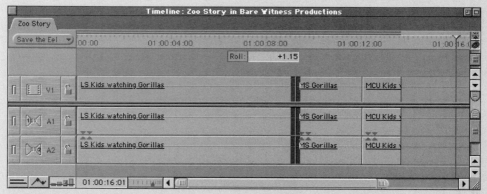

Figure 6.17 If the edit is selected as a roll, the numerical entry will be applied as a roll edit.

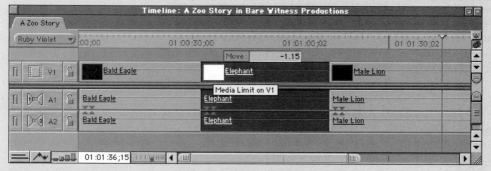

Figure 6.18 If you select a clip rather than an edit point, numerical entry will attempt to move the item by the timecode value you specify. If other clips are in the way, you will get an error; a numerical move operation will not overwrite clips.

Just Type a Number   *continued*

*If no clips or edits are selected, and you begin typing in timecode numbers, Final Cut Pro will direct the entry into the Current Position field and move the playhead by the desired amount (**Figure 6.19**).*

Whenever you make a direct numerical entry, Final Cut Pro translates your entry into timecode values. If you type in more than two digits without a separator (colon, semicolon, period, or comma), the program will assume you are entering a total number of frames and will calculate how many seconds or minutes it equals depending on the current timebase. (NTSC is 29.97 fps; PAL is 25 fps.) (See the sidebar on working with timecode in Chapter 4, "Preparing to Edit.")

Current Position field

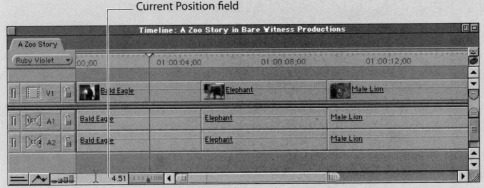

Figure 6.19 If nothing is selected in the Timeline, entering a timecode doesn't pop up a window; the numerical entry goes directly into the Current Position field and moves the playhead. If you omit the + or –, Final Cut Pro assumes you are typing in the destination timecode.

Adjusting Two Edits at Once

It won't take long until you're seeing your way several moves down the chessboard—and you may spot places where you want to adjust two edit points in one operation. I don't mean two sides of one edit point (as with the roll edit just discussed); I mean two entirely different edit points.

Final Cut Pro provides two editing tools specifically for this case: Slip and Slide (**Figure 6.20**). Both tools limit you to adjusting adjacent edits only—and only by the same amount. Nonetheless, you'll encounter many cases where one of these tools is just right for the job.

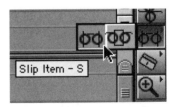

Figure 6.20 The Slip and Slide tools are connected in the Tool palette. The keyboard shortcut for Slip is Ⓢ, and the shortcut for Slide is ⓈⓈ.

Slip Edit

A slip edit changes both the In and Out points of a single clip simultaneously. Essentially, it changes which section of the clip you are using by trimming frames off the front of the clip and adding them to the back—or vice versa. It does not change the duration of the overall sequence, and it has no effect whatsoever on the surrounding clips. Performing a slip is equivalent to doing a ripple incoming and a ripple outgoing on the same clip at the same time.

When to Slip

Here are several situations when the Slip tool can make your day.

Fine-Tune Problem Clips in Finished Sequences

If just one clip in a nearly finished sequence needs adjusting, the Slip function can fix it without messing up your sequence. Imagine we're still working on that zoo video, and you're using a shot of a koala lashing out with her claws right at the camera lens to show why kids shouldn't feed the animals. Unfortunately, the shot begins too early: There's nearly a full second of dead space before the vicious koala strikes. Since the rest of the sequence is locked down, you can't just ripple or roll the edit, because that will modify the other clips. But if you slip the clip about 20 frames to the left, thereby setting a new In point a few frames before the paw swings toward the lens, you're in business (**Figure 6.21**).

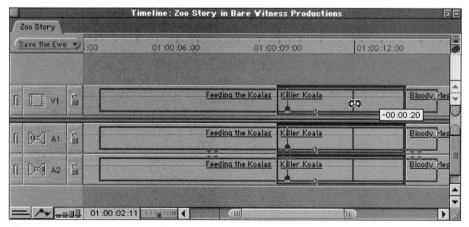

Figure 6.21 You can slip one clip to modify an edit without disturbing the surrounding clips. The marker indicates the frame where the wild beast strikes.

Finesse Continuity Cuts

If you're building a sequence from footage shot with multiple cameras and cutting back and forth between them, sometimes one clip will get slightly out of sync with the shots around it. You can use a slip edit to fix a clip where both sides contain a continuity edit.

For example, suppose a sequence in the zoo video contains a series of shots of penguins playing. The setup involved one camera on land and another one underwater, both shooting simultaneously. As you're editing, you notice a misalignment in a continuity cut from above water to underwater just as one penguin breaks the water's surface. Using the Slip tool, you can adjust the In and Out points of the clip to match continuity across that edit point—and the edit point on the other side of the clip will be adjusted automatically at the same time (**Figure 6.22**).

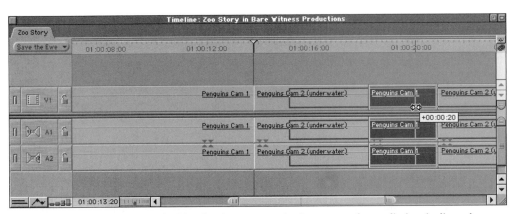

Figure 6.22 When edits on each side of a shot are continuity cuts, and one clip is misaligned on both sides, slipping can fix both edits at once.

How to Slip

Performing a slip edit is as simple as selecting the Slip tool and clicking and dragging a clip in the Timeline (**Figure 6.23**). While you drag, the Canvas window switches to a two-up display showing you the new In and Out points you are selecting. The Timeline feedback tells you how much media is available to you, based on how long the clip is.

Dragging the clip left sets the new In and Out points *later* in the clip, and dragging it to the right sets the new In and Out points *earlier* in the clip. If this seems backward, try to see it like this: Rather than thinking about rippling two edit points, remember that you're simply selecting a different part of the clip—without disturbing the sequence.

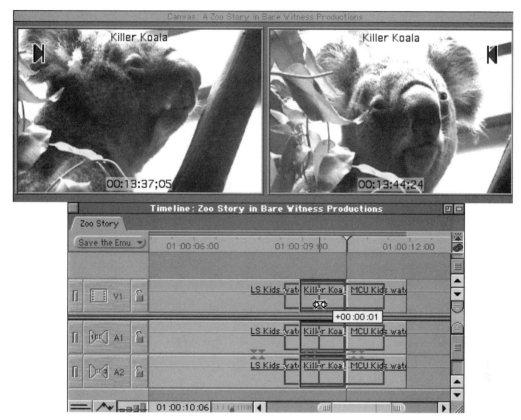

Figure 6.23 Slip a clip by dragging it in the Timeline with the Slip tool. The feedback in the Canvas shows the new In and Out points, and the highlight in the Timeline displays all of the media in the clip to show you what part of the clip you are using and how much spare media exists around it.

Slip With Markers

You can enhance the functionality of the slip edit by using a marker as a midclip guide.

For instance, in another scene in our zoo video, there's a shot of a flock of flamingos taking flight all at once. The narration explains that zoo animals possess a natural urge for freedom. Let's say you want to adjust the timing of the clip so the flock takes off right on the word "freedom." In this case, you can use markers along with a slip edit to align the two events.

First set a marker on the frame where the flamingos fly, and another one on the frame where the narrator says the word "freedom," using the marker controls described in Chapter 5 (**Figure 6.24**).

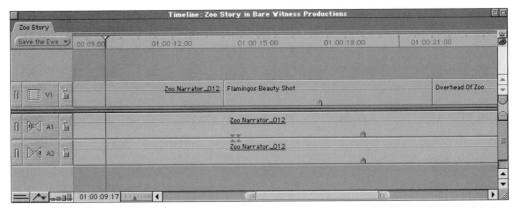

Figure 6.24 First we set markers on the points of interest. One goes on the frame where the birds fly, and another goes in the audio clip on the word "freedom."

Now select the Slip tool, click on the flamingos clip, and drag it until the two markers line up. You must click precisely on the marker in the flamingos clip in order to make the marker act as a snap point. If the markers are not snapping, double-check to make sure that snapping is turned on and that you selected the clip by clicking directly on the marker (**Figure 6.25**).

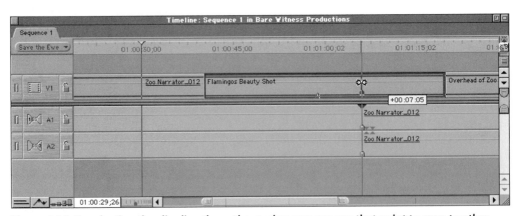

Figure 6.25 By selecting the clip directly on the marker, you can use that point to snap to other points in the Timeline.

Now the flamingos erupt into flight at the very moment the narrator says "freedom," creating a provocative combination of visual and aural elements.

Slip in the Viewer

If you want to perform a slip before you drop the clip into a sequence, you can perform that edit in the Viewer. Simply hold down [Shift] while you drag either the In or Out point in the Viewer, and the other point will move along with you (**Figure 6.26**).

The duration of the clip remains the same, but the section of the clip you're using changes.

When you slip a clip this way, the Viewer window and the Canvas window become a giant two-up display, showing you the In and Out points you are selecting as you drag.

Figure 6.26 You can slip in the Viewer window by holding down [Shift] while you drag the In or Out point. The Viewer and the Canvas become a two-up display to assist you in setting your new points.

Now the hard question: Why in the world would you want to perform a slip edit before you drop the clip into a sequence?

Imagine you have just enough room in your show for a four-second cutaway of seagulls at the beach. The shot you choose is a minute and a half long and includes many different framings of seagulls. Sometimes the gulls are flying; sometimes they're walking around on the sand. Sometimes the shot is zoomed in to show one or two birds; other times it's an ELS of the beach with the gulls as tiny specks in the sky.

The section you pick has to be only four seconds long, but you haven't decided which part of the clip to use yet. So for now, just set an In and Out point anywhere in the clip (as long as they're four seconds apart), and slip around the clip looking for the best four seconds. You can preview this by using the Play In to Out short-cut ([Shift]-[\]), which plays the clip exactly from the In point to the Out. Once you find the section that fits the sequence best, perform the edit and you're done.

Slip by the Numbers

When you look at a problem edit, you may instantly say to yourself something like, "Hmm, that clip probably needs to be slipped by seven frames."

To slip a clip by a precise number of frames, type in timecode numbers while the Slip tool is active. Unfortunately, this isn't quite as straightforward as doing it with a ripple or a roll edit, since you also need a clip to be selected, and the Slip tool doesn't exactly *select* clips. Normally, when you click on a clip with the Slip tool, you drag to perform the edit—and when you let go, the clip is no longer selected.

To slip a clip numerically, you must first select it using the Selection tool by pressing [A], then choose the Slip tool by pressing [S]. Only then can you begin typing numbers.

If you've already selected the Slip tool before you decide to do a numeric operation, you can temporarily select clips in the Timeline by holding down [Shift]. Once the clip is selected, entering a numeric value will perform a slip edit on it (**Figure 6.27**).

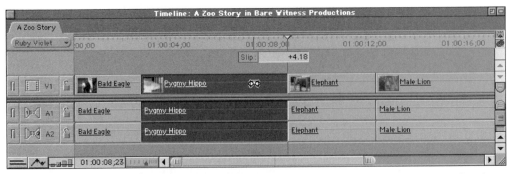

Figure 6.27 If a clip is already selected, and the current tool is the Slip tool, typing in timecode values will perform a slip. To select a clip with the Slip tool, hold down [Shift].

Slide Edit

The slide edit is sort of a reverse slip. Rather than adjusting the In and Out points of the selected clip, the slide edit changes the In and Out points of the *surrounding* clips, allowing you to slide a clip around within a sequence (**Figure 6.28**). Like Slip, Slide will not alter the overall duration of your sequence. Performing a slide is equivalent to making two roll edits in a single step.

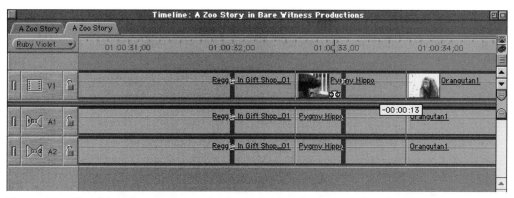

Figure 6.28 The slide edit moves your clip around within the surrounding clips. Here I'm sliding the Pygmy Hippo clip, making the previous clip (Reggie in Gift Shop_01) shorter and the following clip (Orangutan1) longer.

When to Slide

Slide is a more specialized tool than Slip, but for the right situation it's perfect. For instance, in Chapter 5 I described a situation where I put a cutaway on track V2 so I could move it back and forth to decide the best placement without disturbing the clip on track V1. Sliding is a way of performing the same operation when all your clips are on a single track.

How to Slide

Sliding a clip is done exactly the way you slip one: Select it with the Slide tool (see Figure 6.20) and drag the clip—or enter numeric values while the Slide tool is active.

Let's take a scene from *The H Tour*, a short supernatural thriller created by the Bare Witness ensemble. During a confrontation in the toolshed between Jesse and the Entity, I used an insert of a chain saw to remind the audience of the danger Jesse faced, but I didn't bother finding the perfect spot for it. While fine-tuning the sequence, I used the Slide tool to find the best placement for the shot.

The clip leading into the chain-saw shot was an MCU of Jesse, and the clip following the chain saw was a CU of the Entity. (I was also using the insert to bridge my move from MCUs to CUs.)

When I played back the sequence, my first idea was to slide the chain-saw shot earlier and have it begin just after Jesse shivers with fear (**Figure 6.29**). This made a great cut point at the head, but it had the added effect of lengthening the shot of the Entity that followed the chain-saw shot. Because all the shots of the Entity required digital effects (we painted a glow onto the shots to enhance his ethereal nature), I knew that adding extra frames to that shot meant more effects work. So I slid the chain-saw shot to a later spot, setting it to begin after Jesse begins his line, and cutting to the Entity just as he laughs.

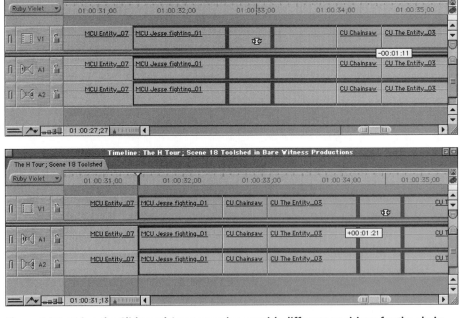

Figure 6.29 Using the Slide tool, I can experiment with different positions for the chain-saw shot.

Slide won't let you move beyond the clip boundaries of the surrounding clips, so you must choose a new location for your cutaway somewhere within the two adjacent clips. If you want to move a shot entirely out of its current position, consider the swap edit (see the section on the swap edit in Chapter 5).

Play Around Your Edit

I've emphasized already how important it is to make your editing decisions while playing your film in real time. You can't judge the nuances of proper timing any other way. So while you're trimming, get in the habit of watching your edit repeatedly as you make adjustments. The best tool for this is the Play Around Current control, which plays from five seconds before the current playhead position to a few seconds after it (**Figure 6.30**). To activate it from the keyboard, just hit ⏎ after each editing operation.

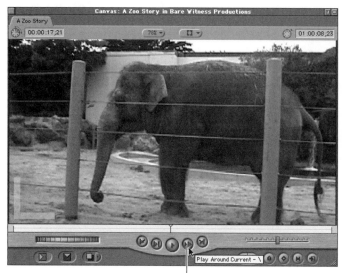

Figure 6.30 The Play Around Current control is a valuable tool to learn about. Although it sits close to the center of both Viewer and Canvas windows, it is surprisingly underused. If you find the button too small to hit easily, use ⏎ on your keyboard.

Play Around Current control

The Trim Edit Window

Fine-tuning your edits is such a critical part of the editing process that Final Cut Pro provides a way to focus your entire desktop on a single edit point. The Trim Edit window (**Figure 6.31**) shows you a zoomed-in view of a single edit point. The left frame (where the Viewer normally is) displays the last frame of the outgoing clip, and the right frame (where the Canvas usually sits) displays the first frame of the incoming clip. The Scrubber areas below the frames provide valuable information about how much media is available to you while you trim, and you'll find a few other unique controls such as the Play Around Edit Loop button.

Outgoing frame   Incoming frame

Additional frames available ⌐   ⌐ Play Around Edit Loop button

Figure 6.31 The Trim Edit window is a good way to view a single edit point.

The truth is, though, that only a few of the cool features in the Trim Edit window are not available when trimming in the Timeline, and I find that the speed and seamlessness of trimming in the Timeline outweigh the value of calling up the Trim Edit window.

So why did we include it? Well, early versions of Avid Media Composer didn't let you do trim operations like ripple, roll, slip, and slide in the Timeline—as you can in Final Cut Pro. As a result, Avid users learned to love its Big Trim mode (which is essentially the model for Final Cut Pro's Trim Edit window), and many of them refused to work any other way. To accommodate those users, we included this feature in Final Cut Pro. No doubt some editors are grateful, and perhaps you will be one of them.

Play Around Edit Loop

The Trim Edit window *does* include several excellent tools, though. For instance, the Play Around Edit Loop button.

If you hit the (Spacebar) while the Trim Edit window is active, rather than just playing forward, Final Cut Pro plays from five seconds before the current edit point to two seconds after. (These values are user-settable in the General Preferences window, which is accessible from the Edit menu.)

As the name implies, this feature loops the area around your edit—which is great, since you can watch the edit again and again. Not only that, while it's playing, you can enter numeric trim commands (such as +3, -8, +11). The next time the edit loops around, the new trim will be applied, so you can keep making tiny adjustments until you're satisfied.

You can create a similar effect while trimming in the Timeline by turning on the Loop Playback switch found in the View menu and using the Play Around Current control described in the previous section. However, unlike with using the Play Around Edit Loop button in the Trim Edit window, each time you trim, playback will be interrupted.

The Trim Viewer

Another really handy feature in the Trim Edit window is the ability to set a new edit point by using the Clip Playback controls. Since you can see the whole clip on either side of the edit point, you can play into the unused area and choose a new spot for the edit.

For example, let's say you've got a dialogue sequence like this one:

Car dealer: My friend, you've got to tell me how much you're willing to spend.

Trey: Well, I really wanted to get it for under sixty...

Trey (continued): There's all those fees and stuff...

Car dealer: My friend. Say no more. Wait right here...

Car dealer (continued): I'll be right back.

Figure 6.32 The clips are arranged in the Timeline as illustrated.

The dialogue is continuous across the edit points. But let's say you want to roll the edit between shots 2 and 3 backward so we cut to the MS just before the dealer says, "Wait right here."

You could roll the edit in the Timeline, but then you wouldn't know exactly where the car dealer begins that line in shot 3—since the media isn't visible. You could make an estimate based on where the line begins in shot 2, but because they're different shots, there's no certainty that the edit will line up properly (**Figure 6.33**).

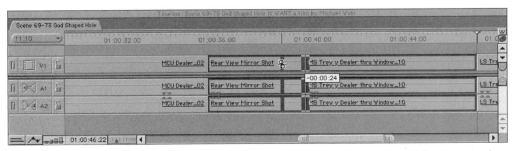

Figure 6.33 You can roll the edit in the Timeline, but you can't hear the section of shot 3 you've just added before committing to the edit.

If you work in the Trim Edit window, you can play clip 3 from beginning to end, find the exact spot the line begins, and stamp down a new In point for the clip. If you select the edit as a roll, this will automatically move the Out point of clip 2 back, and your new edit is complete (**Figure 6.34**).

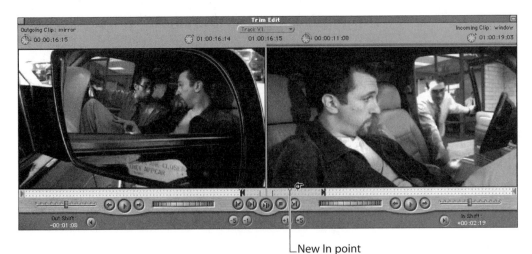

└New In point

Figure 6.34 By trimming in the Trim Edit window, you can see all the media in shot 3 and find the exact spot where you want to set the new edit point.

Trimming Under Transitions

In Chapter 5, I discussed how to edit a transition effect, including the length of the transition, its alignment on the edit point, and its parameters. But since every transition sits on an edit point, you can also trim the edit underneath the transition.

This means you can do all of the trimming operations previously discussed even on an edit where a transition effect has been applied. And you can do it in three places: in the Timeline, in the Trim Edit window, or in the Transition Editor.

Use the Timeline or Trim Edit Window for Edit Decisions

Using the Timeline or the Trim Edit window to trim an edit point with a transition on top of it is a breeze: Just pretend the transition isn't there. You can select the edit point with any of the trim tools and ripple, roll, slip, or slide the edit right underneath the transition (**Figure 6.35**). Because the transition requires additional frames beyond the edit point, the trim tools are smart enough to keep you from editing away the frames required for the transition, but otherwise you hardly have to know the effect is there.

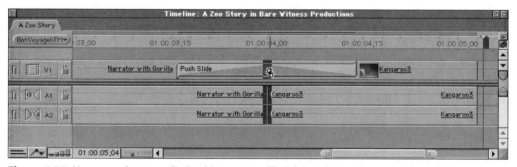

Figure 6.35 You can select an edit (in this case, a roll) right underneath a transition effect and trim it like any other edit point.

If your purpose in making the trim is to adjust overall timing or fine-tune the edit point regardless of the effect, this is the way to go. For example, if you've got a wipe that occurs across an edit that's also a continuity cut, and you want to fine-tune the edit to ensure flawless continuity, trim it just like any other edit.

Use the Transition Editor to Custom-Fit Effects

If your reason for trimming the edit-with-transition is to make the clips fit the transition better, do it in the Transition Editor. For example, suppose that the narrator of our zoo video delivers his lines facing the camera. Then, when he's finished speaking, he turns and walks offscreen-left. A push transition will move the frame of the outgoing clip offscreen from right to left while replacing it with the new clip (**Figure 6.36**). So let's further suppose that we used a push to replace the shot of the narrator with a shot of a kangaroo that's hopping right to left as well (**Figure 6.37**).

There's only one problem: When we play back the sequence, it doesn't work because the narrator starts his walk offscreen too late (**Figure 6.38**).

The way to fix the edit is to ripple the outgoing clip, making it a little bit shorter so the narrator begins walking off just as the transition begins. While we could perform this trim in the Timeline, doing it in the Transition Editor allows us to see how it will line up with the transition effect as we trim (**Figure 6.39**).

Figure 6.36 During a push, the incoming clip bodily shoves the outgoing clip out of the way.

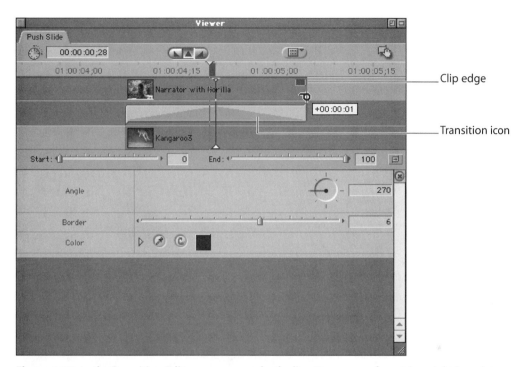

Clip edge

Transition icon

Figure 6.37 In the Transition Editor, you can see both clips. You can perform trims right here by grabbing the edge of a clip (to ripple) or by moving the Transition icon itself right or left (to roll).

Figure 6.38 The effect doesn't work because the timing is wrong on the outgoing clip.

Figure 6.39 The effect is fixed so that Reggie walks off just as the image is wiped off the screen.

Trimming in the Transition Editor

You can roll the edit point in the Transition Editor by dragging the Transition icon itself. (When you move your mouse over it, your cursor automatically becomes the Roll tool.) To ripple either the outgoing clip (above) or the incoming clip (below), click on the clip edge you want to change. Your cursor automatically changes to the Ripple tool, and you can trim the clip. The transition moves along with it (see Figure 6.37).

Canvas Provides the Feedback

As with ordinary trimming, the Canvas provides feedback while you're dragging in the Transition Editor. If you're rolling, it shows you a two-up display, but the frames you're seeing are not the ones on either side of the edit point. You're actually seeing the last-used frame of the outgoing clip and the first-used frame of the incoming clip (**Figure 6.40**).

Figure 6.40 When you roll an edit in the Transition Editor, the Canvas displays a two-up showing you the frames on either side of the transition. Note that the icons in the Transition Editor illustrate which frames are being displayed.

If you're rippling, you'll see a one-up display in the Canvas showing the frame that will become the first or last frame used in the transition (**Figure 6.41**).

Display Frame indicator

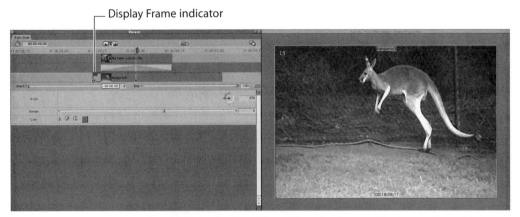

Figure 6.41 When you ripple an edit in the Transition Editor, the Canvas displays a single frame indicating the frame that's changing. The Display Frame indicator in the Transition Editor shows which frame it is.

Trimming Multiple Tracks

The trim tools are immensely powerful, and usually only advanced editors are brave enough to experiment with some of their more esoteric features. For example, many editors shy away from multitrack trimming. In fact, some of them don't even know it's possible. But if you understand exactly what you're trying to accomplish with a particular edit, this feature makes perfect sense—and will let you move really fast.

Whenever you trim, you can modify one edit on each track in your Timeline. The edits don't need to be lined up or to come from the same clips. In fact, they don't even need to be the same *type* of edit. One track can be set to ripple and another to roll. However, all of the edits will move by the same number of frames if they're selected together.

A Simple Multitrack Trim

Let's take a simple example first. Suppose we've got an interview with a lower third title card laid on top of it (**Figure 6.42**). We want the lower third to begin three seconds after the interview starts and stay on-screen for five seconds.

As we trim the beginning of the interview shot, we want the graphic to move along with the clip so it always begins exactly three seconds after the edit. So, in addition to selecting the interview clip and its corresponding audio, I add the lower third to the selection. Now as I roll or ripple the interview clip, the lower third moves along with it, always beginning exactly three seconds after the primary edit point (**Figure 6.43**).

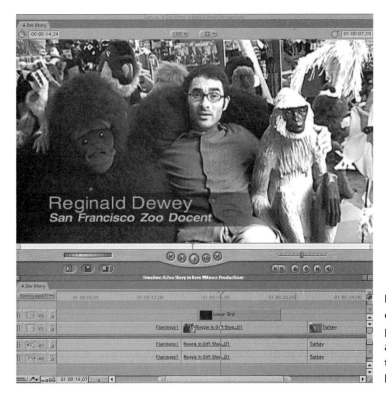

Figure 6.42 The graphic on track V2 appears precisely three seconds after the beginning of the shot below it, and lasts five seconds.

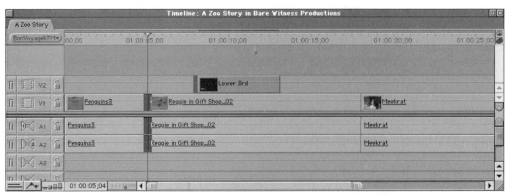

Figure 6.43 With the edit point selected at the beginning of the lower third, any edit I make will move both clips at once. Since I don't want to change the length of the lower third, I select the edit as a ripple outgoing. This ripples the gap exactly as if it were a clip. The result is that the lower third keeps its relative position to the clip below but never changes duration.

Selecting Edits, Part Two

Final Cut Pro will let you create very complex trim operations where you can roll one track while rippling two others, or modify one picture edit and an unrelated audio edit simultaneously. It all depends on what edits are selected and how they are selected when you begin trimming. You already know how to select an individual edit, but how do you add additional edits to that selection?

This is a little tricky, so pay attention.

*If linked selection is turned on, selecting one edit will automatically include edits on linked clips on other tracks (**Figure 6.44**). If you want to select one part of a linked clip as a roll, and the other as a ripple, disable linked selection or temporarily override it by holding down* Option.

Pressing ⌘ *as you click will add edits to the current selection. If you click with the Arrow tool or the Roll tool (while holding down* ⌘*), you will add the edit to the selection as a roll. If you select the Ripple tool, and* ⌘*-click on the edit, it will add that edit to the selection as a ripple (incoming or outgoing, depending on which side of the edit you click on). If you are using either the Ripple or Roll tools, you can temporarily toggle to the other by holding down* Shift.

Once an edit is selected, you can toggle which type of edit it is by clicking on it with the Ripple or Roll tool while holding down both ⌘ *and* Shift *as you click. This will allow you to set any individual edit point to any of the three states (ripple outgoing, roll, or ripple incoming) without deselecting any of the surrounding edits.*

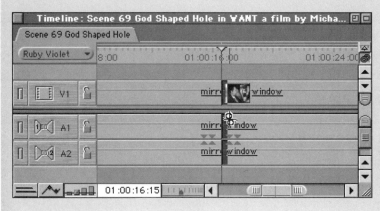

Figure 6.44 With linked selection active, selecting the video edit automatically selects corresponding edits on linked clips.

A More Complicated Multitrack Trim

Now that you get the concept, let's look at a more complex multitrack trim. Suppose you've got a number of tracks lined up together and you need to fine-tune one of the elements. This is a fairly common situation; here's how the pros approach it.

Let's say you've got a sequence with a picture edit on track V1, synced audio on track A1, sound effects on track A2, and stereo music clips on tracks A3 and A4 (**Figure 6.45**). You want to make an adjustment to the picture by trimming nine frames off the end of the outgoing clip. But a sound effect on A2 is lined up with a particular frame in the picture. Likewise, on the music track, the transition from Marrow.aif to Gray.aif is set up to happen at a particular moment in the sequence.

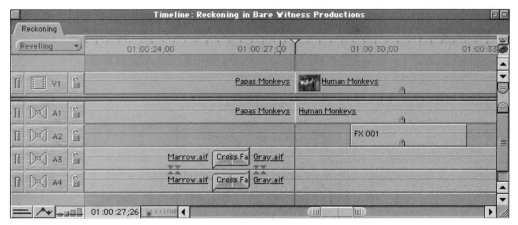

Figure 6.45 In this complex situation, you've got synced elements on five different tracks that should all be trimmed together.

Since your plan is to trim nine frames from the outgoing clip, select that edit and the corresponding audio edit as ripple outgoing edits. Next, select the sound effect as a ripple outgoing also. This ensures that it will stay in sync, no matter what changes are made to the primary edit.

Next, select the audio edit underneath the transition between the clips on A3 and A4. Since the transition can safely occur anywhere in the two songs, we can choose a roll edit here (**Figure 6.46**).

Now that all your edits are selected, you can trim the nine frames by dragging any of the edits, or by typing -9 on the keyboard. Best of all, if it turns out that nine frames isn't quite right, you can keep adjusting the edit frame by frame, as easily as typing in numbers. As long as all the edits are properly selected, they'll all move accordingly.

You could do this in separate operations, of course, but then you wouldn't be able to play back the finished edit until you had completed all three separate trims. More important, once your complex trim is properly selected, you can experiment all you like, checking the result each time. If you were doing this via a bunch of individual edits, you would have to reselect and retrim each edit point for every new frame count you try—opening the possibility of making a mistake and losing the critical timing you previously set up.

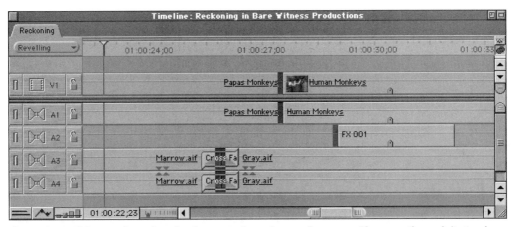

Figure 6.46 This complex edit selection actually makes perfect sense if you go through it step by step: You want the sound effect to stay at the same relative position to the video and main audio (just like the lower third in the previous example), and you want the music to transition from one clip to the next in sync with the picture edit.

Snap and Trim

Once you know where you want an edit to go, if there's a snap point there, you can drag your mouse anywhere nearby and let go. The Snapping function will take over, performing the precise alignment that's almost impossible with a mouse. This makes the Snapping feature one of the most useful tools in Final Cut Pro. Trying to make fine adjustments to an edit point during a trim edit is one of the places you'll appreciate it most.

The Snapping feature can also be one of the most *annoying* tools in Final Cut Pro: If you're not sure where you want to drop your edit, or you're trying to drop it close to a snap target but not right on it, snapping will constantly pull your mouse around, disrupting what you're trying to do and causing you major frustration.

Here's how to use snapping when it's behaving itself:

Most of the time, before you begin a trim operation, you should play your sequence and figure out (while playing) where you want the new edit point to be. Every edit point is a timing decision, and proper timing can best be gauged while playing at normal speed.

For example, let's say you're looking at an edit of someone walking down some stairs. Shot 1 is an LS of the stairway and shot 2 is a CU on the character's foot. Let's presume you've already synced up the shots so wherever you edit will have continuous motion (see the section on the continuity cut in Chapter 2, "Film Language"). Now you want to move the edit so the CU starts as soon as the guy's feet hit a certain step in the LS (**Figure 6.47**).

Figure 6.47 In this sequence, we want to line up the edit on the frame where the feet are about to hit the step.

Play the sequence until the feet in the LS are about to hit the step, and stop playback. You can set a marker at this point, or you can just park the playhead there. You can also use the In or Out point if you're not already using it for something else.

> **TIP:** Using the playhead for marking an edit point is not usually a great idea, since it's easy to forget you were using it as a placeholder and pick it up and move it accidentally.

Once you've marked the desired edit point, drag the edit to the new position and use the Snapping feature to ensure precise alignment (**Figure 6.48**).

Figure 6.48 Once your destination is marked, you can roll the edit right to it and snap it into place.

Turn Off Snapping

In Chapter 5, I mentioned a keyboard shortcut that allows you to toggle snapping, but it's worth pointing out again here, since it's one of the most important controls in the program, and one you'll use a lot while trimming.

One problem with snapping is that most of the time you never know if it's on or off when you begin dragging something. And far too often the only way you find out is the hard way: When you get near your desired end point, suddenly your mouse is pulled over to some nearby marker or edit point you don't care about. Although Final Cut Pro introduced the Snapping indicator (**Figure 6.49**) in version 2, it's so tiny that it's almost impossible to tell whether it's on or off.

Figure 6.49 The Snapping indicator resides in the upper right corner of the Timeline.

The magic fix for this potential frustration is [N], the keyboard shortcut for turning snapping on and off. Best of all, tapping [N] to toggle the snapping state works even while you're in the middle of a drag operation.

REPLACE EDIT

The replace edit is one of the most powerful tools in Final Cut Pro, but for a beginning editor, it can be confusing since it breaks some of the general rules about three-point editing. You can apply a replace edit as easily as an insert or overwrite: It is one of the options on the Edit Overlay and is also available via F11. However, you need to understand when and why to use it before it will do you much good.

Replace is actually a variation on the overwrite edit, but rather than relying only on In and Out points, it allows you to define an additional point somewhere in the middle of the clip to use as the basis for the edit. This is wonderful, because often the element that drives the cut doesn't happen exactly at the edit point. For instance, although a good edit always provides new information, a great edit doesn't necessarily provide it right at the edit point. It's often more effective to make the audience wait for it to appear sometime during the shot (see "New Shot = New Information" in Chapter 2).

The replace edit works based on the current playhead position in both the Viewer and the sequence. It lines up those two points, and then it overwrites the new clip into the sequence, replacing the clip that was previously there.

A replace edit ignores the In and Out points set in the Viewer. And if no In and Out points are specified in the sequence, Final Cut Pro uses the In and Out points of the clip currently under the playhead in the Timeline (on the target tracks). These rules make it work very differently than the basic edits described in Chapter 5.

Show Different Angles of the Same Event

Editors often use a replace edit to choose a different angle of the same event. For example, imagine that you're editing a movie about a jewelry heist. At the climax of the heist scene, security doors begin to close around the thieves, cornering them.

Since this is a big-budget picture, you've got lots of coverage to choose from. In your rough cut you used wide shots to show the doors closing, but after a sneak preview you decide to replace one of the wide shots with a CU of the door latching shut.

First, in the sequence, find the frame where the door shuts completely.

Next, in the new source clip (the CU), find the frame where the door shuts completely.

Finally, drag the source clip onto the Replace target on the Edit Overlay (**Figure 6.50**).

Figure 6.50 By lining up the playhead in both shots to the frame where the door shuts completely, we create a sync point that will enable the entire duration of the shots to sync up. We perform the replace edit by dragging onto the Edit Overlay.

Not only will this replace the WS with the CU, but the timing will be exactly the same. The door in the new clip will shut at exactly the same moment it did in the old clip.

It's helpful to have some clear point on which to sync up your replace edit, but it's not required. For instance, if you want to replace a cutaway of a security camera with a cutaway of a clock ticking, you can place your playhead anywhere in the clip—and as long as the clock shot has enough room to match the length of the security camera shot, you can successfully replace one shot with the other.

Sync a Clip With a Cue Point (Using Match Frame)

You can also use a replace edit to sync up one clip with a cue point on another track. In this case, rather than replacing one clip with another, we're going to reuse the exact same clip, but with different timing. That may sound confusing, but I'll take you through it step by step.

For example, let's stay with the jewelry heist show. In the rough cut, you covered the moment when the thieves grab the 500-carat diamond in a CU that shows the überthief lifting the stone in front of her face and gazing at it rapturously. A moment later, the security alarm goes off, and you cut to an LS showing the thieves huddling together to plan their escape.

However, test audiences are lukewarm on this sequence. According to the comment sheets, there's no suspense: Viewers don't worry about the thieves getting caught, since the robbers have already snatched the diamond seconds before the security alarm goes off.

So...back to the editing room, where you decide to change the timing so the security alarm goes off just at the instant the thief lifts the diamond. Here's how you would use a replace edit to do it.

First, open the Timeline, find the first frame of the thief lifting the jewel, and park your playhead (**Figure 6.51**).

Figure 6.51 Park your playhead on the frame you want to use as a sync point.

Next, use the Match Frame command (found in the Go To section of the Mark menu or by hitting ⬚F⬚ on the keyboard). Match Frame opens a copy of the currently viewed clip in the Viewer. Match Frame also matches the exact frame you are looking at, so the clip in the Viewer is now parked on that exact frame where the thief is about to lift the diamond.

Next, go back to the Timeline and place your playhead at the exact moment the bells go off (**Figure 6.52**).

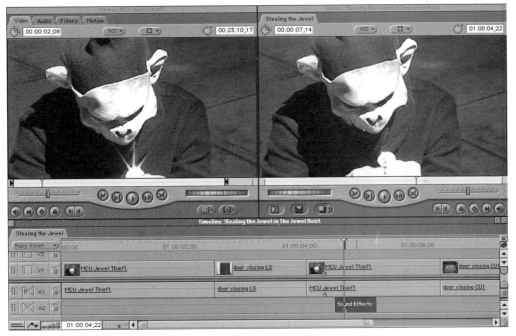

Figure 6.52 After using Match Frame to put your first sync point in the Viewer, find the spot in your sequence that's going to be the second sync point and park your playhead there.

Finally, perform a replace edit. This will line up the frame in the Viewer (the thief about to lift the jewel) with the frame in the Canvas (the sound of the alarm going off), and re-edit the same shot into the sequence with the slightly altered timing (**Figure 6.53**).

The studio loves the new version, the producer signs you on to do *The Jewel Heist II,* and when you test the show again, the audience decides it liked the original sequence better.

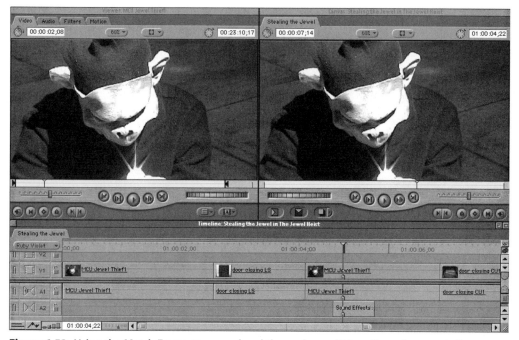

Figure 6.53 Using the Match Frame command and the replace edit together allows us to line up two spots in a few simple steps. I've used markers to show you that the two points are now lined up, but the markers aren't required.

Replace With In and Out Points

The replace edit doesn't require any In and Out points, but you can use sequence Ins and Outs to give you additional control over how the edit works.

For example, let's go back to the shot of the doors closing where we replaced a WS with a CU. Suppose that rather than replacing the whole shot, we just wanted to cut to the CU one second before the door closes. We can do that using an In point and a replace edit.

You would begin the same way, by opening the CU in the Viewer and parking the playhead on the frame where the door closes.

Next, in the Timeline, find the frame where the door closes in the WS and mark an In point one second earlier. Be sure that the playhead is still parked on the sync point, which is the door closing (**Figure 6.54**).

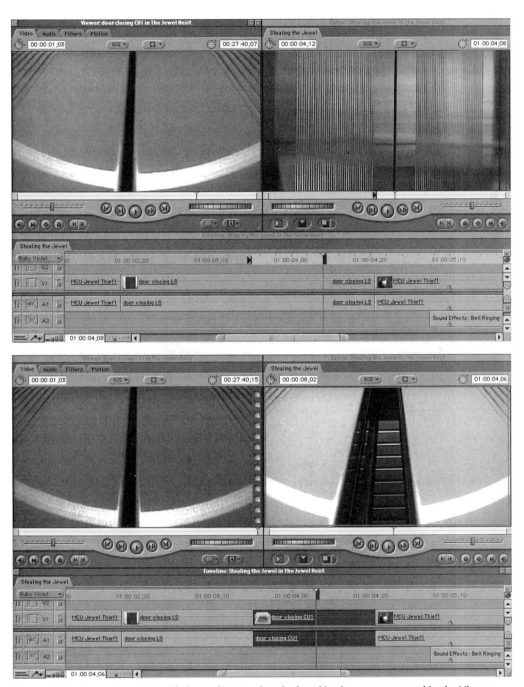

Figure 6.54 The replace edit will always line up the playhead in the sequence and in the Viewer, but if there's an In or Out point in the Timeline, the edit will observe it.

When you perform the replace edit, only the area between the defined In point and the end of the clip is replaced, not the whole clip. Now the WS cuts to the CU one second before the door closes. Continuity flows across the edit point, since the door was closing at the same speed in both shots, and we know that they are synced because Replace lined up the two frames of the door closing.

Sync to a Playhead Position Outside the In/Out Mark

You can take this one step further by syncing to a point *even if it's outside the area being replaced*. If you define an In and Out point in the sequence, and place the playhead outside of that area, the playhead location will still serve as a sync point.

Fiendish, eh? I must admit that in many ways, this is my favorite tool in the entire program!

Let's keep it simple and stay with the same set of door clips. Imagine that instead of cutting to the CU just as the door shuts, we want to cut to the CU for a couple of seconds while the door is closing, and then cut back to the LS as it actually closes. This could be an exciting cut: starting wide, jumping in close, and jumping back out as the action completes. Since we want the action to be continuous across all the cuts, we'll use the moment the door shuts as the sync point and put the playhead on that point in both the Viewer and the Timeline.

But this time, we'll set an In and an Out point in the Timeline just about midway in the door-closing shot—and the same distance apart as the length of CU you want to use (**Figure 6.55**).

When the replace edit is performed, the portion of the source clip used is lined up based on the sync point, but the section actually used is based on the In and Out points provided. The edit points on both sides of the clip will be solid continuity cuts, since everything was lined up on the frames when the door closed.

OK, this is a pretty advanced way to use the Replace tool, but once you begin experimenting you will probably find equally wonderful ways to use it. For instance, you can use this technique to sync up clips that have a slate at the head without having to include the slate footage in the sequence.

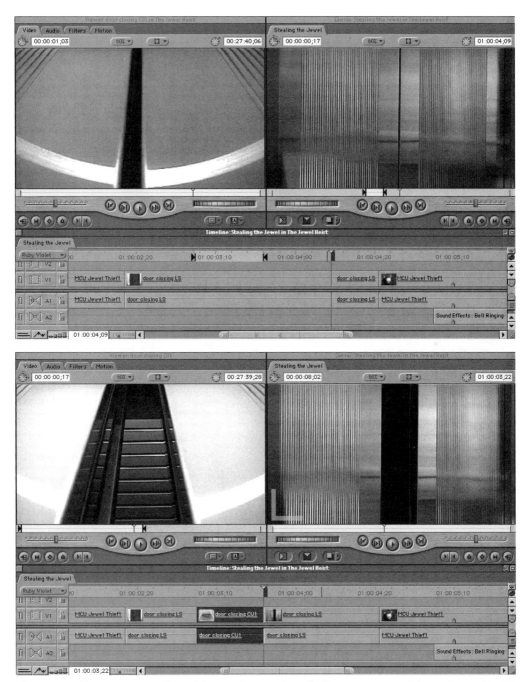

Figure 6.55 You can set your In and Out marks anywhere in the sequence, and the replace edit will back-time the edit based on the two playhead positions. Here we use the door shutting as the sync point even though it's not part of the shot we're replacing.

Make Sure You Have Enough Media in the Viewer

The most common problem editors experience when using a replace edit comes from having insufficient room on one or the other side of the playhead in the Viewer. For example, if you are trying to replace a 10-second clip in the Timeline, and your playhead is parked 7 seconds in, your source clip in the Viewer will need to have at least 7 seconds before and 3 seconds after the current playhead position. If your playhead in the Viewer is only 1 second into the clip (even if the clip is 30 seconds long), the edit will fail and give you an error message saying you have insufficient content for the edit (**Figure 6.56**). To perform this edit, your playhead in the Viewer must be at least 7 seconds into the clip, and there must be at least 3 seconds remaining after (**Figure 6.57**).

Figure 6.56 To execute a successful replace edit, you must have sufficient media in your source clip. Here, the playhead in the Viewer is parked at 1:00, but the playhead in the sequence is parked seven seconds into the clip. Attempting a replace edit at this point gives an error message.

Figure 6.57 By moving the Viewer playhead farther into the clip, you get plenty of room before and after the playhead to replace the target clip in the Timeline.

SPLIT EDITS

I've already talked quite a bit about why and when you'll find yourself using split edits. By separating track edits from picture edits, you can smooth over the inevitable interruption any edit creates. Split edits are essential for almost every dialogue scene and many action scenes as well.

Most editors split their edits after the clips are already in the sequence by rolling the video edit separately from the audio edit, or vice versa (**Figure 6.58**). This works fine, but frequently you need to adjust the new edit point a bit to finish the job.

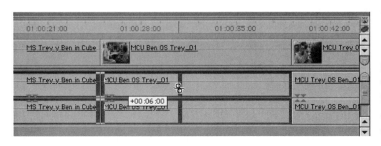

Fig 6.58 The simplest way to create a split edit is to roll either the picture or the track edit point without the other.

Fine-Tuning a Split Edit

Different cases may require different amounts of fine tuning, but a potent combination of rolling and rippling enables you to create and polish the split edits that make transitions smoother, overlap your dialogue to sound natural, and sync up various material across different shots.

I'll use a typical dialogue sequence as an example.

Ben: It's a new video game! I want to call it Senseless Death.

Trey: Ben, that's sick!

Ben: (nods excitedly)

Trey (continued): How do they get away with sending guns through the mail?

Ben: I don't know, dude! It's Thailand. They don't know what the hell's going on!

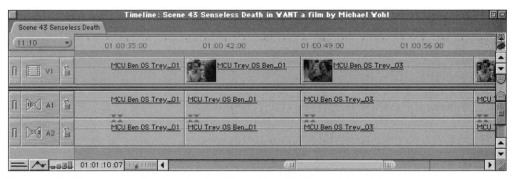

Figure 6.59 The sequence begins with the three clips, all with straight edits.

As is almost always the case, the dialogue runs continuously across the edit points. And so far, all the edits in this sequence line up on dialogue breaks. I haven't made any split edits yet.

Now I want to split the last edit, so the beginning of Ben's line, "I don't know, dude..." is heard over shot 2. Here's how:

1. I play the sequence and stop at the point where I want the new edit. I set the In point or a marker to identify the spot.

2. I roll the video edit forward until it reaches the marker (**Figure 6.60**).

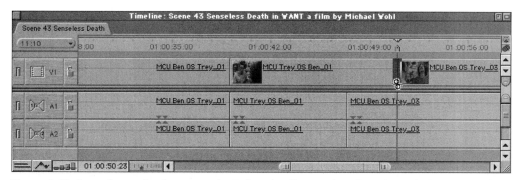

Figure 6.60 Once the marker is set, use the Roll tool to line up the edit point with the desired spot.

In some cases, this may be all you need to do. But sometimes after you roll the edit, you'll spot footage in the first shot that doesn't sync up with the audio underneath it. In this case, even though shot 2 is an OS, where Ben is facing away, his movements don't match the timing of the audio from shot 3. To solve this, we can further trim the edit using the Ripple tool (**Figure 6.61**).

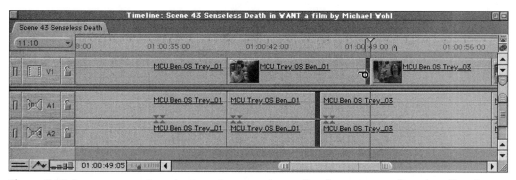

Figure 6.61 In many cases, in order to make a seamless split edit you must adjust the edit point after the initial roll. Here I ripple the clip back to compress the time in between the lines and generally tidy up the timing of the edit.

Now when we play the sequence, the offset of the split hasn't changed, but we've trimmed the end of shot 2. This tightens the edit, allowing less dead space between lines, and more important, it syncs up Ben's movements in shot 2 with the lines heard in shot 3.

Split Marks

Because split edits are such a fundamental part of professional editing, Final Cut Pro has a special feature designed to make creating them easier: split marks. When you're setting your In and Out points in either the Viewer or the Canvas, this feature makes setting different points for your audio and video a snap (**Figure 6.62**). It allows you to define the split edits before you edit the clips into the sequence.

Why would you bother? It's great for cases when you already know from watching the source clip where you want to split the edit. For instance, fairly often when I'm cutting dialogue I'll hear a line or see a gesture that I know will precipitate an edit. I can mark a video only or audio only In point right there in the Viewer and figure out the other point later.

Figure 6.62 Split marks let you set individual In and Out points for your audio and video. Video marks are on the top half and audio, the lower. You can drag one of the points individually by holding down Option .

How to Set Split Marks

Split marks can be set (and cleared) by using the commands in the Mark menu (**Figure 6.63**), or by accessing the Shortcut menu in the Scrubber area of the Viewer and Canvas or the ruler in the Timeline. Of course, as good editors, I know you want to learn how to set them on the fly, and while the key combos are a little convoluted, Final Cut Pro provides one for each case:

Mark Video In	Ctrl – I
Mark Video Out	Ctrl – O
Mark Audio In	⌘ – Option – I
Mark Audio Out	⌘ – Option – O

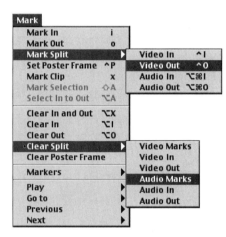

Figure 6.63 The Mark menu contains submenus for marking splits and clearing splits. While you can use keyboard shortcuts for marking individual Ins and Outs, if you want to clear a point you have to use Option – I or Option – O (which clears both Ins or both Outs) or Option – X (which clears everything).

While splitting marks provides impressive power in terms of allowing you to perform a very complex edit in a single step, it also requires more presence of mind in the planning of the edit. You must be able to hold twice as much information in your head as you do with an ordinary edit. Where do you want the picture to begin in the source clip? Where does the audio begin? Do they end at the same point, or is the backside of the clip going to be a split edit as well? And in the sequence, where do you want the split to begin and end? Finally, once you've sorted all that out, you have to decide which of the various points you have to define.

Four-, Five-, and Six-Point Editing

With three-point editing, you need to provide only three of the four necessary points in order to complete the edit. But when you're working with split edits, the number of points you need to define varies. And inexplicably, only some combinations work.

One Split

The simplest arrangement is to split only one of the four points. For example, you might define separate source video In and source audio In points and leave the Out point undefined. You can then set unsplit In and Out points in the Canvas (**Figure 6.64**).

Figure 6.64 The simplest use of split marks is to split only one of the four marks. As with three-point editing, you can leave one of the points undefined.

When you apply the edit, whichever of the split source In points (audio or video) comes first will line up with the sequence In point (**Figure 6.65**).

Figure 6.65 When you edit this clip into the sequence, the sequence In point lines up with the earlier of the two source In marks in the Viewer.

This is the most common way to use split marks—but you need to be aware that the reverse case doesn't work. If you split the source Out point and provide a record Out, Final Cut Pro ignores the audio Out point and treats the video Out as if it were an unsplit Out. This is a bug, and unless you know about it, it may drive you nuts. Unfortunately, you may run into quite a few cases like this (**Figure 6.66**).

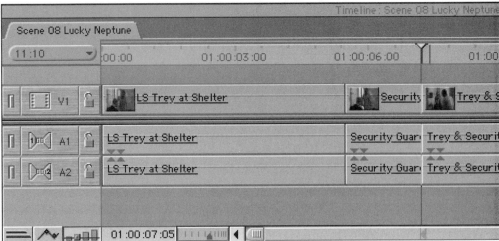

Figure 6.66 One case that doesn't work (for no good reason) is where you split the source Out and don't set a record In.

Two Splits

Often you want to define exactly where the edits land in the sequence. As I explained, the program default causes the sequence In point to sync with the earlier of the two points in the Viewer. If you want to override that default so the sequence In point lines up with the *later* of the two points, you can make that happen by setting a single split mark in the sequence (**Figure 6.67**).

Video only In

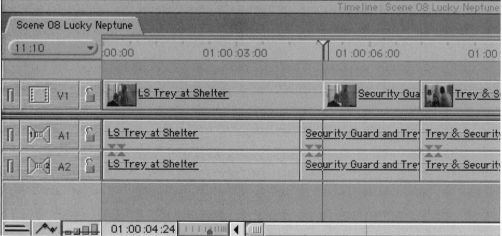

Figure 6.67 If you want to override Final Cut Pro's default (which puts the earlier split source point at the sequence In), set a split sequence In. This will put the edit exactly where you want it.

Why would you want to do this? Well, once you've begun a sequence, each clip you edit in must match up to one that's already there. If you're editing with lots of splits, you're going to have to sync up either the audio or the video as a continuity cut.

For example, let's say you have a sequence of two people talking. You're cutting back and forth between MCUs, and you know that you want to create an L cut so the incoming picture hits before the incoming track arrives.

You can split the respective starting points for audio and video in the Viewer, but when you go to edit it into the sequence, you're primarily concerned about lining up the audio so the dialogue seems continuous; you don't care exactly where the picture edit happens (**Figure 6.68**). To accomplish this, simply mark an audio In at the desired point in the Timeline and the dialogue will line up perfectly. The picture edit may need some fine-tuning, but the L edit will be accomplished in a single operation.

> **TIP:** You can't set two pairs of splits that don't match. If you attempt to set a source split where the audio precedes the video by 20 frames, and at the same time you set a split in the sequence where the audio precedes the video by 10 frames (or the video precedes the audio at all), you'll get an Invalid Edit error.

Banana Split

As you gain confidence and experience, you can get pretty creative, setting a wide variety of split marks to perform very complex edits with a single stroke. (Imagine a shot that's an L edit at the head and a J edit at the tail and gets laid into the sequence at a precise location you've defined with a split mark.) Unfortunately, you'll probably encounter some arrangements of split marks (in addition to the one I identified previously) that just don't work—even though they should. If you run into one, you've probably hit a bug. Call Apple.

While I do recommend fooling around with split marks, I find that if I'm trying to do anything much more complicated than what I described in previous sections, I spend more time *preparing* the edit than I save by doing it in one step. In many cases, it's faster to perform a basic edit (or a simple split) and tweak it in the Timeline after the fact.

└─ Audio only In

Figure 6.68 In this example I want to specify exactly where the audio In point begins in the sequence, and then create an L edit in one step by using the split marks in the Viewer.

Use Subsequences to Manage Large Projects

If you're working with a longer show and you want to simplify the editing process, you should try the Nested Sequences feature—as long as you're willing to work within a few limitations.

You can construct each scene in its own sequence, then create a master sequence and drop in your subsequences one after another so you can see all the scenes in order (**Figure 6.69**). If you do this, swapping scene order is just as easy as swapping individual clips. Simply pick up a scene, drag it to its new location, hold down (Option), and release.

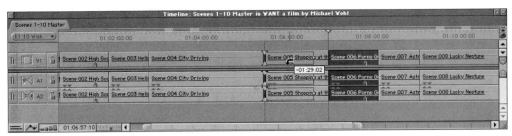

Figure 6.69 You can arrange each scene as a single sequence in a master sequence. This allows you to rearrange sequences just as you would clips.

Unfortunately, the subsequence architecture in Final Cut Pro was not designed to be used for this purpose. It was intended primarily for use in compositing applications (see the section on compositing in Chapter 8, "Special Effects"). So watch out for a few features that don't work the way you expect—or that sometimes don't work at all.

Duration Changes Don't Propagate

Although most editorial changes you make in a subsequence (such as replacing a clip or rolling an edit) will be reflected when you play back the master sequence, changes to the duration of that sequence won't show up.

For instance, suppose you put 10 scenes into a master sequence, and the duration of scene 4 was 2:43. Then suppose you went back into scene 4 and made changes, including some rippling that shortened the scene's duration to 2:20. The master sequence will still think the subsequence is 2:43 and will display black video for those last 23 seconds. If you had made the subsequence longer, the master sequence would simply cut it off abruptly at 2:43.

Workaround: Ripple the Subsequence

The workaround here is fairly straightforward: Go into the master sequence and ripple subsequence 4 to make it longer or shorter to accommodate the changes (**Figure 6.70**).

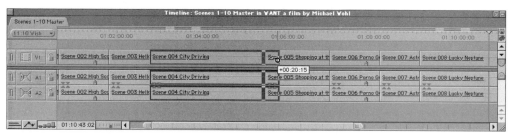

Figure 6.70 You can grab the edge of a subsequence and ripple it just like a clip. Do this to update your master sequence when you've changed the duration of one of the subsequences within it.

No Way to Extract an EDL

Another shortcoming of the subsequence architecture is that while you might expect that you could export an EDL from your master sequence that would cover your whole show, you can't. EDLs can't see inside subsequences, so you'll just get an EDL with ten events, one for each subsequence, which will be worthless.

Workaround: Copy and Paste

The only suitable workarounds are:

• export individual EDLs for each subsequence.

• copy and paste all the clips from each subsequence into a new master sequence.

Neither of these is a terribly elegant solution. If you choose to copy and paste, your new sequence may be a bit unwieldy and will take some time to create. (Final Cut Pro's Copy and Paste tools are notoriously slow.) Moreover, changes you make to the individual subsequences won't be reflected in the master. But if you do this once, at the very end of your edit, it will enable you to export a single EDL for backup or import it into another editing system.

More Media Management Woes

Recapturing, reconnecting clips, and Media Manager operations are all likely to create errors when working with sequences containing subsequences. I don't know of any handy workarounds for these problems, other than to avoid using subsequences if you need any of these media control tools. Hopefully, future versions of Final Cut Pro will address the unreliability of these features and swat the bugs.

THE BIG PICTURE

All these advanced editing techniques tend to focus our attention on the minute details of every edit, and that's important because you'll be employing many of these techniques for thousands of edits in your show.

But don't forget to step back at some point and look at the whole chessboard. The worst editing mistake you can make, far more dangerous than losing an edit point or using a roll when you need a ripple, is losing sight of the big picture.

What Makes a Sequence Work?

When you play back a sequence, ask yourself whether it works.

At the very least, the narrative flow should be smooth: No edit points should jar the viewer and disturb the story. Also, the pacing should be right: no "dead" sections where nothing is happening, no areas so dense that viewers can't make sense of what's going on. Finally, the sequence should be free of blatant continuity errors caused by editing or production mistakes. (For instance, if the hero's hat was on in the CU, it should be on in the next LS.) If you see any of these problems, dive back in and fix them.

But that's just for openers. After you've worked out your various scenes, look at the overall movie and decide how it makes you feel. How does the show *play?* Here are some important things to watch out for.

Awkward Bridges Between Scenes

Pay attention to scene cuts (see the section on scene cuts in Chapter 2). How well do the scenes transition from one to the next? If they don't flow, can you create bridges with sound or compositional elements to help smooth out the scene changes? Sometimes simply rearranging the order of scenes (like swapping shots in an individual sequence) can make a huge difference.

The Overall Story

In most cases, the film embodies thematic elements you are trying to convey or theses you want to prove or disprove. Does the film accomplish those goals? If it's intended to be informative or educational, does it convey the relevant information effectively, economically, and efficiently? If it's a dramatic feature, is it exciting? Is it unique? Is it moving?

Put Away the Script

Sometimes problems are inherent in the script. This may give you a scapegoat, but it won't make your picture better. At some point in the production process, the script becomes irrelevant. You must find a way to make the best movie you can make with the footage available to you.

If the film is in serious trouble, you may have to cut important subplots, or even turn a subplot into the main plot while you downgrade what was supposed to be the main plot to a background event. Obviously, in a drastic revision like this, you'll need to work closely with the director and the writer to decide how to proceed.

Honesty Is the Best Policy

Everyone on the production team must be brutally honest about what works, what doesn't work, and what can be done to improve the film. While I certainly recommend being diplomatic and constructive in offering criticism, you're not doing anyone any favors by pretending something is good when it isn't. You need to be just as honest about your show as you'd be about any show you came across on TV, in a film festival, or at your local theater.

Put Up and Shut Up

Of course, you want to make the best show you can, but if you're editing a film for a corporate client or a governmental agency, all that matters is whether or not your client likes the finished piece. It doesn't really matter whether you like it or your husband likes it or you want to include it on your sample reel. Your job is to give the client what he wants.

Show It to Somebody

On the other hand, if you're cutting a film for public consumption, part of your obligation to the producer and the director is to make it as effective as possible for the audience. This means getting outside input. At some point, you need to show the program to someone completely disconnected from the project (and, ideally, representative of your target audience) to provide some real-world perspective.

Make It Shorter

If a film is too long, it doesn't matter how good it is: Fatigue and impatience will alienate your audience. It's a given in the film biz that you can make almost any film shorter—and nine times out of ten it will be better. But it can be a bloody affair. If you're looking at a show that isn't quite working, start by identifying what can be cut.

Recently I watched a rough cut of a friend's film. She intended it to be a theatrical feature, and the rough cut was 96 minutes, but it had some problems and she wanted advice about how to resolve them. While many of the scenes were terrific— funny, poignant, and honest—a handful of scenes were heavy-handed, poorly acted, even slightly untruthful. On top of which *all* of the scenes went on too long. I decided that about one third of the film was great, one third was mediocre, and one third was poor.

So I suggested that my friend consider turning her feature into a short. At 30 minutes, it could have been a terrific film: entertaining, meaningful, and funny. Sure, she'd have a significant amount of work to do to tie together the great moments, but a great 30-minute film would be a lot better than an uneven one that ran 90 minutes.

The length of a show has a broader impact on your audience than you may realize. Some of it's purely physical. For instance, how long can your audience sit still comfortably? (Movie theater seats are cushioned, but the seats in most classrooms or corporate auditoriums are not.) Will people need a bathroom break? These may sound like silly questions, but for longer projects you must take them seriously.

I remember an early review of *Titanic* in which the reviewer went on and on about how, as the show moved into its third hour, with shot after shot featuring torrents of rushing water, pouring water, dripping water, spilling water, crashing water, all he could think about was how desperately he needed to pee! At the end of the film, he said, the line outside the men's bathroom was out the door.

Unless you have stars like Leonardo DiCaprio and Kate Winslet (and a director like James Cameron) to keep your viewers in their seats, you should consider how distracting that sort of physical discomfort can be and how it can interfere with your audience's appreciation of your film.

Anyone can cut bad footage from a film. The mark of a great editor is knowing how to cut *good* footage to make what's left even better.

Keep Cutting

No matter how many times I've polished it, every time I sit down in front of a scene I'm working on, I see ways to trim a few more seconds. Trust your audience to read your shots quickly, and keep feeding them new ideas and fresh information to hold their interest. I'm not talking about spoon-feeding eye candy to impatient channel surfers; I'm talking about engaging your viewers with meaningful material.

My first rough cut of *Want* was 190 minutes long! My target length was 90 to 110 minutes. I had to find a way to cut at least half the film.

Before I went crazy cutting whole scenes, I reviewed each scene and tightened it up. I removed dead spaces between lines. I cut some lines altogether. I eliminated transitional shots that seemed extraneous. And before I had to cut one single scene, I'd eliminated more than 40 minutes. Five seconds here, ten seconds there, and not only did the film become shorter, it played faster and better. Later, on another tightening pass, I managed to wring out another 12 minutes.

Kill Your Darlings

Even if you are enthralled with the composition at the end of the shot, when two women are walking off of the bridge silhouetted against the sunset, that doesn't justify 15 seconds of dead time between the last line of dialogue and that wonderful image.

Unless you've made a very bad decision about your chosen profession, any film you edit will be packed with moments—sometimes as brief as a single reaction shot, sometimes as long as a whole scene—that fill you with pride when they go by. Maybe you're particularly happy with one continuity edit that took two hours to match, or some serendipitous cut that seems to make a statement about the entire film. Perhaps it's a scene that cost a fortune to produce, or a performance that gave the director chills on set.

Whatever it is, if it doesn't work in the finished film, it's got to go. And you're the one who has to kill it.

I'll tell you a story. In my film *Want,* there was an interesting character, an old woman named Señora Guero. I wanted to draw a subtle connection between Guero and the younger woman Trey is infatuated with, so I asked the same actor to play both roles. We used latex makeup to age her for the scenes where she portrayed the old woman.

The actor hated sitting through the tedious makeup sessions. Applying the latex took more than five hours, and it was quite uncomfortable. To make matters worse, after watching the dailies I decided I didn't like the way the makeup looked anyway, and I wanted to reshoot all of her scenes using a different type of latex. So a series of scenes that was supposed to take two days wound up taking more than six. Hiring the special effects makeup artist was very expensive, and all of the scenes involving Guero were technically complicated and emotionally intense. Those six days were unquestionably the most costly and grueling days of our whole production.

I'm sure you know where this story is going. Late in the editing process, unhappy with the way the film was coming together, I made a drastic decision and cut the entire subplot involving Señora Guero. It was an agonizing decision, but it changed everything—and for the better. Not only did it allow me to trim ten minutes off the total running time, it opened up new opportunities for ways to bring the scenes together. My crew and I grieved for Guero, but in the end killing her scenes was what needed to be done.

Find Redundancies

A certain amount of repetition can be artful, as in comedy or suspense (see "Funnier the Second Time Around" in Chapter 3). But invariably you'll find scenes or shots in your show that are redundant. Perhaps the same point is being made twice, two scenes may communicate the same emotion, or maybe a significant gesture or shot is repeated too many times. You must eliminate these elements. Find the one that does the job best, and cut the others. Most often, repetition merely slows down the story with unnecessary information.

Intercut Scenes

One trick to help you shorten your show is to intercut scenes. You may find that two four-minute scenes can be intercut to make one six-minute sequence, with virtually no loss of impact. Even if you don't stick with the intercut version, I guarantee the exercise will help you find at least one minute from each scene that's expendable.

You can apply this technique to other redundant elements as a way to boil them down to the essentials. If you have three scenes that all basically accomplish the same thing thematically or plot-wise, try intercutting them. You may find that one shot from each scene is all you need.

Game of Inches

I used to race sailboats, and someone once described the sport to me as a game of inches. Not so much because the winning boat might cross the finish line inches in front of its competitor, but because in a tight race, boats can maneuver mere inches apart, nearly colliding and damaging one another. Also, the stiffer the sail, the more precisely you can control the wind, and pulling the main sheet three inches tighter will make a measurable difference that could determine whether you win or lose the race.

In the same ways, editing can also be a game of inches. Tiny changes can have a huge impact on the overall show. An edit point that's off by only three or four frames will make a transition look terrible. One poor edit can make a whole scene play badly. Eliminating just one shot that doesn't fit perfectly will change the entire dynamic of a sequence. And one slow sequence can make the whole show seem too long.

While we're talking about inches, be careful not to oversteer. Make very small changes and see how they impact the whole before you do something drastic. The more experience you get, the more you'll understand how a few subtle changes can make a huge impact on the whole.

Early in my career, I found myself editing a short film about a hotel clerk—and when I showed my first cut to the director, he hated it. He couldn't tell me exactly what was wrong, but he felt I hadn't captured the best performances from the actors.

I spent days going back through bins of outtakes (I was editing 16mm film), desperately watching all the footage and trying to find new shots that would save the film. Then I began to doubt myself and started making broad changes to the cut. After a while, when I detested the way it was coming out, I went back in deep despair and restored the film to a close approximation of what my first rough cut had been. However, in all my reshuffling I had managed to lose a piece of film (easy to do when you're cutting 16mm), and I had to cut the scene together without it.

As soon as I watched the film, I felt different about it. The shot I'd lost was a reaction shot in which the main character had been hamming it up a little. When I showed the new cut to the director, he didn't realize exactly what the difference was, but he agreed that I had made a huge improvement over the last edit.

The moral is: Don't despair, make changes judiciously, and trust the process. You may discover that the scene or sequence you thought was unsalvageable simply needed two shots switched around.

Interview: CHRIS TELLEFSEN

Chris Tellefsen began editing professionally in 1990 on Whit Stillman's *Metropolitan*. Since then he's worked on an amazing variety of projects, everything from Wayne Wang's improvisational *Blue in the Face* to Milos Forman's controversial *The People vs. Larry Flynt*. His credits also include comedies like Harold Ramis's *Analyze This* and David O. Russell's *Flirting with Disaster*. When we spoke, he was right in the middle of cutting *Changing Lanes* for British director Roger Michell.

Michael Wohl: What do you love most about your job?

Chris Tellefsen: What I love more than anything, I guess, is creating and constructing scenes and carving out performances. Making performances really shine and bringing them forward. And shaping the whole.

How do you get from a long rough cut to the final length?

You really have to feel it out, feel where the strengths lie and the weaknesses are, where things feel repetitive. And you only know that from repeated viewings and studying it. Once it's all together, you get more of a sense of overall style and things that feel right. You can get more of an idea of how to keep it interesting rhythmically, pacing the rhythm, keeping it in hills and valleys. Making sure that it doesn't have too even a pace.

Can you talk a bit about cutting comedy?

Comedy has its form: You have to get a laugh. It's very clear what you're trying to achieve. It's a matter of sharpening it and making it really, really razor-sharp funny. That's where the preview process is fun. You feel what's coming off the audience, and in your head you're checking out when those responses are not quite there. With drama it's less well-defined.

What are you looking for in the preview audience for a drama?

Engagement. You're looking for them to be engaged with the characters. To be engaged with the story, to have a satisfying experience. You have to feel their presence, feel their response. Whereas with comedy, you know they've had a satisfying experience if they're laughing.

Has editing on the computer changed the way you work?

Sometimes the most thoughtful cut is a spontaneous cut. That's something I love about digital: You can be very spontaneous. You can suddenly have a thought and go with it. And even if it's the totally wrong way, you can just undo it. It's so flexible. I find it very liberating. I loved film editing, but you can do so much more with digital.

How was working with Milos Forman?

He was very grumpy. I did four versions of a scene one time and he was very intrigued. He said, "Oh, this is better, but not four versions, ten versions!" And it was insanity; I was making 11 cuts of every scene. It was like boot camp. And when we worked together it was like, no joke, we were in the cutting room from 9:30 in the morning till 11:00 at night. We'd never look away.

CHAPTER SEVEN

Cutting the Track

Do you remember *The Blair Witch Project?* I bet while you were watching it you thought, "I can do that!" As far as script and photography go, you probably could. But what you may not realize is that before it was released to your local theater, the distributor probably spent close to ten times the entire production budget on a new sound mix. Without excellent sound, no one would have been able to sit through it.

Even if modern audiences are learning to tolerate lower visual quality (as illustrated by the success of films like *The Blair Witch Project,* with all that miserable hand-held, low-resolution video footage), they show far less tolerance for a soundtrack that falls short of the highest production values. (Maybe it's those THX trailers movie theaters run to demonstrate how good the sound system is.) Without exception, ultra-low-budget films like *Blair Witch* or *El Mariachi* need to have their tracks heavily cleaned up and remixed before showing up at your local theater.

SOUND MAKES THE SHOW

Sound is the current that drives the flow of the entire show: an unseen force guiding the movement of the visual elements. This is why L and J cuts are so important to smooth editing. Creating a fluid and apparently seamless audio track is critical to keeping your audience immersed in the film.

The problem for most inexperienced editors is that sound is literally invisible, which makes it easy to forget. But underestimating the importance of sound is a huge mistake.

A successful film depends more on good sound than it does on good visuals. While it's true that our culture is highly focused on visual information, I believe we are more affected by what we hear than by what we see.

Sound has a direct link to our emotions. If seeing is believing, then perhaps hearing is feeling. Think of how powerful music is, how listening to a symphony or even a well-crafted pop song can move you to tears or exhilaration. Images rarely deliver as immediate an emotional impact.

Of course, it's the combination of image and sound that makes film such a powerful medium. This unique joining touches the audience in a complex way by mixing visual information with the emotional power carried by sound. In this way, film can create a more engrossing experience than any other medium.

It all comes together on the soundtrack, which is created in a process called the sound mix.

WHAT IS A SOUND MIX?

After the picture is locked, the last stage of editing is the sound mix. Here the three kinds of audio—dialogue, sound effects, and music—must be brought together, combined, and arranged. These can be further divided into many separate elements, each of which will get its own track in the mix. These days a movie mix typically includes at least 24 to 48 tracks; some films use as many as 120! Even the smallest projects gobble up to 8 or 10 audio tracks very quickly.

DIALOGUE TRACKS

Dialogue or narration is the most information-heavy of your audio elements, and you want it to sound as clear and natural as possible. In fact, it's common practice to *equalize* or *sweeten* each voice separately so you can optimize its audio parameters. On a traditional mixing board you can assign only one *EQ* setting to a given *pot,* so each voice is placed on a different one.

> **EQUALIZATION (EQ)**   *Fine-tuning an audio track by boosting or lowering certain frequencies (or bands of frequencies). For instance, you can boost higher frequencies to improve clarity or reduce low-frequency rumble.*

> **SWEETEN** *A general term referring to various types of manipulation used to improve the sound quality of an audio element or track. Sweetening might include removing hiss or pops, equalizing a track so it will match a particular environment, and so on.*

The equivalent in Final Cut Pro is to put each voice on its own track in the Timeline. Technically, this is not required, since Final Cut Pro allows you to assign different EQ settings to individual clips even if they lie on the same track. However, it's still fairly common for filmmakers to complete their sound mix outside of Final Cut Pro. If that's your plan, you should break out your voice elements on different tracks to prepare for that eventuality (**Figure 7.1**). This can be a huge amount of additional work, but external audio mixing systems require this type of separation.

> **POT** *Short for potentiometer. A pot is the control knob (or slider) that adjusts the volume of a particular track or input on a multitrack audio control board. The term can also refer to a single track.*

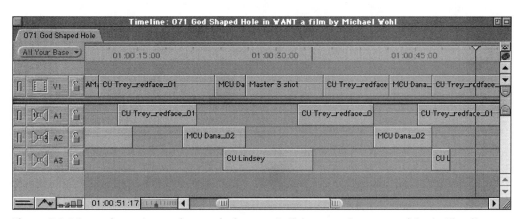

Figure 7.1 It's good practice to place each character's dialogue on its own track in the Timeline.

SOUND EFFECTS TRACKS

Anything in your soundtrack that's neither dialogue nor music is considered part of the sound effects. Sound effects can be divided into environmental sounds and non-environmental sounds.

Environmental Sound

Environmental sound is caused by on-screen objects or events and includes doors closing, footsteps, gunshots, ringing telephones, and so on. While it's common practice to dedicate only a single track to these elements, it's not at all unusual for two or more effects to occur simultaneously. This requires multiple tracks—one for each of these *practical* sound effects (**Figure 7.2**).

> **PRACTICAL** *Any prop or object in a scene that is actually used by the production. For instance, a bedside lamp that is part of the scene lighting is called a practical. Similarly, any device that makes a sound on-screen, such as a car door or water faucet, might be called a practical element.*

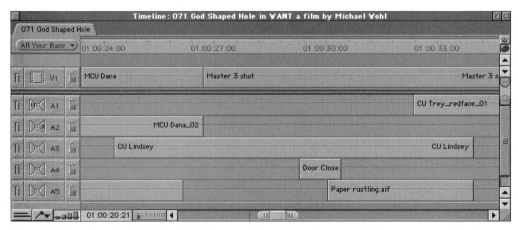

Figure 7.2 You should dedicate a few tracks to different practical sound effects elements. Big-budget shows often break out each element in a scene on its own track.

Creating Sound Effects After the Shoot

Any sound that occurs on-screen can be re-created in post-production. This gives the sound editor more control over the element. For one thing, it can be faded in and out separately from the dialogue track—and creating effects after the fact allows the sound designer to alter the sound for psychological effect.

For example, in the movie *Twister*, about tornado chasers, the sounds of the tornadoes were completely synthetic, fabricated from elements as unlikely as wild animal roars and kitchen appliances such as dishwashers and blenders.

If you don't have the budget or time to build your own sound effects from scratch, you can find libraries of commonly used sounds such as cars, sirens, crowds applauding, gunshots, and so on. Typically, these libraries (available on CD) offer many choices for each sound, so you can search for the one that fits your visuals best. The problem with using libraries is that unless you know the collection fairly well, looking for the effects you need can be frustrating and time-consuming. Even with a good contents list, you can spend hours listening to bird chirps until you discover just the right one—if you ever do. It's not uncommon to wade through two dozen glass-breaking sounds and never hear one that matches your shot perfectly.

Foley

Many sound designers find it's just as easy to record most of these sounds themselves as to rely on libraries. This is the only way to re-create elements that have to be timed precisely to an image, such as footsteps. The act of recording sounds like these is called Foley recording, named after Jack Foley, one of the first sound designers.

Ambient Sound

In addition to the sounds created by on-screen objects and events, environmental sound includes the ambience of a given environment, the sum of the background sounds made by objects or events we *can't* see.

Unless you're floating in outer space, any location has a characteristic sound. If you're reading this in front of your editing station, the hum of your computer is probably one of the loudest sounds you hear, but if you listen carefully you might be able to hear an air conditioner blowing or a clock ticking. Maybe your seat creaks a bit when you shift your weight. If you're really quiet, you might hear your own breathing. Although it takes some concentration to stop and identify all these sounds, if they were absent you would be acutely aware of it.

When a film crew shoots a scene, they make every effort to eliminate all these environmental noises. Streets are closed down, crew members drape sound blankets over the windows to damp out extraneous sounds, noisy machines and air conditioners are turned off. This enables the crew to record the voices of the talent without any distracting elements.

Back in the editing room, however, you have to reconstruct all those elements to create a natural-sounding environment. This is delicate work, but it's one of the most critical components of sound design. You must find just the right mix of background noise to give a realistic ambience. And as with the classic Foley trick of smashing a watermelon to simulate the sound of a body getting stabbed, you may use sounds that vary quite a bit from the actual sounds of the location.

For instance, if a scene is set in an outdoor café, and an extra walks by with a dog on a leash, you can add a dog bark even if the real dog never made a sound. Furthermore, you can add it at exactly the right moment, such as in between the actors' lines. This way you get the requisite neighborhood feeling, but the noise won't interfere with the dialogue.

Room Tone

Even if you eliminate as much background sound as possible during recording, there will still be some white noise in the background. That sound is called room tone, and it's different for every environment. Whenever a crew is finished recording dialogue, they also record some of this unique background noise. Room tone is a critical element for creating realistic environmental ambience.

Room tone is essential for covering up gaps in the dialogue track. For instance, let's say that during a really good shot, one of the crew members had a coughing fit. He managed to do it in between the actors' lines, but you still have to cut out three seconds of the dialogue track so the coughing isn't heard. If you simply drop out the audio, there will be absolute silence for that three-second section—which will sound unnatural. If you lay in room tone, no one will notice the gap, since the background noise *level* will remain constant (**Figure 7.3**).

LEVEL *Refers to audio volume level.*

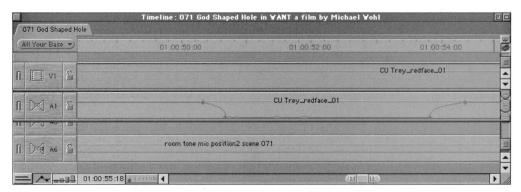

Figure 7.3 Without a room tone track, the audio gap on track A1 would be painfully apparent, since *all* sound would drop out for that section. The room tone provides a constant level of background noise across the whole scene.

Creating Silence From Scratch

What do you do if your sound recordist forgot to capture room tone for "the cough scene"? One option is to steal room tone from another scene, especially if it was shot in the same location or one with a similar ambience. But remember that the actors' dialogue tracks from the cough clip are going to include that same ambient noise, so your room tone track must match closely to blend in perfectly.

*If that doesn't work, scan through the dialogue track of the cough clip to find a section where there's no speech. A fast way to do that is to look at the clip's waveform for silent passages (**Figure 7.4**). Copy that section and edit it into your sequence again and again, slowly dissolving from one piece to the next, until you've stitched together enough room tone for the sequence (**Figure 7.5**).*

Be careful, though: If there's some recognizable sound in the "silence," like a distant car driving by, repeating the clip will sound artificial. In that case, you will need to find multiple sections of silence in the clip and stitch them together.

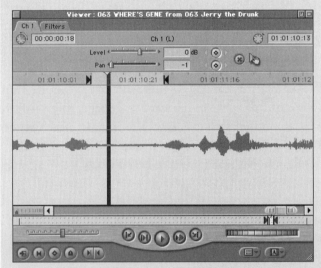

Figure 7.4 Areas where the clip's waveform is flat, or nearly flat, are good places to use as room tone.

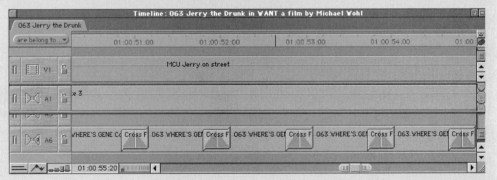

Figure 7.5 By repeatedly copying the silent section into the Timeline, you can create a hand-made room tone track. Dissolving from one piece to the next will prevent audible seams.

Non-Environmental Sounds

For some shows, you may want to include sound elements that are not present in the environment. For example, whenever a chart appears in your training film, you might accompany it with an audio flourish.

In *Want,* as the film progressed, we wanted to give the audience the impression of delving deeper and deeper into Trey's head. One of the main ways we accomplished this was through the sound design: As Trey started to lose his grip on reality, we began incorporating various non-environmental sounds into the mix.

Because one of the factors contributing to Trey's decline was the barrage of marketing messages that saturated his world, we used lots of TV and radio commercials as part of the sound landscape. In the early parts of the film, the sounds of the ads were tied to shots of the TV or radio source. However, later in the film, these ads (with the audio distorted and sometimes layered together) began intruding into Trey's space even when he was nowhere near an actual source.

Using sounds that are not part of the natural environment can break the constructed reality of your film and disrupt the viewer's experience, but artfully employed, this technique can complement the natural elements of the scene, enhance the themes of the piece, and amplify the filmmaker's voice.

MUSIC TRACKS

The most common type of non-environmental sound is music. Music can have a huge impact on the emotional tone of a scene, but it requires a careful match to be successful. Using the wrong music can destroy a scene, but finding just the right *cue* can transform that scene into an utterly brilliant sequence.

> **CUE** *A musical element timed to a specific point in a film. It can be as short as a few seconds or as long as a whole song. A cue point is the moment the element syncs in, and a cue sheet is the list of musical events prepared for the sound mix.*

Don't Use Music to Fix a Bad Edit

Music can make a good scene work better, but it's a bad idea to depend on music to save a poorly edited sequence. You should edit a scene until it works on its own before you lay a song on top of it. If the scene doesn't have the right impact, jacking up its emotional level with some piece of music may help a bit, but it runs the risk of alienating your viewers by manipulating their feelings too openly.

Sophisticated viewers are savvy to the fact that music is often used to tell them what they are supposed to feel, and they tend to resist this kind of mind control— especially if the scene doesn't warrant the emotion the music suggests. For instance, I got up and walked out of *A.I.* as soon as I heard the third swell of violins. And I'm glad I did, because I hear they went on for another hour and a half.

Temporary Music

It may help your editing if you make a quick guess at some music with the right feeling or rhythm to fit the scene you're working on. Of course, if it turns out to be the wrong kind of music, you may have to scrap the cut you produced under its influence.

I recommend listening to the music *before* you edit the scene, rather than putting it on a scratch track so it will play while you're editing. If a song is floating around in your head, its general feeling and rhythm will influence your editing decisions and help make your pacing and timing more consistent and appropriate. However, unless you're absolutely sure the temp music will make it to your final mix, cutting your picture to the beat or structure of the song can lead to problems. If you do that, when you replace the temp track with the final music, your edits won't match.

Some editors play background music while they work, and this can't hurt, since during the hours you spend roughing each scene together you'll hear a variety of different songs or movements. But that's quite different from loading a song into your computer and editing your sequence to it.

Don't get too friendly with your temp soundtrack. If you (or your director) fall in love with the song you're using as a temporary placeholder, you may suffer catastrophic disappointment if you fail to acquire the rights to use that song in the final mix. One of the tricks I used to prevent this when cutting *Want* was to lay in the same two or three temp songs scene after scene. Since I knew I wouldn't want to repeat the music that way in the finished film, it kept me from getting overly attached to any one song.

Selecting Pre-Existing Music

Choosing pre-existing music for your movie can be complicated, and finding the right match is often tricky. It's tempting to pick some song that you really like, but resist the impulse. Select music that's right for the scene.

Complement or Contrast?

The first question to ask yourself is: Do you want the music to complement the tone of the scene, augmenting its emotional impact, or contrast with it for a more complex emotional timbre?

The former strategy comes perilously close to telling the audience what to feel, but of course as an editor you are *always* telling the audience what to feel. The trick is to be subtle about it. Using complementary music can create a clear, consistent message that's easily understood without being patronizing. For example, you might use suspenseful music (a staccato orchestral piece featuring powerful brass and bass lines pouncing on a delicate violin melody) over a scene featuring a character trying to escape his pursuer. The music would emphasize the feeling of suspense. In this case, contrasting the music style might dilute the impact of the scene.

Sometimes, however, contrast can be even more provocative. For example, the general feeling of a key scene in *Want,* between Trey and his father, was slow and melancholy. There were long pauses between the lines, and both characters looked at the ground a lot. My first idea was to use music that amplified that wistful sense, so I chose a moody guitar piece with a big synth bed. It worked fine: The music made the scene feel even sadder. But the scene felt like it was running way too long.

I tried to fix it by cutting the scene until I'd chopped out all but the most essential lines of dialogue. Then it was quicker, all right, but it had also lost a lot of what had made it a great scene in the first place. So I went back to an earlier cut and tried different music instead. I found a clarinet solo that meandered between a peaceful melody and occasional bursts of frantic desperation (the way only a screeching clarinet can). I timed the edit so the musical explosions occurred during moments of silence between the two characters. The result was amazing! The music brought out the underlying tension between the characters, and the scene didn't seem too long at all.

Take the Music Apart

Music can add a lot to a scene, but sometimes it can be an overly broad brush. When music is arranged and recorded, it's designed to be complete, including all the elements necessary to give it the musicians' desired impact. Integrating that song into a filmic sequence adds elements to an already finished work that may convolute the character of the music, even kill it.

One of the best ways to make sure the music in your film works well is to deconstruct it down to its component tracks and lay in the individual pieces one at a time. That way you are essentially remixing the music so your environmental sounds and images can complete the mix. If the music was composed especially for your film, this may be as simple as experimenting with the tracks, turning the various elements of the song (melodic strings, driving trumpet, percussive rhythm section) on and off. How does the scene play with one or more of these tracks removed? Maybe the visuals of the scene can take the place of the melody, and all you need is the musical bed. Perhaps the sound effects in your scene conflict with some of the percussive elements, or maybe they could replace them altogether.

While an experienced film composer will often experiment this way himself before presenting you with the final music, keep these options in mind as you edit in the music for your scenes.

If you're working with pre-recorded music, you might ask a musician friend to re-record the song, one instrument at a time. Maybe she can record just the guitar part or the bass line. It's also pretty easy to throw together a drum track on a sequencer or drum machine; perhaps she'll be able to rebuild pieces of the song one by one. Be aware that manipulating or sampling existing music may infringe on copyrights. Read on to the "No Stealing" section for more information about music copyrights.

Avoid Lyrics

It's generally a good idea to avoid music with vocals, even if it's going to play over scenes without dialogue. Lyrics tend to be too literal, and their images can compete with the visual elements in your film. They may take center stage and make your images seem to merely support the song—as in a music video. Of course, there are many notable exceptions, including the plaintive lament of the Doors' "The End" playing over the opening sequence of *Apocalypse Now*. Perfectly matched vocal music can complement a film sequence successfully, but this is an advanced exercise. Inexperienced editors should beware of creating a competing focus between the narrative of the song and the narrative of the film.

No Stealing

Using copyrighted material without paying for it is illegal, and the music industry has a legion of disgruntled musicians out to catch every violation of their rights. As well they should. Musicians work hard to create their art. If you are integrating their creative work into your own and benefiting artistically or financially from their labor and popularity, they deserve to be credited and paid appropriately.

Contact the music publisher about using a song you want. If your show is a documentary or won't be exhibited publicly, you can often negotiate an agreement to use the music for free or for a nominal fee. But if you get caught showing your film at a trade show or film festival using music for which you don't own the rights, you will probably have to pay a stiff fine.

Hire a Composer

If you have the time and money, hire a composer to create music especially for your film. It's almost always going to fit better than pre-recorded music. The composer can time elements of the music to sync with key moments (even cut points) in your scene. You also have the luxury of modifying the instrumentation or the tempo to better fit your piece.

You can sometimes get the best of both worlds by using a composer to re-create existing music. This gives you a high degree of control while retaining the power of a familiar song. However, it may be less effective, since the original arrangement and production sound are probably big parts of what attracted you to the song in the first place. Although the fee structure is different, re-recording copyrighted materials still requires permission from the publisher.

THE AUDIO PROCESS

The life of a soundtrack moves through four basic stages: The individual sounds are recorded (and captured on your computer); they are edited along with your picture; each clip is sweetened to sound as good and clean as possible; and then all the elements are mixed together to create a final track (or group of tracks) that will be distributed with the finished picture.

RECORDING AND CAPTURING

I won't go into much detail about how to record audio properly. It's more important for an editor to understand how to capture audio correctly to make the best use of it in Final Cut Pro.

You have no way to adjust the levels when capturing DV audio. Whatever was recorded in the field is what goes on your hard disk.

This is not true if you're capturing audio from a source other than DV, such as a DAT player, an analog tape deck (cassette, VHS, Hi8, or Betacam SP), or even a microphone plugged directly into your computer. In these cases you can adjust the audio level by using the Gain control in the Clip Settings tab of the Log and Capture window (**Figure 7.6**).

If you're converting an analog signal (for instance, if you're capturing from Betacam SP tapes or a cassette recorder), line up the 0dB output level on the source deck with -12dB on Final Cut Pro's audio meters. This will ensure that your audio doesn't get *clipped*. To do this, find a section of the tape with a constant output signal of 0dB

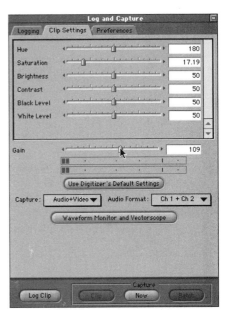

Figure 7.6 The Gain slider is dimmed if you are capturing from DV. Otherwise, use this control to set your input levels.

(the head of your tape should contain a test tone specifically for this purpose) and adjust the Gain slider until the on-screen meters read -12dB.

CLIPPING *Audio that's recorded louder than the capability of the recording device will sound distorted. That distortion is called clipping.*

Audio Shapes

You can capture audio in five different ways, or "shapes" (**Figure 7.7**). In most cases, choosing a shape simply lets the computer know which multichannel format was used when the information was recorded on the tape in the first place.

Figure 7.7 Audio can be recorded in one of five different shapes based on how it was recorded on the source tape.

How Was Your Audio Recorded?

Most videotapes are designed to record sound on one or two audio channels. Some videotape devices let you record four different channels, although they are rarely all used. Professional productions nearly always split the two channels. That means if there's just one microphone, it's recorded on one channel. If there are two mics, they are split discretely on the two channels, one mic per channel. That way you can control their volumes independently so both can be set at optimal levels.

For example, suppose one channel is dedicated to audio coming from a *shotgun,* and the other channel is recording the output from a *lavalier.* Even if both mics are pointed at the same subject, you will probably want to keep the signals separate so you can choose one or the other for your sequence—or mix them together in Final Cut Pro to create a more naturalistic sound than the sound recordist could have achieved with a live mix during the shoot.

> **SHOTGUN** *Microphones are frequently identified by their pickup pattern. A shotgun is an extremely directional mic, picking up signals in a very narrow pattern to the front of the mic. Most films use shotgun mics mounted on a boompole to record dialogue. This allows you to place the mic far enough away from the subject to stay out of the camera's view but still record an adequate signal with very little extraneous noise from the sides or the back of the microphone.*

LAVALIER *A tiny omnidirectional microphone, typically mounted on the shirt collar or lapel. These mics are designed to compensate for the extra low frequencies they record from being adjacent to the resonating chamber of the subject's chest.*

Other times, you may have two wireless mics, each pointing at a different character and each being recorded on a separate audio channel. You can see that this is another case where you would want to keep the channels entirely discrete so you can edit them separately later.

One Channel

If your audio is recorded on only one channel, set the audio pop-up to just that channel. Channel 1 is equivalent to left, channel 2 to right. Final Cut Pro will create a clip with one Audio tab, and the audio signal will be *panned* to the center so it comes out of both speakers at equal volume (**Figure 7.8**).

PAN (AUDIO) *An audio track can come out of the left channel, the right channel, both channels at the same time (centered), or anywhere in between. The control that adjusts this is called a Pan control, and the act of moving the audio track from channel to channel is panning.*

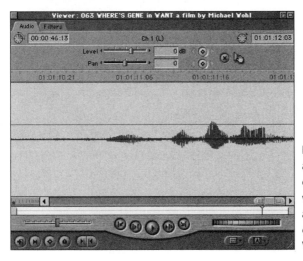

Figure 7.8 If you capture a clip with only one audio channel, you can see the waveform and adjust Level and Pan controls in the corresponding tab in the Viewer.

Two Mono Channels

If your tape was recorded with two audio channels, set the pop-up to Ch 1 + Ch 2. This will bring in the two channels as two distinct tracks, both panned to the center (**Figure 7.9**).

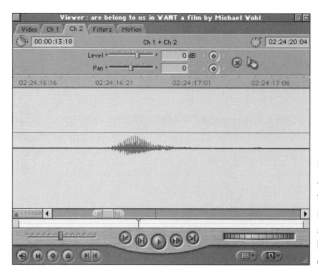

Figure 7.9 If you capture a clip with the pop-up set to Ch 1 + Ch 2 (the default setting), you will get two Audio tabs in the Viewer. Both will be panned to the center.

Stereo Channels

Many consumer-grade camcorders are equipped with a built-in microphone that records sound on the tape in "stereo" format. Although built-in mics are continually improving in quality, they still can't record a true stereo signal. Proper stereo separation requires placing two mics at least as far apart from each other as they are from the subject (forming an equilateral triangle). If you have one of these "stereo" tapes, or if your tape has a stereo signal on it for some other reason (perhaps it was recorded directly from a mixing board at a concert), set the pop-up to Stereo. This will create a clip with one Audio tab but two channels; the channels will be panned "split," with channel 1 going to the left and channel 2 going to the right (**Figure 7.10**).

After the Fact

If you make a mistake while capturing and later realize you want to treat a stereo clip as two discrete channels, or vice versa, you can change a clip's audio shape after it's captured. However, you can make this change only in the Timeline.

The Timeline identifies stereo clips with a little double arrow icon (**Figure 7.11**). If you select a stereo clip, the Stereo Pair menu item (in the Modify menu) is checked (**Figure 7.12**).

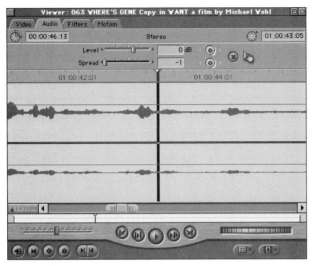

Figure 7.10 A stereo clip displays both tracks in a single tab. The Pan control found in nonstereo audio viewers is replaced with the Spread control, which adjusts the pan of the two channels simultaneously.

Stereo Pair indicator

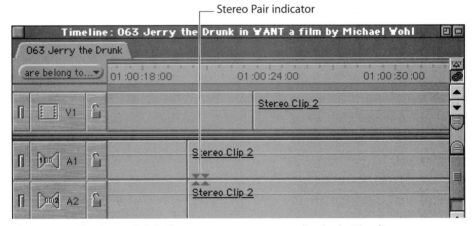

Figure 7.11 The Stereo Pair indicator appears on stereo clips in the Timeline.

Figure 7.12 A check mark next to the Stereo Pair menu item indicates when a clip is stereo.

By selecting the Stereo Pair menu item to toggle it, you can change the audio shape of a clip. To delete one track entirely, choose that item in the Timeline and delete it. None of these changes will affect the master clip in the Browser, but the clip you're working with in the sequence will take on the new properties.

> **TIP:** *Stereo pairs must begin and end at the same time, and they must have identical level and pan keyframes, so if you select two audio clips with different lengths or different keyframe settings and turn them into a stereo pair, Final Cut will conform the second clip to the first clip's settings.*

Mono Mix

Sometimes you'll encounter a tape on which the sound was recorded on two channels, but you would prefer to treat it as a single track. This might occur if your source tape was recorded in stereo but you want to use it as a single mono track while editing. (For example, you might have some sound recorded from a stereo that's going to be mixed as if it were coming out of an AM radio.) In cases like these, you can set the pop-up in the Capture window to Mono Mix. This will mix the two channels into a single track for editing.

EDITING SOUND

The rules for editing sound are mostly the same as for editing video. Here are a few tips that pertain specifically to editing the track.

Play Audio at Slow Speed

When you're trying to find a precise moment in an audio clip, like the first frame of a door slam or the end of a word within a sentence, it's tough to locate the frame you want when playing at regular speed.

For this purpose, Final Cut Pro allows you to listen to your audio at slow speed in two different ways. If you use the Jog control or ⬅ and ➡, Final Cut will play the sound for each frame, one frame at a time, at normal speed. This has the effect of a stuttering sound. What you are hearing is all the sound that occurs within that one frame, played at normal speed.

Alternately, you can listen to the audio at slow speed by using the Shuttle control or by holding down Ⓚ and Ⓛ together. This simulates the sound of a tape playing slowly. The sound plays continuously, and the pitch is lowered so it's easy to hear exactly when a sound begins or ends.

Generally I use the Shuttle control when I'm trying to find the exact beginning or end of a particular sound (especially words or loud sharp sounds). The reason is that sounds can begin or end within the duration of a frame. Even though one second's worth of video contains only 25 or 30 frames, it includes 48,000 audio samples. That means a single frame includes more than 1,600 samples. That's 1,600 possible starting points for a given sound within each frame.

Sync Sounds That Start Midframe

If audio and video don't sync up perfectly because the sound doesn't begin precisely on a frame boundary, you can slip audio by as little as 1/100th of a frame to correct the sync error.

Let's say an explosion begins on picture frame 13 of your sequence, but the corresponding sound doesn't begin until halfway through the corresponding audio frame. While this is a tiny discrepancy, the human ear is very sensitive and viewers will notice. Here's how to fix it:

First, open the clip in the Viewer and zoom in all the way on the audio waveform (**Figure 7.13**). The playhead shows you the duration of a single frame. All of the samples within the width of the playhead occur within the duration of that frame.

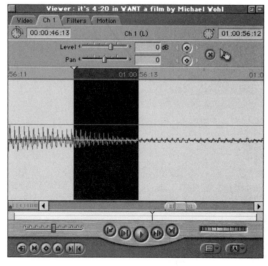

Figure 7.13 When you're zoomed all the way in, you can see exactly how much of the audio signal occurs within a single frame, as shown by the width of the playhead (the dark area here).

You can change the audio so the frame begins at the first sound of the explosion by dragging the front of the playhead to that exact point and stamping a new In point. This also automatically resets the Out point so the clip's duration doesn't change. In this way we are slipping the audio separately from the video.

To move the playhead within the boundary of the frame, you must hold down Shift while you drag (**Figure 7.14**). This allows you to place the playhead precisely where the sound begins. Then, with the playhead parked midframe, hit I to stamp a new In point and perform the slip (**Figure 7.15**).

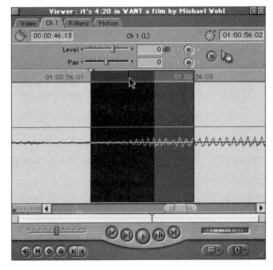

Figure 7.14 Hold Shift to drag the beginning of the playhead to the correct position within the frame.

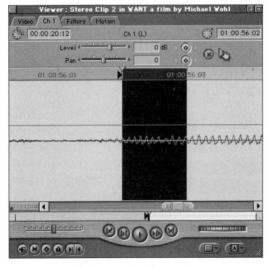

Figure 7.15 Stamping a new In point slips the audio separately from the video, realigning the sound to start at the beginning of the video frame.

SWEETENING

Final Cut Pro provides you with a huge variety of ways to improve the sound quality of your clips and manipulate your sound for artistic purposes.

If you want to create a convincingly realistic soundtrack, one of the most important types of audio improvement you can do is sculpt your sound to match the environment. We've already discussed adding sound effects and environmental elements such as the sounds of the café in my earlier example. Sweetening involves altering the sound quality of a clip to make it fit its environment better.

This is most important when you re-record dialogue after the shoot and have to edit it into the scene. The technical name for this process is automatic dialogue replacement, also known as looping and generally referred to by its initials: ADR.

ADR

Inevitably, some piece of your production sound will be unusable: A plane or truck will be audible in a scene supposedly taking place in the 17th century, or you'll discover that a wireless mic was overwhelmed by static in the middle of a critical line of narration. Whatever the problem, it's quite common to re-record some audio to replace objectionable sound. Occasionally a director will use ADR to replace a line reading to get a different emotional effect, even if the quality of the original sound was acceptable.

Professional post-production facilities usually have an ADR stage specifically designed for this process. The scene in question is projected in a loop, over and over, while the original dialogue is played in the actor's headphones. As she speaks along with the line, it is recorded and lined up with the lip movements on-screen. The film continues looping and the process is repeated until the actor gets the line as close as possible to the original.

If you don't have access to a professional ADR stage, you can do most of this at home. Plop your actor in front of your Final Cut Pro workstation, load the problem clip into the Viewer, and select the Loop Playback function found in the View menu. You'll probably want to record one line or section at a time, so set In and Out points around that section, and use the Play In to Out command (Shift-\). Send the original audio into the actor's headphones and record his new line readings on a new DV tape. Let him repeat the section several times to get the line reading as close to the original as possible. Ideally, you should use the same microphone you used in the original recording to match the original sound quality.

Then, capture the new tape and manually sync up the best reading with the original shot in your sequence.

> **TIPS:** If you're recording ADR at home, be sure to locate the actor in the quietest, most noise-deadened space possible. Surround him with walls of sound blankets, and cover your computer so any fan noise is inaudible.
>
> Here's another handy home-ADR technique: Output the video playback from your computer (with a timecode window burn) on the new DV tape, so that you can line up the new line reading based on the timecode numbers of the original clip.

Integrate the New Clip

Once you've recorded the new dialogue, you're only halfway done. Now you have to sync up the recording with the original picture. If your actor did a good job of matching the pace and timing of the original delivery, this should be fairly easy.

Drop the new clip in the Timeline on a track right below the audio from the original clip (**Figure 7.16**). Zoom in and line up the audio waveforms as closely as possible. When you play back the sequence, you will probably hear a slight echo as the two tracks are playing simultaneously. Select the new clip and move it one or two frames at a time until the echo goes away (**Figure 7.17**).

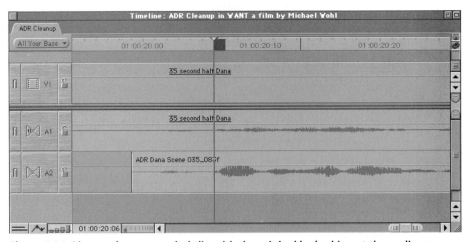

Figure 7.16 Line up the re-recorded clip with the original by looking at the audio waveforms to get them as close as possible. You can turn the waveforms on or off by pressing ⌘-Option-W.

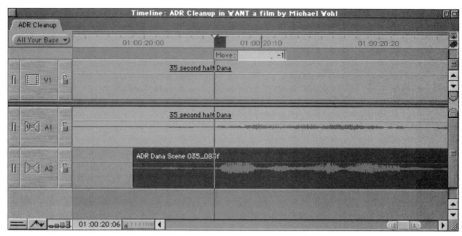

Figure 7.17 Move the clip one or two frames at a time until the echo effect is no longer heard.

If the ADR clip doesn't match the original perfectly, you may never get the echo to go away. If this is the case, find one or two clearly visible lip movements in the picture (plosive sounds like P and B are good ones to choose) and line them up with the appropriate spots in the waveform (**Figure 7.18**). You may have to break up the new recording and add or delete tiny spaces between words to get a good match. Once you have the clips lined up as well as you can, delete (or disable) the original clip so only the new clip is heard.

Figure 7.18 Find a clear lip movement and line up the corresponding waveform as closely as possible.

Sound Quality

Once you've gotten the clip lined up, you need to make sure its sound quality matches that of the other clips in the sequence. The more closely you duplicate the original recording situation (mainly by matching the microphone type and placement), the better the sound quality will match right off the bat. Even so, minor adjustments will help to make the substitution invisible.

> **TIP:** Use headphones. When you're fine-tuning audio clips, it's essential that you listen through professional, closed-ear headphones. Trying to make the kind of minute adjustments audio sweetening requires can't be done any other way.

Equalize It

The first thing to do in order to match the tone of the new clip with the old is to use one of the equalizer filters to modify the sound. Take an acceptable section of the original dialogue, and place it in a new sequence right before a piece of the re-recorded dialogue. Then you can experiment with filter settings on the new clip until the two sections of dialogue sound identical (**Figure 7.19**). Once you've settled on the filter settings you want to use, go ahead and apply them to all the new clips.

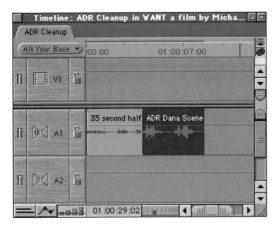

Figure 7.19 Place a copy of the new dialogue right after a piece of the original dialogue and play them back together so you can hear the subtle differences between the clips.

To apply a filter, select the clip and choose the desired filter from the Effects menu. (In this case, we're going to use the 3 Band Equalizer.)

To adjust the parameters of a filter that you're applying to a clip, you must open that instance of the clip in the Viewer. Do this by double-clicking on the clip in the Timeline. To verify that you're editing the instance of a clip used in the sequence, look for the sprocket holes visible in the Scrubber area of the Viewer (**Figure 7.20**).

Figure 7.20 To modify the filter settings for a clip in a sequence, you must load that instance of the clip into the Viewer. The Scrubber area displays sprocket holes when a clip is currently used in a sequence.

Use the Filters tab to adjust the parameters of the filters applied to your clips (**Figure 7.21**). Final Cut Pro's 3 Band Equalizer is quite straightforward and similar to equalizers you may have used on your home stereo or other audio devices.

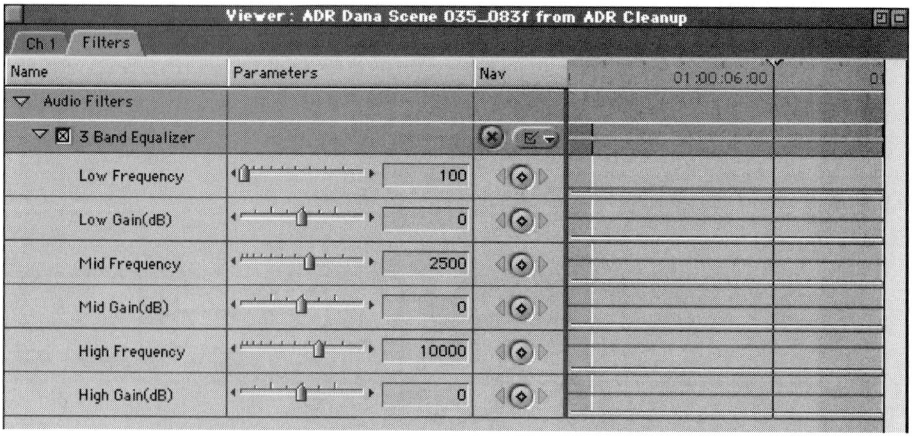

Figure 7.21 Choose the Filters tab to make adjustments to the filters applied to your clips.

For example, if your ADR track is too bassy compared to the original recording, you can reduce the level of the low frequencies in the clip by pulling down the Low Gain slider (**Figure 7.22**).

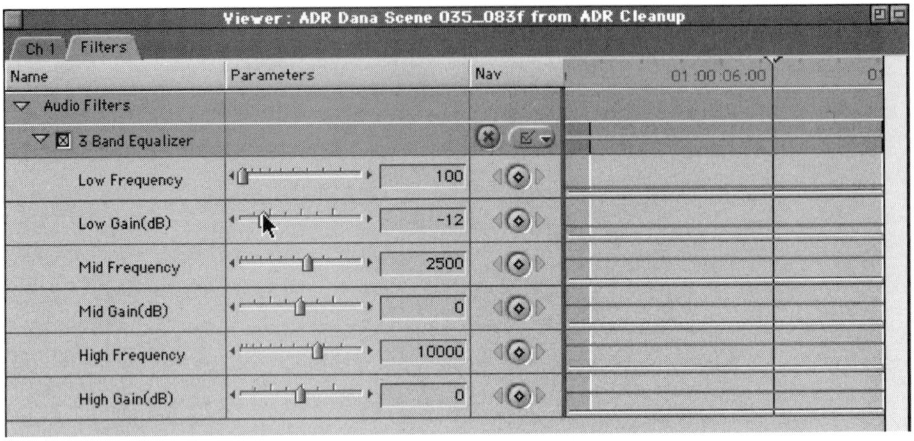

Figure 7.22 By adjusting the Low Gain slider, you can boost or attenuate the level of the low frequencies in your clip.

If the sound you're trying to eliminate is a *very* low frequency rumble that's too low to be affected by the default setting, you can lower the value of the Low Frequency slider to include that particular range. Just pull the slider down until you hear that the rumble is being affected.

Select Specific Frequencies With the Parametric Equalizer

If you prefer, you can use the Parametric Equalizer filter (**Figure 7.23**). This filter has only one frequency adjustment, plus a Q setting. To filter a specific frequency, start by choosing the precise frequency you want to be affected. Smaller numbers (starting at 10 Hz) are lower tones; larger numbers (up to 20,000 Hz) are higher tones. Then adjust the Q control to set the "wideness" of the filter (how many frequencies above and below your target frequency will be affected).

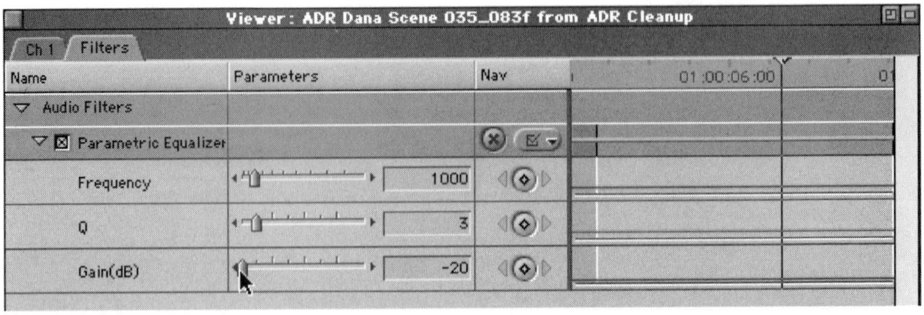

Figure 7.23 The Parametric Equalizer lets you make adjustments to one specific frequency.

For example, let's say you're working with a clip in which some electrical interference produced a high-pitched whistle.

First you need to determine the whistle's frequency. Set your Q setting at 1 (which narrows the bandwidth to virtually a single frequency), and adjust your Gain slider to -20dB (which makes your selected frequency inaudible). Now, run through different frequencies until you hear the whistle go away, or at least get a lot quieter. Since it's a high-pitched noise, you might start at around 8,000 Hz to 10,000 Hz and slowly move up, playing back the clip until you hear the whistle being affected.

Once you identify the appropriate frequency, raise the Q level so surrounding frequencies will be affected as well. When the whistle is completely inaudible, you've found the correct Q setting. Now, slowly raise the Gain slider, bringing it as close to zero as you can without hearing the whistle. That way you're reducing the attenuation to the lowest effective level. Over-attenuating even a very narrow frequency range will sound weird, since voices comprise so many different harmonic frequencies that modifying even a narrow band can noticeably change the quality of the voice.

> **TIP:** It's far better to reduce the level of unwanted frequencies than to boost the ones you do want. Equalization is just a way of changing the sound levels of specific frequencies, and if you set a level too high, it can become distorted when mixed with other sounds.

Give It Some Space

Once you've matched your new clip as closely as possible to the tone of the original, you need to apply some reverb to match the natural space the original sounds were recorded in.

Normally, sound waves bounce off the walls of a room and other flat surfaces, creating subtle echoes that interfere with the waves of the original sound. Those reflections are called reverberations. The larger the space, the farther the waves travel before they bounce back, and the more pronounced the echo sounds. That's why a giant church or a huge arena has such a distinct acoustic atmosphere. This echo can be reproduced synthetically using a digital effect.

Final Cut Pro's Reverberation filter is very powerful and can simulate acoustic environments ranging from a small room to a huge cathedral. The trick to getting a natural result is to use small settings to produce a subtle effect. The default settings are a bit too dramatic for most practical purposes. As with the EQ filters, the best way to match clips for reverb is to put a copy of the original clip alongside the new (filtered) clip. Play them back in sequence while you experiment with the reverb settings. When the two clips sound indistinguishable, you've got it right. Now simply apply that tweaked filter to the other clips you want to affect.

Once you've applied the Reverberation filter by selecting it from the Effects menu, begin by choosing the type of reverb you want to apply (**Figure 7.24**). For realistic effects, I find the Thin Plate settings create excellent natural-sounding effects.

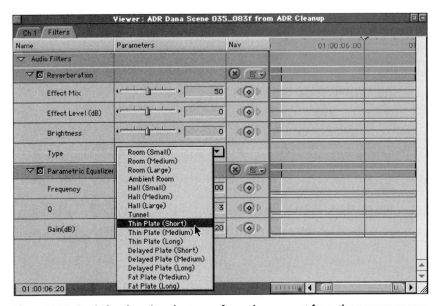

Figure 7.24 Begin by choosing the type of reverb you want from the pop-up menu.

The Effect Mix slider controls how much of the reverb effect gets mixed in with the original. The Effect Level controls how loud the reverb itself is. I recommend leaving the Effect Level control at its default setting of 0dB and controlling the amount of reverb by lowering the Effect Mix slider.

The Reverberation filter also contains a Brightness slider. In a natural acoustic environment, sounds become muddy as they reverberate around a large space and the lower frequencies overpower the higher ones. The Brightness control allows you to counteract that phenomenon, resulting in a cleaner, crisper effect.

Don't Forget the Room Tone

Once you've got your new clip thoroughly filtered to match the surrounding clips, mix in your room tone track. Now, with any luck, the sound of the new clip should be indistinguishable from the original.

Check It Out

If it still sounds (or looks) funky, go through the steps again, one by one.

First, check that the clip is synced up as accurately as possible. Although the same actor said the same lines while watching her own lips, she may have spoken in a subtly different way that just doesn't match up. Ultimately, you may not be able to do anything about the discrepancy. This is why medium and wider shots always make for better ADR than close-ups.

Then, recheck the EQ settings, the reverb settings, and the room tone mix—and adjust any of the settings and levels as needed, until the clip sounds as natural as possible.

CLEAN UP YOUR SOUND

There are many additional types of cleanup you can do as part of the sweetening process. All of them make a difference.

Remove Pops

Suppose you have a track that sounds great except for one little pop caused by a faulty audio cable, or perhaps a mixing error. You can remove it easily by fading down before the pop and back up after it—so quickly viewers will never notice. Here's how:

As with the slipping control I described earlier to micro-sync sound and image, Final Cut Pro allows you to make audio keyframe adjustments down to 1/100th of a frame. That's not quite down to sample level (there are between 1,600 and 2,000 samples per frame), but it's good enough for most pops.

First you have to find the pop. Open the offending clip in the Viewer, and zoom in until you identify the pop in the waveform (**Figure 7.25**).

You can set level keyframes by Option-clicking on the level envelope (the pink line). Set three keyframes, one directly on the pop and the other two on either side. Then drag the center keyframe down as far as it will go (**Figure 7.26**). The clip will fade out and come back in so quickly that no one will hear the sound of the pop. The closer together you set the surrounding keyframes, the quicker that fade-out/fade-in will be.

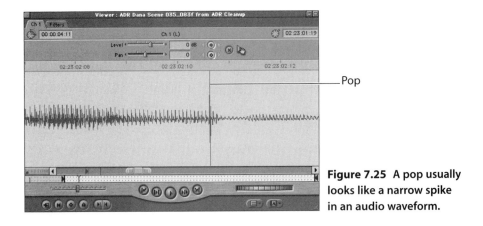

Figure 7.25 A pop usually looks like a narrow spike in an audio waveform.

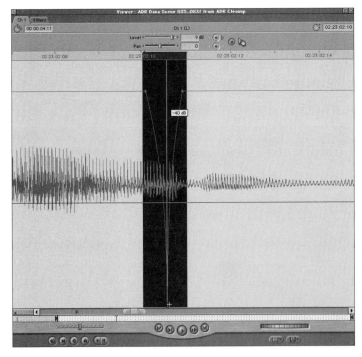

Figure 7.26
By setting three keyframes, you can create a very quick fade-out/ fade-in effect to hide the pop.

If the pop lasts longer or there are two close together, you may need to set four keyframes and drag the middle two points down so the clip stays silent for a longer period of time (**Figure 7.27**).

Notice that the fade-outs you just created have a curved line. Final Cut Pro automatically makes all audio level adjustments logarithmically to match the way the human ear hears sounds. A sound at -10dB is twice as loud as a sound at -20dB, not ten times louder. For the most part you don't need to think about this at all, except when you're trying to adjust audio levels numerically.

Just as I recommend making all editing decisions while playing, I also recommend making audio level adjustments based on how the sequence sounds while it's playing. One of the biggest limitations of Final Cut Pro, though, is that you cannot make audio adjustments on the fly. You have to listen, pause, adjust, listen again, pause, adjust, and so on. Still, this works well enough for most situations.

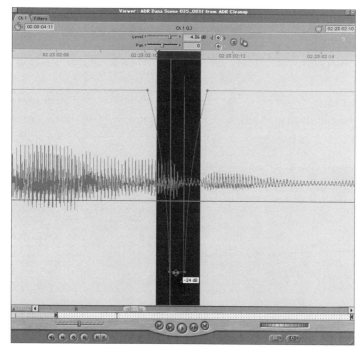

Figure 7.27 If you want to silence a longer area of a clip, set four keyframes and drag the two middle ones down. The portion of the clip between the second and third keyframes will be completely silent.

Problem-Solving Filters

Final Cut Pro is richly endowed with filters, and you'll find several of them are quite useful for solving common problems with audio tracks.

Reduce Background Noise

There are actually several filters for the same purpose: eliminating unwanted background noise. Unfortunately, the nature of audio recording precludes any fail-safe methods of removing one frequency without affecting others. Also, as I mentioned earlier, voices occur over such a wide range of frequencies that if you remove even a narrow band of lows to get rid of a rumble, it's likely to take some of the bassy punch out of the voice.

Eliminate Unwanted Frequencies With Pass Filters

When you want to *roll off* frequencies above or below a certain pitch, you can use the High Pass or Low Pass filters (**Figure 7.28**). The High Pass filter allows all the frequencies above a selected frequency to "pass" into the mix. All frequencies below that are eliminated. You can use the High Pass filter to quickly get rid of too much bass or rumble in your track.

> **ROLL OFF**   *Eliminate unwanted ranges of frequencies.*

The Low Pass filter does exactly the opposite and can be used to eliminate high-frequency noise such as static or the sound of water crashing. (While the narrator might look great in front of that waterfall, don't forget how the location will impact the sound!)

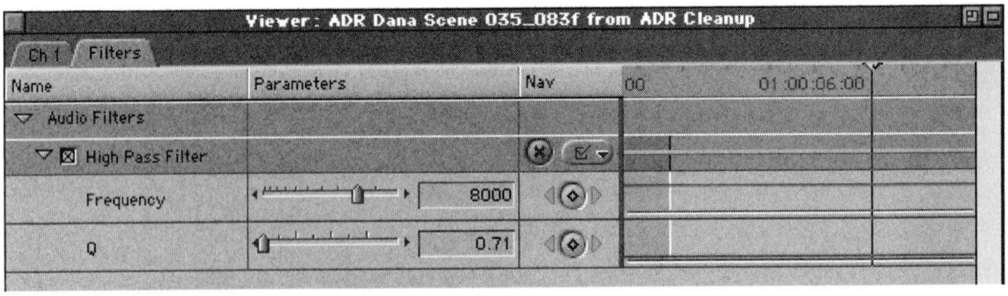

Figure 7.28 High and Low Pass filters enable you to define a frequency below which (or above which) sounds will be muted.

Filter Out Unwanted Noise

Every audio signal includes a certain amount of noise that's audible in between the parts you want to use (**Figure 7.29**). This is essentially room tone, and in many cases it's desirable. But occasionally you want to eliminate that noise.

For example, let's say you recorded a voice-over narration in a park, and whenever the narrator pauses you can hear a certain amount of traffic noise in the background. You plan to run the narration over a section of the film that occurs indoors. Naturally, you want to remove as much of that traffic noise as possible.

This is a job for the Expander/Noise Gate filter (**Figure 7.30**), which is designed to eliminate all signals that fall below a certain volume level.

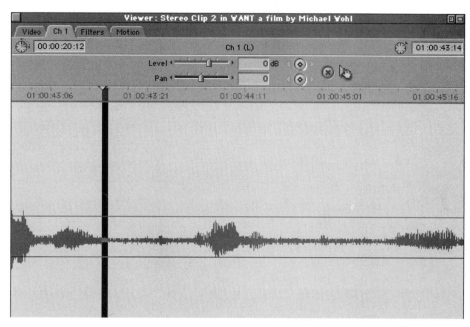

Figure 7.29 The areas where the waveform is small but not flat indicate the environmental noise recorded in between sections of useful information.

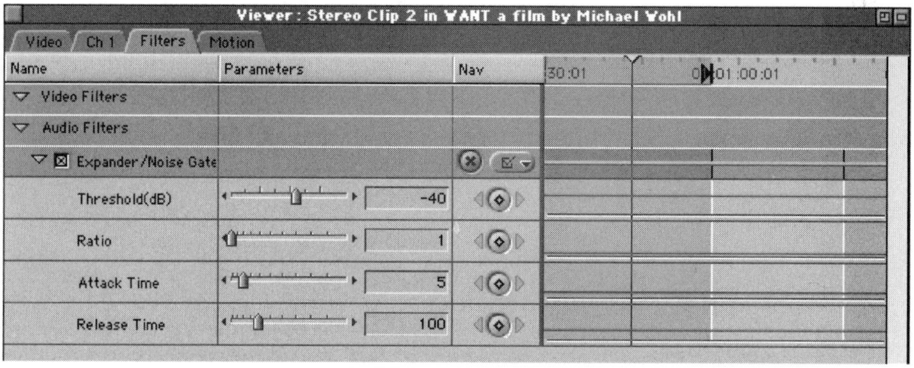

Figure 7.30 The Expander/Noise Gate filter can be used to cut unwanted segments of room tone from a clip.

Adjust the Threshold slider to the proper value for removing the noise, and use the Attack Time and Release Time settings to determine how quickly the filter takes effect and how long it waits before turning off. (Generally you don't want to drop out the tiny pauses between words, but you do want to eliminate longer pauses at the ends of phrases and sentences.)

Lose Hum

Use the Hum Remover filter (**Figure 7.31**) to eliminate common hums. This filter works exactly the same way as the Parametric Equalizer described earlier, but the default settings are designed to remove 60-cycle hum—the most common audio problem. American electricity runs at 60 Hz, and if an electrical signal interferes with your audio (as often happens if a microphone cable runs parallel to an electrical cable on the set), you'll get a 60-cycle hum. (In other parts of the world, electricity runs at different frequencies and produces different hums.)

Since a hum may cause reverberations on additional frequencies (due to the nature of audio harmonics), the Hum Remover has check boxes to apply similar attenuation to harmonic frequencies. If, after setting the main parameters, you still hear remnants of the hum, check the Harmonics check boxes one at a time until the noise goes away.

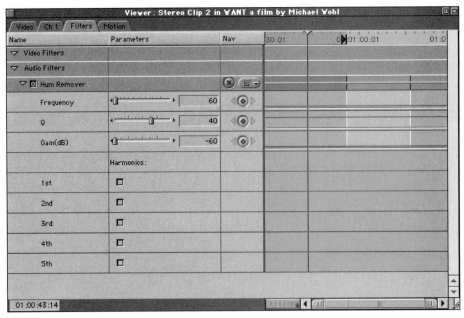

Figure 7.31 The Hum Remover filter is designed to (surprise!) remove hum. Use the Q slider to control the breadth of the effect.

DePop and DeEss

Recording voices is a more of an art than a science. You must choose between many microphones, experiment with various mic placements, and overcome a variety of esoteric problems. Voices that are close-mic'd (recorded at very close range) frequently contain sibilants (hissing S's) and plosives (popping P's, B's, T's, and D's) that can be distracting.

Final Cut Pro provides tools aimed specifically at solving these problems. Use the Vocal DeEsser filter to remove excessive sibilance. Use the Vocal DePopper filter to remove excessive plosives (**Figure 7.32**).

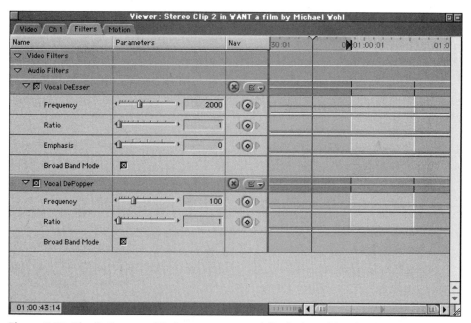

Figure 7.32 The DeEsser and DePopper are especially designed for cleaning up problems with vocal recordings.

MIXING IN FCP

Final Cut Pro provides 99 tracks per sequence, and since you can nest one sequence inside of another, you end up with virtually unlimited tracks to play with. This makes Final Cut Pro a viable tool for creating your final mix.

Start by separating all your elements on individual tracks, performing the various sweetening operations described previously, and using the Level and Pan controls to balance the different tracks and create effective stereo separation.

Adjust Level and Pan Settings

You can control level and pan in many different ways.

One way is to adjust an individual clip's level or pan settings in the Audio tab in the Viewer (**Figure 7.33**). You can set either parameter to change over time by using keyframes. Add keyframes by Option-clicking a point on the line, and set the desired value by dragging the point or the line. If you prefer, you can click the Add Keyframe button and set your desired value with the slider.

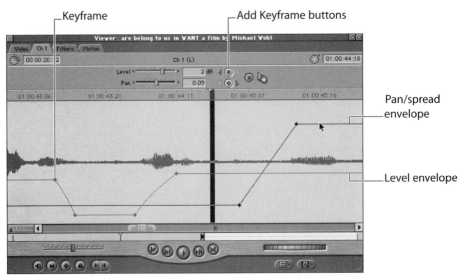

Figure 7.33 Adjust audio settings in the Audio tab by clicking and dragging the envelopes drawn over the waveform. Pink is for level, purple is for pan/spread.

Alternately, you can adjust levels in the Timeline. To do that, first turn on Clip Overlays by clicking the control in the lower left corner of the window (**Figure 7.34**) or hitting Option-W. When Clip Overlays is turned on, you can see the level envelope (or rubber band) drawn right over the clips. You can set and add keyframes here exactly the same way that you do in the Viewer: Option-click to add a keyframe, and drag the point to the desired level.

You might want to make an adjustment to multiple clips at the same time—perhaps to boost the audio on all the shots containing a particular character's dialogue or to attenuate background noise in certain shots simultaneously.

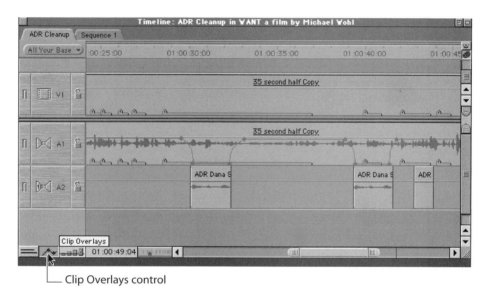

Clip Overlays control

Figure 7.34 Levels can also be adjusted in the Timeline.

To make changes to multiple items, select the clips and choose Levels from the Modify menu. This opens the Gain Adjust dialog box, which lets you set all the selected clips to a new dB level, either by making a relative adjustment (moving all levels up from their current setting by, say, 2dB) or making an absolute adjustment (setting all levels precisely to that value) (**Figure 7.35**).

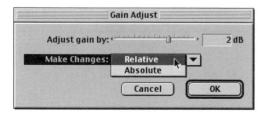

Figure 7.35 The Gain Adjust dialog box allows you to change the level of multiple clips at once.

You can also make simple level and pan adjustments to clips either in the Timeline or the Viewer by using the Audio submenu of the Modify menu (**Figure 7.36**). Here you can nudge audio levels up or down by 1 or 3dB and pan clips left, right, or center. The menu lists corresponding keyboard shortcuts.

The Real Real Time

The main disadvantage of mixing in Final Cut Pro is that it has limited real-time capability.

Final Cut Pro advertises that it can mix eight tracks of audio in real time.

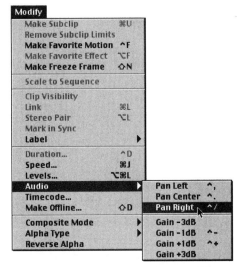

Figure 7.36 The Audio submenu enables you to make simple adjustments quickly and easily.

That means if you have eight audio tracks stacked up in your Timeline, you can hit Play and hear them mixed together with all your level settings correctly applied to each clip. In reality, depending on the video being decompressed and played back at the same time, this can require so much processing power that only the most powerful computers can actually play all eight tracks without dropping video frames. Most systems choke as soon as you get above five or six.

It doesn't take long to use up eight tracks when you're trying to build a complex natural environment. To make matters worse, any filters you apply have a "track cost." One track with an EQ filter applied is the equivalent of four unfiltered tracks. As you can imagine, you run out of tracks and time—real time— very quickly.

Once you exceed the computer's real-time audio playback capability, you must *render* your sequence before you can play it and hear the mixed audio. Depending on the length of your sequence (and the power of your editing station), rendering can take a while—and having to re-render each time you make a small adjustment is not very conducive to a good creative workflow as you do your final mixdown.

This is why many editors prefer to do their final sound mix outside of Final Cut Pro. The most popular tool for this purpose is Digidesign Pro Tools.

RENDER *When Final Cut Pro can't perform the calculations necessary to play an effect in real time, it needs to stop, process the effect, and write it to a file. This process is called rendering. Thereafter, when you hit Play, Final Cut Pro reads the file and plays the effect in real time.*

EXPORTING FOR PRO TOOLS

Final Cut Pro allows you to export the audio tracks from your sequence into an OMF file. (OMF stands for open media format.) This file contains all the audio information for your sequence, including the actual sound media as well as the track information. When you import the OMF file into Pro Tools (or another OMF-savvy application), all the tracks from Final Cut Pro appear in your new document, with all the clips on them—ready to be edited, sweetened, mixed, and output to tape. You can even add handles when you export to allow a little fudge room for editing (**Figure 7.37**).

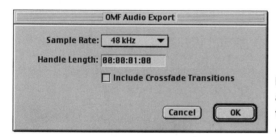

Figure 7.37 When you export to an OMF file, keep the sample rate the same as the sequence you're exporting from (usually 48 kHz).

The advantage of using Pro Tools is that you can perform all of the sweetening adjustments I described earlier, as well as many more types of manipulations, in real time. Some Pro Tools systems can even output sound in multitrack formats like Dolby Surround.

Final Cut Pro's audio capabilities are fairly robust, but systems like Pro Tools are dedicated to doing audio editing and sweetening. If your mix is going to be relatively simple, Final Cut Pro may be all you need. But if you're trying to do something complex, Pro Tools is the right tool for the job.

Interview: JOHN WILSON

John Wilson's professional editing career is unique. For ten years he worked exclusively with Peter Greenaway, the highly regarded British artist and filmmaker. Among his credits are *The Draughtsman's Contract, A Zed and Two Noughts*, and the memorable and controversial *The Cook, the Thief, His Wife & Her Lover*. In 2000 he cut the international sensation *Billy Elliot,* directed by Britain's premier theater director, Stephen Daldry. At the time of this interview, he was working with veteran director Lewis Gilbert on a film tentatively entitled *The Memory of Water*.

Michael Wohl: How does your editing cycle work?

John Wilson: Good directors will make it quite clear by the way they have shot the material how it should go together. So, for the seven-week period of the shoot I'll be putting stuff together as I see fit. Then, when the shoot's finished and the director and I can work together, everything gets particularly interesting. It opens up the possibility of throwing away the script and starting again, if necessary. One has to work with the material rather than following any sort of script, start getting the pace, transitions between scenes, addition of temp music, just to see how it's going to flow and develop. And when we get down to that stage, after maybe four or five weeks of hard editing, we show it to our producers.

Have you ever looked at the scene and just said, "I have no idea what to do with this?"

Certainly. There are always scenes that I call my bête noire scenes. Some scenes require a lot more input from an editor than others because of the very nature of the material. Maybe two or three cameras have been run on something, and it's up to the editor to make sense of it. So, yes, there are one or two scenes in every film where you think, "Now that's going to be tricky."

Sometimes you'd like to go off and shoot some more, but often it's very expensive and very difficult: You can't always get your actors back, or the time of year has changed. All these little problems can get in the way. So you have to be creative. There's an early scene in Billy Elliot where we see Billy plunking out notes on the family piano, and the father comes in with coal for the fire, and the brother comes in and says he's going to join the picket line for a strike—we needed to set up an awful lot of things, but that sequence didn't exist in the script. So we stole bits from other scenes later in the film.

How do you know when you're done?

You're never done. No film is ever finished. It can always be improved, but you know you're done when the sound editor is screaming at you for reels to work on and you keep putting him off. Once the executives and the producers have all climbed off, then the film is done. But there are times when you're in the dubbing theater and you think, "If we could only extend that shot there…" You're never really finished, never really satisfied. But that's the organic process of filmmaking, I suppose.

CHAPTER EIGHT
Special Effects

OK, you've been working with Final Cut Pro for a couple of months now, and you've probably edited a few shows. You've been good, too, diligently staying away from all those weird menu items—the ones that look intriguing even though you don't know exactly what they're for. Still…there's that secret longing deep inside. *You've got to know!*

Or maybe it's day three, you've mastered all the editing stuff, and all you want to do is make some cool-looking pictures.

Either way, you're sick of waiting. And you've come to the right place.

One big thing that sets Final Cut Pro apart from all the other nonlinear video editors is its seamless integration of editing and effects. Sure, most other programs have a set of features for doing special effects, too, but the way editing and effects are integrated into Final Cut Pro is both unique and extremely cool. Basically, you can apply *any* effect to *any* clip at *any* time—and that means seamless workflow.

GETTING STARTED

What is a special effect, anyway?

Any time you alter the video data from the image that was captured in the camera, you have created an *effects shot*. (I'll get to in-camera effects momentarily.) An effects shot can be as simple as applying a noise reduction filter or as complicated as creating a traveling *matte* that composites a video image inside a moving title over a computer-generated background (**Figure 8.1**).

Figure 8.1 This effect is called a traveling matte. It requires three different layers: the background, the text, and the image inside the text.

ALPHA CHANNEL   *The part of a graphics file that indicates which areas of the image are opaque and which areas are transparent.*

MATTE   *More or less synonymous with an alpha channel. When working in film, it refers to a piece of film that blocks out the background in one shot during printing so you can drop in the background from another shot. In the digital realm, it tells programs like Final Cut Pro which areas of the clip are transparent and which are visible. The only difference is that while an alpha channel is embedded in the clip, a matte might be an entirely separate clip.*

Before we get into the nuts and bolts of how, why, and when to create which effects, here are a few general notions to think about first.

Become a Specialist—or Hire One

Just because the software manual says that Final Cut Pro is designed to produce a wide variety of stunning visual effects, many novice editors assume that they can make their cooking video look like *The Matrix*. There's an easy way to disabuse yourself of this notion: The next time you see a major "effects" film, stay in your seat, watch *all* the credits, and try to count how many people were involved in the creation of the special effects. The number can easily run into the hundreds.

You will become very frustrated very fast if you buy into the myth that says one person can do everything herself. She can't—and neither can you.

Performing special effects is a specialized art, one that's quite different from editing. The two activities require different skill sets and very distinct dispositions. For instance, a word processing program is capable of outputting everything from a love letter to a mystery novel or a technical manual on disarming nuclear submarines—but that doesn't mean the same author is up to all three of those tasks!

Of course, you should experiment with the tools available to you, both to understand what they do and because you *might* have a propensity for effects design in addition to (or instead of) straightforward film editing. But be honest with yourself and with your clients. There are far too many dilettantes dabbling in every area of digital media creation. If you're serious about a career in post-production, you must find a single focus and develop it. Even though Final Cut Pro can do all types of image manipulation, and you'll need one or another of its effects tools from time to time, you don't need to master the whole program.

Employ the Right Tool

If you choose to delve seriously into the realm of special effects, Final Cut Pro may not even be the right tool. You can perform many types of effects much more adroitly with a different application. Some effects, like rotoscoping or 3-D rendering, can't be done in Final Cut Pro at all; others, like organic movements and color correction, are possible—but are a lot easier to do in a program dedicated to the job.

If you're serious about developing your effects skills, Final Cut Pro is a great place to start. You can experiment with layering, keyframing, alpha channels, and many other elements of *motion graphics,* and the skills you learn will translate easily into the more specialized tools to which you'll graduate.

MOTION GRAPHICS *A subset of special effects focusing on clip motion and layering.*

But it's important to recognize the limitations of Final Cut Pro. Rather than spending hours trying to simulate a randomly generated keyframe pattern by hand, try Adobe After Effects instead and check out The Wiggler. Applications like After Effects, Discreet Combustion, and the like have specialized features expressly designed for the challenges involved in creating special effects. (See the section called "Getting In and Out of After Effects," at the end of this chapter, for details on the mechanics of moving files between After Effects and Final Cut Pro.)

Don't Do Effects in the Camera

Most modern video cameras are designed with a collection of built-in effects you can apply while shooting. This set of effects generally includes mosaics, posterization, slow-motion capture, and so on, and while they can be fun to fool around with, I strongly recommend against using them on a serious project.

The reason is simple: Once you record the footage, it's all you have. If you record it with some sort of filter applied (such as a pastel effect, which adds a painterly texture to the images), you can never remove that effect.

On the other hand, if you record it clean, you can usually apply the same effect in Final Cut Pro and exert even finer control over the result: You can adjust the intensity of the filter and customize various parameters. You can make the effect begin slowly or appear and disappear on a certain cue. If you're applying the filter to an edited sequence, you can apply it evenly across all the edit points. And if you change your mind about the effect, you can remove it easily—and the original footage will still be perfectly usable.

If you're planning to edit your footage (which is why you bought your G4 and the Final Cut Pro software in the first place), you're far better off doing effects like these in post.

OK, I Lied

There is one exception to that rule: The slow shutter speed effect. When you slow down a camera's frame rate to only five or ten frames per second, it creates a unique and often beautiful smearing effect. This was used with great impact in Wong Kar-Wai's *Chung King Express*. The film was peppered with slow shutter tracking shots of Hong Kong at night in which its colored lights erupted into dramatic bursts of smeared color, making the city seem simultaneously overwhelming and enticing. That picture was shot on film, but modern video cameras can create the same effect.

I have yet to see a filter in Final Cut Pro or any other desktop tool that simulates this convincingly. If you are looking for that particular effect, do it in the camera—at least until some software wizard comes up with a suitable equivalent.

Save Effects for the End

Another rule that will save you time and wasted effort is to avoid doing effects until your editing is complete. The reason? Most effects have to be rendered before you can play them in real time—and rendering takes time and can degrade image quality.

For instance, imagine you are applying a color correction filter to a particular sequence. If you apply the filter before the sequence is fine-tuned, you'll be rendering frames that may get trimmed out in the final edit—and each of those frames takes rendering time. Additionally, you may perform a trim that will add frames to a clip. Those new frames will need to be rendered all over again.

Nor do you want to apply an effect to a clip that's already been rendered. If you're working in DV, each time you render, the process introduces a certain amount of image degradation. It's not a lot, but you don't want to compound the problem by rendering a shot more times than is absolutely necessary.

In most cases, Final Cut Pro takes care of this for you. If you apply a filter to a clip that already has another effect on it, Final Cut Pro will throw out the old render file and re-render from the original (clean) clip. That way you get only one generation of loss even though there are two effects.

The time you can run into trouble is when you output your clips manually and then reimport them to do more effects. For example, let's say you're making a documentary about the Russian American community in Chicago. The interviews are primarily in Russian, so you generate subtitles in English and superimpose them over the video. Since you've now changed the pixels in the picture, you need to render this effect. Once your rough cut is complete, you might (for any number of reasons, including making a backup copy) lay out the edited sequence, subtitles and all, to a DV tape.

When it comes time to do the fine cut, you recapture the edited sequence (instead of recapturing your original source footage, without the subtitles) and begin fine-tuning. When all the editing is done, you apply a filter to give the video a more film-like look. When you render *that* filter, the software won't know that the clip has already been rendered once and will render it a second time.

While this case may seem a bit farfetched, there are many reasons you might be tempted to render something more than once. Don't do it.

TYPES OF VISUAL EFFECTS

Visual effects can be grouped into four major categories: speed effects, filtering effects, compositing effects, and *CG* effects. Of course, these are not mutually exclusive. You will frequently combine different categories to create compound effects, such as applying a filter to a title that is composited over a CG background image. You might even filter the background as well, or play it in slow motion, or both.

> **CG** *Short for computer generated, or computer graphic.*

Organic Versus Inorganic Effects

Before we run down that list of effect categories, perhaps we should first distinguish between effects that subtly enhance or distort a realistic image and those that leave reality behind. This distinction has ramifications similar to those I described earlier in the book, in which certain editing decisions allow the viewer to lose herself in the narrative, while others interrupt the illusion of reality.

Recognizing which is which in terms of special effects is harder than it seems. For example, in real life we *never* experience episodes during which time suddenly slows down to a crawl. Nonetheless, a slow-motion shot is a fairly subtle effect that most viewers will accept without experiencing a disruption of the narrative flow.

On the other hand, compositing two unrelated images into a double exposure would seem to be a jarring, unnatural effect that challenges viewers to make sense of the competing images. It's tempting to classify such a double exposure as a "cinematic" technique with little connection to the real world. But in fact, we see double exposures all the time: When you look out the window of a train, or even out the window of your office, part of the interior is reflected back at you, superimposed over the image of what lies outside.

So, while you can generally drop a slow-motion shot into a narrative sequence with far less disruption than a double exposure, trying to classify effects can get you into deep water. Even though more and more big-budget movies seem to rely on special effects, the current fashion is to create effects that seem entirely real. In most cases, with films like *The Perfect Storm* or *Saving Private Ryan,* the tens of millions of dollars the producers spent on visual effects went to create images that showed no trace of digital manipulation.

Still, part of what makes this medium so powerful is its ability to distort and manipulate images for dramatic effect. Finding a unique balance between real and fake is one important way of defining your own cinematic style. Remember the "bullet time" effect popularized in *The Matrix?* Although that completely disrupted any pretense of realism, the flow of the story was unimpeded.

Speed Effects

The most familiar types of special effects involve the manipulation of time. A speed effect is any modification to a clip's playing speed: slow motion, fast motion, ramping, and so on. As I mentioned in the previous section, speed changes tend to be one of the least disruptive types of effects.

You can change a clip's speed in Final Cut Pro by selecting the clip and choosing Speed from the Modify menu. This opens the Speed dialog box (**Figure 8.2**). You can enter a percentage of the clip's normal speed or you can simply define a new duration. In either case, only the frames between the In and Out points will be affected. If you want to play a clip backward, enable the Reverse check box. If you want it to play at double speed backward, check the Reverse box and set the speed to 200 percent.

Figure 8.2 The Speed dialog box allows you to set a clip to play at a constant speed, in forward or reverse. Call it up by hitting ⌘-Ⓙ.

Since modifying the speed of a clip also changes its duration, Final Cut Pro has to make adjustments to the surrounding clips in the Timeline. Speed changes cause the sequence to ripple forward or backward to accommodate the change in duration.

For example, if you took a 10-second clip and set the speed to 50 percent, the clip would become 20 seconds long. This would ripple the following clips 10 seconds downstream (**Figure 8.3**). If you're not sure how long you want your clip to be, or if you've got items on adjacent tracks that you don't want rippled, drag your clip onto a new track and lock all the other tracks (**Figure 8.4**). That way any speed changes you make won't affect the surrounding clips until you've decided on the desired speed. At that point you can unlock the rest of the tracks and integrate the clip back into the sequence.

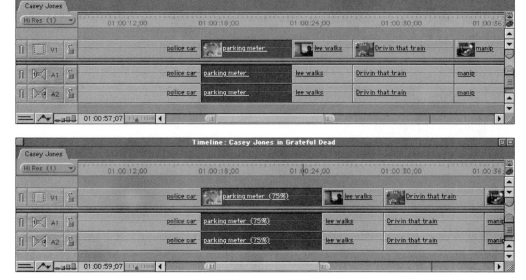

Figure 8.3 Speed changes ripple the sequence to accommodate the new duration of the affected clip.

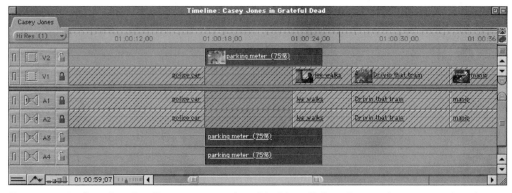

Figure 8.4 By dragging the clip to a new track and locking all the other tracks, you can alter the speed without disturbing the surrounding clips. (Option)-clicking the Lock icon for a track "solos" that track, opening it for changes while locking all the others.

Slow Motion

The ubiquitous slo-mo shot is the most common speed effect. Slow-motion shots are used to highlight a dramatic moment (Rocky holding the World Champion belt over his head), enhance the significance of a particular event (the necklace sinking through the depths in *Titanic),* and draw special attention to an event so the details can be understood even though it happens very quickly (the re-enactment of the assassination in *JFK*).

When you slow down a clip, Final Cut Pro has to create new frames to fill in the spaces. Look for a setting in the Speed dialog called Frame Blending (see Figure 8.2). When you enable this check box, Final Cut Pro calculates the new images by mixing together the surrounding frames. If this setting is turned off, Final Cut Pro creates intermediate frames by duplicating the preceding frames, creating a strobe-like effect. The latter technique renders more quickly than Frame Blending but creates a much less natural effect.

How far you can slow down a clip depends on the details of the shot. You can only go so far before smooth movement deteriorates into "steppiness" (even with Frame Blending enabled). And while audiences will tolerate a beautiful slow-motion shot without bouncing out of the story, if the shot begins to step rather than flow, all illusion of continuity is lost.

Fast Motion

It's just as easy to speed up a shot when you want to quicken the pace, increase the excitement, and accelerate how quickly things happen. This is far less common than slowing images down, but it does have its place. While slowing down an event can make it seem overly dramatic, speeding it up tends to reduce its dramatic impact and slide it in the general direction of comedy. Good examples of this are the driving sequences in Steven Soderbergh's *Schizopolis,* or Robert Downey Jr. designing his costume as the title character in Richard Attenborough's *Chaplin*.

Time Lapse

Sometimes you'll want to speed up events so much that what might take hours or days in real time plays out on-screen in only a few seconds. This method is commonly applied to slow-moving natural events such as sunsets or flowers blooming. Traditionally, the effect is performed in the camera using a technique called time-lapse photography. Time-lapse-capable cameras record a single frame at intervals you set: for instance, one every minute, or one every hour.

You can apply time lapse in post, much the same way that you apply other speed effects. You might take an entire one-hour tape and speed it up so it plays in just ten seconds.

Ramping

Ramping—changing the speed of a clip while it's playing—is currently enjoying great popularity. You'll see it quite often in TV commercials, music videos, and even a few feature films. In a ramp effect, the clip may begin playing at regular speed, gradually accelerate until it's playing at 2,000 percent, and then slow back down to a crawl. Director Guy Ritchie featured this effect in the opening sequence of *Snatch,* introducing each character with a ramp shot that slowed to a freeze frame—at which point a title showing the character's name and credit appeared over the frame.

Ramping can even be used to go from forward motion to backward motion. You can begin a shot by playing forward at half speed, then slow it down to a stop, play it backward, slow to a stop, play it forward again, and so on ad infinitum. Think of this as a visual equivalent of the way a DJ scratches a record. I've seen ramps employed comically in sports coverage, where they show a basketball dunk, then back it up and show it again and again: ball goes in, ball comes back out, ball goes in, ball comes back out. It's a bit nauseating, but it does have a certain charm.

Now that I've inspired you to try this exciting effect, I have bad news for you. Final Cut Pro can't do it. You'll need to use After Effects to perform this particular effect. Still, you can make a pretty close approximation in Final Cut Pro by using the Razor Blade tool and the speed controls.

1. Drag a clip into a new sequence and chop it in half with the Razor Blade tool.

2. Select the first half and set the speed to 150 percent.

3. Cut the second half in half.

4. Set the first half of that clip to 200 percent.

5. Cut the remaining clip in half and set the first half to 300 percent.

6. Repeat as needed.

The result is that the clip gets faster and faster as it plays. Although this is somewhat clunkier than using the feature in After Effects, the result is quite similar (**Figure 8.5**).

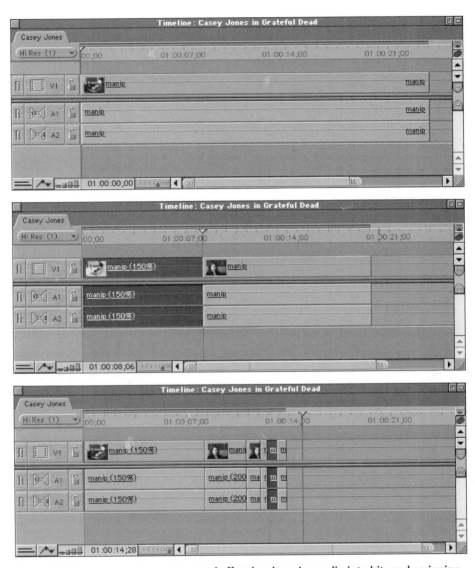

Figure 8.5 You can create a ramp speed effect by chopping a clip into bits and assigning different speeds to each section.

Freeze Frames

A freeze frame—stopping the action on a single frame—is a common way to end a sequence when you want to leave your viewers in suspense. You can also use one as a background for a chart or title.

Performing a freeze frame in Final Cut Pro is a snap: Select a clip and choose Freeze Frame from the Modify menu, or press Shift-N. This selects the current frame and opens it up as a still frame in the Viewer. Set In and Out markers to determine how long you want it to run, and drop it into your sequence like any other clip.

Fit to Fill

If you need a clip to fill a certain gap in your sequence, but the clip is too short or too long, you can use the fit-to-fill edit style. For instance, suppose you've got a 22-second clip in which the narrator describes how to fold a flag. You also have a B-roll shot of a flag being folded, but that shot lasts only 15 seconds. You want the clip to fit the narration exactly, and you don't care if the action is slowed down a little.

Fit to Fill will change the speed of the source clip to make it fit the space you've allotted in the sequence. It's one of the choices on the Edit Overlay, or you can hit Shift-F12.

To execute a fit-to-fill edit, you must provide all four points—source In, source Out, record In, and record Out (**Figure 8.6**). If one of these points is missing, you'll get an Invalid Edit error. (OK, that's not entirely true; if you don't provide a source In or Out, the beginning or end of the media will be used. You'll get the error only if one of the record points is missing.)

Use Fit to Fill with caution. Many clips can't be slowed down or sped up without the effect being obvious. In general, you can get away with speed changes below 10 percent without anyone noticing, but once you push it much above that, the effect is impossible to hide.

Figure 8.6 Fit to Fill modifies the speed of the source clip, stretching or squeezing it into the space defined in the sequence.

Speed and Audio

Final Cut Pro can apply speed effects to an audio clip just as easily as to a video clip. The good news is that audio speed changes don't require rendering. The bad news is that there's no way to change speed without altering the pitch of the sound. That means if you speed up an audio clip, it will get higher pitched, and if you slow it down, it will get lower. Sometimes this effect is desirable, but if you're trying to make a subtle speed change, this pitch alteration can give you away. It *is* possible to change speed without shifting audio pitch…in Pro Tools.

Render Quality

Rendering takes a long time. Even on the most powerful computer, once you start working with the types of effects described in this chapter, you will be desperate to find ways to speed up rendering any way you can.

Final Cut Pro offers four different render quality (RQ) settings to enable quicker rendering. The idea is that you switch to a lower quality render setting while you're making your rough decisions about edits and effects, and once you've finalized your decisions you switch back to a full-resolution RQ and re-render.

*You can see the current render quality (or change to a different one) via the RQ menu in the upper left corner of the Timeline (**Figure 8.7**). The contents of this menu are also available in the Render Quality submenu under the Sequence menu.*

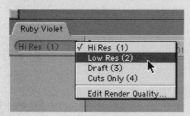

Figure 8.7 The Render Quality menu displays the current RQ. You can change this setting by selecting it in the menu. You can also toggle between the four states by pressing Y. Each time you hit that key, the current RQ changes to the next one in the list.

*Each RQ controls a collection of settings that affect rendering time. You can customize these settings by selecting Edit Render Quality from the RQ menu. This opens the Render Quality Editor (**Figure 8.8**).*

Don't change the settings hastily; the default settings are quite useful.

The first RQ (called Hi Res) is designed to give you the highest quality playback possible. Use this setting after you've made all your decisions and you want to see the final quality output. This is the slowest rendering option.

*Low Res (**Figure 8.9**) speeds up rendering by disabling Frame Blending, Field Rendering, and Motion Blur. All three of these are huge time-sucks while rendering. The advantage to disabling them here, globally, is that you can leave your individual clip settings at highest quality (with things like Frame Blending turned on). While you are set to Low Res, all those individual settings will be temporarily ignored, but later, when you return to Hi Res, you won't need to reset them.*

Additionally, Low Res renders images at 50 percent of the frame size. Because of all these compromises, rendering speed will probably be greatly accelerated. (Naturally, it depends on the specifics of the sequence: If you don't have any clips that use Frame Blending or any of the other "turned-off" settings, it won't give that much improvement.) However, the trade-off is that your images will be uglier, and you may not be able to see some of the fine details.

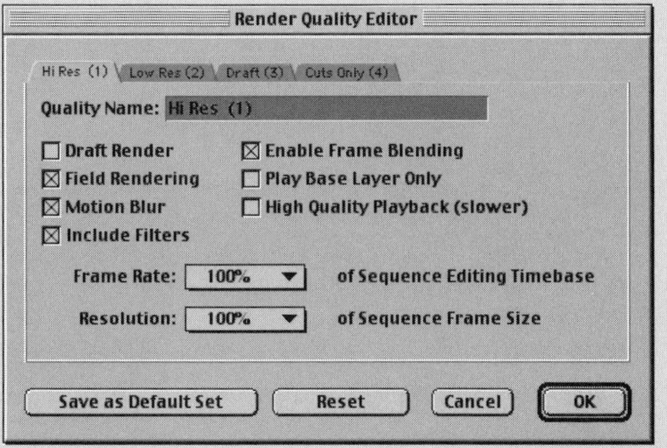

Figure 8.8 The Render Quality Editor allows you to choose which settings will be affected in each RQ.

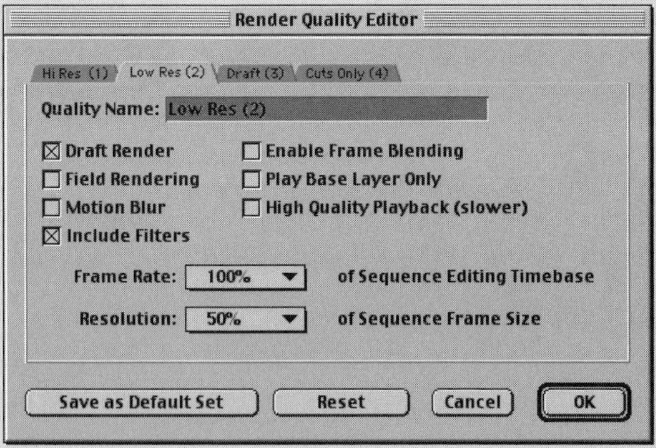

Figure 8.9 Low Res usually provides a significant improvement in rendering time. However, it also degrades the image quality.

Feel free to customize the RQ settings all you want, but it's a good idea to leave the Hi Res setting alone. You want to be sure you keep at least one RQ at full resolution for your final output.

One more useful nugget about render qualities: When Final Cut Pro plays over an area in your Timeline that requires rendering, it displays a warning frame that reads "Unrendered" (**Figure 8.10**). While this reminds you not to send an unfinished tape to the client, it's an annoying interruption if you're watching your show for timing purposes. If you enable the Play Base Layer Only check box in the Render Quality Editor, Final Cut Pro will attempt to play the base layer of video (usually V1) instead of displaying the "Unrendered" warning.

continues on next page

Render Quality *continued*

This means if you have a title on V2 and it isn't rendered, Final Cut will play the clip on V1 and ignore the title. Also, if you have a dissolve between two clips on V1, the edit will be played as a cut instead of the transition effect that requires rendering.

The fourth render quality, called Cuts Only, is identical to the Hi Res setting except that the Play Base Layer Only checkbox is enabled.

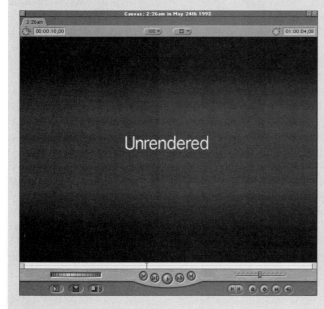

Figure 8.10 The evil "Unrendered" warning can be avoided by setting Render Quality to Cuts Only.

FILTER EFFECTS

Filter effects are modifications to the pixels within an image. They might include anything from lightening a dark shot to making it look like an oil painting. Final Cut Pro performs these manipulations with the use of filters. More than 80 different filters are built into Final Cut Pro, and each comes with different parameters that can create an amazing variety of effects (**Figure 8.11**). Final Cut Pro will also let you use certain third-party filters designed for After Effects. That brings hundreds of additional effects to your fingertips.

Many filters are designed to clean up images or modify them in a naturalistic way, not to create a flashy effect. This includes color correction filters, noise reduction filters, blur or sharpen filters, and certain perspective filters like Rotate or Flop. (Of course, any of these filters can be used to create a dramatic distortion of the original image, if you like.)

Applying a filter is as easy as selecting the clip you want to modify and choosing the desired filter from the Effects menu. You can also drag and drop filters onto a clip from the Effects tab in the Browser.

Once you've applied a filter, you can modify its parameters in the Filters tab for the affected clip (**Figure 8.12**). Remember that each instance of a clip is unique. So if you want to modify the

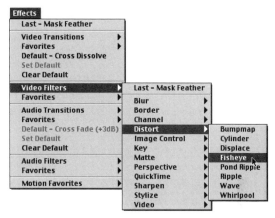

Figure 8.11 Filters can be accessed from the Effects menu or from the Effects tab in the Browser.

parameters of a filtered clip that's currently in a sequence, you must double-click that clip to open it into the Viewer.

This area shows the keyframes for each parameter.

The Reset button restores default settings for all parameters. — Add Keyframe

This check box turns the effect on or off.

The revealer enables you to hide the parameters for a particular filter.

Filter parameters

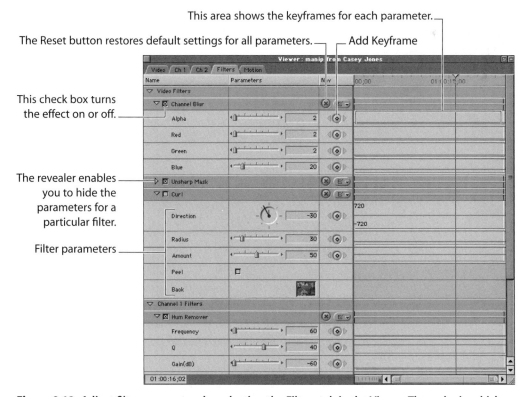

Figure 8.12 Adjust filter parameters by selecting the Filters tab in the Viewer. The order in which the filters appear in the list governs the order in which they will be applied.

Most filter parameters can be keyframed so the effect changes over time. This could be as simple as a clip that gets more and more blurry—or it could be a complicated effect where many parameters change at different times.

When you modify a setting in the Filters tab, the image is processed and the newly generated frame is displayed in the Canvas window. This requires that your playhead in the Canvas be parked on the clip being modified. Alternately, you can tear the Video tab out of the Viewer, and changes you make in the Filters tab will be visible there (**Figure 8.13**).

Figure 8.13 By pulling the Video tab out of the Viewer window, you can get immediate feedback on your filter manipulations.

Color Correction

If the color, lightness, or contrast of your image leaves something to be desired, check out Final Cut Pro's modest selection of color correction filters. Many of these filters, such as Brightness and Contrast or Tint, will be familiar to you if you've spent any time playing with Adobe Photoshop or another image manipulation program. These filters work much the same way in Final Cut Pro as they do in Photoshop. Other filters, like Proc Amp and Gamma Correction, work more like traditional analog video color correction hardware.

The term "color correction" implies that something needs correcting. Usually this means you've got a shot (or series of shots) in a sequence that doesn't match its neighbors. Perhaps the shot is a pickup, recorded under different lighting conditions, or maybe the sun moved during the course of the day. In any case, before you can fix an image you have to know what "correct" looks like.

Once you've applied your filter and opened the Filters tab to change the settings, select a frame from a "good" clip and load it into a new viewer by choosing Clip in New Window from the View menu (**Figure 8.14**). Drag that window so it's adjacent to the Canvas (between the Filters tab and the Canvas). And be sure the sequence playhead is parked on a good frame of the clip to be corrected (**Figure 8.15**).

Figure 8.14 The Clip in New Window command will open a new Viewer window for your clip.

Figure 8.15 By arranging the windows like this, you can easily compare the changes made to the clip in the sequence with the reference frame in the second viewer.

Compare Similar Frames

Don't try to match the color for a close-up with a frame from a long shot. Find another close-up so you can compare skin tones apple to apple. Ideally you'll have a shot of the same actor under the proper lighting conditions to use as your reference frame. If not, you may need to find another element in the scene to use as a comparison.

The first things to look for are whites and blacks. Find a spot that should be the same tone of white in the two images. Then adjust the filter parameters until the whites match. Next match the blacks. Finally, find a color that should be the same in both images—maybe some wallpaper, or the leaves of a tree. A single bright color that appears in both shots is ideal. Match that color by adjusting the hue (or phase) and saturation (or chroma) until it looks as close as possible.

Beware! You probably won't be able to make a perfect match. First of all, the tools available to you are fairly crude: Four sliders just aren't enough! Also, the nature of color correction makes it difficult to adjust one color without distorting another.

Frankly, I recommend doing color correction in Discreet Combustion, which offers more advanced tools. For instance, it allows you to limit the correction to a single color range so you can adjust skin tones without affecting the background colors.

Do It Last

If possible, save your color correction until you're nearly finished with the show. All films can benefit from a color-correcting pass to adjust the fine details. If a shot is just a touch underexposed, you can lighten it; if a scene looks weird because too much blue light was leaking in through the window, you can warm it up.

In fact, nearly every shot can benefit from some minor adjustment—but don't be too quick to blame your DP. Traditionally, one of the last steps in making any feature film is the *answer print,* which includes a critical process called *color timing.* Color timing is vital to creating the uniform visual tones you're used to seeing in movie theaters. If you could see the untimed cuts of even the most expensive films, you'd be shocked at how inconsistent colors and exposures are from shot to shot.

ANSWER PRINT   The first print back from the lab with all color timing and dissolve effects included. Once this print is approved, the lab can make multiple release prints, which are sent to theaters for distribution.

COLOR TIMING   A film-specific process in which each individual shot in a film is tweaked so it looks its best and matches the others.

Do It Uncompressed

If you're going to be making color adjustments (or any other kind of adjustments) to nearly every frame of the movie, don't do it on DV in Final Cut Pro. Doing that would mean re-rendering *your entire movie,* which would be horribly time consuming, and it also means that every frame would get recompressed, introducing rendering artifacts into your film.

If your budget permits, I strongly recommend making your color correction pass at an online editing facility using an uncompressed format like D1. That's right, abandon the nonlinear digital world and make a tape-to-tape transfer, applying color correction shot by shot as you go. While this is fairly expensive (these suites cost between $100 and $1,000 per hour), it gives the best results. Not only will you find state-of-the-art color correction tools (million dollar machines with names like Henry, DaVinci, Alex, and Inferno), but they will be operated by specialists who know exactly how to make the most of your images.

Abstract Filters

If you're looking to create interesting artistic effects, you can also use filters to make a shot look like a moving painting or a ripple spreading across a watery surface. It's rare for an editor to apply these sorts of severe distortions in traditional narrative films, but if your object is to keep the viewer's eyes open during a dull sequence, this sort of eye candy can be just the thing to help the medicine go down.

For example, speaking of medicine, I produced a series of films for a medical equipment firm: educational sales tools designed to explain the details of high-tech medical machinery to doctors and hospital staff. The material was unbearably dry, and even though we used dramatizations to show how the tools were put to work in a hospital, we still needed something to keep the doctors' eyes from closing. So to brighten up the transitions between sections, we used a filter called Find Edges, which identifies areas of contrast in the image and gives them a sort of neon glow (**Figure 8.16**). This abstract visual element helped to offset the methodical details about the medical equipment.

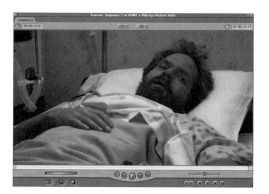 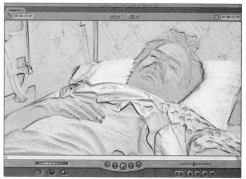

Figure 8.16 The Find Edges filter is just one abstract effect available in Final Cut Pro.

You can find most of the abstract filters listed in the Distort and Stylize categories (**Figure 8.17**), but a few more cool ones are hidden in other places. I recommend playing with the Color Style filter in the QuickTime submenu (**Figure 8.18**). And check out the Zoom Blur filter in the Blur section (**Figure 8.19**). Don't be afraid to try combining multiple filters: Sometimes just the right combination can create a truly unique eye-pleasing effect.

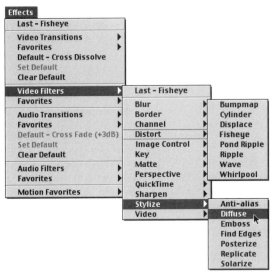

Figure 8.17 The Distort submenu contains filters that apply a physical distortion or texture to your image, like Pond Ripple or Fisheye. The filters listed under Stylize modify the image itself, reinterpreting the pixels in some abstract way.

Figure 8.18 The Color Style filter can create something that looks like an image in a comic book.

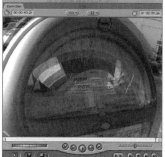
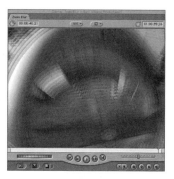

Figure 8.19 Zoom Blur can simulate the exact effect of a super-fast zoom (called a smash-zoom) with the camera lens, but by experimenting with the parameters, you can create some very interesting variations.

Keyframes and Filters

Final Cut Pro's keyframe architecture is consistent across the program. Once you understand how keyframes work, you can use them for audio levels, filter parameters, motion effects, even titles.

*The basic controls for all keyframes are the Add Keyframe button, the parameter control (usually a slider), the keyframe graph, and the keyframe navigation controls (***Figure 8.20***).*

continues on next page

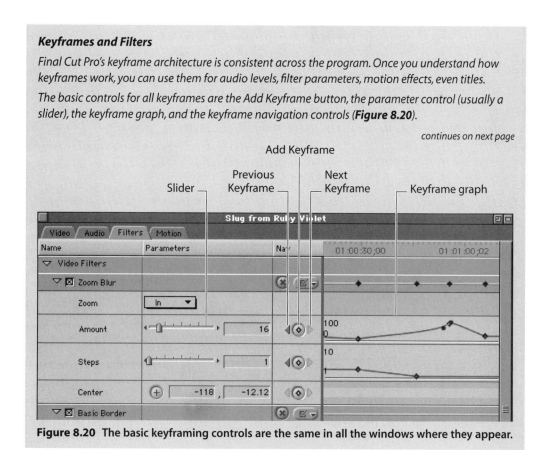

Figure 8.20 The basic keyframing controls are the same in all the windows where they appear.

Keyframes and Filters *continued*

Since keyframes are time-critical, be sure to check your playhead position before creating a new keyframe. Also, once your first keyframe is set, all it takes to set a new keyframe is changing the parameter value at a different point in time.

*For example, if you set the Gaussian Blur filter to a value of 12, it will be 12 across the duration of the clip. If you then tell the filter you want it to be 5 at some other point in the clip, the value will have to change over time to get from 12 to 5. This change will be reflected in the keyframe graph (**Figure 8.21**).*

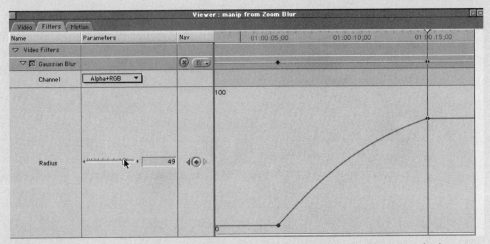

Figure 8.21 Keyframe graphs are very flexible. You can stretch them by dragging the bottom edge of the graph, and you can zoom in or out on them just as you can in the Timeline. You can also drag the keyframes around in the graph to change their values.

*You can change a keyframe to a smooth point by ⌃Ctrl-clicking on the keyframe. That will add Bezier handles that allow you to control the curvature of the keyframe envelope (**Figure 8.22**). This has the advantage of smoothing out the time changes of the effect. In the case of the blur, it will go down from 12 to 6 linearly, but it will slow down as it goes from 6 to 5. This creates a more organic-looking effect (see "Ease In and Out," later in this chapter).*

*Once you've set multiple keyframes, you can navigate between them using the little Previous Keyframe/Next Keyframe buttons. If there are no more keyframes in one direction, the button will dim (**Figure 8.23**).*

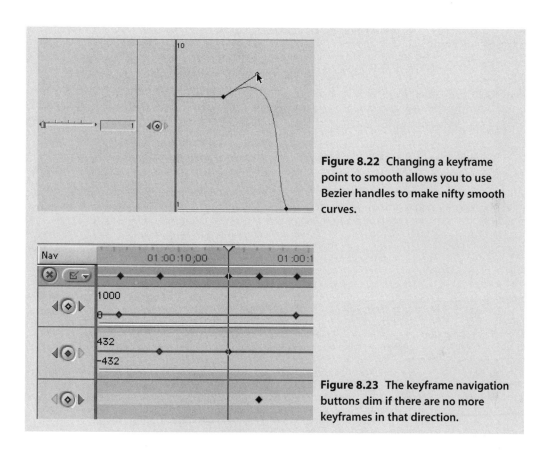

Figure 8.22 Changing a keyframe point to smooth allows you to use Bezier handles to make nifty smooth curves.

Figure 8.23 The keyframe navigation buttons dim if there are no more keyframes in that direction.

COMPOSITING

For many people, this term conjures up images of 3-D football helmets flying across the TV screen, or fancy title sequences for movies like *The Island of Doctor Moreau* or *Seven*. But most compositing is far simpler than that. In fact, any time you put two or more images on the screen at once, that's a form of compositing. Every lower third is a composite. So is every split screen or picture-in-picture.

In Final Cut Pro, a composite is represented by two or more clips in the Timeline occupying the same point in time. You can accomplish this easily by placing them on separate tracks.

Superimpose Edit Style

You can drag clips right to the Timeline and put them directly on whatever tracks you want, but sometimes you'll want to line up a clip using traditional In and Out points before you edit it in. The last edit style you'll find on the Edit Overlay is Superimpose; its keyboard shortcut is F12.

A superimpose edit places your clip into the sequence on the track *above* your target track (**Figure 8.24**). One of the most common uses for the superimpose edit is adding a graphic like a lower third. You can set your In and Out points in the sequence and drag the title right to the Canvas. If you select Superimpose, Final Cut Pro will automatically drop the clip exactly where you want it.

Once the clip is positioned in time, you must decide where you want to place it in the frame.

Figure 8.24 Superimpose will add a new track, if necessary, in order to put the new clip above the current target.

Motion Effects

Any clip can be moved, rotated, scaled, distorted, and cropped to change its placement in the frame. These are all called motion effects. To perform a motion effect, simply grab the clip in the Canvas and drag (**Figure 8.25**).

Figure 8.25
You can modify nearly any aspect of a clip's size and shape by clicking and dragging it in the Canvas window.

If you're going to be moving clips around in the Canvas window, you must set the View pop-up to Image+Wireframe (**Figure 8.26**). Once this setting is enabled, you will see a frame around each clip; when a clip is selected, an "X" will connect the four corners of the clip (**Figure 8.27**).

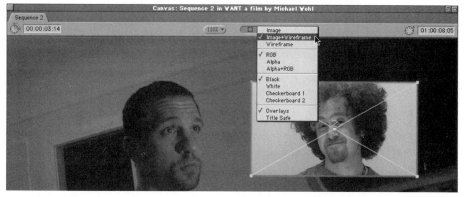

Figure 8.26 The View pop-up lets you set various display options for the Viewer or Canvas window. When Image+Wireframe, or Wireframe, is set, you can drag items around in the window to reposition them. Toggle between the states by hitting Ⓦ.

Figure 8.27 You can tell if an item is selected by the highlight around the clip and the "X" connecting the corners.

Design a Picture-in-picture

Suppose you are doing a picture-in-picture effect and you want to make clip 2 appear in the upper right corner of the frame, superimposed over clip 1 (**Figure 8.28**). Start by putting both clips in the Timeline at the same point in time (**Figure 8.29**). If you remember from Chapter 5 ("Basic Editing"), clips on higher tracks obscure clips below. In this case we're going to shrink clip 2 so it obscures only part of clip 1.

Figure 8.28 A simple picture-in-picture effect.

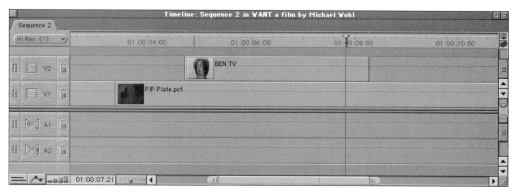

Figure 8.29 Items on higher tracks obscure items on the tracks below them.

Once the clips are properly lined up in the Timeline, you're ready to shrink and position clip 2. Make sure the wireframe is enabled. Then click on one of the corner points to scale the clip. If you click on one of the clip edges, you can rotate the clip. And if you click anywhere within the boundaries of the clip, you can move it (**Figure 8.30**).

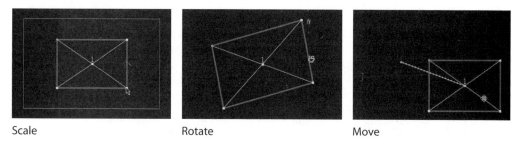

Scale   Rotate   Move

Figure 8.30 Depending on where you click, you can modify the clip in different ways.

> **TIP:** (Shift) *constrains or unconstrains clip movement. When you're changing the position of a clip, holding down* (Shift) *limits your movement to left-right or up-down. When you're scaling a clip,* (Shift) *releases the default aspect-ratio constraint so you can change the horizontal and vertical scale independently (squeezing or stretching the clip). When rotating,* (Shift) *constrains movement to 45-degree angles.*

Start and End the Effect

You still need to decide *how* clip 2 will appear and disappear. At this point, it's just going to pop on the screen and then pop off, based on the duration of the clip as set in the Timeline. But suppose you want it to fade in, and then, when it's finished, shrink to a point and vanish.

I introduced the Clip Overlays control (**Figure 8.31**) in Chapter 7 ("Cutting the Track"), when I discussed setting audio levels in the Timeline. But that control has an additional function. Not only does it turn on the audio level rubber band, it also turns on the clip *opacity* rubber band.

> **OPACITY** *The opposite of transparency. The more opaque an object is, the more it obscures objects behind it. The more transparent it is, the more background objects show through.*

Opacity graph

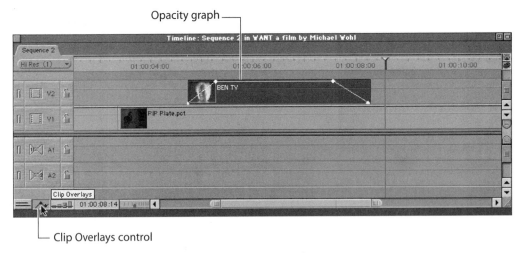

Clip Overlays control

Figure 8.31 The Clip Overlays control is found in the lower left corner of the Timeline window. Turning it on displays an opacity envelope that lets you fade clips in and out right in the Timeline.

You can add keyframes to the rubber band by [Option]-clicking the line. Then simply drag your new point to the desired setting. See Figure 8.31, which shows our picture-in-picture fading in from completely transparent (invisible) to completely opaque (solid).

To make the picture-in-picture disappear by shrinking into a point, we'll need to fire up the Motion tab.

Setting Keyframes Near Edges of Clips

One of the trickier aspects of working with keyframes in the Timeline is adjusting them when they're positioned near the edges of the clip.

The problem is, when you try to grab a keyframe that's right next to the clip edge, Final Cut Pro grabs the clip edge instead, assuming you want to trim the clip. This might not seem all that rough, but in real life, almost every time you set a keyframe in the Timeline, you are setting it right at the clip edge. This is how you perform fade-outs and fade-ins. Far too often, you innocently Option-click to set your first keyframe where you want your fade-out to begin. But then, when you try to set the second keyframe at the end of the clip, the program won't let you!

There are two ways to work around this.

*The first is to set the keyframe farther into the clip and then drag it to the edge (**Figure 8.32**). This is the most common solution because it can be done with the least interruption to your workflow.*

The second option is to switch to the Pen tool by pressing P. Use the Pen tool to set all the keyframes you want, anywhere your heart desires. Then switch back to continue editing.

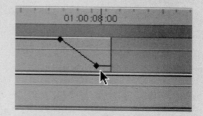

Figure 8.32 Set your keyframe far away from the edge, and then drag it to the edge to set it.

Use the Motion Tab for Precise Control

You can make a clip shrink by dragging its corner point in the Canvas—but it's difficult to get it to a precise setting, especially when you're trying to set the scale to zero! This is why Final Cut Pro also allows you to set the value numerically.

Double-clicking the clip in the Canvas will load it into the Viewer (just like double-clicking a clip in the Timeline). Once in the Viewer, select the Motion tab (**Figure 8.33**). Here you can make numeric changes to every aspect of the clip's size and shape.

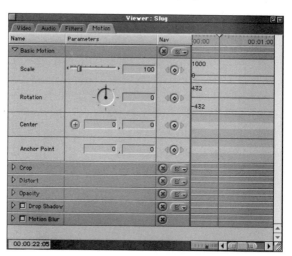

Figure 8.33 Every clip in Final Cut Pro has a Motion tab.

To make the scale change over time (in this case, move from 35 percent to 0 percent), we must set two keyframes. The first keyframe goes one second before the end of the clip, and the second goes on the last frame of the clip (**Figure 8.34**).

Voilà! A vanishing clip.

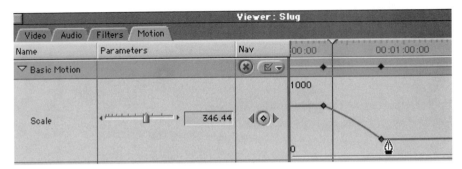

Figure 8.34 Set keyframes in the Motion tab exactly the same way you would in the Audio tab or the Filters tab: Option -click to add a keyframe and then drag it to the desired value. Or click the Add Keyframe button and adjust the slider.

Control Clip Motion With Position Keyframing

Let's say that instead of fading in our picture-in-picture effect, we want it to fly across the screen and land in the designated spot. The trick to position keyframing is to figure out your landing position first, and then go back and set the starting point. This is because in most cases, the ending point of the move is where the item will stay once the move is complete.

First find the point in time where you want the move to end, and place the clip at its final position. In this example, we want the opening move to be complete exactly one second into the clip, and the resting position to be in the upper right corner of the screen. Once you've set the time and place, add a keyframe in the Canvas by clicking the Add Keyframe button at the bottom of the window (**Figure 8.35**). That's to let Final Cut Pro know that this is the ending point of the move.

Figure 8.35 The Add Keyframe button in the Canvas (or Viewer) adds keyframes for almost all motion parameters: Scale, Rotation, Center, Anchor Point, Aspect Ratio, Crop, and Distort. Ctrl -click on the button to set or clear any of these parameters individually.

You may notice that there's no keyframe graph for the Center setting in the Motion viewer. That's because the Center parameter determines the clip's position, and those keyframes show up right in the Canvas. When you change the position of a clip over time, a dotted line appears in the Canvas showing the path that the clip will follow (**Figure 8.36**).

Figure 8.36 Motion paths appear in the Canvas and the Viewer to show you how your clip will move over time.

Move the playhead backward until it sits on the first frame of the clip (a perfect time to use ⬆, which moves you back to the previous edit). Drag the clip to your desired starting position in the Canvas. As soon as you drag, a line appears showing the path the clip will follow. Why does the line appear even before you set a new keyframe? Because you've already established that it must be at that ending position at a later time. By dragging it while the playhead is parked at an earlier time, you are automatically setting a new position keyframe (**Figure 8.37**).

Figure 8.37 Drag the element to its starting position.

TIP: Use the Canvas Zoom pop-up menu to control how much of the viewable area you can see in the current window. If you wish to position a clip offscreen (as we're doing for the starting position in the picture-in-picture example), zoom out so you can see the pasteboard around the viewable area (**Figure 8.38**).

The Canvas Zoom pop-up allows you to set the current zoom level on the window.

The Fit All setting will display as much extra space as necessary to show every clip currently on the pasteboard.

The Fit to Window setting will force the viewable area of the window to fill the current window size regardless of the zoom level.

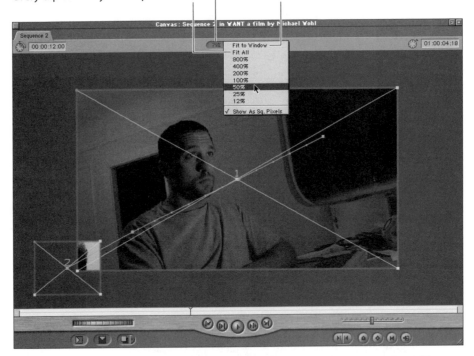

Figure 8.38 When the Canvas (or Viewer) is zoomed out, you can see areas that will never be seen in the finished movie. This allows you to place clips "in the wings" so they can move on- and offscreen.

At this point, the picture-in-picture will fly in from offscreen (lower left) and land in the upper right corner. But you're still not satisfied. Now you think it would be much more natural looking if the picture-in-picture followed a curved path. You can add keyframes to a motion path by clicking and dragging a point in the path (**Figure 8.39**). That will add a keyframe, and, as you can see in the figure, it will create a curved path by default.

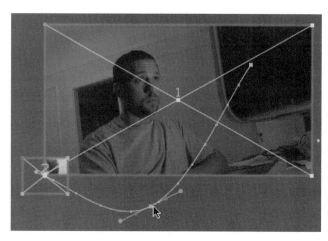

Figure 8.39 Adding points to a motion path is as simple as clicking and dragging. New points appear automatically, set to be smooth points complete with Bezier handles for adjusting the amount and type of curvature.

Ease In and Out

In addition to creating a curved path, you may want to make your picture slow down and stop gradually when it reaches its final destination, rather than slamming to a sudden halt.

This kind of smooth deceleration is called easing in, and the corresponding change at the beginning of a move (slowly accelerating until it reaches full cruising speed) is called easing out. When you're flying clips around on the screen, you should generally use this type of acceleration/deceleration control in order to observe the rules of inertia and simulate the way objects move in real life. Here's how.

You can set any keyframe to ease in and out via the Shortcut menu that appears when you Ctrl-click the keyframe (**Figure 8.40**).

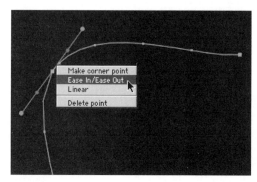

Figure 8.40 Ctrl-clicking a keyframe brings up a Shortcut menu that lets you set the point to Ease In/Out. You can also toggle a point between being a corner point (a hard change in direction) and a linear point (with Bezier handles).

If you're trying to perform precise moves, you will probably want more control over the speed and amount of acceleration and deceleration than the preset Ease In/Out setting provides. You can change the acceleration manually by adjusting the tiny subhandles on each keyframe's Bezier handles (**Figure 8.41**). Unfortunately, while this looks kind of cool, I find these controls virtually useless. There is no way to get a precise result, and the range of variation is extremely limited.

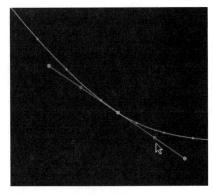

Figure 8.41 The Bezier controls contain a second set of handles for controlling acceleration.

To get more precise control I recommend using After Effects. After Effects has wonderfully flexible and accurate control over acceleration settings. And it allows you to control acceleration for every parameter of every clip or filter, so you can control how quickly your blur takes effect, or how slowly a pond ripple slows to a stop.

Preview Motion Without Rendering

*As you know, you have to render the sequence in order to see your final effect. However, if you want a quick preview of the movement your clips will make, you can do it by setting the Canvas view state to Wireframe (**Figure 8.42**). In this state, all clips turn into simple outlines, but when you play the sequence, the objects perform their movements in accurate real time. This includes all Ease In/Out settings, so you can use this to adjust the timing of your movements. Audio is played as well, so you can time movements to line up to specific audio cues.*

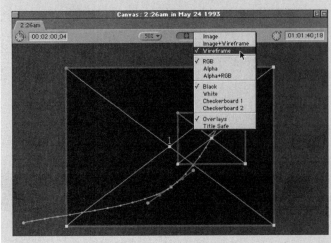

Figure 8.42 Setting the Canvas View menu to Wireframe enables the real-time motion preview. You can toggle between the three view states by hitting W.

Apply Motion Blur

The perfect precision of computer-generated movement can make your motion effects seem phony. One way to counteract this is by applying an effect called Motion Blur. Motion Blur simulates the slight fuzziness that occurs when a camera photographs an object that's moving too fast for the camera's limited shutter speed.

You might expect that viewers would prefer images to be as sharp as possible, but our eyes are so used to seeing this slight blur that when it's absent, moving objects look stiff and unnatural (**Figure 8.43**). This becomes particularly apparent when you combine camera images with movements created synthetically in Final Cut Pro.

Motion Blur affects only clips that have motion applied via the motion controls in Final Cut Pro. Objects moving within the frame are unaffected.

Figure 8.43 Motion Blur creates a subtle blurring effect on moving objects.

You can turn on Motion Blur in the Motion tab of the Viewer (**Figure 8.44**). There are two parameters you can assign. % Blur controls how dramatic the effect is. You'll need to experiment, since the result can vary depending on how large your object is and on how quickly it's moving. A fast-moving object generates much more blur than a slow-moving object. You can counteract this by cranking up the blur

Figure 8.44 Turn on Motion Blur in the Motion tab. It will be applied only when rendering in Render Qualities with the Motion Blur check box enabled.

percentage for slow-moving objects, but that defeats the purpose of the control. Raising the blur amount is similar to lowering the frame rate in the camera, causing more blur in each frame. As an object slows down (as it would during an ease-in), the blur decreases.

The second parameter is Samples. This refers to how many frames are used to create the blur. If this setting is too low, you will see steppy frame edges instead of a smooth blur effect. In general, you should set this value as high as possible to create the smoothest blur, although with slow-moving objects you may not see much benefit from the higher settings. Just remember that the higher you set it, the longer the effect takes to render. Setting it to 8 will take twice as long as setting it to 4, and 16 will take twice as long as 8. Rendering motion blur is pretty slow to begin with, so a high setting like 16 will increase your rendering time dramatically.

Of course, you can set one of your render qualities to ignore motion blur so once you've determined the correct settings, you can switch RQs and finish your editing and timing decisions without it. Then, when you're ready for final output, switch back to Hi Res and come back in the morning.

Move Clips in 3-D Space

Another common motion effect involves making the clip or graphic seem as if it's moving forward or backward in three-dimensional space, as though there were physical depth to the screen. You'll see many examples of this effect in show openers, title sequences, and so on, although, like most motion effects, they rarely show up in narrative films.

Flashy motion effects like 3-D can help keep viewers alert, especially when you need to make information on a chart or graphic more interesting. Objects moving in the frame create action, and action creates engagement. So even if your show doesn't include a motorcycle chase, you can add a few 3-D motion effects to spice up that list of safety instructions.

Unfortunately, Final Cut Pro's 3-D options are very limited, so this is another case where you should probably turn to After Effects (version 5; earlier versions do not support 3-D) or Discreet Combustion.

Both these packages offer true 3-D capability, allowing you to move objects along a Z axis as well as the X and Y. You can make one image pass through another on its approach to the front of the screen. Additionally, objects themselves can have depth as they fly around and flip over, so they look like books or boxes rather than flat objects that vanish when seen edge-on, as well as cast shadows.

But if you have no other option, and you want to create 3-D effects within Final Cut Pro, you're not totally out of luck.

Final Cut Pro's Basic 3D Filter

The Basic 3D filter (found in the Perspective submenu of the Effects menu) allows you to make a clip *look* as though it's moving in 3-D space (**Figure 8.45**). This is accomplished by applying graphic distortions to make the 2-D object appear to be tilted or skewed in three dimensions. For a single image the result is nearly indistinguishable from what you get with true 3-D tools, but the Basic 3D filter lacks any way to define the three spatial coordinates. That means objects neither bump into nor break through objects behind or in front of them.

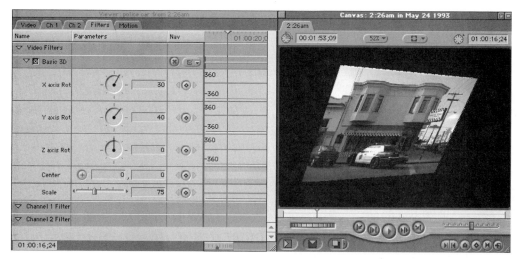

Figure 8.45 The Basic 3D filter allows you to simulate 3-D movement for a clip.

Use the Secret 3-D Tool

Another cool way to simulate 3-D in Final Cut Pro is to use a fairly esoteric feature of the Distort tool. The Distort tool (**Figure 8.46**) allows you to grab any corner point of a clip and move just that point—which stretches and distorts the clip's shape (**Figure 8.47**).

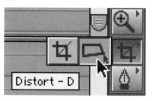

Figure 8.46 The Distort tool is hidden beneath the Crop tool. Access it from the keyboard by hitting D.

Figure 8.47 You can distort the shape of a clip by pulling on one corner point.

Very few people know that the Distort tool can be transformed into a magic 3-D tool by using the (Shift) modifier. When you view a clip in 3-D space, it's distorted based on the rules of perspective so that the side of the image closer to the front of the screen is larger than the side farther away. When you hold down (Shift) while dragging a point with the Distort tool, it automatically forces the clip to simulate this effect (**Figure 8.48**).

Figure 8.48 The magic 3-D tool is really just the Distort tool with (Shift) held down.

If you combine this special type of distortion with changes to the Scale parameter (which make the whole clip look closer or farther away), you can create convincing three-dimensional effects without ever needing another program.

Saving a Favorite Motion

Motion settings can be saved and applied to a different clip. Let's say you're doing a training film about environmental responsibility that includes six different episodes providing examples of environmentally responsible behavior. During each section, as soon as the character realizes the right thing to do, you drop in a little animated light bulb from the top of the frame. It swings back and forth a couple of times as text fades in explaining the point you just illustrated.

Once you define the exact motion that the light bulb will follow in section 1, you can save that motion path. Then, in the next section, rather than redesigning that motion, you can simply apply the saved motion path so the second light bulb follows the same exact path of movement as the first.

*Saving a motion path is simple. If you have a clip in the Viewer with the motion applied, or if you have the clip selected in the Timeline, choose Make Favorite Motion from the Modify menu. This will add that motion to the Favorites folder in the Browser (**Figure 8.49**). Once you have it there you can rename it and drag it onto another clip. Alternately, you can apply it just like a filter from the Motion Favorites section of the Effects menu (**Figure 8.50**).*

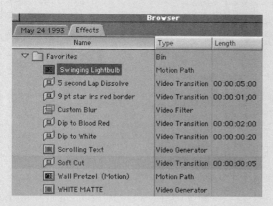

Figure 8.49 The Favorites folder can hold motion paths as well as other effects.

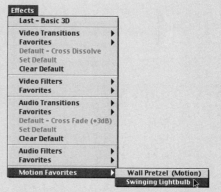

Figure 8.50 Favorite motions can be applied just like filters via the Motion Favorites section of the Effects menu.

Check the Manual

Once you begin playing with clip motion, you'll discover that Final Cut Pro includes quite a few features to make your life easier. I can't possibly cover all of them here, but I suggest that you check the Final Cut Pro User Manual for more information on Drop Shadow, Aspect Ratio, Anchor Point, Bevel, and Border.

Mixing Layers

Once you've mastered the art of moving clips around, you'll soon find yourself in situations where you've got two overlapping clips on the screen. If you don't want one image to completely obscure the other, you'll need to decide how they should interact visually.

Sometimes you'll want to mix multiple images together to create a background for a title or chart. Other times you may need to create a poetic combination of images. There are no rules, so feel free to make up your own.

Final Cut Pro includes a number of tools to help you resolve situations like these. It's difficult to describe exactly when to fire them up, but if you understand something about what they can do, you'll probably begin developing your own ideas about how and when to put them to use.

Set Opacity

All clips have opacity, and by default the level of that opacity is set to 100 percent opaque. As you lower opacity, the clip becomes more and more transparent, revealing the clips or background behind it.

I've already discussed how to adjust a clip's opacity by using Clip Overlays in the Timeline. And you may have noticed that there's an Opacity slider in the Motion tab. These controls are identical: Changing one will change the other. It's exactly like the way the audio level rubber band in the Timeline is identical to the graph in the Audio tab.

Mix Your Pix With Composite Modes

Any time a clip is layered over another clip, you can choose different ways for the images to interact visually. In Chapter 5, I discussed additive and non-additive dissolves as two variations on how clips could be combined during a cross-dissolve. By setting a clip's composite mode, you can gain access to more than ten different ways of combining superimposed clips.

Just as every clip has an opacity level, each one has a composite mode. By default it's set to Normal. That means that at 100 percent opacity, the clip will be entirely opaque, and as opacity decreases, the clip will fade away in a linear fashion, as in an ordinary cross-dissolve.

However, if you set Composite Mode to one of the alternate settings, such as Multiply, Hard Light, or Lighten, you can create wildly different effects (**Figure 8.51**). I can't describe exactly what each setting does, because they are based upon complex mathematics and results vary widely. But I can recommend a few settings. In all these cases, I'm assuming that the bottom clip is set to normal (100 percent) opacity, so the changes I'm describing will be applied only to the top clip.

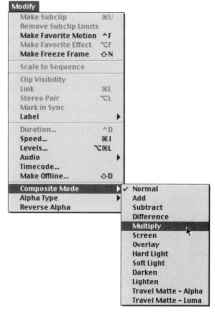

Figure 8.51 You can set Composite Mode for each clip in the Modify menu. (Ignore the Travel Matte choices for now.)

Add Lightening and Darkening Effects

Some modes make your image lighter and some darker. This can be tempered somewhat by the effect of the opacity of the clip. Some modes will not change the overall lightness or darkness value of the image at all.

If you're trying to create a background for a logo or title, it may be helpful to create a lighter background (for a dark logo) or vice versa. The composite modes Add, Screen, and Lighten tend to make your image lighter, while Subtract, Multiply, and Darken tend to make the image darker.

I find the Multiply and Screen modes (which are roughly opposites) to produce some of the most beautiful and useful results. Multiply will combine lighter elements (darkening them) but leave the darker areas alone. Screen will lighten darker elements but leave lighter areas unaffected (**Figure 8.52**).

Figure 8.52 Multiply and Screen are two of the most versatile and attractive settings to use for combining images.

Since Multiply will always remove any areas of absolute white in the combined clips, and Screen will automatically remove any areas of absolute black, you can use them to remove white or black from a clip. For example, if you had an image of a lens flare effect on a black background, compositing that lens flare using Screen would ignore all the black and combine only the flare itself with the bottom image (**Figure 8.53**).

Figure 8.53 Screen will remove the black areas so only the lens flare is combined.

The Overlay setting is unique because it actually combines the effects of Multiply and Screen. Multiply affects only pixels darker than 50 percent gray, and Screen affects only the lighter half. Overlay combines them, creating an entirely new type of effect.

Additional settings include Difference and Hard and Soft Light. Difference has the effect of inverting the image based on its combined values (**Figure 8.54**). Hard and Soft Light are more difficult to describe. They are supposed to give the impression that a harsh spotlight, or a diffuse soft light, is shining on the image. I don't think they achieve that result, but they can make for pretty pictures regardless (**Figure 8.55**).

Figure 8.54
The Difference mode creates a type of inverted look.

Figure 8.55 Hard and Soft Light create unique effects that are dependent on the contents of the clips.

Control Transparency With Alpha Channels

Frequently, when you're dealing with elements such as logos or other graphics, you will need to control the shape of transparent areas in your frame. For example, if you have a round logo, you wouldn't want to see its square outline when you use it in a sequence. Final Cut Pro (as well as most other computer graphics programs) controls transparent areas in the frame by using something called an alpha channel. You'll find alpha channels in still images like PICT or TIFF files, you'll find them in 3-D animations, and you'll even find them in some video files (**Figure 8.56**).

Whenever you bring a clip with an alpha channel into Final Cut Pro, the alpha channel is automatically recognized and the appropriate areas will be treated as transparent whenever you use that clip in a sequence. Different programs store this information differently, but Final Cut Pro can determine the precise format of the alpha channel and interpret it appropriately.

Figure 8.56 The alpha channel for an image contains the details of which areas are opaque and which are transparent. Black areas are treated as transparent, and white areas are treated as opaque. Gray areas are semi-transparent.

Occasionally you may import a file whose alpha channel is interpreted incorrectly—or, more commonly, is inverted. (In the latter case, what should be transparent appears opaque, and what should be opaque shows up as transparent.) In these cases, you will need to override the program's assumptions manually.

You can reset the alpha channel state for any clip in the Modify menu. You can fix an inverted alpha by selecting Reverse Alpha, and you can fix an incorrect alpha setting (usually identified by a halo or crunchy edge around the transparent object) by selecting a different setting from the Alpha Type submenu (**Figure 8.57**).

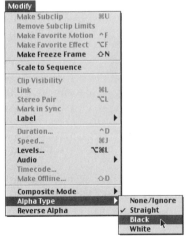

Figure 8.57 Clips with an alpha generated against a white background should be set to White. Ditto for Black. Clips with alpha that was generated against no background at all should be set to Straight. Normally this setting is determined automatically when you import a clip. You need to adjust it only if something looks wrong.

View the Alpha Channel During Wireframe Preview

If you've got a clip with an alpha channel, and you go into Wireframe mode, Final Cut actually shows you the outline of the alpha channel as a pattern of dots (**Figure 8.58**). This enables you to predict how graphics will show up on the screen. This pattern sticks around even during the real-time preview I described earlier.

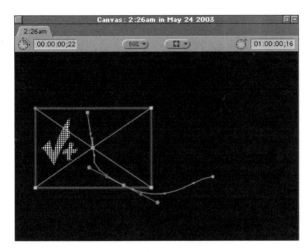

Figure 8.58 Graphics with alpha channels are visible when playing a clip in Wireframe mode.

Alternately, you can choose to view the alpha channel for a clip (or sequence) by choosing Alpha from the Viewer View menu or the Canvas View menu (**Figure 8.59**). If you choose Alpha+RGB, the alpha will be overlaid onto the image as a semi-transparent red layer.

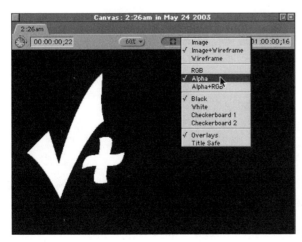

Figure 8.59 Choose Alpha from the View menu to view the alpha channel for the clip you're looking at.

As long as the artist preparing your graphics (in Photoshop or some similar program) understands what she's doing, you can usually forget about alpha channels entirely. Final Cut Pro will see them and take care of them, and the transparent hole for your circular logo will be wonderfully round. But it's important to understand how Final Cut Pro uses alpha channels any time you need part of your image to be transparent.

Which leads us to keying.

Keying

Want to insert a person or object from one shot into a background from a second shot? A *key* is the special effect that lets you accomplish this. First, the subject needs to be shot in front of an evenly lit, solid color field. Then you remove the color digitally, creating a transparent alpha channel where the color used to be. Finally, the subject is composited over an alternate background that shows through the transparent areas (**Figure 8.60**). This process is called keying, short for chroma-keying. The color that's removed is called the *key color.* Most often the key color is blue or green. That's because a solid, primary color is easiest for the computer to identify, and human skin tones mostly fall outside of the blue and green range. These backgrounds—and therefore the shots themselves—are called green screens or blue screens.

Figure 8.60 In the keying process, the key color is removed from the shot, leaving behind a transparent area where the color used to be. Then the image is combined with a new background, creating a composite shot.

Construct a Killer Color Key

Final Cut Pro provides sophisticated tools to help create your matte, but even so, you'll need to invest serious effort in choosing foreground and background elements that match convincingly.

First, make sure that the lighting matches. If the key light in the foreground shot is coming from the left, don't use a *plate* where the light source is coming from overhead.

PLATE *The background element of a key.*

The same goes for lighting style and color: If your goal is to hide the fact that two shots are being combined into one, don't expect a shot filmed in the studio, with diffuse, cool light sources, to match a plate filmed in strong, warm afternoon sun.

Account for Camera Position and Movement

If the blue screen shot is low angle, the plate must be as well. If you intend to use camera movement, you must create tracking marks on the set to allow the computer to record the movement. In many cases you will want to use a *motion control* rig. Motion control can re-create the camera moves that were used in the studio so they can be repeated for the plate.

MOTION CONTROL *A mechanical, computerized system that records and re-creates camera moves.*

Perform the Key

Final Cut Pro can perform a key by using one of several filters (**Figure 8.61**). To extract the background from the most common shots, which use a green or a blue screen, choose the Blue and Green Screen filter.

Blue and Green Screen is specially designed for shots where the background is not just any blue or green color but the precise and specific blue and green used for this purpose in professional studios.

First you need to arrange the clips in the Timeline. Because the Key filter will make the colored areas transparent, simply put the plate on the track beneath the key shot. That way the background will show through any transparent areas.

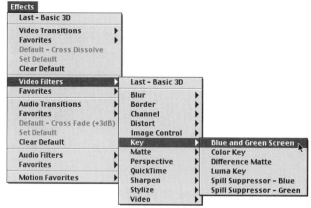

Figure 8.61 Final Cut Pro's keying tools are applied as filters.

Apply the Blue and Green Screen filter to the clip you wish to key, and double-click it to open it into the Viewer (**Figure 8.62**).

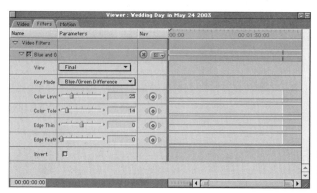

Figure 8.62 The Blue and Green Screen filter is the best choice if your clip was shot against a properly lit, professionally colored backdrop.

TIP: If you can't read the names of the parameters, you can resize the columns by dragging the column header edge (**Figure 8.63**).

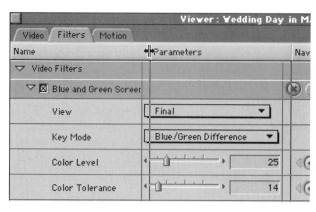

Figure 8.63 You can resize any column in any window by dragging the divider in the column header area.

Now you must adjust the parameters in the Filters tab to key the shot properly.

The first thing to do is set Key Mode to Blue/Green Difference. Regardless of whether your shot is a blue screen or a green screen, this is the setting I recommend. If you still can't get a clean key after adjusting all the other parameters, then go back and try another key mode. (How do you know if you've got a "clean key?" Hang on and I'll tell you!)

Next, reset the Edge Feather parameter to zero. By default, it's set to 10 pixels—but this is all wrong, since it softens the edge of the key you're creating. It's very difficult to see how accurately the key is working with this setting turned up so high.

Now, adjust the Color Level and Color Tolerance sliders until you get the key as clean as possible. I can't tell you where to set these sliders, since that will vary depending on your source footage. But I *can* tell you what to look for so you know when you've got a good key. To set your key using the two color sliders, you'll need to closely examine the alpha channel that the key effect is generating.

The View parameter gives you the option of seeing either the unfiltered source clip, the matte itself, the final output of the filter (in which the green areas become transparent and the plate shows through), or a nifty display where you can see all three at the same time (**Figure 8.64**). For now, set it to Matte.

Figure 8.64 Changing the View parameter will change what's displayed in the Canvas.

You'll know you've got a good key when the background turns completely black and there are no black spots anywhere in the opaque part you want to keep (**Figure 8.65**). Any murky gray areas will be semi-transparent. Raise the color tolerance until the whites and blacks are as solid as possible.

Figure 8.65 Use the Matte view to make your first pass at setting the key. You want to see as clear a separation of black and white as possible. Black will be transparent, white will be opaque.

Once you get close, switch the view to Final. Because the quality of your key depends on the specific interaction between the foreground and the background, you should make your final adjustments while looking at the actual composited image. Zoom into the Canvas and examine the edge of the key. Make sure you're not seeing any of the green screen and that you haven't gone too far and eaten away at the foreground image.

Finally, once you've got the key as clean as possible, use Edge Thin (which shrinks or expands your matte shape uniformly) and Edge Feather (which softens the edge of the matte) to make the background and foreground combine as well as possible.

Get the Spill Out

Quite often when you're shooting a green (or blue) screen shot, a bit of the screen color reflects or spills onto the subject, especially if it has any reflective surfaces. That means that your actor might have a slight green hue reflecting off his shiny face. So, even though you may have created a perfectly clean edge between the subject and the background, the foreground shot may still need more work.

You can remove this subtle green haze by applying a Spill Suppressor filter to the source clip. This will extract all the green (or blue) from the image. Choose green or blue, then set the Amount slider to control how much of the color is removed. Slide it down until all the color is gone; then bring it back up very carefully until you start to see the green spill reappear. Bring it back down a hair, and you're there.

Remember that the order in which filters are listed in the Filters tab indicates the order in which they will be applied to the clip. If you apply the Spill Suppressor before you apply the Blue and Green Screen filter, you will extract all the green from the shot, and the key won't work.

Plug in Ultimatte

It's easy to plug third-party After Effects filters directly into Final Cut Pro. Although different packages have different installation procedures, once you complete the setup, they will appear in the Effects menu with the rest of your filters. Several of these are specifically designed for keying. The best-known one is called Ultimatte.

The Ultimatte filter is a very powerful plug-in that can create a killer key. But it's designed for footage shot specifically to Ultimatte specs, and ideally created with special Ultimatte hardware that generates a "live" matte during the shoot.

You can still use the Ultimatte filter on any blue or green screen shot, but before you lay out the bucks, I recommend doing some tests with Final Cut Pro's built-in keying features and filters. Final Cut Pro's keying algorithms are sophisticated and can produce excellent results—and you have only five parameters to adjust. The Ultimatte package actually consists of three different filters, and you'll end up having to tweak dozens of sliders and settings. All those extra parameters do give you more fine control, but mastering them requires a lot of patience and experience. That fancy Ultimatte filter won't do you any good if you don't spend the time learning how to use it properly.

Don't Key With DV

Now that you know everything about keying (yeah, right!), let me issue a major, serious warning: Don't do it with DV footage!

That's right: If you plan to shoot a blue screen shot, don't shoot it with DV. Rent a Betacam, a Digital Betacam (usually referred to as Digibetacam), or even a DVC Pro camera and shoot it with that. Why? Remember that DV is highly compressed—and while the compression is extremely intelligent, it is also specifically optimized to fool the human eye. It's not that good at fooling the computer, which stumbles over all the missing data.

The human eye is far more sensitive to changes in light and darkness than to changes in color, so one of the ways DV stays svelte is by throwing away a lot of color data. In fact, it throws away almost three quarters of the color data for each frame! Given that, it's amazing how good it looks. But unfortunately, when it comes time for Final Cut Pro to find the exact pixels where the green screen ends and your actor's curly brown hair begins, the data doesn't exist.

If your final "release print" is going to be a highly compressed Web movie, shooting your blue screens on DV may work just fine—but if you intend to show the finished shot on a movie screen or a high-resolution TV, the key that seemed perfectly acceptable on your computer screen may suddenly look embarrassingly crunchy.

Other Types of Keys

Not all keys are shot against blue or green screens. And sometimes you want to make a key from a shot that wasn't originally shot with that intent at all. For these cases, try one of the other keying filters in Final Cut Pro.

Color Key Filter

Traditionally, people use blue and green to key off of, but in reality you can key off any color—and sometimes you have to. Once I needed to key a dollar bill, so we shot it against a red screen. (The blue-green ink would have made a blue or green background harder to isolate.) In a case like this, choose the Color Key filter. It will let you pull a key from any color in your image.

Difference Matte

This key compares two frames and generates a matte based on what's different between them. Imagine you have a static shot of someone standing in front of a mural, and for some reason you want to isolate her (maybe so you could add a halo effect around her). If you can find a frame of the mural without the actor in it, and compare that frame to a frame of the actor *and* the mural, the difference would be…the actor! And the matte would be generated based on that shape.

Luma Key

You can treat the luminance value of an image as if it were a transparency. Remember that an alpha channel is nothing more than a grayscale image in which black means transparent, white means opaque, and anything in between is only partially visible. If you extract the luminance values of a clip, you end up with a black-and-white version of that clip you can use to determine what parts of the image are transparent. This will create some striking visual images.

Making Mattes

Keying is based on making a matte from the information in a clip, usually a clip that's been shot against a blue or green background specifically for that purpose. But you don't need a colored background; sometimes you can use a separate element to create a matte. Since a matte is just a way of determining what part of the image shows through and what part is hidden, you could use a matte to apply an effect to any part of a picture.

For example, let's say you had a shot that included a window, and the window was overexposed. You want to darken the window without darkening the whole image (**Figure 8.66**). You can create a matte using one of the tools I am about to discuss and isolate the window. Then you can apply a Gamma Correction filter to the window and counteract the overexposure.

Figure 8.66 The window is overexposed, but the inside of the room is fine. You can use a matte to apply an effect to just the window.

Crop It

For very simple mattes, Final Cut Pro allows you to crop the visible area of any clip. That means you can hide problems around the edges of your clip such as a light stand peeking into the frame or some video noise introduced during capture. (Some analog capture cards create a few lines of black or colored noise at the bottom or right edge of each clip.)

To crop an image, select the Crop tool (**Figure 8.67**) and drag from one of the edges of your clip to eliminate the objectionable material (**Figure 8.68**). If you drag from a corner point, you can crop two sides at once.

Figure 8.67
The shortcut key for the Crop tool is Ⓒ.

Figure 8.68 You can crop an image from any side, or from a corner to crop two sides at once.

Since you're replacing the cropped area with transparency, cropping makes the viewable image smaller. So if the cropped clip is on the bottom track, that area will appear black. If it's on a track with a clip beneath it, that clip will be visible in the cropped areas.

Create Custom Mattes With After Effects

Cropping is very limited, since you can create only straight edges and rectangular mattes. When you want to design a matte that's a custom shape (suppose that overexposed window was a porthole in a ship's cabin), the Crop tool's functionality is clearly inadequate.

Here again, I recommend that you cut your losses and launch After Effects. This trusty motion graphics behemoth allows every clip to have custom-shaped mattes you can control via Bezier curves, and what's more, you can have as many of them as you like. So not only can you quickly isolate that round porthole, you can matte three windows shaped like boat anchors.

Final Cut Pro does include some additional matte tools, and for simple cases they can be useful. Furthermore, they have the advantage of creating the effect right in your editing tool, with no need to pass files back and forth. But they are unquestionably inferior to After Effects' offerings.

Lose Junk With Garbage Mattes

Functionally, a garbage matte is no different from any other matte; it gets its name because you use it to get rid of junk you don't want in the frame. It's most frequently combined with tools like the keying filters. For example, if your blue screen shot included a tiny corner of the stage that wasn't painted blue, you could apply a garbage matte to make that corner turn transparent as well.

Final Cut Pro's garbage mattes are an attempt to emulate the functionality that After Effects provides, but they are quite awkward to use. You apply the matte as a filter, which you select from the Matte submenu of the Effects menu (**Figure 8.69**).

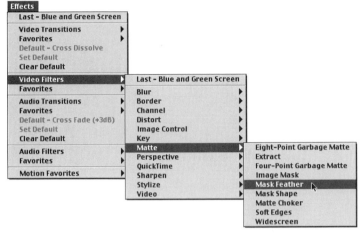

Figure 8.69 All of Final Cut Pro's matte tools are applied as filters, accessible through the Matte submenu of the Filters section of the Effects menu.

Rather than dragging the points of the matte to where you want them, you must use the Point control in the Filters tab (**Figure 8.70**). You have to click once on the Point control in the Viewer, and then click in the Canvas where you want the point to be.

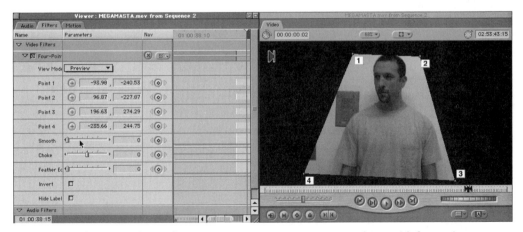

Figure 8.70 The Four-Point Garbage Matte can create a transparent shape with four points.

Furthermore, forget about true Bezier curve controls. If you want your matte to have a curved edge, you'll have to settle for the Smooth slider. All this does is uniformly round the entire matte (**Figure 8.71**). You can also create a soft edge to your matte by adjusting the Feather Edges slider (**Figure 8.72**). Don't get me wrong, you can create some cool and useful effects using these tools, but to me it still feels like hammering with a wrench.

Figure 8.71 The Smooth control rounds the edges of your matte.

Figure 8.72 The Feather Edges control softens the edge of your matte.

Design Simple Forms With Mask Shape

You can create mattes in simple shapes like diamonds, ovals, and rectangles with the Mask Shape filter. (In Final Cut Pro, "mask" and "matte" are synonymous.)

Image Mask

This filter lets you select another clip and use its luminosity as a matte.

Put It in Widescreen

Try the Widescreen filter to create a letterbox matte at the top and bottom of your image. This simulates the wide-screen aspect ratio of theatrical film formats. The advantage to using this filter instead of the crop controls is that the Widescreen filter allows you to slide the image up and down underneath the matte. That way, if your subject's head is being cut off by the letterbox, you can lower the image until it fits. Of course, you're just cutting off more of the bottom of the image, but if you want to make a wide-screen image out of a full-frame picture, you have to cut something.

Soften It Up With Mask Feather

You can apply the Mask Feather filter to soften the edges of any of the mattes you create with these other tools.

Build Traveling Mattes

The term "traveling matte" refers to any matte that moves. Technically, all of the mattes I've described so far are traveling mattes, since they are all keyframable—which means you can change their positions or shapes over time.

What I'm referring to here is a little different: using one clip to act as a mask for another clip, where both can be moving independently of each other. For instance, a good example of a traveling matte would be titles in which images are moving inside the letters while the text is scrolling across the screen. This is one of the most useful mattes in Final Cut Pro.

Travel Matte (abbreviated to save space on the menu) is actually a composite mode. If you set a clip's composite mode to Travel Matte, it will use the clip beneath it as a mask. To use this feature, place the mask clip (for instance, the letters of the text scrolling across the screen) on one track, and place the video you want to show through the mask (for instance, exciting footage of explosions or flames) on the track above it. Set the upper clip's composite mode to Travel Matte – Alpha, and the clip will show through the lower clip's alpha channel (**Figure 8.73**).

If you want to use the luminance of a clip rather than using its alpha channel, set the upper clip's composite mode to Travel Matte – Luma. This is perfect if you've got a simple graphic such as black text on a white background (**Figure 8.74**). If you have white text on a black background and need to invert it, simply apply the Invert filter (found in the Image Control submenu of the Filters section of the Effects menu) to the mask clip.

Figure 8.73 A classic traveling matte is created by using one clip's alpha channel to act as a mask for a second clip.

Figure 8.74 If you're using a clip's luminance for the mask, remember that black is transparent and white is opaque.

If you want to go for broke, you can put a third clip beneath the traveling matte clips to create a background for your matte (**Figure 8.75**). Be careful to choose something that won't compete for focus with your matte image; otherwise it will just be a big mess.

Figure 8.75 Most traveling mattes are used with a background element. Pick a muted image that won't make the matte hard to see.

Nest Sequences

Sometimes you may want to apply a single effect to a group of clips. Let's say you've got a two-word title with the words in different clips, and you want to fly them on as one entity. Or you might want to apply two effects to the same clip in a carefully controlled order. For situations like these, Final Cut Pro allows you to nest one sequence inside another.

In the simplest case, you may have an interview and a lower third you want to treat as a single item so you can dissolve them together into another clip (**Figure 8.76**). This is a perfect example of how nesting the items can make your task easier.

Whenever you nest items, the sequences become live-linked. So if you go back and fix a spelling error on that lower third, the correction will also take effect in the parent sequence.

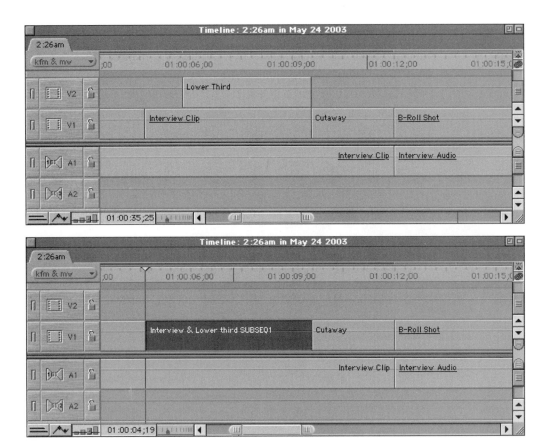

Figure 8.76 We want to dissolve both the interview and the graphic at the same time. By nesting them, we can treat them as a single clip.

There are two ways to create a nested sequence:

Drag One Sequence Into Another

You can build the two sequences separately and drag one sequence from the Browser right into the second sequence, treating it like a clip. This is fine if you know about it ahead of time. For instance, in the lower third example I just gave, if you knew before you started that you were going to nest the sequences, you could create a new sequence, lay in the interview clip and the lower third, and then drag that whole sequence into your master sequence, where you could dissolve it with the adjacent clip.

Use the Nest Items Command

If you don't think about doing a nest until after you start (which is usually the case), use method number two, the Nest Item(s) command.

Select the items that you want to nest in the Timeline, and choose Nest Item(s) from the Sequence menu—or press Option-C. This will open the Nest Items dialog box (**Figure 8.77**).

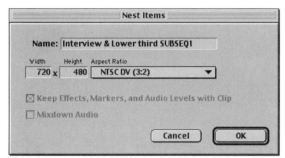

Figure 8.77 The Nest Items dialog box allows you to define the new sequence you are about to create.

Don't fail to immediately give the new sequence a good name. Once you begin nesting sequences, if you're not careful you can quickly create a complicated mess. Name the subsequence something that will tell you what's in it, and also that it's used in a parent sequence.

Once you dismiss the dialog box, a new sequence will be created replacing the clips right there within the sequence. The new sequence will be placed on the lowest available track, and from that point on you can treat it as a single clip. The only difference is that if you double-click it, rather than opening into the Viewer it will open as a new tab in the Timeline, revealing the clips inside the sequence. (If you want to open it into a Viewer—to adjust filter or motion parameters—hit Enter or choose Sequence in New Window from the View menu.)

CG

This last type of effect (the acronym stands for computer graphics, or computer generated) refers to elements created in your computer. These can include titles, background elements such as a solid color field, or 3-D objects (everything from a static logo to an animation of a realistic-looking dinosaur).

In most cases you will import these elements into Final Cut Pro from other applications, but first I want to talk about the ones you can create right inside the program.

Generators

Final Cut Pro includes a group of effects called generators. These are clips that are generated by the program and can be used just like any other clip. They include titles, color mattes, gradients, and noise. You can use the motion controls to fly these clips around on the screen, distort or scale them, and add drop shadows. You can add filters, use them as part of a complex composite, and customize the titles to suit the aesthetic of your program.

Generators are born in the Viewer window. You can select the type of clip you want to create by choosing an option in the Generators menu (**Figure 8.78**).

Figure 8.78 This menu in the lower right corner of the Viewer provides access to all the generators available in Final Cut Pro.

Titles

When you need to create basic titles, try the generators you'll find in the Text category (**Figure 8.79**). When you select an item from the Generators menu, it opens into the Viewer with a new tab called Controls (**Figure 8.80**). All of the generator's parameters can be adjusted there.

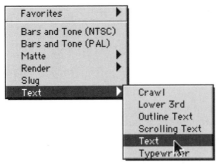

Figure 8.79 Final Cut Pro includes several different types of text generators. The simplest one is just called Text.

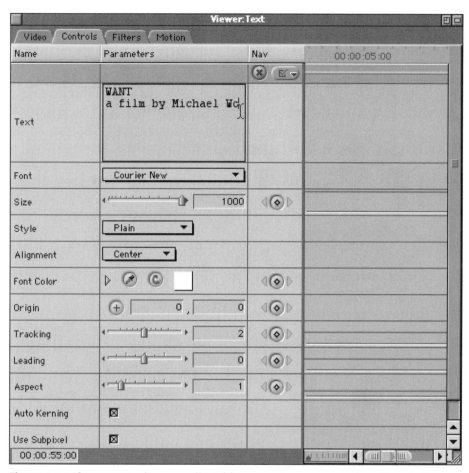

Figure 8.80 If a generator has any adjustable parameters, you can access them in the Controls tab.

The best way to use a text generator is to edit it into your sequence *before* you customize the text and set the various controls. That way you can see the changes you make update live in the Canvas window. Here's how:

1. Select the text generator from the pop-up menu.

2. Set your In and Out points in the Viewer and the Canvas, and perform an edit to get the title into the sequence.

3. Park the Canvas playhead somewhere over the title.

4. Double-click the generator in the Timeline to open that instance in the Viewer. (Be careful! If you skip this step you will modify the wrong instance of the clip.)

5. Open the Controls tab, and change the text and other parameters to create the title you want.

If you follow this procedure, the changes you make in the Controls tab will update live in the Canvas. While the controls are fairly rudimentary, this still allows you to create attractive titles.

> **TIP:** *Final Cut Pro can read only TrueType fonts. If you have a Type 1 font that you absolutely must have for titling, use a shareware utility to convert it to TrueType.*

Use Readable Fonts

You can use only one font for each title. If you want multiple fonts, you must create two generators. Be sure to select a fairly thick typeface. Remember that video is *interlaced* and if you select a font with thin horizontal lines, it will flicker during video playback.

> **INTERLACING** *Video images consist of hundreds of horizontal lines. Televisions display this information by splitting the image into two fields, with each field containing every other line. The upper field contains lines 1, 3, 5, and so on, while the lower field contains lines 2, 4, 6, and so on. When the TV plays the signal, it paints each field on the screen alternately, creating the illusion of smooth movement. This is called interlacing.*

In general, sans serif fonts are best, since they lack the tiny ornaments (serifs) that characterize serif fonts. It's also a good idea to use a large font size. Anything smaller than 30 points will be too small to read comfortably on-screen. In general, I recommend sizing screen fonts between 36 and 96 points.

Final Cut Pro's text generators suffer from overzealous kerning. You'll probably want to adjust the tracking (the space between letters) to a setting of 1 or 2. Another problem with text kerning is that the Tracking slider only works if the Auto Kerning check box is enabled. Go figure.

I recommend changing the font color, too. Bright 100 percent white can be harsh when seen on a video screen, and on some TVs it will cause smearing or bleeding. If you want a white title, set the color to 90 percent white. This will still look plenty white but will avoid distortion.

More Text Generators

Final Cut Pro provides an additional handful of other text generators for more specialized puposes. Lower Third is a quick and easy way to whip up title cards for your interview subjects and includes several different styles to choose from. Typewriter creates your indispensable *X Files* type-on effect. (Unfortunately, there's no built-in sound effect.)

Scroll Your Credits

The Scrolling Text generator is perfect for creating those scrolling credits so familiar from the end of every film (**Figure 8.81**). You can enter as much text as you want. I recommend typing the list in your word processor and then copying and pasting the text into the generator.

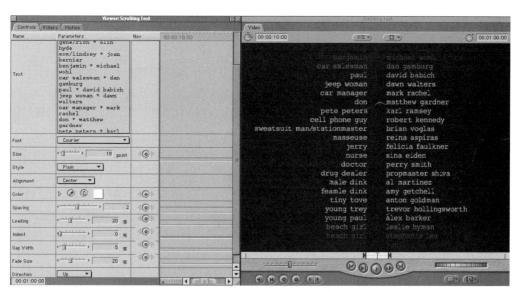

Figure 8.81 The Scrolling Text generator provides that essential for every film: scrolling end credits. The asterisk character is a secret message to Final Cut Pro indicating you want to insert a gap between two columns of text. Only the first * is recognized.

You might want to adjust a couple of special settings for this generator.

Fade Size

Want to set an area at the top and bottom of the screen where the titles will fade in and fade out? Use the Fade Size slider.

Gap Width

This slider has absolutely no effect unless you know the secret (undocumented) way to use it. If you place an asterisk (*) in each line of text, Final Cut Pro will read that character as a request to add a tab (or gap) at that point in the line. The Gap Width parameter controls the size of that space. This is especially cool for creating the two columns of information commonly found in credits.

To create your columns, type the text for the first line of the first column, then type an asterisk, then type the text for the first line of the second column. Repeat this for every line of text (see figure 8.81).

Create Color Mattes

Final Cut Pro can generate fields of color. While this capability may seem fairly unimpressive, you'll be surprised how often you need it. First of all, at the end of your movie, when the lead character goes to heaven, you might want to fade the last shot to white instead of black. Or you might want your titles to be black text on an orange background for that big Halloween special.

Also, the Crop and matte tools can turn any clip into a custom shape. That includes generators. Need a small blue diamond to go under your company logo? How about a tiny white oval to fly through a shot of the night sky looking like a UFO?

The most basic generated clip is the simple color matte. By default it is 50 percent gray. The only parameter you can modify in the Controls tab is the color. But remember, as with every parameter, you can change the value over time, so your UFO can cycle through the spectrum as it races across the sky. Also, as with every other clip, you can modify a generator's opacity, add a drop shadow, or apply filters to it to broaden its usefulness.

One great thing you can do with a white color matte is mix it with another clip using the composite modes. If you apply a white matte onto an image and experiment with the opacity and the composite mode, you can lighten and soften the image, creating a dreamy, washed-out look that might be good for a flashback. Alternatively, you can create a nice, light background to use behind a dark title. Try the Soft Light, Overlay, or Add settings.

Regeneration

Just as with filters and motion paths, you can save generators in your Favorites folder. I recommend creating a white color matte and adding it to your list. That way you'll always have quick access to it in the Favorites section of the Generators menu (**Figure 8.82**). As you figure out which generators you use most frequently, you can make them into favorites, too.

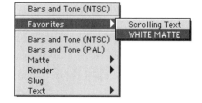

Figure 8.82 If you save a generator as a favorite, it will show up in the submenu of the Generators menu.

To create a favorite generator, open the generator and set the parameters to the way you like them. (In this example, we're setting a basic color matte to White.) Next, select Make Favorite Effect from the Modify menu. If you want to rename it, you can find it in the Favorites folder in the Effects tab of the Browser window (**Figure 8.83**).

Figure 8.83 The Favorites folder is where the generators you use the most can be edited.

Gradients

A gradient is just a color matte that uses two colors instead of one. Choose the colors in the Controls tab, then set the gradient's direction and shape. Gradients make nice backgrounds, although they look a bit conservative.

If you need a background for a chart, or even for a narrator who was shot against a blue screen (or some other background you can replace), try this recipe for an elegant moving background:

Set your gradient colors to two shades of a similar hue, such as a medium blue and a dark purple. Next apply a distort filter, such as Wave or Whirlpool. This will create a very slight movement in the background. You don't want something so dramatic that it detracts from the subject in the foreground, just enough movement to make the shot feel dynamic.

A Word About Slug

When you're cutting actual film, it's essential to keep the picture reels and sound-track reels exactly the same length so they stay in sync. If you add a shot you don't have sound for yet, you have to fill in the space on the track reels temporarily with random scraps of film. This filler is called slug. Final Cut Pro borrows this metaphor for the Slug generator.

When you launch Final Cut Pro, the Viewer window is black—but that doesn't mean it's empty. It actually contains slug. That means if you want to throw a place-holder clip into your sequence, you can drag right from the Viewer into the Canvas without ever loading a clip. Slug has both audio and video (the audio is silent and the video is black) so it can be used as placeholder on any track.

Slug is also handy if you need a black matte. Rather than creating a favorite color matte set to black, you can just use slug. For example, there are some third-party After Effects plug-ins that create effects like fire or snow and completely replace the shots you apply them to. If you want to use those filters in Final Cut Pro, you can apply them to a piece of slug.

Importing Files

In most cases, when you use a computer-generated element while editing, it's not created in Final Cut Pro. If it's flat art, it probably comes from an illustration pro-gram like Freehand or Illustrator or an image manipulation program like Photoshop. If it's 3-D art (still or animated), most likely it comes from Maya, Lightwave, or 3-D Studio Max. Final Cut Pro can read a wide variety of file formats, but here are a few tips to make your life easier.

Import Flat Art as a TIFF, PICT, or TGA File

Final Cut Pro can't rasterize vector graphics. That means if you're working for Greenpeace, and someone sends you its logo as an EPS file, Final Cut Pro won't be able to read it. Solution? Open the EPS file in Photoshop and save it in TIFF format. That will convert it from vector art into actual pixels.

Final Cut Pro can read almost any graphics format, including BMP, JPEG, SGI, PNG, PSD, TIFF, PICT, and TGA as well as some Macintosh-specific formats like MacPaint and QuickTime Image. However, not all these file formats can hold alpha channel information. Since PICT, TIFF, and TGA can, any of these formats is ideal for use with Final Cut Pro.

Import 3-D Animations

If your 3-D program can output its file as a QuickTime movie—and most can—go ahead and save it that way. You'll be able to import it right into Final Cut Pro. Just remember to use the Animation codec, with the color depth set to 32 bits. That way, the alpha channel (the one that separates the dinosaur from the background) will be imported into Final Cut Pro along with the file. The Animation codec is lossless (when set to highest quality), so you won't be throwing away data during the transfer process.

Try to avoid outputting your 3-D file in DV, since that will compress it even before you get it into Final Cut Pro. Nor will it have any alpha channel information. Then, when you incorporate it into your sequence, you'll have to re-render it (I'm presuming you'll be compositing the 3-D element with some other shot), recompressing it and causing further degradation.

Use a Series of Stills

If you can't export the 3-D animation as a QuickTime movie, your only alternative is to export a series of still images from the 3-D program. The stills can be in any of the graphics formats I just listed. While Final Cut Pro won't automatically recognize the series of images and turn it into a single clip, you can achieve the same result if you follow these instructions.

1. To import the individual frames of your animated sequence, start by changing the Still/Freeze Duration setting in General Preferences to one frame (**Figure 8.84**). This setting defines the duration of every still image you import, as well as how long freeze frame clips last.

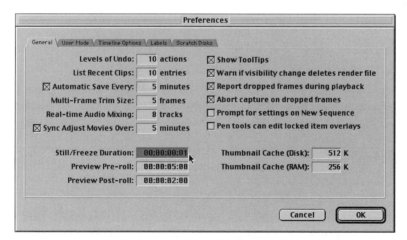

Figure 8.84 Change the Still/Freeze Duration setting to one frame.

2. Make sure your 3-D program saves all the still images in a single folder, and then import that folder into Final Cut Pro. When you direct Final Cut Pro to import a folder, it creates a bin in the Browser with all of the folder's contents inside (**Figure 8.85**).

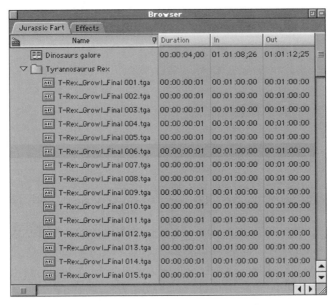

Figure 8.85 The bin contains all the still images for your animation sequence.

3. Drag the folder right onto the Canvas window. Final Cut Pro will edit the images into a sequence one after another, automatically reassembling your animation (**Figure 8.86**).

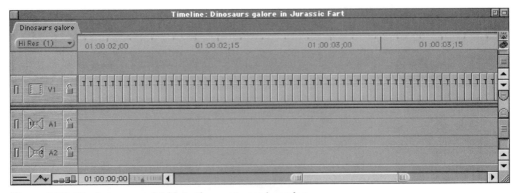

Figure 8.86 The images are laid into the sequence in order.

That's it! Since the stills are in a different format than your video, this sequence will need to be rendered before you can play it back—but at this point you are rendering it as part of your sequence, so it will be rendered only once.

Import Layered Photoshop Files

When you create a file in Photoshop, you can store different picture elements on different layers. When you import a layered Photoshop file into Final Cut Pro, you get a sequence with each of the layer elements on its own track—allowing you to animate and manipulate each of them independently. This is one of the coolest special effects features in Final Cut Pro (**Figure 8.87**).

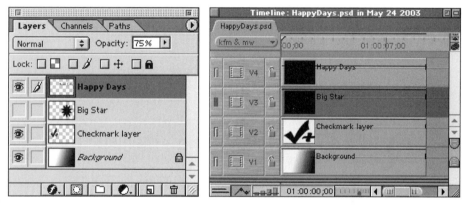

Figure 8.87 On the left is the Photoshop Layer palette. On the right is the same file imported as a Final Cut sequence.

You don't need to do anything special to make this work, either. Whenever you import a Photoshop document (PSD), Final Cut will interpret it this way.

Why is this so cool?

Photoshop is the ideal tool for image manipulation and the best place to design all the graphics you want to use in your video. For example, you can create a chart with each element on a different layer. Once you bring that file into Final Cut Pro, you can animate the bars independently or fade them in one by one. Or let's say you want to do a title where each of the letters is animated individually. You can create each letter on a different layer in Photoshop, and do the animation in Final Cut Pro.

Even existing images can benefit from doctoring in Photoshop before you animate them. I did a job once where the director wanted to animate a series of Marc Chagall paintings. First I imported the images into Photoshop, where it was easy to isolate each element onto its own layer. Then I moved the layered Photoshop file into Final Cut, where I could apply the movement: I made the lamb in *I and the Village* blink, and in *Au-Dessus De La Ville* I made the couple flying over the farmhouse actually fly!

Final Cut Pro imports quite a lot of vital information from Photoshop, such as each layer's opacity, whether the layers are currently visible or hidden, even composite modes. Each element gets its own track and its own alpha channel in Final Cut Pro and inherits the transparency it had in Photoshop. You cannot import Text layers, Layer Effects, or Shapes. So if you're using any of those features, rasterize those layers before importing the file.

GETTING IN AND OUT OF AFTER EFFECTS

Final Cut Pro is my editor of choice, but it will never replace After Effects as the premier tool for creating motion graphics. So how do you move your files back and forth between them?

After Effects is QuickTime savvy, which means it can open the files you captured in Final Cut Pro right off your disk. So go ahead and open your clips in After Effects, perform amazing feats such as ramping or creating awesome keyframe effects, and export a QuickTime movie you can suck right back into Final Cut Pro.

If the shot you're creating in After Effects doesn't need to be dissolved, supered-over, or combined with any other elements in Final Cut Pro, you can export the After Effects file compressed in the DV codec so it will play immediately in your Final Cut sequence. However, if the After Effects output is going to face potential re-rendering in Final Cut Pro, export it in the Animation codec as I described earlier for 3-D animations. This way you'll avoid unnecessary recompression and retain the highest possible quality.

The only problem with output from After Effects is that it doesn't know about the timecode track Final Cut Pro creates during batch capture (so you can export EDLs or recapture your footage later). For that reason, you should always keep the original clip in your Final Cut Pro sequence when you drop in the doctored After Effects version (**Figure 8.88**). Put the new clip on a higher track than the original, so you'll see only the doctored version when you play back. EDLs and recapturing will still identify the original clip.

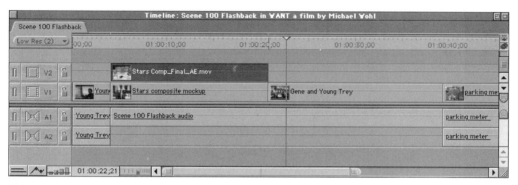

Figure 8.88 Place your After Effects output directly above the original source clip in the Final Cut Pro Timeline.

Interview: PAUL HIRSCH

Paul Hirsch is best known for the Academy Award he won for editing *Star Wars,* but his credits are even more impressive than that, and his career has covered more ground than most editors dream of. He collaborated with Brian DePalma on ten films, including *Carrie, Blow Out,* and *Mission Impossible,* and has cut films as stylistically diverse as *Ferris Bueller's Day Off, Steel Magnolias, The Empire Strikes Back,* and Joel Schumacher's *Falling Down.* Just before we did this interview, he had completed an Eddie Murphy comedy, *Pluto Nash.*

Michael Wohl: Can you describe the process of getting from the first cut to the final cut?

Paul Hirsch: Well, it's a bit like doing a mural in mosaics. You have a design that you've been working from, but you've been placing each tile in place from very close up. So, when you step back and look at the whole mural, you say, "Oh God, the eyes are too close together," or "The nose is too big," or "That woman is standing to the left of the tree, and she should be to the right of the tree," or whatever. And it's only by looking at the whole that you get a sense of what needs to be corrected. It's a combination of stepping back and looking at the whole, and then going in and focusing on the details.

How has editing changed in recent years? Not necessarily from a technological point of view, but in general?

When you were working with film, there was an industrial quality to the workplace that kept the executives and the suits out. Editing rooms were always grungy. But as the technology changed, the editing rooms have gotten more inviting and comfortable for executives and producers. At the same time, I mean, all generalizations are false, but many of these people have short attention spans, and very few of them had the patience to sit while you made changes on film. But now electronic editing can happen so quickly that they can see things change in front of their eyes. So the process has begun to be more micro-managed than it used to be.

Are there different problems in different genres, such as comedy, drama, and action?

The problems are always the same. You have to make a beginning, a middle, and an end. You have to have effective transitions. You want them to be dramatic or comedic in one way or the other. You have problems with pace. You have problems with clarity. You have problems with performance.

Do you give priority to any of those?

You have to make it all work. You approach the problems one by one and try to make them go away. My wife once asked me, "Can you tell if a picture is well-edited?" I said, "Sweetheart, sometimes the biggest contribution I've made on a film is taking a scene out. Take that out and everything flows, it all makes sense. So how can you tell what's been done?" If we do our work really well, the picture should look as if there's nothing to it. If you look at it at the end, you've struggled for months trying to make everything clear and all the transitions work and the scenes the right length and the emotions the right pitch, and so forth, and you get to the end and everyone looks at it and says, "Well, of course."

CHAPTER NINE

The Digital Future

I don't know about you, but I'm sick of the choices at the local multiplex. As bigger and bigger companies take over the major film studios, we're seeing a striking conservatism limit the kind of material they're willing to produce and distribute. Increasingly, Hollywood is forcing us to choose between:

- TV sit-com-quality comedies that rely primarily on sight-gags and fart jokes to make audiences laugh.

- giddy, shallow romantic comedies that reinforce stereotypical gender roles and focus on the helplessness of being in love.

- action comedies that depend on ever-more-violent images to whip audiences into a heightened state of blood-lust, the equivalent of a roller coaster with too many loops.

Commercial film scripts have often been written by committee (even if the committee is just the director, the producer, and the writer), but lately these committees are getting bigger and dumber—and they are tossing away Joe Campbell's marvelous rules of storytelling. Instead of turning to myth or character for inspiration, they are poring over the box-office charts, trying to repackage whatever shred of innovation made last year's hits sell.

And so, rather than offering us a variety of fresh voices telling unique stories, mainstream movies have begun to resemble a kind of pornography. Plots are just threadbare fabrics serving to tie together the moneymaking scenes of violence (for men) or romance (for women). Formulas abound in which hearts are broken or cars get demolished, all glossed over with well-timed, smart-alec punch lines delivered with clever cynicism by this season's bankable actors.

The secret subliminal message? Movies are cotton candy. They vanish in your mouth and still spoil your supper.

IF YOU DON'T LIKE THE MOVIES, GO OUT AND MAKE SOME OF YOUR OWN

Is this it? Is this all? Is this what cinema, the culmination of over a century of technological and aesthetic innovation, adds up to? Well, it doesn't have to be!

In fact, thousands of independent movies are being made all over the world that do not suffer from the cowardice and failure of imagination that has beset the film studios like a disease of the spirit. If there's one thing I hope you have learned from this book, it's this:

Anyone can make a movie. (Anyone with access to a few relatively inexpensive pieces of equipment, that is.) A DV camera, a computer, and Final Cut Pro are all you need to make films equal to, or better than, the pictures being produced in Hollywood right now for tens of millions of dollars each.

HOPE FROM THE INTERNET

There is a deep irony at work in the film industry right now. While it's getting less and less expensive to make a movie, budgets are growing larger and larger. Stars, sets, and special effects are all costly, of course, but the most outrageous expense is incurred in marketing a film. Since more movies are being released, it costs more to make sure a film rises above the crowd so the public will hear about it.

If your movie costs $40 million dollars to produce and market, you need to sell nearly 5 million tickets (at $8.50 each) to earn a profit. This is exactly why studio execs fall back on lowest common denominators when they plan their next money-making venture. But hope is in sight. The Internet provides a new medium for marketing movies to a more select audience—and maybe even for distributing the movies themselves. If your movie costs only $50 grand, you can earn back your money by selling just 6,000 tickets. The problem of finding 6,000 people and seducing them into seeing your movie is of a completely different level of magnitude than trying to find 5 million viewers.

MARKET ON THE WEB

I'm not going to give you a lesson on how to use the Web to market your movie; plenty of other books and Web sites out there are waiting to help you with that. But I *can* tell you that in one year Bare Witness Productions, my improvisational film company, received more than 50,000 hits from 20,000 different visitors to our Web site. And that was entirely through word of mouth; we did absolutely no intentional publicity or marketing, other than submitting our films to festivals.

Doing your own marketing on the Internet is particularly easy if a project is aimed at a clear target audience. For instance, if you're making a film about the human rights abuses of the Taliban government in Afghanistan, you can probably find a wide audience quite quickly by advertising your film on sites devoted to the Taliban government, Afghanistan, or human rights. At the very least, you might be able to get a mailing list from one of the sites' organizers.

If your project is aimed at a more general audience, it may be harder to find such a rich concentration of potential viewers, but you can still post a trailer for the film on general-interest Web sites focused on independent film such as ifilm, Atom Films, Filmfilm, or Eveo. And you'll find dozens of other resources for independent filmmakers online, many focused primarily on marketing and distribution. (See the Appendix for URLs.)

> **TIP:** Don't forget what director Roger Corman said about marketing: Even the most expensive advertising and publicity campaign will fill theater seats only for the first weekend. After that, if people don't tell their friends how great your movie is, you'll die like a dog. In other words, a great movie is the best marketing strategy you can have.

With just a minimal effort like this, you can spread the word about your films to a very wide audience. Combine that with as much traditional marketing (direct mail and ads in magazines and newspapers) as you can afford, and you can probably convince a few thousand people that your film is worth checking out. Then all you need to do is hope they like it. If they do, go ahead and book a *four-wall* tour of a few targeted cities. Who needs a major distributor?

> **FOUR-WALL** Rather than placing a film with a traditional distributor (a company that will put it in theaters and pay the producer a percentage of the box-office take), independent producers may choose to rent a theater themselves and present their film directly to the public (thereby keeping more of the box-office money). This is called four-walling.

DISTRIBUTE VIA THE INTERNET (WEB CINEMA)

All signs point to the inevitability of Web-based video delivery. Of course, it hasn't happened yet, but the only serious question is how long we have to wait.

I don't want to get *too* starry-eyed about the promise of the Internet, but video delivery over the Web is one of your best avenues for finding enough paying customers to offset your production costs. Let's say only 15,000 of the 6 billion people in the world are interested in ancient Mayan archery; you could conceivably find two-thirds of them on the Internet. If you can also sell them the opportunity to actually *view* your latest production, *Shafts Over Iztacíhuatl,* online, the $25,000 you spent on production would turn out to be a good investment. Filmmaking could actually become a sustainable career without your having to produce ads for tennis shoes or makeup.

Of course, a lot of technological innovation still needs to take place before this dream becomes a reality. For one thing, no one will take Web video seriously until it downloads instantaneously, with image quality equal to or better than television's. For another, that same problem of getting your voice heard above the din exists on the Internet. You will need to develop effective, nonintrusive, personalized marketing to ensure those Mayan archery fanatics find out about your Web site without having to suffer through advertisements for Bullseye brand cologne or plastic replicas of Mayan art.

For films aimed at more general audiences, I predict we'll become largely dependent on curators, critics, and popular review sites where the wheat can be separated from the chaff.

Web Video Today

Setting the future aside for the moment, there's not one thing preventing you from putting your video content on the Web right now. Your work will be seen, and you will be communicating the information in your movie to the public (albeit a mostly white, urban, and affluent public). At the very least, you'll find out if anyone responds to it.

If you're creating instructive or educational content, it will be added to the wealth of information that already makes the Internet such a powerful and versatile research tool. Essentially, you'll be joining the discussion on your topic of choice and contributing your views to the discourse. And thanks to the compelling nature of film, you'll be presenting those views in the most convincing way possible.

Just don't expect to make any money showing video on the Web. Internet video quality isn't worth charging eight bucks per viewing yet. But a Web presence can help attract the attention of a distributor, who might buy the rights to distribute your film in a more traditional channel.

Outputting Video for the Web

What does it take to put your video on the Web?

Not much! It's incredibly easy to make your show Web-ready. And if you already have a Web site of your own, it's no more difficult to include a video clip on a page than it is to include a static graphic. If you don't have your own site, dozens of sites will eagerly host your video for you.

DV is a highly compressed format, but it's still far too bulky to use online. Uncompressed video is approximately 27 MB/sec, while DV is approximately 3.6 MB/sec. In order to stream video across the Web at a reasonable speed, you need to reduce the data rate to between 10 and 50 KB/sec. That's a *lot* more compressed than DV!

Format Wars

How do you select the best format, file size, and type of compression to use for your Web video? There are so many issues to address that I'm going to skip most of them. (A number of other books and Web sites cover nothing *except* those three questions. I've listed a few of my favorites in the Appendix.) However, here are some general guidelines that should be helpful no matter how you approach the problem.

Currently there are three competing formats for compressing video: RealPlayer, Windows Media Format, and QuickTime. In most cases, it doesn't matter which format you choose. All three are capable of relatively high quality, all three are viewable on most computers connected to the Internet, and all three are fairly easy to host.

No matter which format you decide to use, I can tell you right now which software to use to create the compressed files: Media 100's Cleaner. (I don't know why they call it Cleaner, since what it does is make your beautiful video dirty.)

Apple bundles a limited version of Cleaner called Cleaner EZ with Final Cut Pro, so if you've bought a copy of Final Cut Pro, you already own a copy of Cleaner. One of the main limitations of the EZ version is that it compresses only to the QuickTime format.

Still, I must admit that I do like using QuickTime—maybe because I spent so much time in those hallowed halls down in Cupertino. The format is very versatile, you can optimize your compression for audio and video separately, and best of all, it has extensive interactive capabilities. (I'll talk more about interactive video in a bit.)

You can actually create and export a Web-ready QuickTime movie right from Final Cut Pro's export menu, but I recommend using Cleaner instead. Cleaner has dozens of options and optimizations that allow you to create a clip of the smallest size with the highest quality.

Cleaner can not only compress to your Web format of choice, it can compress to as many different ones as you want. And it can also convert between formats. I expect that over the next few years, the format wars will see some dramatic changes and consolidation. I strongly recommend not becoming attached to any one format. Learn the general concepts required to make nice-looking Web video so you'll be able to apply them to the format du jour, whatever it may be.

Export a Reference Movie

To use Cleaner on your finished sequence in Final Cut Pro, you do need to know one special trick. Cleaner works on single clips, and your edited Final Cut Pro sequence is actually hundreds of tiny clips carefully positioned and timed. To turn your sequence into a Web movie, you'll need to export a single file that contains your whole show.

But if you export a new clip with all the data in it, the file will be gigantic. Even if your show is only 15 minutes long, that can still take quite a while to export, and you'll end up with a 3 GB file! To address this, Final Cut Pro allows you to export a *reference movie*. This is a file that contains nothing but pointers to all your original media clips. The file itself is quite small, but it's all that Cleaner needs to turn your show into a Web movie.

Unfortunately, this feature is quite hidden. To export a reference movie, you must select Final Cut Pro Movie from the Export submenu (**Figure 9.1**). Then, when the dialog box appears, uncheck the check box called Make Movie Self-Contained (**Figure 9.2**). By unchecking that box, you will be instructing Final Cut Pro to make a reference movie instead of generating a new clip that contains all the video and audio data from the sequence.

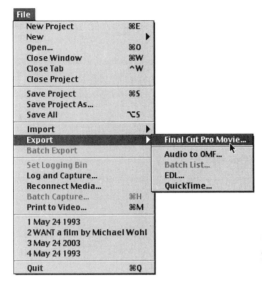

Figure 9.1 To make a reference movie, you must export a Final Cut Pro movie (not a QuickTime movie).

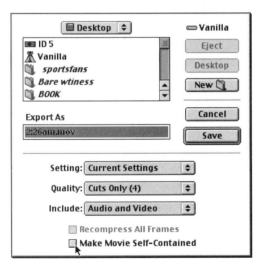

Figure 9.2 Uncheck the Make Movie Self-Contained check box. The movie that is created will require the source clips to which it refers.

A reference movie does not contain any actual video data for the movie; that's what keeps the file size so small. It refers to the video data in your original source clips, though, so be careful not to throw any of those away. If one of those files is missing, the reference movie won't play, and it will be unusable in Cleaner.

Garbage In, Garbage Out

This age-old adage is the first and most important rule of Web compression. The better your video and audio quality is before you compress it, the better it will look and sound after it's compressed. And the smaller the file will be, too.

Unfortunately, even the best Web video is ugly. The frame is tiny, the frame rate is reduced from 30 fps to 10 or 15 fps, compression creates distracting artifacts like blockiness or noise patterns, and the audio quality is mediocre. However, if you feed poorly lit, poorly shot, and poorly recorded video and audio into Cleaner, not only will the end result be even uglier than necessary, but the compression won't be able to function well, and your resulting file will be significantly larger. That means slower download times for your viewers and more space eaten up on the server's hard disk. The higher the quality of the original, the better a job the compressor can do to preserve that quality and make your file as small as possible.

Prepare for Your Web Audience

If you know you're making a video that will be distributed over the Internet, you should make certain editing decisions differently than you would if you were aiming for television or theatrical distribution.

For example, if the end result is going to be a movie that runs in a postage-stamp screen inside a Web browser, wide shots won't play very well. The details in longer shots will be completely lost on so small a screen. Web video works best with CUs.

Similarly, since the frame rate may be reduced to only 10 or 15 fps, fast cutting might not look right once the video is compressed. In order to reduce the frame rate, every other frame (or even two out of every three frames) is discarded. If you use edits shorter than one second, the sharpness of the cuts can be completely lost, resulting in a muddy mixed frame. Or sometimes cuts simply won't line up properly with audio cues.

Also, short cross-dissolves look horrible at reduced frame rates. If you have a 5-frame dissolve, and you play that back at 10 frames a second, you'll see only frame 1 and frame 4 of the dissolve. That means you'll get two partially dissolved frames without a smooth transition between them—which will look like a mistake. The same is true for any short-duration transition effect.

Even the production team should think differently if final distribution is slated for the Web. Compression does very badly with busy backgrounds, so if the camera crew shot an interview in front of waves of grain, or a sparkling lake, or a busy freeway, that background is going to turn into a mushy blob at compression time, or the file will get huge, or both.

Another thing compressors hate is camera movement—especially zooms and hand-held shots. Part of the way compression works is that pixels that remain unchanged from frame to frame can be thrown out; rather than redrawing the pixel, the compressor just says, "Same as last time." But when the camera is moving, every pixel changes in every frame, making your compressed movie bigger. Or, if you insist on a small data rate, it will turn the image to video noise when it can't keep up.

Hosting Your Video

If you are your own Webmaster, you can embed your compressed video clip into your Web page, or create a link so the clip will be played in a special helper application like Windows Media Player. Depending on your HTML authoring program, this is usually no harder than inserting a simple JPEG graphic.

If you don't have your own site, you can send your finished video to one of the popular online movie sites, such as ifilm, which will take care of everything for you. In most cases you can send a DV tape through the mail, and the online site will even do the compression for you. Of course, compression is compression, and the same rules apply.

Also, keep in mind that while your video is extremely precious to you, and you are perfectly willing to stay up all night experimenting with different compression settings to make it look its absolute best, most movie sites compress hundreds of movies every day. Your film will probably get tossed into an automated system that will lack the optimization you could do yourself.

Some sites evaluate your film before they agree to host it and may turn it down if they don't like it or it fails to fit the themes or style of their site. Some sites will host just about anything (except outright pornography). A quick Internet search on "web cinema" or "virtual theaters" will turn up scores of sites that will host your movie, usually free of charge.

For instance, not only will ifilm host your movie, the film will be rated by anyone who visits the site. ifilm claims at least a dozen success stories in which unknown filmmakers posted their work and the films were purchased for distribution in other channels—or the filmmakers sold subsequent screenplays or got jobs in advertising or television. Some have even signed multi-picture movie deals.

What's the Web Good For?

The biggest problem facing the success of Web cinema is bandwidth. If the quality and immediacy of Web video matched that of television, the Internet's unlimited channels and on-demand capabilities might allow it to actually replace the boob tube. But bandwidth isn't the only issue.

While it's not impossible to gather a small crowd around a computer monitor, watching Web video is usually a solo activity. One of the most unique and characteristic elements of moviegoing is the collective experience of sitting in a theater and sharing your experience with 200 other people. Comedy is always funnier when a crowd is laughing, and even the collective silence created by the tension of a drama or suspense film is palpable. Sitting alone in front of a computer, the "movie theater" experience is impossible.

But it doesn't have to be.

The Web has the potential to support a virtual theater experience where hundreds, thousands, or even millions of other viewers could be present with you when you watch a program online. I'm not sure exactly how this would be implemented (and I'm not talking about laugh tracks), but it seems to me that technology offers the potential to address this issue, creating something combining the best of what television offers with a unique experience based on the community of the World Wide Web.

Already, files can be downloaded from the Internet into existing movie theaters equipped with digital projectors. This allows a true movie theater experience but saves the cost of making and distributing film prints (which can cost tens of thousands of dollars).

Interactive Cinema

And there's something else, something that (for lack of a better name) I'll call interactive cinema—though it's not simply interactive and it's not really cinema (at least as we understand it today). One of the most exciting and dramatic possibilities offered by Web video is the ability to create films that incorporate a certain kind of audience involvement never seen or experienced before.

Take just one parallel example: When it was first invented, the telephone was considered military equipment. It was highly sophisticated technology for its time, but the only application its inventors could conceive of was to convey brief, urgent messages between high-level officers. The idea of a hot line between Washington and Moscow was inconceivable. So was the concept of ordering a pizza from your car so it arrives at your home just as you do, or trading stocks, or sending faxes, or any of the other things we use the telephone for today—including accessing the Internet. These commonplace functions were literally unimaginable when the technology was invented.

I believe we are currently in a similar state of ignorance with regard to interactive cinema. Right now, the most intriguing explorations of an interactive interface between the video medium and the computer have been implemented only in games. Many experts feel that interactive video might be more of a sport than an entertainment, and the very nature of interacting is incompatible with the narrative experience. I don't believe that. I think we can create an entertainment experience that lies halfway between a modern movie and *Star Trek*'s holodeck. If you're unfamiliar with it, the holodeck is fictional technology where the viewer literally steps into a 3-D virtual reality, interacts with narrative elements, and creates an entirely personal experience comparable only to a dream state.

DO WHAT'S NEVER BEEN DONE

Why am I talking about this here? Because I believe it's you, the new generation of video editors, media creators, and filmmakers, who can bring about this reinvention of the medium. I don't think we need machinery as sophisticated as a holodeck to find new ways to use the film medium. The simple technology of making marks on paper was transformed from a primitive accounting machine into an art capable of creating novels that captivate the human imagination in ways theretofore unknown. I believe we are on the verge of a similarly significant transformation in film.

Final Cut Pro is just a tool, a way to make the art of film and video editing easier and less expensive. But the intersection of affordable filmmaking tools and the exploding potential of the Web as a distribution medium creates possibilities that exceed the sum of these parts.

I challenge you to see this opportunity with new eyes. Don't simply re-create what's come before. Do what's never been done. A movie streaming to a Web page can have multiple video streams simultaneously. The viewer can click and type and speak to affect which images and sounds he sees and hears. The content of the video image can originate on edited film, or it can be computer-generated material. Live camera feeds can be incorporated on the fly into the video stream. A camera pointing at the viewer, or pointing at a live performance, can be mixed with preexisting images and sounds in real time. The possibilities are limitless!

I'll give you two examples of how I've tried to explore these concepts in my own work. Last semester, in my Future Cinema class at San Francisco State University, we constructed a Web site about commuting and public transportation that incorporated many types of media. We started with four streams of video, all downloading simultaneously to the viewer's computer. Each was a different fictional commute story, edited so they were all exactly the same length. By clicking on different areas of the screen, the viewer could switch focus from one story to the next by controlling which audio stream was heard. Simultaneously, text messages containing traffic statistics scrolled over part of the screen, and a live, interactive map showed the paths of the four different fictional stories. Finally, the site was supported by extensive links to other Web sites about transportation, plus editorial content pertaining to the impact of commuting on the students' lives.

Our goal was to merge the immediacy of the video medium with the entertainment value of four fictional stories to serve as the backbone for a comprehensive multimedia experience about our chosen subject.

Another project I've been developing with my improv company, Bare Witness Productions, is an interactive movie loosely based on Ryunosuke Akutagawa's novella, *Rashomon*. *Rashomon* is a story about a rape and murder, showing how different narrators perceive different versions of "reality." As a written text it was a seminal exploration of subjectivity, comparable to and contemporary with Joyce's *Finnegan's Wake* and Einstein's theory of relativity.

In 1950, when Akira Kurosawa made a film version, it was a masterful artistic statement that reflected (among many other things) the incredible schizophrenia that beset post-war Japan as the USA, its former enemy, spent billions of dollars transforming it into a modern first-world nation.

I plan to bring the same questions of subjectivity and multiple perspectives to bear in order to explore the nature of the interactive cinema experience. How can each viewer create her own narrative experience of an event? And is there one true version, or are all the versions tainted with an inescapable human subjectivity?

We will shoot each event multiple times, from different psychological perspectives, and then present the finished piece as a Web movie in which the viewer can switch between versions, joining any one of the perspectives at any time.

TELL YOUR STORIES

Telling stories is how we make sense of the world and how we bring communities together. Some would argue that it's the single most important cornerstone of civilization. Storytelling is power.

And we all have stories to tell. Nonetheless, over the last few decades the number of voices telling stories has been systematically diminished. Mainstream media has become a bully pulpit on which a tiny minority of storytellers present narratives that are little more than shallow advertisements promoting a culture of consumption and passivity.

Now we have an opportunity to rediscover our true voices.

The tools at your disposal are revolutionary. Take a risk and tell your stories.

The economics of filmmaking have been redefined. Take advantage and tell your stories.

A new medium is being born. You and I are the pioneers who are discovering what is possible. We live at an incredible time in the history of the planet. Get out there and tell your stories.

Someone's got to.

Interview: *WALTER MURCH*

Walter Murch is one of the most admired and respected editors of our time. His inspiring book, *In the Blink of an Eye,* is a definitive theoretical text on editing. More than just a great film editor, he is also one of the most renowned sound mixers in the history of cinema. His editing credits include *The Conversation, Julia, Apocalypse Now, The Unbearable Lightness of Being, American Graffiti, The Talented Mr. Ripley,* and *The English Patient* (for which he won an unprecedented double Oscar for sound and picture editing). His credits as a writer and director include the dark, moving (and woefully underrated) *Return to Oz.* He took time out from cutting Kathryn Bigelow's *K-19: The Widowmaker* for this interview.

Michael Wohl: What do you think makes the film medium unique?

Walter Murch: I think every age has a medium that talks to it more eloquently than the others. In the 19th century it was symphonic music and the novel. For various technical and artistic reasons, film became that eloquent medium for the 20th century. It's partly because cinema synthesizes all of the arts: it's photography, and in a certain sense painting, and it's theater, and it's architecture, music, and the novel—all rolled up into one. And then—at its best—it has become something else which synthesizes and transcends all of its parts.

How do you think the lower cost of technology is going to affect the industry?

People become excited about any new technology, particularly when the cost becomes significantly more affordable. A tool like Final Cut Pro, for instance, is at least an order of magnitude less expensive than the Avid. Ultimately, I'm not sure where it will go. Film editing is now something almost everyone can do at a simple level and enjoy it, but to take it to a higher level requires the same dedication and persistence that any art form does. The price of the ticket to get into the park is now much lower than it has been, but the cost of the ride is still ultimately very high in terms of time and dedication. I am excited that there is now the opportunity to give film students copies of uncut dailies from professional films, so that they can practice their craft on top-quality material and then compare their results with the finished film.

What do you think is the biggest challenge facing independent filmmakers right now?

Finding innovative ways to take advantage of the new forms of distribution. By which I mean the Internet—both as a way to publicize the work and a means by which that work can be distributed.

Distribution has been the bugaboo of independent films. You can always make a film somehow. You can beg, borrow, steal the equipment, use credit cards, use your friends' goodwill, wheedle your way into this or that situation. The real problem is, how do you get people to see it once it is made?

What do you like most about editing and sound design?

At a very early age I fell in love with the tape recorder. What I loved about it (and this is true about film editing now) is that you could instantly capture a fragment of reality, and then you could manipulate that fragment and juxtapose it with other fragments in unpredictable ways. That was intoxicating to me in the early 1950s, and it still is in

continues on next page

the early 21st century. I also love the collaboration, working with other people, and I'm very interested in emerging technology, how it can be applied, and how parts of the old technology can be maintained and integrated into these new systems.

Can you think of specific examples of problems you face in the editing room?

Well, on a certain level there's always the basic question of "How do you put the shots together?" Like every editor, I have to find ways to choose the right material, and to cut to the right shot at the right time, and be on the right character at the right moment, and make action scenes dynamic and interesting, and come in on schedule, and all that kind of stuff. But those are not primary issues for me any more. I suppose it is a little like learning how to play a musical instrument: Once you get past the issues of fingering and learning how to read a score, you don't think about them so consciously.

The things that I do struggle with are the issues of structure, length, and what you might call redundancy. The moving image is inherently redundant: Twenty-four times a second it's the same image, but slightly different. That's a metaphor for the whole process, because the art director will read the script and interpret the characters and the situation with set construction. The cinematographer does the same thing with light. The camera operator does the same thing with framing and camera movement. Actors do the same thing with how they act, how they speak the lines. The costumer does the same thing with the costumes.

For instance: Because of something the art director did in scene 3, you may find that the audience already understands something about a certain character. "Oh, if he owns that kind of entertainment center, then I know exactly how much money he makes." So we don't need a later scene about how much money he makes. Nonetheless, that other scene might get shot, and it's only when you see the whole film put together that you realize the extent and nature of all of these kinds of redundancies. Then it becomes a question of what and where to eliminate, at ever more subtle levels.

When you're cutting an individual scene, does that same sort of mentality apply? Eliminating redundancies?

Exactly. It's kind of a fractal situation. How long do you hold this shot? Is that look redundant given the fact that the character gave a similar *look just before? You don't see all these things immediately. They reveal themselves over time. Looking at a first assembly is kind of like looking at an overgrown garden. You can't just wade in with a weed whacker; you don't yet know where the stems of the flowers are. So you have to gently go through and discover, "OK, that's a weed, that's a weed, there's a flower." Then you start to see the outlines of the garden, and you discover that it might look better if these flowers were over on the left side where they'll get more sun. Then you start transposing, and things start to get interesting.*

How do you go about cutting a long rough cut down to final size?

You need the time to find all of the redundancies. On The Conversation, *which was the first film that I edited, our rough cut was four and half hours long. And a wonderful one hour, 52 minute film came out of it. But we spent a long time getting it down to that length, and had to jettison many things that seemed at the time to be important parts of the script. So it's not that it cannot be done, but it will take time, and you're putting the patient (the film) at risk. And you're naturally kind of depressed at all of the work that went into the things you are now taking out.*

Any advice for young editors?

When you're starting out in your career, pay close attention to the material you decide to work on. You may not be able to be selective yet, but ultimately don't be afraid to turn things down. There's a common fear that if you turn a certain project down, you'll never work again. But I think what's more to the point is that if you take whatever comes your way without really looking at it, you're potentially chaining yourself to something that doesn't suit you. And therefore you won't be able to do your best work on it, and the result may damage your reputation.

You also have to realize that most of the time you're in the same room with somebody —the director—whose baby this really is. It's not your baby. Well, part of it is, and you have to take responsibility for that part, but there's a good deal of a certain kind of psychoanalysis that goes on in the editing room, in which you're finding ways to ask the director, "What were you trying to get at here?" And beyond that: "Why are you trying to get at this?" You have to develop a feeling for knowing how to ask those questions, because some directors will respond favorably and some might resent it. This applies to many film jobs, not just editing: Half the job is doing the job, and the other half is finding ways to get along with people and tuning yourself in to the delicacy of the situation.

Appendix

There's so much to learn about film editing, Final Cut Pro, and the world of digital video that no single book (even mine) could possibly cover it all. So here's a sampling of some of the best places to find more information and continue your education.

Don't forget, though: Reading is good, but cutting is better. Start editing! Nothing can teach you like experience.

BOOKS

In the Blink of an Eye, Walter Murch (Silman-James Press, 2001)

Read this book. It'll change the way you think about editing forever.

First Cut: Conversations With Film Editors, Gabriella Oldham (University of California Press, 1992)

If you like the interviews in *my* book, *First Cut* is a collection of 23 insightful and inspiring discussions with an incredible selection of film editors.

On Film Editing, Edward Dmytryk (Focal Press, 1984)

This simple, elegant look at the aesthetics and technical considerations of film editing is nearly 20 years old, but it's still one of the best books I've read on the topic.

The Hero with a Thousand Faces, Joseph Campbell
(Princeton University Press, reprinted 1972)

This book will give you essential information about life in general, but it's especially useful for understanding the underlying structures of stories—something that must become part of every good editor's sensibility.

The Writer's Journey: Mythic Structure for Writers, Christopher Vogler
(Michael Wiese Productions, 1998)

Based in large part on the work of Joseph Campbell, this is required reading for screenwriters, and it'll help editors understand the fundamental elements of storytelling.

Nonlinear 4, Michael Rubin (Triad Pub Company, 2000)

You'll find this an indispensable reference on the technology of computer-based editing, especially DV. Also check out the companion Web site: *www.nonlinear4.com.*

Creating Motion Graphics with After Effects, Chris and Trish Meyer
(CMP Books, 2000)

From the best teachers on the planet, the definitive guide to my favorite motion graphics program.

Final Cut Pro 2 for Macintosh: Visual QuickPro Guide, Lisa Brenneis
(Peachpit Press, 2001)

The fundamental guide to daily use of Final Cut Pro. 'Nuff said.

The Final Cut Pro 2 User's Manual (Apple Computer, 2001)

This essential reference is not just a detailed description of every bell and whistle in Final Cut Pro; it's full of practical production advice, too.

WEB SITES

2-pop *(www.2-pop.com)*

The 2-pop community of Final Cut Pro editors has been around since Day One. The site is a wonderful resource and the perfect place to waste hours procrastinating instead of working on your show.

ifilm *(www.ifilm.com)*

This a very useful site for independent filmmakers—not just because it might host your work but because it tells you what's going on in the realm of Web video and in the film world at large.

The Internet Movie Database *(www.imdb.com)*

Here's everything you ever wanted to know about the movies, searchable by title, filmmaker names, even plot elements. This is the single most useful film reference work available in print or online. Check out the glossary of movie terms in the Fun & Games section.

Adam Wilt's DV Page *(www.adamwilt.com/DV.html)*

Adam is a DV master. His site is a sharp, clearly written source of information about the technology that underlies your editing system. Although it can be a bit technical at times, it's a required bookmark.

Codec Central *(www.codeccentral.com)*

Designed and run by the people who created Cleaner, this is an excellent source for prime information on compressing video for the Web. It's also a great place to find updates on new codecs and streaming technologies.

DV Creators.net *(www.dvcreators.net)*

This site is host to FCP411, a Final Cut Pro–specific message board, and it provides excellent resources in the way of tech support, tips, and techniques for Final Cut Pro. DV Creators.net also runs the DV Revolution workshops, a three-day crash course in digital filmmaking. All in all, it's an informative introduction to every aspect of digital filmmaking, and tons of fun (especially if I'm instructing).

The DV Guys *(www.dvguys.com)*

Another handy source for tips and techniques on Final Cut Pro and digital video in general. The Guys host a weekly Internet radio program featuring interviews, discussions, reviews, and usually some humor.

Filmmaker magazine *(www.filmmakermagazine.com)*

Look here for intelligent commentary and news on the world of the independent filmmaker, as well as nuts-and-bolts articles with titles like "12 Tips for Selling Your Film." If you like the site, check out the magazine.

Res *(www.res.com)*

These guys are pioneers in the digital video revolution, as well as the founders of Resfest, the first digital film festival. This site and its corresponding hard-copy magazine are always a great read. Both include lots of useful product and service comparisons. Don't miss Rob Nilsson's monthly commentary. I learn something new with every issue.

DV Magazine *(www.dv.com)*

DV is a solid source of reliable product reviews, how-to articles, and current information on the state of the video art—always well written and intelligent. This site contains much of the magazine's content plus some Web-only features that make it a great bookmark.

Indie Bin *(www.indiebin.com)*

This new site, aimed at the independent film community, is developing a large selection of original content and contains an outstanding set of links to the world of indie film on the Web.

Bare Witness Productions *(www.barewitness.com)*

My humble improv group. Come see some of our movies online.

Want the Movie *(www.wantthemovie.com)*

This is the site for my current film project. You've seen so many images from the film in this book, you should pop over, see the trailer, and let me know what you think!

Glossary

ADR Short for "automatic dialogue replace-ment," also known as looping. This is the process by which actors in a sound studio re-record dialogue while watching playback of a loop of the shot so they can match lip movements on-screen. ADR is frequently used to replace poor production sound or to change the delivery of a line.

ALPHA CHANNEL The part of a graphics file that indicates which areas of the image are opaque and which areas are transparent.

ANSWER PRINT The first print back from the lab with all color timing and dissolve effects included. Once this print is approved, the lab can make multiple release prints, which are sent to theaters for distribution.

ASSEMBLY The first rough cut of a show, which contains all the material in approximately the correct position but not yet cut for style or pacing.

AXIS An imaginary line based on the eyeline of the on-camera subject.

B-ROLL A catchall term used in documentaries to describe all the footage that is neither interview nor narration.

CAMERA ANGLE Refers to camera position: high angle (camera shooting down from above the set), low angle (camera shooting up at the set from the ground), and so on.

CAMERA LOG A detailed journal, made on set during production, recording essential informa-tion that will enable the camera crew to re-create the shot if necessary: the camera's f-stop, focal length, position, and so on. It also usually includes information for the editor, such as length of shots, where they are on the film or tape, and comments on their content.

CAPTURE Transferring audio and video from your original videotapes to your computer's hard disk.

CG Short for computer generated, or computer graphic.

CINELOOK Cinelook, Filmlook, and Magic Bullet are all post-production processes that manipulate color balance, frame rate, and aspect ratio to make content shot on video appear as if it were shot on film. Filmlook and Magic Bullet require you to send your video to a facility for processing, but Cinelook is a plug-in that works with Final Cut Pro or Adobe After Effects.

CIRCLE TAKES At the end of the shooting day (or the next morning), the crew usually gathers to watch the dailies. The director will identify the takes she prefers, and an assistant will circle her choices in the camera log. (In the old days, economy dictated that only the circled takes would be printed onto film for editing.)

CLIPPING Audio that's recorded louder than the capability of the recording device will sound distorted. That distortion is called clipping.

CLOSE-UP A shot that usually cuts off mid-neck, showing the face or entire head.

COLOR CORRECTION Part of finishing a show is fine-tuning the color matching for every shot.

COLOR TIMING A film-specific process in which each individual shot in a film is tweaked so it looks its best and matches the others.

COMPOSITE See *compositing*.

COMPOSITING The act of combining two or more images on-screen at the same time. This can be as simple as superimposing a title card on top of an image or as complex as mixing multiple layers with special effects, transparency, and motion. The end result is a composite shot.

COMPS Short for composites, rough versions of completed special effects sequences.

CONTINUITY CUT Any cut that preserves continuity of action, space, time, and screen direction across the edit point.

CONTINUITY In order to make a seamless edit between two shots, it's important that both shots match up in as many ways as possible: props, key lighting, focal length, speed of motion in the frame, screen direction, room tone, and so on. If all the elements match, the shots maintain continuity.

CONTINUITY REPORT Similar to a camera log, this report is made during production and lists every shot and every take in the order in which they appear on the tape. It focuses on continuity elements within the shots: props, costumes, makeup, gestures, and blocking.

COVERAGE The number and variety of shots and angles that were filmed during production in addition to the "master shot." Good coverage means you have lots of editing choices; poor coverage means you have only one or two choices for cutting each scene.

CRANE SHOT A shot in which the camera is mounted on a crane, allowing it to move freely in three-dimensional space.

CROSSCUTTING The process of showing two events that are taking place in two different locations at the same time by alternating shots from each of the events.

CROSS-DISSOLVE See *dissolve*.

CUE A musical element timed to a specific point in a film. It can be as short as a few seconds or as long as a whole song. A cue point is the moment the element syncs in, and a cue sheet is the list of musical events prepared for the sound mix.

CUT A transition between shots in which the second image replaces the first image instantaneously.

CUTAWAY A shot of a neutral element from the location that's *not* part of the current shot but *is* part of the current scene. For a scene that takes place at the beach, a classic cutaway would be a shot of seagulls flying.

CUTTING Another word for film editing. For many years, editing involved physically cutting pieces of film, scraping off some of the emulsion, applying special cement, and reassembling the pieces using a handy gadget called a splicing block. In this book, I used the term generally to refer to any aspect of the editing process.

DAILIES To make sure that the scenes have been photographed successfully, each day's work is reviewed either at the end of a day or the next morning (to allow some sleep after a long or late shooting day or, if you're shooting on film, to give the lab time to print the film). These screenings are called rushes or dailies.

DISSOLVE A transition between shots in which the first shot starts to fade out while the second image is fading in. In the middle of the dissolve, both shots are briefly superimposed.

DOWNSTREAM Events or clips that exist later in the sequence from the point where you're working are described as downstream. Events or clips that exist earlier in the sequence from the point where you're working are upstream.

DP Short for director of photography.

DUTCH ANGLE A shot in which the horizon is tilted.

DV The term "digital video" (in lowercase) refers to any video information that is stored digitally, but the acronym DV (in uppercase) refers to the latest digital technology for recording video images and the specific format it uses. That format may be further specified as MiniDV, DVCAM, or DVCPRO. Some variants include DV50 and DV100.

EDIT POINT The precise moment when one shot ends and the following shot begins.

EDL An edit decision list (EDL) is a text file containing the bare minimum of pertinent information to allow you to re-create your sequence. These files are commonly used to transfer projects from one editing system to another, such as from Avid to Final Cut Pro (or vice versa).

EFFECTS SHOT Any time you alter the video data from the image that was captured in the camera, you have created an effects shot.

EQ See *equalization*.

EQUALIZATION (EQ) Fine-tuning an audio track by boosting or lowering certain frequencies (or bands of frequencies). For instance, you can boost higher frequencies to improve clarity or reduce low-frequency rumble.

ESTABLISHING SHOT A shot (sometimes called a locator shot) that shows the environment in which the events to follow take place. Usually the first shot of a sequence.

EXTREME CLOSE-UP (ECU) A shot in which the subject exceeds the boundaries of the frame.

EXTREME LONG SHOT (ELS) A shot that shows a vast area.

FINE CUT Sometimes called picture lock, this is the final edit of the picture.

FIREWIRE (or IEEE 1394) allows high-speed data transfer over inexpensive cables. FireWire is the technology that connects your DV tape deck to your computer and transmits video, audio, and time-code information all at once, and very quickly. Before FireWire, connecting a deck to a computer meant hooking up as many as six different cables and having a special interface on the computer to plug all those cables into.

FLOP A digital effect where the image is reversed left to right.

FOLEY The art of re-creating incidental sound effects (such as footsteps) in the sound studio, in synchronization with the images on-screen. The term is named after Jack Foley, one of the first sound designers.

FOLLOW SHOT A shot where a dolly is used to move the camera along with a moving subject (for example, a car-to-car shot).

FOOTAGE All the video and audio shot during production.

FOUR-WALL Rather than placing a film with a traditional distributor (a company that will put it in theaters and pay the producer a percentage of the box-office take), independent producers may choose to rent a theater themselves and present their film directly to the public (thereby

keeping more of the box-office money). This is called four-walling.

GAP Final Cut Pro–speak for any empty space in a sequence. If you play across areas of gap, you'll either see black video or hear silent audio, depending on which tracks contain the gap.

GRIP The technical crew on a film shoot is usually separated into two categories, based on whether they handle electrical equipment or nonelectrical equipment. A grip handles nonelectrical equipment.

HANDLES Extra footage before and after the selected In and Out points. Final Cut Pro can add handles automatically during capture.

HEADS AND TAILS Extra footage at the beginning and end of a shot.

HIGH-ANGLE SHOT A shot filmed with the camera above the subject and looking down.

IN AND OUT POINTS When you're working with a clip, Final Cut Pro allows you to set special markers identifying the frames that begin and end each shot you want to use. These markers are known as In and Out points.

INSERT A close-up of an object or detail within a scene.

INTERLACING Video images consist of hundreds of horizontal lines. Televisions display this information by splitting the image into two fields, with each field containing every other line. The upper field contains lines 1, 3, 5, and so on, while the lower field contains lines 2, 4, 6, and so on. When the TV plays the signal, it paints each field on the screen alternately, creating the illusion of smooth movement. This is called interlacing.

JOGGING A way of moving through a clip frame by frame, using the Jog wheel or → and ← to go forward or backward one frame at a time.

JUMP CUT Any cut or transition that breaks the continuity of time, space, or screen direction—deliberately or accidentally—or where the action doesn't match across the edit point.

KEY COLOR See *Keying*.

KEY LIGHT The primary source of light in a scene.

KEYFRAMING Any time you tell Final Cut Pro to make changes (such as fading to black) over time, you must provide different values at different points in time. These markers are called keyframes, and the act of defining them is called keyframing.

KEYING Special effect that allows you to insert a person or object from one shot into a background from a second shot. The subject needs to be shot in front of an evenly lit, solid color field. Then you remove the color digitally, creating a transparent alpha channel where the solid color used to be. Finally, the subject is composited over an alternate background that shows through the transparent areas. The color which is removed is called the key color.

LAP DISSOLVE A cross-dissolve that lasts longer than 2 seconds; in fact, it may last as long as 15 or 30 seconds.

LAVALIER A tiny omnidirectional microphone, typically mounted on the shirt collar or lapel. These mics are designed to compensate for the extra low frequencies they record from being adjacent to the resonating chamber of the subject's chest.

LENS FLARE A spot of haze or discoloration created when a light source shines directly into a camera lens.

LEVEL Refers to audio volume level.

LINKING Final Cut Pro links clips that should remain in sync (such as stereo audio tracks, or clips originating from the same file). If you edit a linked clip, the other clips to which it is linked are affected, too. A Timeline state called linked selection controls whether selecting items in the Timeline observes linking or ignores it. Deactivating linked selection makes it easier for clips to get out of sync but permits finer control of individual elements. Whatever the current state, Shift-L temporarily overrides it.

LOGGING The process of cataloguing your footage and preparing your original source tapes for capture.

LONG SHOT (LS) A shot in which the camera is set back far enough to include the full human figure. While the point of focus is the human being, the environment is clearly visible as well.

LOW-ANGLE SHOT A shot filmed with the camera beneath the subject and looking up.

LOWER THIRD When you superimpose a title or other graphic element over the bottom third of the screen to identify the person speaking in an interview, it's called a lower third.

MARKER A placeholder or bookmark you can use to identify a specific frame (or a range of time) within a clip or sequence.

MASTER CLIP The clip from which a subclip was generated.

MASTER SHOT A shot that is framed to capture all the action in the scene and usually runs from the beginning of the scene to the end.

MATTE More or less synonymous with an alpha channel. When working in film, it refers to a piece of film that blocks out the background in one shot during printing so you can drop in the background from another shot. In the digital realm, it tells programs like Final Cut Pro which areas of the clip are transparent and which are visible. The only difference is that while an alpha channel is embedded in the clip, a matte might be an entirely separate clip.

MEDIUM CLOSE-UP (MCU) Usually a shot that frames the head and upper torso, cutting off midchest.

MEDIUM SHOT (MS) A shot that frames the subject from the waist up.

MONTAGE An extended sequence of short images that are tied together thematically but break the rules of continuity of time and space.

MOTION CONTROL A mechanical, computerized system that records and re-creates camera moves.

MOTION GRAPHICS A subset of special effects focusing on clip motion and layering.

OPACITY The opposite of transparency. The more opaque an object is, the more it obscures objects behind it. The more transparent it is, the more background objects show through.

OVER-THE-SHOULDER (OS) SHOT A shot in which two people are facing one another—one in the foreground with his back to the camera, the other facing the camera.

PAN A shot that turns from side to side. Short for "panoramic."

PAN (AUDIO) An audio track can come out of the left channel, the right channel, both channels at the same time (centered), or anywhere in between. The control that adjusts this is called a Pan control, and the act of moving the audio track from channel to channel is panning.

PICKUPS Additional shots requested by the editor, to be collected after principal photography is complete.

PLATE The background element of a key.

POINT OF VIEW (POV) SHOT A shot that lets us look through a character's eyes and shows us exactly what she's seeing.

POST See *post-production*.

POST-PRODUCTION Everything that happens after the film is shot, including editing, sound design, special effects, and so on. Also known as post.

POT Short for potentiometer. A pot is the control knob (or slider) that adjusts the volume of a particular track or input on a multitrack audio control board. The term can also refer to a single track.

PRACTICAL Any prop or object in a scene that is actually used by the production. For instance, a bedside lamp that is part of the scene lighting is called a practical. Similarly, any device that makes a sound on-screen, such as a car door or water faucet, might be called a practical element.

PRE- AND POST-ROLL In order for Final Cut Pro to capture clips accurately, the deck needs a few seconds before the clip gets up to speed—and a few seconds after the clip ends so Final Cut Pro can close the file properly. Different decks require different amounts of pre- and post-roll; you can set the values in the General Preferences window.

PROCESS SHOT An old-school film term for compositing. On film, if two images are to be optically combined, an additional lab "process" is required.

RACK FOCUS A technique that involves the camera operator shifting (or racking) the focus from one character or object to another within a single shot.

RAMPING Manipulating the playback speed of a clip so that it varies over time. For example, a shot can begin at normal speed, slow down smoothly to a few frames a second, then speed up to a superfast playback rate that's three or four times the normal speed.

REACTION SHOT A shot that reveals how a character reacts to something that just happened.

REFERENCE MOVIE An intermediary file exported by Final Cut Pro and used by Cleaner to turn your show into a Web movie. The reference movie is a relatively small file that contains pointers to all your original media clips.

RENDER When Final Cut Pro can't perform the calculations necessary to play an effect in real time, it needs to stop, process the effect, and write it to a disk file. This process is called rendering. Thereafter, when you hit Play, Final Cut Pro reads the file and plays the effect in real time.

REVERB Echo, usually produced electronically.

REVERSE SHOT Any shot that is taken from the opposite angle of the previous shot. Also known as reverse angle.

RIPPLE EDIT Rippling an edit modifies an edit point by changing the duration of only one of the clips involved. This changes the duration of the entire sequence.

RIPPLE The act of pushing all the items in a sequence forward or backward in time to make room for new material. However long the new material is, that duration ripples through the entire sequence like a wave traveling down a rope.

ROLL EDIT Rolling an edit shortens one clip while lengthening the other—with a single adjustment. It doesn't matter whether it's the outgoing clip getting shorter and the incoming clip getting longer or the other way around; the overall sequence length doesn't change.

ROLL OFF Eliminate unwanted ranges of frequencies.

ROLLING Moving an edit point forward or backward in time by lengthening one clip while shortening another.

ROLLING OUT THE TAPE To make sure they don't run out of tape in the middle of a shot, videographers commonly swap a new tape into the camera two to five minutes before the current tape runs out. However, since editing software like Final Cut Pro requires at least three to five seconds of recorded footage after the last Out point, it's good practice to record a few moments of "junk" after the last shot on the tape so the very last recorded frames aren't ones you intend to use. Filming that junk is called rolling out the tape.

ROOM TONE Unless you're in outer space, the environment around you has a characteristic sound. In a house it might be the soft hum of the refrigerator and the ticking of a clock. In a park it could be wind in the trees and a chattering squirrel. These sounds make up what filmmakers call room tone, an important consideration when recording and editing the soundtrack.

ROTOSCOPING The process of painting digitally on individual frames of the film. It's used primarily for cleaning up mistakes or removing the wires from a model shot.

ROUGH CUT An interim cut of the show, usually containing incomplete sound, placeholders for special effects shots that aren't done yet, and some editing areas that require further work.

RUBBER BAND CONTROL One way to set keyframing. You click and drag a line that represents various values over time—and it stretches like a rubber band.

SCENE CUT A cut that takes the viewer from the end of one scene to the beginning of another.

SCREEN DIRECTION The direction (left or right) that a subject is facing, or moving, in the frame.

SCRUBBER AREA A graphic representation of the length of the clip or sequence. The playhead, In and Out points, and markers are all indicated.

SHOOTING RATIO A comparison of footage shot to finished film.

SHOT Every time the camera frames a different angle or image of the events being filmed, the resulting video or film is a shot. The word also refers to different ways of framing the action, as in "close shot" or "long shot."

SHOT LIST Breakdown of how a scene will be filmed, shot by shot. May be supplemented by a matching series of shot sketches known as a storyboard.

SHOTGUN Microphones are frequently identified by their pickup pattern. A shotgun is an extremely directional mic, picking up signals in a very narrow pattern to the front of the mic. Most films use shotgun mics mounted on a boompole to record dialogue. This allows you to place the mic far enough away from the subject to stay out of the camera's view but still record an adequate signal with very little extraneous noise from the sides or the back of the microphone.

SHUTTLING A way of moving through a clip at variable speed by using the Shuttle control. Hitting the play keys ⎣J⎦ and ⎣L⎦ multiple times serves as the keyboard equivalent.

SINGLE Any shot of one person.

SLATE Also known as a clapboard, this tool is primarily used to identify a shot. On productions where the sound and picture are recorded on separate media, clapping the top bar gives a "sync" point that allows the editor to line up the separate recordings in post. The Final Cut Pro icon and box art show a typical slate.

SLIDE EDIT Rather than adjusting the In and Out points of the selected clip, the slide edit changes the In and Out points of the *surrounding* clips, allowing you to slide a clip around within a sequence. Slide will not alter the overall duration of your sequence.

SLIP EDIT This edit changes both the In and Out points of a single clip simultaneously. Essentially, it changes which section of the clip you are using by trimming frames off the front of the clip and adding them to the back—or vice versa. It does not change the duration of the overall sequence, and it has no effect whatsoever on the surrounding clips.

SNAPPING A Timeline state. When snapping is turned on, certain items attract and grab other objects (such as clip edges, edit points, In and Out points, the playhead, keyframes, and markers) that are dragged nearby.

SOFT CUT A very short dissolve that lasts between three and five frames.

SOUND MIX This is the final stage of post-production, after the picture is locked. It involves mixing the sound from many individual tracks into the final, balanced track that will be distributed with the film.

SOURCE/RECORD Traditional videotape-based editing systems comprised two tape decks: one to play back the source tapes, and one to record the master sequence. This model has carried over into the digital realm, even though tape decks are no longer required.

SPLIT EDIT Any edit where audio and video are cut at different points.

STRAIGHT EDIT A cut, as opposed to a dissolve or an L or J edit.

SUPERING Short for "superimposing."

SWEETEN A general term referring to various types of manipulation used to improve the sound quality of an audio element or track. Sweetening might include removing hiss or pops, equalizing a track so that it will match a particular environment, and so on.

SYNC SOUND Audio that's synchronized with the image. For instance, the sync sound for a wine-tasting sequence might include the clink of glasses being set on the counter and the tasters' discussion of the grassy overtones of the Sauvignon Blanc.

TAKE A single iteration of a scene or shot, as in take 1, take 2, and so on.

TALENT Film-biz talk for actors.

THERBLIG Term coined by Frank and Lillian Gilbreth, behavioral scientists whose analysis of human behavior made huge contributions to the technological advances of the 20th century. It refers to the most basic mechanical action a human can make. The Gilbreths came up with 17 or so unique therbligs. Note that "therblig" is Gilbreth spelled backward (almost).

THREE-POINT EDITING Every edit you make has four points: the starting point of the source clip, the ending point of the source clip, the point where it will begin in the sequence, and the point where it will end in the sequence. If you supply three of the four points, Final Cut Pro can figure out the fourth.

TILT A shot in which the camera tilts from down to up—or vice versa.

TRACK Film editors refer to all the sound elements as "the track." It's short for "soundtrack."

TRACKING SHOT A shot that begins in one physical location and moves along the ground to another. Also known as a dolly shot, crab shot, and truck shot.

TWO-SHOT Any shot with two people in it.

UPSTREAM See *Downstream*.

VOICE-OVER An audio-only shot.

WIDE SHOT (WS) A shot in which the camera is far away from the action and captures roughly what might be witnessed with the naked eye.

WINDOW DUB Some video decks can display timecode numbers in a window right on top of the video image, so you can see the exact time-code number for any given frame on the TV monitor. This is known as BITC—short for burned-in timecode, and pronounced "bit-see." A dub made with that window visible is called a window dub. This makes it possible to record timecode values even from a non-professional tape format like VHS.

WIPE A transition between shots in which the second image replaces the first image by taking some recognizable shape such as, for instance, an expanding circle or a moving diagonal line.

ZOOM SHOT A shot that involves changing the focal length of the lens while the shot is rolling to make the subject seem larger or smaller in the frame.

Index

non-environmental sound, 308
noseroom, 19, 74
numbers
    frames, 244–246, 252
    reels, 165

O

Ocean's Eleven, 166
offscreen action, 92
OMF files, 339
opacity, clips, 384
organic effects, 348–349
orientation, left-to-right, 74–75
OSs (over-the-shoulder shots), 47–48
Óskarsdóttir, Valdís, 230–231
OTSs (over-the-shoulder shots), 47–48
Out points. *See* In and Out points
over-the-shoulder shots (OSs, OTSs),
    47–48
Overlay composite mode, 386
overwrite edits, 195–196, 198–199

P

pacing of films, 81
pans, 40–42, 315, 336–338
Parametric Equalizer filter, 326–327
Pass filters, 332
pasting clips, 203
patterns. *See* editing patterns
pauses, cutting, 101, 125
pedestal shots, 45
Pellington, Mark, 28
People vs. Larry Flynt, The, 298
Perfect Storm, The, 348
persuasive films, 4–5
Photoshop, 415–416
pickups, 11–12, 21
PICT files, 412
picture-in-picture effects, 370–371
picture locks. *See* fine cuts
plates, 391
Play Around Current control, 255
Play Around Edit Loop button,
    256–257
Play Base Layer Only check box, 357
playback, keyboard shortcuts for, 205
playheads, 276–278
plosives, removing from tracks, 335
plot, emphasizing mood over, 132–133
Pluto Nash, 418
PNG files, 412
point of focus, 19–20, 34
point-of-view (POV) shots, 49–50
points

cue, 271–274
edit, xix, 101, 215–218, 242–243, 265
In and Out, 143, 145–147, 181,
    186–194, 274–277
pops, removing from sound, 329–331
position keyframing, 374–377
positive space, 17
post-production, xx, 26
post-roll, 147, 165
potentiometers. *See* pots
pots, 303
Potter, Sally, 134
POV (point-of-view) shots, 49–50
Power of Myth, The, 85
practical sound effects, 304
pre-roll, 147, 165
Previous Marker control, 183
prints, answer, 363
Pro Tools (Digidesign), 338–339
process shots, 63
Prompt check box, 152
ProTools (Avid), 6
PSD files, 412
punch-up-from-black, 67
punctuation in films, 65–68

Q

Q setting, 326–327
quality of sound, improving, 321–329
QuickTime, 412–413, 425–426

R

Rabinowitz, Jay, 132
rack focus, 65
Rage in Harlem, A, 86
Raging Bull, xiii
Raising Arizona, 26
Ramis, Harold, 298
ramping, 131, 352–353
Range Selection tool, keyboard shortcut
    for, 206
ranges, time, 182–183
ratios, shooting, 16
Razor Blade tool, 206, 211–213
reaction shots (RXN), 50–51
real time, mixing tracks in, 338–339
reality-based programs, revealing tools
    of film creation in, 21
RealPlayer, 425
Reason to Fear, 126
recaps, 93
recording tracks, 313–318
Reel field, 144–145
reel numbers, 165

reference movies, 426–427
reflections, in shots, 20
Release Time setting, 333
Remains of the Day, The, 26
render quality (RQ), 356–358
rendering, 338–339, 378
repetition in comedy, 122–123
replace edits, 270–279
Reposition Marker command, 186
Requiem for a Dream, 132
reshoots, 12
Resize tool, 213
Return to Oz, 434
Reverberation filter, 327–328
reverse angles, 49
reverse shots, 49
reviews, 93
Ripple Delete command, 125, 200–203
ripple edits, 240–246
ripples, 196
Roadkill Jim, 9
Rocky, 350
roll edits, 235–239
roll offs, 332
rolling Dutch, 39
rolling edit points, 101
rolling out the tape, 139
romantic comedy, chase patterns,
    118–119
room tone, xix, 306–307, 328
rotoscoping, 54
rough cuts, 7, 12, 437
RQ (render quality), 356–358
rubber band control, 67
rubber bands, adding keyframes to, 372
Rule of Four T's, 36–37
Rule of Motivation, 42
Russell, David O., 298
RXN (reaction shots), 50–51

S

Samples parameter, 380
saving
    generators, 410–411
    motions, 383
Saving Private Ryan, 348
scene cuts, 58–59
scenes
    bridges between, 292
    choosing music for, 309–312
    described, 142
    finding shots in, 151–152
    starting, 90
    transitions between. *See* transitions

Need a quick software refresher before diving into *Editing Techniques with Final Cut Pro*?

Magnet Media has the solution—video-based training on HyperCD™.

Check out the enclosed HyperCD from Magnet Media. It contains over an hour's worth of video training—free—featuring award-winning editor Zak Tucker, owner of Swete Studios in New York. Additional valuable resources are available from the associated Web site. This CD uses a patented technology called HyperCD that delivers broadcast-quality video along with updateable Internet-based graphics and resources.

Edit a professional commercial

Magnet Media's complete course runs approximately three hours and takes you through the entire process of editing a professional commercial with Final Cut Pro.

You'll learn how to:
- ◈ set up and organize a project
- ◈ log and digitize your clips
- ◈ assemble a sequence of audio and video clips
- ◈ use motion effects
- ◈ perform advanced compositing
- ◈ output to tape
- ◈ use Final Cut Pro 2's new media-management tools
- ◈ relocate projects
- ◈ and more

To access your **1 hour of free training**, simply insert the CD, enter **PPSCT2** when prompted for your access code, and you're off.

To take full advantage of this interactive video, you must have a connection to the Internet while viewing the training program (connection speed will not affect the quality of the video). Minimum requirements: 14.4 kbps modem or faster, Netscape Navigator 3.0 or later, Internet Explorer 3.2 or later.

Here's what you need to run the HyperCD: Power Macintosh (166 MHz or faster) • 16 MB RAM (32 MB recommended) • 640 X 480 monitor displaying thousands of colors (16-bit color) • Multi-session-capable CD-ROM drive • Mac OS 8.1 or better • QuickTime 4 or better